Kim Il Sung

A Study of the East Asian Institute, Columbia University

KIM IL SUNG
The North Korean Leader

Dae-Sook Suh

Columbia University Press
New York   1988

COLUMBIA UNIVERSITY PRESS
New York   Chichester, West Sussex
Copyright © 1988 Columbia University Press

Printed in the United States of America

LIBRARY OF CONGRESS CATALOGING-IN-PUBLICATION DATA
Suh, Dae-Sook, 1931-
Kim Il Sung : the North Korean leader.

Bibliography: p.
Includes index.
1. Kim, Il-Sŏng, 1912-   . 2. Heads of state –
Korea (North) – Biography. 3. Korea (North) – Politics
and government. I. Title.
DS934.6.K5S84   1989   951.9'3043'0924   [B]   88-6106

ISBN 978–0–231–06573–3 (pbk.)

Casebound editions of Columbia University Press books are
printed on permanent and durable acid-free paper.

To James William Morley

Contents

Illustrations

Preface to the
Paperback Edition

When he reached his eightieth birthday in 1992, Kim Il Sung began to write his memoirs, entitled *Segiwa tŏbur* [with the Century]. He published five volumes in two years, covering the period from his birth in April 1912 to March 1937; the fifth volume was released only two weeks before his death on July 8, 1994. The account ends before the Poch'ŏnbo battle of June 1937, which is the most important event of his guerrilla fighting days in Manchuria. His memoirs fit neatly into the official North Korean history of the period. Since he revealed only a few facts concerning his boyhood friends and the benefactors who helped him when he was poor and hungry, these writings offer no significant new information that could change our understanding of his early life.

It is unfortunate that Kim passed away without telling us his own version of his long and illustrious life. He could have told us the fate of his guerrilla groups in Manchuria and later in the Russian Maritime Province, as well as his opinion of what was heralded as the triumphant return of his partisans. Even more important would have been his stories of the Russian occupation of North Korea after the end of World War II; of the establishment of the Democratic People's Republic of Korea; of the Korean War; and of the purges and the consolidation of his political power. He could have described his successes at indoctrinating the people of North Korea with his ideology of self-reliance, *chuch'e*. He must have had a lot to reminisce about concerning his creation of a dictatorial regime that survived him in the hands of his son Kim Jong Il.

Kim Il Sung's life spanned eighty-two years of the twentieth century. He spent thirty-three years preparing for his political career and he ruled North Korea almost single-handedly for forty-nine years, longer than any Korean political leader of this century. During the course of his political life, Kim was many things to many different people. According to his supporters, Kim Il Sung was the supreme leader, *suryŏng,* of the North Korean people. He was admired as the sun of the nation, peerless patriot, national hero, ever-victorious iron-willed brilliant commander, an outstanding leader of the international Communist movement, an ingenious thinker, the red sun of the oppressed people of the world, and the greatest leader of our time. A statue built for him is larger than any built for other Korean leaders, past or present. Other monuments to him include a huge museum, a tall tower commemorating his political ideas, and a triumphal arch, larger than the one in Paris, that signifies his victorious return to Pyongyang after the liberation of Korea. These tributes to his accomplishments were dedicated at the time of his sixtieth and seventieth birthdays.

To his enemies, however, Kim was a nonentity, a fake who fabricated his entire life's story, from his family background to his revolutionary past. He was considered a potentate backed by the Soviet Union to create a small Communist satellite state in the northern half of Korea. Detractors claimed that he started the fratricidal war at the command of his Communist masters. When he survived the war and consolidated his power, he was perceived by them to be a dictator who purged every political enemy standing in his way. When he was able to finally declare independence from his Communist masters, he was accused of building a cult of personality unparalleled in the annals of Korean history.

Because he lived in a country that had been subjugated to Japanese colonialism for thirty-five years and then divided into two disparate political regimes for nearly fifty years, the existence of such vastly contradicting opinions of Kim Il Sung seems inevitable and, to a certain extent, understandable. However, the truth of his successes and failures lies somewhere between these extreme and biased views. Kim Il Sung was a Korean patriot who gallantly took up arms for his country against the Japanese militarists and can claim a place in the annals of modern Korea for what he accomplished. He deserves recognition for his persistence and his resolve to fight to the end without submitting to his enemies. It is notable that he attained recognition as a political leader of the Korean people from the Soviet occupation forces that liberated North Korea. Like other political leaders of Korea at the time, he wished to reunify the divided country—thus starting the Korean War—but he failed to achieve this goal. It is to his credit that he was able to survive the aftermath of the Korean War and consolidate his political power in the north. On the international level, he maneuvered very skillfully during the Sino-Soviet dispute and charted a new course of self-reliance by building connection with third-world countries. For better or worse, Kim Il Sung is the best-known Korean politician of this century.

Kim did have his share of failures, among which is his attempt to reunify the country. He never abandoned his hard-line policy intended to subjugate the South Korean people to his rule. Although he built a stable government that lasted fifty years, he failed to establish and refine a socialist political system in Korea. Blinded by the ambition to be an absolute ruler, he introduced a system that more resembles a monarchy than a socialist or communist government. In this sense, he betrayed the hopes of all those Koreans who fought to establish a communist system in Korea and who died for that cause. He seems to have succeeded in leaving his kingdom to his son, but this consists of a poor, economically underdeveloped country isolated from technologically advanced and industrialized nations of the world. To secure the succession, Kim has given his son a huge standing army with one or two nuclear bombs, but this inheritance is expensive to maintain.

This book was published six years before Kim's death. He still represented North Korea as the supreme leader of its people, but he left most of the daily political chores for his son to manage. North Korea suffered setbacks in its relations with former allies after the Soviet Union and fraternal socialist countries in Eastern Europe collapsed, but Kim and his son maintained absolute control domestically. Even when the North Korean economy had begun to deteriorate, the people pledged their loyalty to the father and the son. When China established diplomatic relations with South Korea, North Korea sought to negotiate with the United States to join the family of technologically advanced and industrialized nations. However, these problems belong not to the father but to his son.

Speculations abound as to whether Kim Jong Il will be successful in his bid for power in North Korea or will fall prey to North Korean political maneuvers without the protection of his father. Those who predict doom for Kim Jong Il have already begun to forecast the collapse of the regime by denigrating his character. His enemies portray him as a playboy, a womanizer, and an irresponsible person of little or no analytical mind. It is often alleged that he inherited his father's kingdom but none of his charisma or leadership skills. I see these, however, as politically motivated accusations of little substance. Kim Jong Il may well be better equipped to govern today's North Korea than his father would have been. In fact, Kim Il Sung was becoming too old-fashioned for modern North Korea. Unlike his father, whose formal education ended at the eighth grade, Kim Jong Il is a college graduate who worked his way from the bottom to the top of the party's highest organs. He may have received undue favors when he worked as a secretary to his father, but he was also trained for his current job for more than two decades.

In my opinion, there are at least five reasons why Kim Jong Il will be successful in assuming power. First, his father prepared him for the task for a long time. He was named successor as early as 1972 and so was an understudy for at least twenty-two years. Second, Kim Jong Il was careful not to upstage his father, whereas many of his father's partisan comrades have already been replaced by younger supporters of Kim Jong Il. Without formally taking over the position of head of state, Kim Jong Il already has control of the military and is in the process of becoming the supreme commander of the North Korean armed forces. Third, we may surmise that a Chinese-style gerontocracy will not be created in Kim Jong Il's North Korea. Of the twenty-one plenums of the Central Committee held during the past fourteen years, from the Sixth Party Congress in October 1980 until April 1994, sixteen plenums dealt with "organizational problems" and ordered the replacement of important party leaders with younger people. Kim Jong Il will most likely remove his father's partisan comrades from positions of power and give them more ceremonial duties. Fourth, Kim Jong Il has precedence over other aspirants of his generation, because few of his peers are known to be in the top leadership group. Among his relatives, Kim Jong Il can indeed claim legitimacy, as the eldest son of Kim Il Sung's first wife. Fifth, and perhaps the most important reason for Kim Jong Il's likely success, is that there is no recognizable opposition group or any identifiable individual to challenge him.

In the end, the people of North Korea may honor the wishes of Kim Il Sung in order to maintain political stability, but as his successor Kim Jong Il must chart a new course for the country. The future of North Korea depends on how well Kim Il Sung trained his son for the role of head of state.

Preface

Kim Il Sung has ruled the northern half of Korea for four decades, the only political leader the North Korean people have known. While he is still general secretary of the Workers' Party of Korea and still president of the republic, he has effectively turned over the daily operation of the party and the government to his son. Kim Il Sung is called the supreme leader and the sun of the nation.

The record of Kim's accomplishments is indeed impressive. He fought the Japanese despite insurmountable odds and persisted to the end without submitting to the Japanese. Returning from the Manchurian plains at the end of World War II without political roots in Korea, he served under the Soviet occupation authorities in order to consolidate his power. Supported by his partisan guerrillas, Kim used the political division of Korea to his advantage by eliminating his rivals. In an effort to reunify the divided country militarily, Kim launched an attack on the South, thus starting the Korean War, and he was saved from sure defeat only by the Chinese volunteers. By the time the Chinese troops withdrew from Korea, he was able to claim undisputed political leadership.

Except for a few anxious years at the beginning of the Sino-Soviet dispute, he exploited the quarrel between his two neighbors and proclaimed self-reliance and independence. He even introduced his own political concept of self-reliance, but this idea placed more emphasis on the rejection of things non-Korean than on the domestication of communism. His search for Korean identity often led him to exaggerate and at times fabricate his past record, and he often projected himself as leader of the entire Korean people in both North and South Korea. Endowed with apparently infinite self-esteem, he even tried to promote himself as leader of the entire bloc of nonaligned nations. He has built monument after monument to himself until the countryside has become scattered with memorials extolling his achievements. What he has built in the North however, resembles more a political system to accommodate his personal rule than a communist or socialist state in Korea. It is not the political system he built that will survive him; it is his son, whom he has designated heir, who will succeed his reign.

This is a study of Kim's life and politics. Voluminous biographies have been written about him, but amid the effusive praise and grossly distorted accounts only a few hard facts have emerged. An attempt will be made here to distinguish fact from fiction and to present a critical analysis of his life and politics; however, details of the lives of Communist political leaders are closely guarded secrets, and the available sources are less than adequate for a life story. Even the accounts of Kim's political record, particularly the earlier version dealing with the first two decades, have been revised to befit the glory and splendor of his rule in the third and fourth decades. He has undertaken many times to rewrite his own record, suppressing the unfavorable and inventing the appropriate to glorify his rule.

The distortions, exaggerations, and absurd tributes to himself notwithstanding, it is important to study Kim Il Sung and his rule – not merely to document the unsuccessful effort by the Korean Communists to establish and refine a Communist or socialist political system but to assess the true record of Kim's accomplishments and failures. Since his "wise and benevolent" leadership pervades every corner of the North, the study of Kim and his rule is the study of North Korea.

This book examines Kim Il Sung's revolutionary past, his rise to power, his efforts to reunify the country, the challenges to his leadership, his altercation with both the Soviet Union and China in the search for Korean identity, his problems in a self-reliant but isolated Korea, his exploits in Third World countries, and his adventures in South Korea. This book also analyzes North Korea under Kim's rule, his political thought, his shifting of political power from party to state in his effort to train his son to succeed him. Barring unforeseen calamities, Kim seems to have succeeded in appointing his son heir and has transferred the daily operation of the party and government to his son and his son's generation.

The materials needed for a study of this nature are difficult to obtain. North Korean sources are highly propagandistic and unreliable for ascertaining factual information about specific events. In an effort to justify the system's present posture, many original records are suppressed and many more are rewritten to promote Kim. The problem is compounded by anti-Communist materials emanating from South Korea that denigrate Kim and his regime. An effort will be made to distinguish the original from the revised and to evaluate objectively both Communist propaganda and anti-Communist denunciation.

Some of the more important sources used for the first time in this study are worth brief mention here. An exhaustive search was made for Kim's writings, speeches, interviews, and proclamations as well as for other materials about him. All the available unclassified works of Kim in their original form, amounting to more than seven hundred items, were read and studied (*Korean Communism, 1945–1980*). As for his family and educational background, the North Koreans seem to have settled finally on the three-volume biography by the party (*The Great Supreme Leader, Comrade Kim Il Sung*). This version includes elaborated tales of his revolutionary past as well. As to that past, however, there are both Chinese and Japanese sources that put the record of Communist guerrilla struggles in Manchuria in more proper perspective than Kim has made it out to be. The Chinese have published, for example, biographical information on those guerrilla fighters who were Kim's contemporaries in the United Army (*Dongbei kangri lishichuan* in three volumes), revealing much of what actually took place. Furthermore, the Japanese have also published some of their government records to show how they suppressed the "Communist bandits." The Japanese veterans' association of the Manchurian police has published its history (*Manshū kokugun*), and the Manchurian police have also published their records (*Manshūkoku keisatsushi* and *Manshūkoku keisatsu shoshi* in three volumes) to show how they maintained order.

On the liberation and occupation of North Korea by the Soviet Union, the Academy of Sciences of the Soviet Union has published a collection of reminiscences by members of the Soviet occupation authority. Contrary to Kim's claims, their essays reveal many details of their effort to implant a Communist system in the North (*Osvobozhdenie Korei*). These were written by prominent members of the occupation forces: General Ivan M. Chistiakov, who commanded the 25th Division of the Soviet Army, which occupied North Korea; Major General Nikolai G. Lebedev, who was in charge of political affairs of the occupation; Major General B.G. Sapozhnikov, a historian; and others. The Soviet Union has also made public the documents and materials dealing with their relationship with North Korea from 1945 to 1980 (*Otnosheniia Sovetskogo Soiuza s narodnoi Koreei: Dokumentii i materialii*).

For the early period of the republic, there are important North Korean source materials seized by the U.S. military forces during the Korean War. The collection was declassified in 1977 and contains hitherto unavailable party and government documents, books, journals, newspapers, photographs, personal papers, and other items. There are, for example, minutes of the First and Second Party Congresses and the proceedings of the Supreme People's Assembly sessions and the minutes of its Standing Committee. These documents reveal much about the inner struggle for power in the early period.

For the later period, there exist few objective studies that have scrutinized the available North Korean sources. There are four sets of Kim's selected works, for example, and the first set has undergone two subsequent revisions to support his inerrant prophecy and justify his infallibility. The North Koreans have published still another collection of Kim's works (*Works of Kim Il Sung*), and the publication of the latest version is still in progress. It is essential to compare them and to study the writings that were added or discarded for subsequent collections.

Emerging from the seclusion of the first three decades, North Korea expanded its horizon to the outside world in the 1970s, and a few non-Communist scholars and Western journalists have been given opportunities to visit the forbidden country. Much of the harsh and Spartan life was described by reporters, who asked hard questions about Kim's rule, but no serious effort was made to analyze his life and politics. I was fortunate to have been able to visit the North in 1974 and learned much both from firsthand observation and my conversations with North Korean scholars. It was also possible during the visit to acquire a number of rare books and source materials not available elsewhere.

Undoubtedly, Kim Il Sung is one of the important leaders of divided Korea. He established a separate regime in the North and has ruled the people of North Korea for four decades. Understanding his political successes and failures is instrumental to understanding the nature of his regime and the Korean division. It is hoped that better understanding of Kim and his politics will contribute to the reunification of the Korean people.

Note on Transliteration

Except for commonly accepted usage in English of Korean names, such as Pyongyang, Seoul, and Kim Il Sung, the McCune-Reischauer transliteration system is used for Korean. In romanizing Korean first names, the sound change only in the second syllable is observed – for example, it is Ch'oe Yong-gŏn and not Ch'oe Yong-kŏn, Han Sŏl-ya not Han Sŏr-ya, and O Kŭk-yŏl not O Kŭng-nyŏl. The Pinyin system is used for Chinese, the modified Hepburn system for Japanese, and the Library of Congress system for Russian transliteration.

Acknowledgments

Because of the unusual difficulties involved in acquiring source materials for this study, I am indebted to many scholars, librarians, and research institutes in the Soviet Union, China, North Korea, Japan, South Korea, and the United States. I want to express my appreciation to all those who helped me, but because of the large number of people in various countries who provided valuable assistance, as well as the kind of information I have acquired from them, I cannot acknowledge them individually here. I would like to thank the Institute of Oriental Studies of the Academy of Sciences of the Soviet Union for inviting me there and giving me opportunities to consult Soviet scholars on Korea. The Soviet scholars gave me valuable insight into the Soviet occupation of North Korea.

I would also like to express my appreciation to the North Korean scholars whom I met in Pyongyang for inviting me there and helping me to acquire source materials not available elsewhere. As much as I appreciate their unbounded affection and loyalty to Kim Il Sung, I hope that they will also understand my effort to be objective, although critical at times, in analyzing his life and politics. I have received generous help from my colleague, Masaaki Ichikawa of Tokyo, who secured many valuable source materials from Japan for this study. His unfailing friendship has been a source of encouragement.

Special appreciation is expressed here to Bruce Cumings and the School of International Studies of the University of Washington, where I spent the fall semester of 1982 under a grant from the Henry Luce Foundation. I have made a number of trips to the National Archives and the Library of Congress, where I received valuable assistance from many colleagues and friends. I want to thank Sun-joo Pang of Amerasian Data Research Services and Rinn-Sup Shinn of the Foreign Area Studies Division of American University for helping me to find valuable sources and secure rare photographs. I also want to thank Key P. Yang for helping me at the Library of Congress.

I am grateful for the assistance provided by the Woodrow Wilson Center for International Scholars, Washington, D.C., in 1985, and I am deeply indebted to Ronald Morse, Director of its Asia Program, for his kind advice and encouragement. Without his support and constant reminders, this study might not have been completed. I want to thank the Wilson Center for supporting me and providing me with a quiet place to work, and I want to thank Eloise S. Doane and Fran Hunter of the Wilson Center for their assistance. To Bertrand Renaud and Young-key Kim Renaud, I express my sincere thanks for making my stay in Washington comfortable.

Grateful acknowledgment is made to Kate Wittenberg, Executive Editor of Columbia University Press, for her unfailing support, and to Don Yoder, who edited the entire manuscript. Last but not least, I want to acknowledge the able assistance of Charlotte Oser, Administrative Officer, and Jean Tanouye, Secretary, of the Center for Korean Studies at the University of Hawaii for taking up many of my administrative chores, thus providing extra time for me to devote to this study.

Kim Il Sung

I

YOUNG KIM AND THE UNITED ARMY

An official account of Kim's early life appeared for the first time during the Korean War, seven years after his return to Korea. It was a simple account of bare facts and basic information of his birth and early guerrilla activities in the plains of Manchuria. In view of subsequent revisions of this version, perhaps its significance lay in the timing of its release. The Soviet occupation authorities, who had put Kim into power, had left, and the initial setbacks of the war had been reversed by the Chinese Volunteer Army. It helped to remind his political rivals as well as the Chinese volunteers that he had earlier fought the Japanese imperialists under the Chinese command, and the Chinese and Koreans were once again fighting shoulder to shoulder against another imperialist, the United States, in the Korean War. This biography, written by the party and published in its official organ, stressed that there was a firm and unbreakable camaraderie between the peoples of China and Korea that was begun in an eight-year joint struggle against the Japanese in the 1930s.[1] There are earlier versions: one by Han Sŏl-ya published by the North Korean Arts Federation in 1946 and another by Yun Se-p'yŏng in the North Korea historical journal in 1949. These are not official accounts, however.

The official version has undergone two subsequent revisions, once by Yi Na-yŏng in 1958,[2] and again by two members of the Academy of Sciences of North Korea, Song Chi-yŏng and Kim Ŭl-ch'ŏn,[3] in 1961. What seems to be the official biography of Kim was written by Paek Pong (Baek Bong) in 1968, and it is this version, translated into many languages including English, that the North Koreans promote internationally as the official account of Kim's biography.[4] A full-page advertisement of this three-volume version appeared in the *New York Times* on October 27, 1969, with a caption stating that the history of Kim's revolutionary struggle is the history of the Korean people's struggle for freedom and independence. The latest version of the three-volume biography, published in 1982 to commemorate his seventieth birthday, is an updated version of Paek Pong's work.[5] Kim's life story is still filled with exaggerated claims and unsubstantiated assertions.

What comes through clearly in all these versions is an attempt by the biographers to build an image of Kim as a model revolutionary who led the Korean Communist revolution and succeeded in building a viable Communist state in Korea. North Korean historians and party officials are serious in their effort to trace the tradition of Korean communism to Kim and his guerrilla forces. His birthplace has become a sacred ground of the Korean revolution, and his family has become a source of inspiration for modern Korea. Even the founding of the present Korean People's Army on February 8, 1948, was backdated in 1978 to coincide with the alleged founding of Kim's first partisan force on April 25, 1932. Kim is proud of his statues, monuments, and slogans of the "glorious tradition" of his guerrilla activities. But it is more important to register the true record of his revolutionary past upon which the tradition of Korean communism is being built.

1

Background

Kim's life from his birth to his return to Korea in 1945 is not a complicated story. His obscure past and the relatively minor role he played make it difficult to decipher the details of his accomplishments, but the basic information is known. Kim was born Kim Sŏng-ju on April 15, 1912, in Pyongyang to a peasant couple named Kim Hyŏng-jik and Kang Pan-sŏk. He was the eldest of three sons, Sŏng-ju, Ch'ŏl-chu, and Yŏng-ju, and followed his family into Manchuria and attended elementary school there. He returned briefly to Pyongyang to attend the fourth and fifth grades, but he finished grammar school and two years of middle school in Manchuria attending Chinese schools. His formal education ended in 1929 at the eighth grade when he was expelled from school for participation in unlawful activities.

His father died early in 1926 when Kim was only fourteen. In the spring of 1930, when he was released from jail, he began to follow various bands of guerrillas, leaving his widowed mother and two brothers behind. His mother died two years later, in 1932, and his brothers became orphans. When the Chinese anti-Japanese forces absorbed most of the Korean partisans for operations against the Japanese and Manchukuo forces, Kim fought in a group organized predominantly among Koreans within the Chinese groups, changing his name from Sŏng-ju to Il Sung in the process. He led a small band of Korean partisans several times into Korea attacking Japanese outposts in remote northern villages. He fought well within the Chinese guerrilla groups during the peak of the Chinese Communist guerrilla activities from 1937 to 1939. The Japanese expeditionary forces eventually crushed the guerrillas, and the survivors of these groups fled to the Russian Maritime Province in 1940 and 1941. Kim survived the Japanese drive and fled to the Soviet Union, where he joined others who fled there from 1940 to 1945. He returned to Korea with the Soviet occupation authorities when Korea was liberated in August 1945.

To these basic facts, North Koreans have added a great deal of information to build a towering image. Many important characteristics of his early life have had a bearing on his political maneuvers as ruler of the North, and it is worthwhile to examine his record of accomplishments carefully.

Family

Every visitor to the North is urged to visit the so-called cradle of revolution, Man'gyŏngdae, the birthplace of Kim Il Sung. It is located southwest of the capital on the banks of the Taedong River, one of the most scenic places near Pyongyang. The North Koreans explain that Kim was born in such a choice spot because his great-grandfather, Kim Ŭng-u, had moved to the place as a tenant farmer with the promise that he would take care of the ancestral graves of a rich landlord named Yi P'yŏng-t'aek. The graves are nowhere visible today, but this hallowed ground is complete with a swing site, wrestling site, sliding rock, study site, and a favorite tree that Kim used to climb. The pine tree that stands there is a young tree, in fact too young for him to have climbed when he was a boy. The house he was born in is a shrine including, among other things, an old wooden desk sitting smartly on a bright red carpet. Poems and songs have been written about the place, and a modern museum was built nearby.[1] It gives visitors an eerie feeling to know that all these tributes are paid to a still-living head of state.

North Korean historians trace Kim's ancestry back twelve generations, a family moving north from Chŏlla pukto to Pyongyang. They claim that his great-grandfather participated in the fight against the U.S.S. *General Sherman* which invaded Korea and that his grandfather fought gallantly against the Japanese. These are politically motivated fabrications of little importance. When it comes to his father and mother, their lives and revolutionary activities are described in more detail, but none of the assertions about revolutionary activities can be verified in any Korean or other records. His father, Kim Hyŏng-jik, was born on July 10, 1894, and, at the age of fifteen, married the seventeen-year-old daughter of a local schoolteacher. He spent most of his life in Manchuria operating a herb pharmacy and died early in 1926 at the age of thirty-two. His mother, Kang Pan-sŏk, was born on April 12, 1892, in Ch'ilgol, near Pyongyang, and died on July 31, 1932, at the age of forty in Manchuria. Kim has erected a monument for his father in Ponghwari and one for his mother in Ch'ilgol on the outskirts of Pyongyang, both with museums and statues.[2]

In fact, Kim's father attended Sungsil School, established by American missionaries in Pyongyang. He may have joined an anti-Japanese nationalist group, but his activities were of little importance. His father had two brothers, Hyŏng-nok and Hyŏng-gwŏn. Hyŏng-gwŏn was arrested in Hongwŏn in a small skirmish with the local police and interned in Seoul, where he died on January 12, 1936. A statue has been erected for him in Hongwŏn, Hamgyŏng namdo.[3]

These efforts seem to be directed more toward upgrading the attributes of Kim as a pious son who reveres his parents rather than substantiating obscure facts of his family record. To be sure, his parents were ordinary people who suffered the poverty and oppression of the time and died early without giving much education or assistance to their children. Contrary to the efforts to build Kim's image as a person coming from a long revolutionary tradition and dedicated parents, his image may be more resplendent if he is described as he was: a "dragon from an ordinary well," so to speak. At least that would be closer to the truth.

Early Years

From his official biographer, it has become clear that Kim's formal education ended at the eighth grade when he was expelled from the middle school he was attending for participation in illegal student activities. Earlier versions insist that he had finished the middle school, returning to the school after his release from jail.[4] In the course of six years of grammar school, he attended three different schools: the first four years at Badaogou Elementary in Manchuria, two years at Ch'angdŏk Elementary in Ch'ilgol near Pyongyang, and finally graduating from a Chinese school, Fusong Elementary in Manchuria. During his two years of middle school he attended two schools, a Korean school named Hwasŏng School and a Chinese school named Yuwen Middle School, both in Manchuria. Kim's attendance in Chinese schools is important not so much because the North Korean historians and his biographers deliberately omit this fact in their efforts to build a "Korean leader," but because his Chinese education and his facility in the Chinese language helped him in his future association with Chinese guerrillas in Manchuria.[5] The latest version corrects a number of dates, adjusting the transfers and graduations from one school to another, but these changes are of minor importance.

Earlier biographies filled the gap from the end of Kim's education in 1929 to his active participation in guerrilla activities in 1932 with the claim that he had joined a Communist party, a Communist youth group, and had organized numerous student groups and led the anti-Japanese struggles in Manchuria, traveling from Jilin to the Changchun, Yitung, and Harbin areas. It was made abundantly clear in later studies outside of North Korea that there was no Korean Communist Party or Korean Communist Youth Association in Manchuria after their dissolution in 1930, and the latest version has dropped these claims.[6] To maintain such a claim, North Korean writers would have to admit that he had joined a branch of the Chinese Communist Party, if indeed he had joined, and this is contrary to the Korean image they want to build. They now claim that Kim was engaged in an edification campaign of Korean peasants in Gelun, a village located halfway between Changchun and Jilin, a short distance west of where he went to his last school.

They claim that he established a number of four-year elementary schools, such as Chinmyŏng and Samgwang, and taught students from the first to the fourth grades the basic doctrines of Marx's *Das Kapital*, dialectical materialism, and histories of the Soviet Union and Korea. The idea of an eighth-grade expellee teaching fourth-graders is curious enough, but teaching them dialectical materialism and the writings of Karl Marx is beyond belief. It is this sort of assertion that casts doubt on the true record of his achievements.

In the great halls of the revolutionary museum built in marble to commemorate Kim's sixtieth birthday in 1972, one Japanese document was enlarged and prominently displayed covering nearly half of the wall. It is a report made by the Japanese consul-general of Jilin of a communist youth organization in the region.[7] The document mentions among others one student of Yuwen Middle School named Kim Sŏng-ju (Kim Il Sung) for participation in the group and is perhaps the earliest record of Kim's participation in any group activities and the cause of his subsequent imprisonment and expulsion from his school. The organization was simple and short-lived, involving fewer than a dozen people. It was organized and headed by a man named Hŏ So, a member of the South Manchurian Communist Youth Association. Han Sŏk-hun was head of the organization section, and Kim Tong-hwa was chief of the propaganda section. Yi Kŭm-ch'ŏn and his wife, Song Suk-cha, were in charge of liaison with other groups, and there were five or six students of local schools including Sin Yŏng-gŭn, a student at the Political and Law Institute, Ch'a Sik, a graduate of the South Manchurian Institute, Kim Sŏng-ju (Kim Il Sung), a student at Yuwen Middle School, and a few others. The individual initiation fee to the group was thirty cents and annual dues were twenty cents. The students were organized in early May 1929 and were arrested after their third meeting on May 10 of the same year.

It is not unreasonable to expect a seventeen-year-old boy without his father and away from his family to wander into a subversive organization of this nature, or to join a subversive group, even one that was Communist, but it is quite different to claim that he organized and led the group. Kim was not only one of its youngest members – other students were either graduates of middle and high schools or college students – but also the organizers were much older persons and seasoned revolutionaries: Yi Kŭm-ch'ŏn and Kim Tong-hwa were both in their early thirties and were eventually expelled from Manchuria.[8] To support the claim of Kim's leadership role, the North Koreans have deleted names of other members of the group from the document they so proudly display in their museum. Regardless of their claims, Kim's learning about communism or association with Communists began at the tender age of seventeen. Kim claims that he read the classics of Marxism and Leninism, including *Das Kapital*, when he attended Yuwen School. The school was a Chinese private school where no instruction was given on communism. In fact, it is doubtful that such literature in Chinese or Korean was available at this time in a remote town of Jilin in Manchuria. Even if he were exposed to such literature, his level of comprehension at the age of seventeen as an eighth-grader is questionable.

It is futile to challenge every assertion made by Kim's sycophantic writers, and their errors are too obvious to warrant detailed refutation. Kim's learning about communism was not through formal education, an intellectual awakening to the doctrines of Marxism and Leninism, as the North Koreans would lead us to believe. His education came through random association with anti-Japanese Korean Nationalists and Chinese Communist guerrillas, and his belief hardened through his own anti-Japanese activity under the Chinese Communist guerrilla forces in Manchuria.

The person with the most profound influence on Kim's understanding of communism was perhaps Wei Zhengmin, Kim's immediate superior and comrade during his guerrilla days from 1935 to 1941. Wei was sent to Manchuria by the Chinese Communist Party in 1932, and he was secretary of the East Manchurian Special Committee in 1934. Wei participated in the Seventh Congress of the Comintern in Moscow in 1935 as a delegate of the Chinese Communist Party, and upon his return he served as chairman of the Political Committee of the Northeast Anti-Japanese United Army under its commander Yang Jingyu. Kim Il Sung fought in this army as well, and Wei is the one who comes closest in teaching him about communism.[9]

Wei wrote often to Kang Sheng in Moscow and later in Yanan,

Kim Il Sung in his school days.

Commander Wei Zhengmin, Kim Il Sung's Chinese mentor and political commissar of the First Route Army of the Northeast Anti-Japanese United Army

Officers and men of the First Route Army, 1939

Kim Il Sung and his soldiers of the Second Directional Army, 1938

reporting his own activities and the various campaigns of the Chinese guerrillas toward the end of the 1930s in Manchuria. He made efforts to propagate communism to the guerrillas, teaching them about Lenin. He used to ride a white horse with pride, and in one of his last letters to Kang Sheng on April 15, 1940, he mentioned that his horse had died. Wei himself was suffering from ill health and was killed on March 8, 1941, in Manchuria.

Kim seems to have learned much from Wei and tried to emulate him in many ways. There is a huge painting in the revolutionary museum that has Kim sitting smartly on a white horse, but in another section where an authentic photograph of the guerrillas is displayed, Wei's picture has been cropped out.[10] Many people, Koreans and Chinese alike, helped Kim Il Sung and led him to the cause of communism during these guerrilla days, but Kim recognizes none.

It was during this period between his release from jail and his active participation in an organized Chinese guerrilla force in the early 1930s that Kim adopted the pseudonym of Kim Il Sung. The

North Koreans claim that his comrades in Wujiazi bestowed the name Il Sung, meaning "one star," on him, citing a South Korean publication of 1945. He later changed to his current name, the same Korean pronunciation of different Chinese characters.[11] There is considerable controversy related to his name and identity, but suffice it here to state that there were others with the same name. The current North Korean President Kim Il Sung is unmistakably the Kim Il Sung who participated in an anti-Japanese Chinese Communist guerrilla force in Manchuria. There are still a few South Koreans who insist that the present North Korean president and a Korean revolutionary named Kim Il Sung are two or three different persons with the same name, but this is idle speculation.[12] Both names, Kim Sŏng-ju and Kim Il Sung, appear in the Japanese police records, and there are more than adequate records of his partisan activities in both Chinese and Korean publications published before the liberation of Korea in 1945.[13] There are even photographs taken by the partisans themselves and captured by the Japanese in the late 1930s that show his guerrilla groups and identify him specifically. These photographs are displayed in the revolutionary museum in the North, and they were also reproduced by the Chinese Communists in Manchuria shortly after the defeat of Japan.[14]

Partisan Activities

Kim's partisan activities are important for several reasons. The first is that it was his participation in the anti-Japanese guerrilla activities in Manchuria that won him his first recognition, and toward the latter part of his campaign he was important enough for the Japanese to post a reward for information leading to his arrest. Another is that it is his partisan activities to which the North Koreans trace their revolutionary tradition. They maintain that other revolutionary activities, Nationalist and Communist alike, are unimportant. Their revolutionary history is filled with details of his partisan activities, and others are mentioned only to show how unimportant they are in comparison. Still another reason is that it is this partisan group that constituted the core political leadership of the North. Kim used this group to consolidate his power against all other factions that challenged him, and it is the children of this group and those who were trained by this group that hold the key to power in North Korea today.

For these reasons and because Kim's biographers and North Korean historians make outlandish claims, it is important to put partisan activities in proper perspective – not so much to discredit Kim's considerable accomplishments, but to distinguish fact from fiction. It should be stated at the outset that the major organized efforts to resist the Japanese in Manchuria during the life of the Japanese puppet regime, Manchukuo, from 1933 to 1945, were carried out by the Chinese Communists and not Koreans. They were carried out against incredible odds by the Chinese Communists, and while Koreans in Manchuria joined the Chinese individually, there was no separate organized effort by the Korean Communists. Furthermore, it should be pointed out that the Chinese Communists were defeated and ultimately driven out of Manchuria into the Soviet Union by 1941, long before the Japanese defeat in World War II by the allied forces.

Kim claims that he first organized a partisan group in Antu, a small village in southern Manchuria, on April 25, 1932, and expanded his forces to create a Korean People's Revolutionary Army (*Chosŏn inmin hyŏngmyŏnggun*) in February 1936. He was a commander of this army throughout his numerous and successful campaigns against the Japanese in Manchuria until 1945, when he returned to Korea. He admits that he went into a small-unit operation in 1940, a tactical dispersion of this army to continue his fight against the Japanese.

The date of April 25, 1932, when Kim is alleged to have organized his first partisan group, was not revealed until 1968 when his biography was published. This version reported that Kim organized the group with eighteen members, naming only one partisan other than Kim himself, Ch'a Kwang-su. Ch'a died in July of that year.[15] The earlier version reported that it was organized in the spring of 1932 with Yi Yŏng-bae and Kim Ch'ŏl-hŭi, neither of whom North Korean histories mention in any subsequent writings.[16] Another version reports that it was organized in the winter of 1931, and still another version reports that Kim had joined a partisan group in Antu that was already in operation.[17]

It has been difficult for biographers and historians to piece Kim's past together, not because it is nonexistent but because they want to claim the earliest date possible for the beginning of his guerrilla activities. The North Koreans suddenly announced in February 1978 that the Korean People's Army of the Democratic People's Republic of Korea, which was created on February 8, 1948, was in fact founded on the day Kim's partisan group was organized, April 25, 1932. For the succeeding twenty-nine years, they marked February 8 as the founding date, celebrating the twenty-ninth anniversary in 1977, but since 1978 they have celebrated April 25 as the founding date of the army, proclaiming that April 25, 1978, was the forty-sixth anniversary.[18] The Korean People's Army celebrated its fiftieth anniversary on April 25, 1982.

North Korean historians also claim that other Korean partisan groups were formed in southern and eastern Manchuria about this time and list some of the members and localities involved: Yi Kwang, Kim Ch'ŏl, and Ch'oe Ch'un-guk in the Wangqing area; Ch'oe Hyŏn and Kim Tong-gyu in the Yanji area; Yi Pong-su and An Kil in the Hunchun area; and Nam Ch'ang-su and Pak Yŏng-sun in the Helong area.[19] They claim that Kim organized these and other Korean partisan groups to form what he called a Korean People's Revolutionary Army in the spring of 1934. Here again the later version of Kim's biography has changed the date to February 1936. More important than the juggling of dates is the formation of the army itself. There is, of course, no record of such an army. It is a name that has been invented to designate a Korean group that operated under a Chinese guerrilla army. There was a group with a similar name, the Korean Revolutionary Army, but this was a Korean Nationalist army commanded by Yang Se-bong,[20] who was twice the age of Kim and who received a posthumous medal of honor for his contribution to Korean independence from the South Korean government in 1962.

Members of Kim's partisan group and his army fought under a Chinese guerrilla army. They were many, but they were scattered all over southern, eastern, and northern Manchuria under different units of the Chinese forces. There was no unified command of all Koreans who participated in this army. It should be pointed out, however, that the largest concentration of Korean partisans was in eastern and southern Manchuria, and that is the region where Kim Il Sung proved himself. Kim is one of the better-known Korean guerrilla leaders, but there were others equally, if not more, famous among the Koreans, and in fact many were Kim's superiors and close comrades at one time or another. There were Yi Hong-gwang, An Pong-hak, Chu Chin, Kim Ch'aek, Yi Hak-man, Ch'oe Yong-gŏn, Ch'oe Hyŏn, and Chŏn Kwang, to mention only a few. Some of them fought in different regions, and Kim may not have had personal contacts, but he knew of their guerrilla activities.

Many members of the various units were killed by the Japanese, and a number of them surrendered. Those who survived the war and returned north to tell the story of their struggle number approximately 120 men and women.[21] Almost all survivors were asked to reminisce, and their tales are published in many books and reprinted time and again in magazines and newspapers.[22] They remembered no other leader but Kim and refused to remember those who surrendered to the Japanese. Only the most important ones, such as Kim Il and Ch'oe Yong-gŏn, withstood the pressure and abstained from recounting their partisan activities. Other partisans who are not encouraged to remember are those who fought in northern Manchuria where Kim had no operational ties. Yim Hae, Kim Ch'ang-dŏk, and Kim Kwang-hyŏp, for example, have not revealed how they fought the Japanese in northern Manchuria without Kim.

It is conceivable that Kim began his guerrilla activities as early as 1932 when he was barely twenty years old. In some of the earlier accounts, Kim was said to have worked under a partisan named Yang Sŏng-yong. Yang was reported by the Japanese police to be a common bandit near the Wangqing area, but Yang later did fight under the Chinese guerrilla army and died in September 1935.[23] The reason for these and other contradictory claims is not difficult to understand, but they certainly do not do justice to Kim's true record, which, as we shall see, is considerable.

2

Kim and the Northeast Anti-Japanese United Army

The army that ultimately unified the scattered Chinese and Korean guerrillas in Manchuria was the Northeast Anti-Japanese United Army (*Dongbei kangri lianjun*), led by a Chinese commander, Yang Jingyu.[1] It is under this army that Kim Il Sung and his guerrillas fought against the Japanese in Manchuria from approximately 1932 to 1941. This army was unmistakably Communist but it was not Korean. Thus Kim Il Sung did fight against the Japanese in Manchuria, but he did so under Chinese, not Korean, command. It is not my purpose here to examine fully the operation of this army, but since Kim traces his revolutionary tradition to the guerrilla activity against the Japanese in Manchuria, it is important to scrutinize the United Army and the Korean participation in it.

The United Army

The origin of the Northeast Anti-Japanese United Army began in 1932 when a guerrilla group in Panshi prefecture in southern Manchuria was reorganized as the 32nd Red Army. It is said that the 32nd Red Army of Panshi prefecture was so named to follow the

31st Red Army of the Chinese Communists in Sichuan province.[2] In January 1932, the headquarters of the Manchurian Provincial Committee of the Chinese Communist Party was moved from Shenyang to Harbin, and various Communist guerrilla groups were organized under its command. On the second anniversary of the Japanese invasion of Manchuria, September 18, 1933, Yang Jingyu reorganized the 32nd Red Army to found the first independent division of the Northeast People's Revolutionary Army (*Dongbei renmin gemingjun*) with approximately three hundred partisans. The following year, in November 1934, Yang expanded by adding the second independent division, and both divisions operated primarily in southern Manchuria. Yang became commander of the army and appointed Yi Hong-gwang,[3] a Korean, commander of the First Division, and Cao Guoan, a Chinese, commander of the Second Division.

In eastern Manchuria, the Second Army was established under the command of a Korean guerrilla fighter named Chu Chin in March 1934 in Santouwai. This army was expanded into two independent divisions in May 1934 in commemoration of the Jiandao May 30 Communist Incident.[4] Chu Chin commanded the first independent division with Wang Detai as his political commissar, and he appointed a Chinese, Fang Zhensheng, commander of the second independent division. This army united a number of scattered Chinese and Korean guerrillas amounting to nearly a thousand strong, including Chinese fighters led by Dong Changying. The majority of this army consisted of Korean recruits from Jiandao. In northern Manchuria, the Third Army was established under the command of Zhao Shangzhi, putting together the Communist guerrillas in the Zhuhe region in the autumn of 1933. During the following year, Zhao and his comrade Li Zhaolin fought the Japanese with approximately four hundred guerrillas. However, the formation of the Third Army was not announced until January 28, 1935.

In northeastern Manchuria, the guerrilla fighters of Wang Delin were united under Li Yenlu to form the Fourth Army. Li had united the fighters of Shi Zhongheng and other guerrilla leaders, putting together a sizable group headquartered in the Mishan area. There were a number of Koreans participating in the Fourth Army including Kim Chin-guk and Yi Chin-bok.[5] In the area near

Mudanjiang, Ningan guerrilla groups were formed shortly after the Japanese took over Manchuria; this group began with approximately two hundred guerrillas, but it expanded under the leadership of Zhou Baozhong and guerrilla groups led by Ping Nanyang. Zhou at times worked with the guerrillas of the Second Army, but in September 1934 he formed the Fifth Army and appointed such able commanders as Chai Shiying and Liu Hanxing of Jidong guerrilla groups. Farther to the north near Jiamusi on the lower reaches of the Sungari River, Tangyuan guerrilla groups were reorganized into the Sixth Army under the leadership of Xie Wendong. Tangyuan guerrilla groups were reorganized a number of times, moving from region to region on both banks of the Sungari River, and they were later commanded by Xia Yungjie.

Soldiers of these six armies consisted of members of the Chinese and Korean Communist parties, youth volunteers, and other anti-Japanese Nationalist armed groups. Even the Japanese estimated that the total number might have reached as many as 15,000.[6] There were many casualties as well as defections from these groups, but by the mid-1930s these six armies were under the direction of the Manchurian Provincial Committee of the Chinese Communist Party, receiving directives from Kang Sheng in Moscow. Han Shoukui, who was sent to Manchuria from the Comintern to direct the activities of the Chinese Communist Party in January 1936, was arrested soon after his arrival on April 16, 1936, and he revealed much about Chinese Communist activities in Manchuria.

The Seventh Congress of the Comintern in 1935 called for a united front of all anti-imperialist forces, and the Chinese Communist Party issued the August First Declaration in 1935. In response to the declaration, the leaders of these six armies issued a declaration of their own addressed to the leaders of the entire Chinese anti-Japanese movement, including both Mao Zedong and Chiang Kai-shek, on October 12, 1935, pledging a united front of these groups and other anti-Japanese forces in Manchuria. Shortly thereafter, on January 28, 1936, some of the leaders of these armies held a meeting in Tangyuan prefecture in Sanjiang province to announce the formation of a united army named the Northeast Anti-Japanese United Army (*Dongbei kangri lianjun*) on February 20, 1936.[7]

There was much fighting by these groups, and casualties were high. But when the Japanese intensified their drive into Manchuria in 1931 and continued into the China mainland in 1937, the resistance in Manchuria against Japanese rule also intensified. The major force of resistance was in southern, southeastern, northern, and northeastern Manchuria, and during the mid-1930s more guerrilla armies were formed and joined the United Army. In Raohe, near the Soviet border, south of Khabarovsk, the Seventh Army was organized by a Korean guerrilla leader named Yi Hak-man, known to the Chinese as Li Baoman. In this manner the United Army was expanded to include eleven armies. The Eighth Army was expanded from the Sixth Army and was headed by Xie Wendong in the Yilan and Fangzheng areas; the Ninth Army was expanded from the Third Army and was headed by Li Huatang in Tonghua, Sanjiang province. In November 1936, Wang Yachen announced the formation of the Eleventh Army in Fuyuan near Khabarovsk on the banks of the Amur River.

With the proliferation of various armies operating in different regions, coordination from one army to another became difficult, and since all were engaged in guerrilla activities in the countryside and forests away from towns and villages, strict control of eleven armies was virtually impossible. Each army, more or less, operated on its own, and hence there were no large-scale challenges to the Japanese army or the Manchukuo police force. In an effort to coordinate their activities, these eleven armies were reorganized according to their operational regions into three route armies at various times from 1936 to 1938. The First Route Army was announced on May 11, 1938, by combining the First and Second Armies to operate primarily in southern Manchuria under the command of Yang Jingyu. The Second Route Army was organized with the Fourth, Fifth, Seventh, Eighth, and Tenth Armies in January 1937 and operated in eastern Manchuria under the command of Zhou Baozhong. The Third Route Army was organized with the Third, Sixth, Ninth, and Eleventh armies in 1936 and operated in northern Manchuria under the command of Zhao Shangzhi.

The leadership of the United Army during the latter half of the 1930s changed rapidly. The roster of officers presented in table 2.1 was put together by combining information from a number of Chinese and Japanese sources.[8] For a better understanding of their guerrilla activities, see map.

NORTHEAST CHINA
(MANCHUKUO)

Legend
1. First Army
2. Second Army
3. Third Army
4. Fourth Army
5. Fifth Army
6. Sixth Army
7. Seventh Army
8. Eighth Army
9. Ninth Army
10. Tenth Army
11. Eleventh Army

■ Headquarters

Khabarovsk

Fuyuan (11)

THIRD ROUTE ARMY

Fujin (10) Raohe (7)

Jiamusi

Tangyuan (6)
Yilan (8)

Fangzheng

Tonghua (9)

Mishan (4)

Harbin

Zhuhe (3)

SECOND
ROUTE
ARMY

Mudanjiang
Ningan (5)

SOVIET
UNION

Changchun   Jilin   Emu

Vladivostok
Nakhodka

Santouwai (2)

Tomen

Yitong
Panshi (1)

Yanji

Longjing

Antu

Fusong

Paektusan

FIRST ROUTE ARMY

Shenyang

Hyesanjin

Padaogou

KOREA

Area of Operation by the northeast Anti-Japanese United Army

*Table 2.1. Leadership of the Northeast Anti-Japanese
United Army from 1936 to 1941*

First Route Army (Commander-in-Chief: Yang Jingyu)
First Army (Commander: Yang Jingyu; Political Commissar: Yi Hong-gwang*)
    First Division (Commander: Cheng Pin)
    Second Division (Commander: Cao Guoan)
    Third Division (Commander: Chen Hanzhang)
Second Army (Commander: [Chu Chin], Wang Detai; Political Commissar: Wei
    Zhengmin)*
    Fourth Division (Commander: An Pong-hak*; Ch'oe Hyŏn*)
    Fifth Division (Commander: Fang Zhensheng)
    Sixth Division (Commander: Kim Il Sung*)

Second Route Army (Commander-in-Chief: Zhou Baozhong)
*Fourth Army (Commander: [Wang Delin], Li Yenlu; Political Commissar: Huang
    Yuqing)*
    First Division (Commander: Li Yanping)
    Second Division (Commander: Zou Yŏuyan)
    Third Division (Commander: Guo Fude)
Fifth Army (Commander: Zhou Baozhong; Political Commissar: Song Yifu)
    First Division (Commander: Ping Nanyang)
    Second Division (Commander: Fu Xianming)
    Third Division (Commander: Guo Fude)
Seventh Army (Commander: Yi Hak-man*; Political Commissar: Ch'oe Yong-gŏn*)
Eighth Army (Commander: Xie Wendong; Political Commissar: Liu Shuhua)
Tenth Army (Commander: Wang Yachen)

Third Route Army (Commander-in-Chief: Zhao Shangzhi)
*Third Army (Commander: Zhao Shangzhi; Political Commissar: Feng Zhongyun, Kim
    Ch'aek*)*
    First Division (Commander: Zhao Shangzhi)
    Second Division (Commander: Li Xishan)
    Third Division (Commander: Li Fulin)
    Fourth Division (Commander: Shi Guilin)
    Fifth Division (Commander: Li Zhaolin)
Sixth Army (Commander: Xia Yunjie; Political Commissar: Chang Shoujian)
    First Division (Commander: Xia Yunjie)
    Second Division (Commander: Feng Zhingang)
    Third Division (Commander: Chang Chuanfu)
Ninth Army (Commander: Li Huatang)
Eleventh Army (Commander: Qi Zhizhong)

Note: Among these leaders of the United Army, only a few survived World War II. Zhou Baozhong of the Second Route Army survived the war and later became an alternate member of the Central Committee of the Chinese Communist Party in its Eighth National Congress. Zhou died in February 1964. When a North Korean military delegation visited Beijing shortly before his death, Zhou was hailed as their former leader in Manchuria. Li Yenlu was elected to the Standing Committee of the Third National People's Congress in January 1965. Feng Zhongyun was twice elected to the National People's Congress from Jilin. See their activities in Donald W. Klein and Ann B. Clarck, *Biographic Dictionary of Chinese Communism, 1921-1945*; Howard L. Boorman, ed., *Biographical Dictionary of Republican China*, 1:415-416; and *Who's Who in Communist China*, pp. 367-368. See also a similar chart in the Chinese People's Revolutionary Museum that was reproduced in Nishimura Shigeo, *Chūkoku kindai tōhoku chiekishi kenkyū*, pp. 290-304.
*Korean officer

It is this United Army that most of the Korean partisans joined to fight the Japanese from 1932 to 1941. The top leadership of this army was held primarily by the Chinese Communists. Koreans were scattered in all of these armies, but they were heavily concentrated in the Second Army because it operated in eastern Manchuria, where Koreans had emigrated and settled for a long time, outnumbering the Chinese in the region. There were many gallant Korean partisans in all armies, including Yi Hak-man who later became commander of the Seventh Army.[9] It was the Second Army in which Kim Il Sung began his armed guerrilla activities.

Kim and the Second Army

When the Second Army was first organized in March 1934 the commander was a Korean named Chu Chin, and his political commissar was Wang Detai, a Chinese who later succeeded him as commander. Chu Chin was a good fighter, well known for his exploits against the Japanese. He was eventually arrested in February 1935 by the Yilan branch of the Japanese police, whose members were rewarded with money and trophies.[10] Kim Il Sung began in this Second Army as a fighter in the third detachment of the First Company of the Second Independent Division and rose through the ranks, eventually reaching the rank of Sixth Division commander. His activities along with such other Korean guerrillas as Kim Il, Ch'oe Hyŏn, and An Kil were notable, and Kim consolidated his position within the army.[11]

When the Second and Fifth Armies were regrouped for a joint operation against the Japanese in 1936, the rise of Kim's prominence within the guerrilla group was obvious. Kim was assigned to the Chinese commander Chai Shiying and deputy commander Fu Xianming as political commissar of the Central Command. He also commanded his own division, named the Kim Il Sung Division, of approximately one hundred men in the Emu area halfway between Jilin and Mudanjiang.[12] However, for a Korean to rise in the Chinese army was a difficult matter, even for a man with Kim's background of attendance at Chinese schools and fluent in the Chinese language. The commander of the Second Army, Wang Detai, was killed in a battle against the Japanese Seventh Cavalry Division in the Fusong area on November 7, 1936. He was succeeded by another Chinese, Zhou Shudong, but he too was killed, on April 24, 1937, in the battle of Antu.[13] The command of the Second Army was taken over by still another Chinese, Wei Zhengmin, Kim's mentor. There were a number of important casualties among Korean guerrillas too; Kim Myŏng-p'al, for example, who was four years senior to Kim and had an illustrious record of guerrilla activity against the Japanese, was killed in October 1937. On the Japanese side, Major General Ishikawa Shigeyoshi was killed by a company of guerrillas led by An Pong-hak, a Korean partisan, in the battle near Tunhua prefecture on October 10, 1936.

In an effort to control the Communist guerrillas, the Japanese in Manchuria launched a number of expeditionary forces. The Japanese army, particularly the *Kantōgun* (Guandong Army), was interested in securing their bases in Manchuria to support their advance into the China mainland. The Japanese wanted to develop and secure coal mines, timber industries, and other natural resources in Manchuria without interference from organized Communist resistance groups. This effort, together with the measures taken by the police of the Manchukuo government, eventually brought an end to the operation of the United Army.

The final push to stamp out the Chinese Communist guerrilla forces in Manchuria came when the *Kantōgun* appointed Major General Nozoe Shōtoku commander of the Second Independent Security Division in Jilin. In October 1939, leaders of the Japanese military and the Manchurian government met, and Nozoe's expe-

Zhou Baozhong, commander of the Second Army

Li Yenlu, commander of the Fourth Army

Feng Zhongyun, political commissar of the Third Route Army

Kim Il Sung and his soldiers, autumn 1940

ditionary force was given thirty million yen to wipe out the Communist guerrillas by March 31, 1941.[14] Major General Nozoe was assisted by an able man and veteran "bandit hunter," Lt. Col. Fukube Kunio, who proposed a two-prong policy of defeating the guerrillas in combat and persuading them to surrender. The latter was called a submission operation that promised the guerrillas money and immunity from punishment if they would abandon communism and surrender. Fukube's policy was successful. Those who surrendered not only abandoned communism but assisted the Japanese in capturing the leaders of the guerrilla forces.

   In anticipation of the intensified Japanese expedition, the First Route Army in southern Manchuria reorganized themselves. The First and Second Armies of the First Route Army were organized into three directional armies (*Fangmianjun*). In this final reorganization of the First Route Army, Kim Il Sung was appointed com-

*Commanders of the Japanese and Manchukuo Expeditionary Force:
Major General Nozoe Shōtoku, Yu Chenzhi, and Lieutenant Colonel Fukube
Kunio*

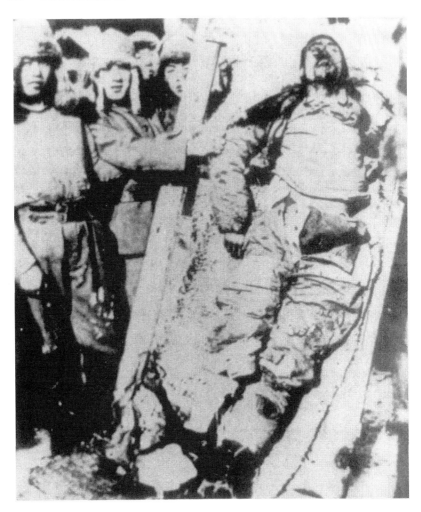

Body of Yang Jingyu, commander-in-chief of the Northeast Anti-Japanese United Army, February 23, 1940

mander of the Second Directional Army operating in Jiandao province where the majority of residents were Korean. The leadership of the First Route Army in November 1938 was as follows:[15]

Japanese Expeditionary Force that killed Yang Jingyu

Commander-in-Chief: Yang Jingyu
Deputy commander: Wei Zhengmin
Chief of staff: Fang Zhensheng
Political commissar: Chŏn Kwang (Korean)
First Directional Army commander in Tonghua province: Cao Yafan
Second Directional Army commander in Jiandao province: Kim Il Sung (Korean)
Third Directional Army commander in Jilin province: Chen Hanzhang

When the Japanese expeditionary campaign under General Nozoe intensified, all of these leaders except Kim Il Sung were either killed or surrendered. In the most famous campaign to capture the commander-in-chief of the First Route Army, Yang Jingyu, the Japanese forces were guided by one of Yang's most trusted comrades, the former First Division commander Cheng Pin who submitted to the Japanese. Yang was killed on February 23, 1940, in the battle of Mengjiang in Tonghua province. He was tracked down for about a week by Cheng Pin, and it was claimed that the detachment which eventually killed Yang was commanded by Nishitani Kiyojin of the Mengjiang Prefectural Police Expeditionary Force, which belonged to the Tonghua Provincial Police headed by Kishitani Ryūichirō.[16]

Yang's chief of staff Fang Zhensheng was arrested and executed by the Japanese on February 15, 1940, and the commander of the First Directional Army, Cao Yafan, was killed by his own men in an internal squabble on April 8, 1940.[17] The commander of the Third Directional Army, Chen Hanzhang, was killed by the Japanese on December 8, 1940, after a long chase from southern to northern Manchuria. After Yang died, the deputy commander Wei Zhengmin assumed leadership of what was left of the First Route Army. Shortly after the death of Yang, Wei called a small meeting, March 13–15, 1940, at the camp of the political commissar, Chŏn Kwang, in Huaxun. This meeting was attended by eleven leaders of various groups left in the First Route Army including Han Inhwa, Kim Kwang-hak, Ch'oe Hyŏn, Kim Chae-bŏm, Kim Il Sung, and Chŏn Kwang. In view of the mounting casualties, Wei cautioned that all units, whenever possible, should avoid direct confrontation with the Japanese and change tactics to work more closely with the people. Even this new tactic did not work, however, as two members of this group, Kim Kwang-hak and Kim Chae-bŏm, were arrested when they went into villages to work with the people.[18]

The end of the First Route Army came when the political commissar, Chŏn Kwang, surrendered to the Japanese submission operation on January 30, 1941, and turned against his comrades-in-arms. Chŏn led the Japanese expeditionary troops to the hideouts of his fellow guerrillas. Soon thereafter, Wei Zhengmin was killed on March 8, 1941, in Huaxun. Others either surrendered or were arrested and later submitted to the Japanese, including Pak Tŭk-bŏm, who gave the Japanese much information on the remaining guerrillas and their activities, making it almost impossible to continue fighting. Among the leaders of the First Route Army, Kim Il Sung was the only one who neither surrendered nor was captured and killed. Kim continued to fight to the end, but when it became obvious that the United Army was defeated, and the Second and Third Route Armies were also defeated in the north and northeast, Kim fled to the Soviet Union. It is reported that Kim told Wei

Zhengmin he wanted to follow Zhou Baozhong, commander of the Second Route Army, into the Soviet Union, but Wei was said to have withheld permission. Kim fled shortly after the death of Wei in March 1941 by way of Hunchun prefecture, using a wooded area called Meili across from Vladivostok.[19] General Nozoe's expeditionary forces had succeeded in their campaign to wipe out the United Army, and General Nozoe ordered dissolution of his own force on March 12, 1941. The Japanese and Manchukuo joint victory celebration was said to have been held on March 19, 1941, about two weeks ahead of schedule.[20]

There are various reports on numbers of Communist guerrillas in Manchuria, but both Chinese and Japanese accounts are either exaggerated or discounted. The Japanese estimated that approximately 15,000 guerrillas were operating from 1932 to 1940, and the Chinese claim there were more than 30,000 guerrillas in the eleven armies of the United Army.[21] Irrespective of their claims, Communist revolutionary struggle in Manchuria was an ordeal to be remembered by both Chinese and Japanese forces.[22]

3

Guerrilla
Accomplishments

This account of the United Army is not intended to deny or belittle the many successful exploits of Kim Il Sung and his partisans. The fact that he outlasted his Chinese superiors and Korean comrades in the First Route Army to the end is commendable. Kim survived as a true Communist guerrilla without surrendering, despite numerous Japanese campaigns to defeat him and without submitting to the many invitations to defect. The reward posted by the Japanese for information leading to his arrest in 1936 was only 20,000 yen compared to 200,000 yen for Yang Jingyu, but by 1939 Kim commanded the same amount as Yang.[1] At one point, one of the Japanese expeditionary forces thought they had killed him, and the money was paid and a citation was issued to the commander of that force, but Kim turned up in another region.[2]

Kim's accomplishments are impressive, as we shall see, but what is most damaging to his record is his exaggerated claims. Kim has built an image of a benevolent and righteous leader who took from the rich and gave to the poor and still fought for the Korean Communist revolution. His fame as a successful guerrilla fighter comes not from his benevolence but from the ruthlessness with which he dealt with Japanese and Korean collaborators. It is a good record for a young man to have taken up arms against the Japanese while many of his compatriots were collaborating with the enemy. Kim claims many campaigns in southern and eastern Manchuria prior to 1935, but these seem to have been small-scale operations. His most illustrious campaigns do not start until about 1936 and they end in 1940.

Koreans in the United Army

Kim does not mention his former affiliation with the United Army; he claims that he organized a Korean anti-Japanese partisan group on April 25, 1932. He says that he fought the Japanese in Wangqing prefecture in March 1933, in Xiaowangqing in April, in Dongning prefecture in September. He also claims that he reorganized his partisan groups into a Korean People's Revolutionary Army in March 1934, twice going to northern Manchuria to Ningan prefecture near the city of Mudanjiang from 1934 to 1936. Kim's effort here is to establish a Korean identity and to build a Korean tradition out of his association with the Chinese Communist guerrilla group.

Kim began his guerrilla activities early in a Korean Nationalist group, led by Yang Se-bong, but soon changed to fight for the Chinese group headed by Wu Yicheng who was not a Communist guerrilla leader. Kim said that his first encounter with the Chinese commander Wu was in June 1933 when he visited him in Luozigou to resolve the problem of Chinese killing some thirty Korean partisans led by Yi Kwang in April 1933. Kim is supposed to have had a conference in which he was able to persuade Wu to work with and not against Koreans. As a result of this meeting Kim is said to have brought Wu's forces, including Shi Zhongheng and Li Sanxia, under his command.[3] These claims are absurd to say the least.

Wu was a well-known Chinese commander who inherited most of the soldiers of Ma Zhansan and Li Du, both of whom fled to the Soviet Union after the Japanese took over Manchuria in 1931. The Japanese at one time reported that Wu's command had several thousand Chinese soldiers. It should be remembered that Kim had organized his own partisan forces in April 1932, only a year earlier, with eighteen men. Friction between Chinese and Koreans was not uncommon, and at times the Chinese discrimination against Korean partisans was intolerable. Many Koreans who were uncertain about their role in the Chinese guerrilla force left to join a partisan group headed by a Korean commander. This was the Second Army of the United Army, headed by a Korean commander named Chu Chin, that operated in the Jiandao region where Korean residents outnumbered the Chinese. In the Jiandao region of eastern Manchuria, 78 percent of the population were Koreans compared to 22 percent Chinese, and in southern Manchuria the percentage was reversed, about 80 percent Chinese and 20 percent Koreans. Most of the Koreans were engaged in farming, working about half of the arable land in this region.[4]

The racial conflict in the United Army came out in the open in January 1935 through the Minsaengdan Incident. The Minsaengdan was a Japanese police front organization of Korean residents in Manchuria established to curb the constant looting by bandits. Members would disguise themselves as bandits, penetrate the camps of the guerrillas, and return with information of their whereabouts, numerical strength, condition of arms, and the like. This organization was in existence for only a short period, from February to July 1932, but its name became a catchword among the partisans and any Korean agent was called a *minsaengdan*.

A similar organization named Hyŏpchohoe was organized to perform more or less the same function on September 6, 1934, by a Japanese gendarme, Lt. Col. Katō Hakujirō of Yanji prefecture. The president of the organization was a Korean collaborator named Kim Tong-han, and it had a membership of 8,195 men in the Jiandao region. This group openly advocated assassination of guerrilla leaders, induced the surrender of partisans, and rewarded informers. It was in operation until December 27, 1936, when it merged with still another organization known as Kyōwakai or Hyŏphwahoe.[5]

The incident that touched off the open hostility between Korean and Chinese guerrillas was the penetration by an agent of Hyŏpchohoe into the armed camp of the Second Army. The agent knew that a certain guerrilla named Han Yong-ho had gone to fetch food in nearby Baicaogou. Acting as Han's friend, he had entered the campground and escaped with vital information about the guerrilla base. When he returned to the base, Han insisted on his innocence but was executed after interrogation. Han named others before his death, and a wave of interrogation and execution spread throughout the Second Army, eventually reaching as far as the commander, Chu Chin, and his political commissar, Yi Sang-muk. Chu was able to escape, but he was later captured and executed by the Japanese; Yi Sang-muk surrendered to the Japanese and revealed much information about the impact of the *minsaengdan* on the Sino-Korean relationship in the United Army.[6]

After this incident, Wang Detai, a Chinese, was appointed to succeed Chu Chin as commander of the Second Army, and its leadership was taken over by the Chinese. Worse than the change in leadership was the suspicion hanging over every Korean partisan. Many innocent Koreans were suspected and tortured. Hŏ Yŏng-ho, for example, was immediately dismissed from his position as Second Company commander, and Ch'oe Hak-ch'ŏl and some sixty men in Hunchun prefecture were expelled from the army. According to one report, the enraged Korean partisans even conspired to assassinate the new Chinese commander, Wang, in retaliation.[7]

A conference to solve the problem of *minsaengdan* was held from February 24 to March 3, 1935, in Daihuanggou in Wangqing prefecture under the new political commissar of the Second Army, Wei Zhengmin. Some of the excessive punishments were recognized and rectified by the Chinese. While there was no change in the composition of leadership circles, the Chinese persuaded the Koreans to stay and fight with them in the United Army. Kim Chae-su, who later defected, reported that in some areas the Chinese and Koreans organized separate detachments. In others, however, the prejudice against the Koreans continued, and many Koreans left the United Army. In Tangyuan, for example, the commander, Xia Yunjie, was a heavy opium smoker who ordered his Korean subordinate Yi In-gŭn to cut off the ear of a kidnapped Korean hostage; when Yi refused, Xia called him a *minsaengdan* and shot him to death on the spot. Five Korean partisans in that army escaped and reported the incident to the commander of the Third Army, Zhao Shangzhi. Zhao rectified the situation by relieving Xia from his post.[8] However, the United Army was no longer the same place for Koreans and many left.

North Korean historians claim that Kim played a leading role in mediating the differences between Chinese and Koreans in the incident. The records of the conferences held under the auspices of Wei Zhengmin in February and March 1935 are available, and Kim was not present at those meetings, let alone playing any role in them. The earlier version of Kim's biography condemned the leaders of the Korean delegation to these meetings, Song Il and Kim Sŏng-do, as factionalists, but the latest version omits their names. Kim Sŏng-do was not even present. Song Il headed the delegation, but he was later falsely accused of being a *minsaengdan* himself and was executed.[9]

The more important consequence for Kim Il Sung was his future role in the United Army. Most of the fainthearted Koreans defected, and cooperation between the Chinese and Koreans was difficult at best. Kim was one of the few Koreans the Chinese had trusted because of his facility in the Chinese language and his Chinese educational background. For those who remained, the Chinese leaders paid extra attention and treated them well, particularly after the August First Declaration of the Chinese Communist Party that called for a united front of all ethnic groups in Manchuria.

The Poch'ŏnbo Raid and the Korean Association

The largest and most successful campaign Kim waged during his guerrilla days was the raid on Poch'ŏnbo, a Korean town just over the Manchurian border. Kim's Sixth Division of the Second Army of the First Route Army, consisting of nearly two hundred guerrillas, attacked the town on June 4, 1937, destroying local government offices and setting fire to the Japanese police box, the local elementary school, and post office. He took four thousand yen from the local people and inflicted damage estimated at sixteen thousand yen. He took the town and occupied it for that day, but early the next morning he retreated to Manchuria. The stunned Japanese police pursued Kim's unit to the Yalu River on June 5, but Kim Il Sung turned around and defeated the Japanese police force, killing seven Japanese police officers including Police Chief Ōkawa.[10] In a related campaign, Kim was joined by the Fourth Division commander, Ch'oe Hyŏn, who was returning from a similar raid on Musan on June 9, 1937, in Ershidaogou in Changbai prefecture in Manchuria. The combined forces raided the outpost of Yokoyama timber camp and attacked the Japanese forces, killing more than ten and taking nine hostages as well as guns and ammunitions. This was the raid that made Kim famous and known to the Japanese.

The raid was important for its military impact alone, but more important to the Japanese was the fact that the raid on Poch'ŏnbo was coordinated by the anti-Japanese united front organization known as *Hanin choguk kwangbokhoe*, the Korean Fatherland Restoration Association. Members of the association were in touch with Kim Il Sung's Sixth Division for nearly half a year planning for the raid. Kim claims that he was president of the association, but the facts on the association are well documented and its operation is known.

The association was created to form a united front of the anti-Japanese Koreans in Manchuria following the August First Declaration of the Chinese Communist Party in 1935. The association was founded on June 10, 1936. Its declaration, platform, and bylaws of eight chapters and fourteen articles are documented.[11] The person who played the most important role in organizing the association was Chŏn Kwang, Kim's superior in the United Army. Chŏn Kwang was directed in turn by Wei Zhengmin who came from the Comintern. Branches of this association were created in various border towns within Korea; for example, Kwŏn Yŏng-byŏk organized the Changbai Operation Committee (*Changbaek kongjak wiwŏnhoe*), the Kapsan Operation Committee was organized by Pak Tal and Pak Kŭm-ch'ŏl, and the Kangguri Operation Committee by Ch'oe Kyŏng-hwa. Kim Il Sung did have a role because he used the members of the Kapsan group to attack Poch'ŏnbo in June 1937, but his connection did not go beyond his military campaign. The organizational work of establishing various branches seems to have been the work of Chŏn Kwang.

Chŏn Kwang is a celebrated revolutionary known to the Korean revolutionary movement as O Sŏng-yun. The declaration of the association was signed by an initiatory committee consisting of three men: O Sŏng-yun, Ŏm Su-myŏng, and Yi Sang-jun. Of the three, O Sŏng-yun is most famous. Together with an accomplice named Kim Ik-sang, O tried to assassinate a Japanese general, Baron Tanaka Giichi, in Shanghai on March 28, 1922. He missed Tanaka, however, and killed an innocent woman who was getting off the boat behind Tanaka. O was immediately arrested and interned in the Japanese consulate jail in Shanghai. He escaped on May 2, 1922, and eventually made his way to Manchuria through Europe and the Soviet Union and joined the United Army.[12] O was known in the United Army as Chŏn Kwang and worked closely with Yang Jingyu and Wei Zhengmin. In fact, O was Kim's superior in the United Army, serving as political commissar under Wei, while Kim was one of its division commanders. Wei Zhengmin held one of his last meetings of the First Route Army at O's operational headquarters. Kim Il Sung did participate in this meeting, and Kim knew O Sŏng-yun, known to him as Chŏn Kwang, very well, but he does not mention Chŏn Kwang or O Sŏng-yun at all.

Even without his claim to membership in the Korean Fatherland Restoration Association, his military exploits are impressive. The raid on Poch'ŏnbo was particularly important because he crossed the border and came into Korea from Manchuria, using an underground group that was organized by the United Army. Kim's earlier guerrilla activities in Manchuria were reported in Korea as early as October 1936. An article in *Chosŏn ilbo* described Kim with about forty men descending on a Korean farmer named Pak Hŭng-yong in a small village named Shiliudaogou and taking his cow and grain on October 4, 1936.[13] There are many more articles about Kim's activities of this kind, but they deal with Kim's banditry and general condemnation of his plundering, sympathizing with the suffering of the Korean immigrants in Manchuria. It was difficult for Korean-language newspapers of the 1930s under strict Japanese censorship to report any patriotic and Communist activities.[14] However, the Japanese made a big issue of Kim's raid into Poch'ŏnbo, because Kim's activities did not stop with Korean farmers or Korean collaborators but extended to killing Japanese police officers in Korea. Kim's guerrilla activities in both Manchuria and Korea commanded the immediate attention of the Japanese because he was an able guerrilla leader efficient in killing Japanese soldiers and police.

Guerrilla Activities: 1937–1940

Many Japanese accounts of Kim's guerrilla activities report on this period, and there are even more claimed by Kim in North Korea. There is no need to describe them all in detail, but it is important to know how Kim fought, recruited guerrillas, procured supplies and arms, and conducted himself.

Even before his raid into Korea, Kim's force of nearly 150 guerrillas, joined by an equal number of partisans headed by Cao Guoan, met the Japanese expeditionary force in February 1937 and engaged them in a number of battles in Changbai prefecture near Paektusan. Especially noteworthy is the battle of Limingshui on February 26, 1937. A small detachment of approximately 50 guerrillas challenged the Japanese forces, but when the Japanese expeditionary force gave chase to the retreating guerrilla detachment, Kim Il Sung's main group of 250 guerrillas attacked from the snow-covered highland where they were hiding, covering their heads with white cloth. It is reported that nearly five feet of snow fell the night before. Kim and Cao's guerrillas defeated the Japanese, killing thirteen officers under Lieutenant Kawada, wounding fourteen Japanese soldiers, and taking seventeen prisoners including Lt. Murayama Masashige.[15]

Kim Il Sung fought all during 1938 and 1939, mostly in southern and southeastern Manchuria. There are numerous accounts of his activities, such as the Liudaogou raid of April 26, 1938, and his raid into Korea once again in May 1939. Another noteworthy engagement was Kim's battle with the Japanese Special Police headed by Maeda Takeshi that tracked Kim's group for months in early 1940. When Maeda's forces finally caught up with Kim in March 13, 1940, at Daimalugou in Helong prefecture, they were attacked by Kim's guerrillas. After the attack, Kim is said to have released his captives because he had to move on quickly. Maeda's police pursued him for nearly two weeks, catching up with him in Hongqihe, Antu prefecture, on March 25, 1940. In this battle, Kim deployed 250 guerrillas against 150 of Maeda's force and defeated him completely. Kim killed the commander Maeda Takeshi, 58 Japanese police officers, and 17 workers attached to the police force and wounded many police officers and workers. He took 13 prisoners and much ammunition and weapons from Maeda's force. To the

Korean captives, Kim is said to have preached Communist revolution in Korea, and he asked them to join his guerrilla forces voluntarily. He promised them he would someday invade Korea.[16] Kim's force expanded to approximately 340 guerrillas in July 1940, and such trusted comrades as Ch'oe Hyŏn, Ch'oe Ch'un-guk, Kim Tong-gyu, and An Kil worked closely with him. However, his force became one of the main targets of Major General Nozoe Shōtoku's expeditionary forces, and Kim himself admits that he went into a small-unit operation from August 1940.

Kim's largest command was approximately 300 men, both Chinese and Koreans, at the height of his operation from 1937 to 1940, but at times he operated with fewer than 50 men. This is not to belittle his efforts. The nature of his operation was such that the forces were divided into many small companies and detachments, constantly moving from one location to another in deep mountain forests and difficult-to-reach areas. It was an arduous undertaking with the Japanese expeditionary forces constantly following their trail. To avoid heavy casualties, his campaigns in most cases were hit-and-run operations. There were many casualties, particularly in the winter months. Kim said that the winter of 1936–1937 was so harsh that he spent most of the time in the snow-covered impassable mountains with only a few soldiers.

Kim recruited Chinese coolies and Korean farmers, and in many of his raids into towns and villages he kidnapped young men and trained them to fill the ranks. In his raid on Poch'ŏnbo, for example, Kim recruited nearly ninety Koreans into his company. For the recruitment of officers, the Second Army advertised a training school and printed handbills to announce the recruitment of officers. Among several qualifications listed, such as age and loyalty to the cause of China and Chinese communism, was a provision that the prospective candidate should not smoke opium. These handbills were printed in Chinese and were directed to the Chinese and Korean residents in Manchuria. Kim's principal method, however, was to take hostages.[17]

The guerrillas acquired their provisions in several ways. The most commonly used methods were demands made on rich Koreans, enforced by taking hostages. At times they attacked small villages and trains to replenish their supplies. At other times, they

In commemoration of the capture of Chu Chin by the Yilan Branch of the Japanese police, February 1935

offered opium and ginseng farmers their protection and exacted their crops. Kim often used threats against farmers to collect supplies and money. One of the phrases he often used against the farmers and Japanese collaborators was to give "guns if you have guns, people if you have people, money if you have money, and goods if you have goods." Kim used to threaten people that if they did not comply, he would cut off the ears of the hostages, and if they still did not comply he would cut off their heads.[18]

Numerous reports in Korean newspapers cite Korean immigrants who suffered at the hands of the guerrillas. Kim's partisans took 5,000 yen from a rich Korean miner named Kim Chae-hŭng; from those who did not have cash on hands, they took promissory notes to be collected later.[19] Kim spoke often of the dire need for food and described grievous circumstances with little clothing in the dead of winter. Kim and his men had to go for more than two or three days without food, and at times they maintained a diet of salt and water. The methods they used to acquire provisions were not unusual for an underground guerrilla force.[20]

Li Zhaolin of the Third Route Army.

Li's Korean wife and children

Leaders of the Korean Fatherland Restoration Association arrested after the Poch'ŏnbo raid, December 1937

From left to right, seated front row:
Sŏ In-hong, Yi Che-sun, Chi T'ae-hwan, and Kwŏn Yŏng-byŏk (all executed); standing back row:
Pak Nok-kŭm (free), Hwang Kŭm-ok (six months), Chang Chung-yŏl (eight months), and Pak Kŭm-ch'ŏl (life imprisonment)

Ch'oe Hyŏn and his men in Dunhua prefecture, winter 1938

Members of the First Route Army, summer 1939

In an effort to find out more about the internal operation of Kim's guerrilla force, the Japanese police sent in a woman named Chi Sun-ok whose husband had earlier joined the force. She joined ostensibly to look for the husband she had not seen for three years, but in truth she was sent in by the Japanese police equipped with a poison pill to swallow if she was unmasked and unable to withstand the torture. She joined the Seventh Detachment commanded by O Chung-hŭp of Kim's guerrillas in August 1939 and worked nearly a year as a cook and seamstress. She was released from the guerrillas by Han Ik-su because she was weak and unable to move fast when the guerrillas had to retreat into mountain forests. Chi Sun-ok reported that when she first joined the guerrillas, she was interrogated by Kim Il Sung in person for nearly four days, and she was allowed to join the women's detachment consisting of about thirty-two women.

A guillotine in Manchuria.

Public display of the beheaded.

Shortly after she joined, Kim's group raided a wealthy Chinese landlord named Liu and took him hostage to get food and clothing. She and other women made clothes from the fabric for the

Chŏn Kwang (second from left), Kim Il Sung's superior in the First Route Army, surrendered January 30, 1941

Pak Tŭk-bŏm surrendered September 28, 1940.

Kim Il Sung in the Soviet Union, 1943
Left to right: Kim Il Sung, unknown, Ch'oe Hyŏn, and An Kil

Kim Il Sung, his wife, Kim Chŏng-suk, and son Kim Jong Il

guerrillas. After repeated requests, she was allowed to see her husband once, but her husband was transferred to another unit. In November 1939, the Seventh Detachment commander O Chung-hŭp was killed in a raid and O Paek-yong succeeded him as commander. She reported that Kim Il Sung was an able leader, constantly preaching to his men about international communism and Korean nationalism when they were not fighting or retreating. She also said that on October 11, 1939, eight Russians came with two interpreters and stayed nearly ten days discussing something with Kim in the forest near Sandaogou, Helong prefecture. She suspected that the Russians supplied ammunition and arms from the Soviet Union at least once in three months. She confessed that the most difficult part of her guerrilla life was the hunger and cold.[21]

As for the procurement of arms, Kim said that he fought with weapons he took from the Japanese. This was one method the partisans used to acquire arms, but in most cases the Korean partisans received weapons from their Chinese counterparts, and sometimes they bought ammunition locally. There are many Japanese arrest reports dealing with the illicit sale and purchase of firearms, particularly those attempts by Ch'oe Hyŏn, who was the supply officer for the Second Army. At times the Manchurian police, after faking an encounter with the guerrillas, sold their weapons and ammunition for profit. It was reported that Fang Zhensheng, one of the Chinese commanders, regularly obtained arms and ammunition in this way.[22]

Still another method was to *make* arms. Pak Yŏng-sun made a crude form of grenade, for example, which the Koreans called *yŏn'gil p'okt'an* (Yanji bomb).[23] Simple repairs of guns and pistols were all done by the partisans themselves. Perhaps most noteworthy was the fact that the guerrillas often crossed the border into the Russian Maritime Province and bought arms from the Soviet Union. This practice was common in the northern region across from Khabarovsk where the Second Route Army, and more specifically the Seventh Army, operated. The commander of the Seventh Army, Yi Hak-man, used to cross the border into the Soviet Union and bring back large numbers of arms and ammunition.[24]

Kim's accomplishments as a guerrilla are therefore many. He fought the Japanese expeditionary forces at great odds. He was ultimately defeated, but he never feared the Japanese. What he feared more was the hunger, the cold, and the defection in his ranks. Many of his men, including Kim Pong-jun, Yim U-sŏng, Pak Tŭk-bŏm, Han In-hwa, and Kim Chae-bŏm, did defect. Even his superior officer in the First Route Army, Chŏn Kwang, surrendered to the Japanese and then helped the Japanese expeditionary force hunt Kim down, but Kim escaped and survived. There was strife in his own ranks also, such as the quarrel between Ch'oe Hyŏn and Pak Tŭk-bŏm. When Pak defected, he joined the Japanese in the search for Ch'oe Hyŏn. Among those captives and hostages Kim took in his numerous raids into timber camps and coal mines, few believed in his Communist revolution and virtually all looked for an opportunity to defect.

In the Soviet Union: 1941–1945

While Kim is silent about his retreat into the Soviet Union, there are many reports of his trek there. He is said to have entered the Soviet Union to evade the pursuing Japanese forces soon after the death of Wei Zhengmin on March 8, 1941. Wei was Kim's superior and mentor, and his death convinced Kim that his guerrilla activities in southern Manchuria had come to an end. In the biographical sketch of Wei, there is a story of camaraderie between Wei and Kim, signifying the joint effort by Chinese and Koreans against the Japanese. Kim always cared for Wei, who was in ill health, securing rare herb medicine for him and giving him food when it was scarce. Wei, in turn, is said to have prepared Korean buckwheat noodle soup (*naengmyŏn*) when Kim visited him in his camp. Wei said that Kim's love for *naengmyŏn* was well known, and he prepared it properly, even when it was difficult to get foodstuffs.[25]

Kim is said to have left from Hunchun prefecture, using the wooded area called Meili, along the banks of the Tumen River into the area west of Vladivostok. It is said that Kim had only six men with him when he crossed the border and that he was temporarily interned until his identity was verified by Zhou Baozhong, the commander of the Second Route Army who had earlier retreated to the Soviet Union in 1940.[26] Kim eventually joined the Chinese guerrilla group led by Zhou Baozhong in three training camps.

One defector from North to South Korea related that when he was a reporter for the North Korean newspaper *Minju Chosŏn*, he was told by Kim Il Sung himself that he had fled to the Russian Maritime Province in 1941. He said his article to that effect appeared in the paper on August 15, 1947.[27]

Chinese and Korean partisan retreats, either tactical or by necessity, were not uncommon. One of the more famous Chinese leaders, Li Du, fled to the Soviet Union in the early 1930s. In addition to Zhou Baozhong, Kung Xienying and Chai Shiying also fled to the Soviet Union, and Yi Hak-man, the Korean commander of the Seventh Army, crossed the border into the Soviet Union. In a Russian study about the liberation of Korea, Major General B.G. Sapozhnikov relates that there were many partisan crossings as early as 1936 and 1937. He recounts one incident that he investigated while stationed in the Russian Maritime Province. He was asked on February 22, 1936, to investigate a crossing of armed guerrillas into Soviet territory. Accompanied by one Korean interpreter named Kim Soy (Kim So-i, or Lieutenant Kim), he found that some sixty partisans, of whom two-thirds were Koreans and one-third Chinese, under the command of a Korean partisan named Pak In-ch'ŏl, had come into the Russian Maritime Province. He said that many were wounded and hungry, and the commander, Pak, was wounded in his left arm. Sapozhnikov related that after he had helped them he sent them back to Manchuria in April 1936. He also expressed the general concern of the Russians at the time that it was difficult for them to distinguish between genuine anti-Japanese partisans and Japanese agents disguised as partisans.[28]

The Soviet Union seems to have welcomed the Chinese and Korean guerrillas from Manchuria in the 1940s after they had forcibly relocated Korean residents from the Russian Maritime Province to the Central Asian republics of Kazakhstan and Uzbekistan in the latter half of the 1930s. Survivors of all units of the United Army eventually retreated at various times from 1940 to 1941 into the Soviet Union. They were camped and trained in three locations: Okeanskaya Field School near Vladivostok, Voroshilov Camp in Nikolsk, and a training camp in a wooded area south of Khabarovsk.[29] Korean partisans were scattered in all three Soviet training camps, and Kim Il Sung was trained at Okeanskaya Field School.

Kim eventually met all Koreans from the Second and Third Route Armies including those under Zhou Baozhong, among them Ch'oe Yong-gŏn, Kim Ch'aek, and Kim Kwang-hyŏp, but survivors of Kim's own group from the First Route Army, including Sŏ Ch'ŏl, An Kil, and Ch'oe Ch'un-guk, stayed with Kim in the southern camps near Nikolsk and Vladivostok.

The purpose of the Soviet Union in training these men seems to have been to use them against the Japanese if ever the Soviet Union had to fight the Japanese in Manchuria. These guerrillas, though defeated in Manchuria, had both the experience and the will to fight the Japanese. There are scattered reports that Kim Il Sung led a small detachment and reentered Manchuria near Dongning prefecture and fought the Japanese. One report says that Kim Il Sung, Ch'oe Hyŏn, and Chai Shiying and their partisans of 150 men were reorganized into three detachments with fifty guerrillas each in the Voroshilov Camp commanded by a Soviet officer of the 57th Guard Unit in Iman. The same report says that Kim Il Sung headed the second detachment and taught anti-Japanese songs and trained his men. Kim is said to have returned to Manchuria and fought the Japanese police unit headed by Koga on April 26, 1941.[30] There are other reports of his men fighting in Manchuria after the retreat to the Soviet Union, among them were An Kil, Kang Kŏn, Kim Il, and Yi Pong-su.

The most important revelation is a report made in February 1943 when a Soviet-trained Korean guerrilla named Pak Kil-song was arrested. Pak was one of the Korean detachment leaders arrested on January 4, 1943, after entering Manchuria from the Soviet Union.[31] Pak revealed there were approximately 700 men in Khabarovsk Camp taking orders from a Soviet officer named Vassiliev, but such Chinese leaders as Zhou Baozhong and Chang Shoujian appealed unsuccessfully to the Soviet authorities to let them be autonomous and take orders only from the Chinese Communist Party. Pak also revealed that, when he returned to Manchuria, he discovered that the Korean underground leader in Manchuria, Hŏ Hyŏng-sik, was killed on August 3, 1942, and the operation in Manchuria had had to undergo reorganization. In this reorganization Kim Ch'aek was elected leader of the underground organization in September 1942, but he was ordered to return to the Soviet Union.

Among others who returned and were arrested were Han Hŭng-sŏn and Kim Ch'un-sŏp, who told of their training in the Soviet Union in anticipation of the Soviet war against Japan. Details of the Soviet training of partisans are not known, but some sort of sophisticated training seems to have taken place, including parachute exercises. Major General Sapozhnikov has related that when the Soviet army entered Manchuria at the close of World War II, they dropped paratroopers near Harbin and were able to link up with them after crossing the border in August 1945. In a jovial mood shortly after his return to Korea, Kim Il Sung said that he and his men were planning a dramatic entrance into Pyongyang by parachute, but the confounded Japanese had surrendered before their plans could be realized.[32]

Pak Kil-song also revealed that the Soviet Union was in the process of creating an international military unit under their Far Eastern Command by recruiting and training the anti-Japanese guerrillas from Manchuria, an army 10,000 strong, to prepare for their campaign against the Japanese. In an effort to train the retreating guerrillas from Manchuria, the Soviet Far Eastern Command appointed a few officers of the international unit. Pak said that in the camp near Khabarovsk, Zhou Baozhong, commander of the Second Route Army, and Chang Shoujian were appointed colonel; Kim Ch'aek and Feng Zhongyun were appointed lieutenant colonel; and Wang Minggui, Bian Fengxiang, Chang Guangdi, and Pak himself were appointed to the rank of major.[33] Similar organization must have taken place in Voroshilov Camp and Okeanskaya Field School, and Kim Il Sung is said to have been appointed major in the 88th Division of this international unit of the Far Eastern Command of the Soviet army. When Kim first appeared in Pyongyang, he was reported to have returned to Korea in a Soviet army uniform wearing the rank of captain or major.

It was during his five-year stay in the Soviet Union that Kim was married to Kim Chŏng-suk, a member of his partisans who fought with him in Manchuria. The record of Kim Chŏng-suk appears in Japanese police files, and the North Koreans recognize her as a partisan who was a close comrade of Kim Il Sung, but not his wife. Kim Chŏng-suk, was born on December 24, 1919, the elder of two daughters of a poor farmer in Hoeryŏng, Hamgyŏng pukto. She was seven years younger than Kim and had a background similar to Kim's own. She followed her mother to look for her father in Yanji, Manchuria, but found that he had already died there. Soon thereafter she lost her mother and became an orphan. She is said to have joined Kim's guerrilla force in 1935 at the age of sixteen as a kitchen helper. She worked at many odd jobs for the guerrillas and was arrested by the Japanese in the summer of 1937 while working as an undercover agent to procure food and supplies.

When she was released, she rejoined the guerrillas. She is said to have cooked, sewed, and washed for the guerrillas and even saved Kim's life once in 1939.[34] Japanese Major General Nozoe Shōtoku, whose expeditionary force hunted Kim and his partisans during his last days in Manchuria, related that his able military police sergeant Nagashima Tamajirō had captured a woman partisan named Kim Hye-sun who claimed that she was the wife of Kim Il Sung. She was arrested on April 6, 1940, and has related that she and another woman along with three male partisans were left behind because she was wounded. The Japanese tried to use her to lure Kim to surrender, but they were not successful. There is no record of such a woman partisan in any of the Chinese or Korean sources.[35]

Kim Chŏng-suk followed Kim Il Sung into the Soviet Union, apparently married him there, and bore him a son on February 16, 1942. This son was given the Russian name Yura and the Korean name Chŏng-il (Kim Jong Il). While in the Soviet Union, she bore him another son. Kim's second son, named Shura (Kim P'yŏng-il), was born in 1944, but he drowned in a swimming accident in July 1947 in Pyongyang. She also bore him a daughter (Kim Kyŏng-hŭi) in Pyongyang, but the whereabouts of this daughter are not known. Kim Chŏng-suk died on September 22, 1949, in Pyongyang while delivering a stillborn baby.[36] She was affectionately called Vera by the generals of the Soviet occupation forces in Pyongyang, and for one year after the establishment of the republic in North Korea until her death in September 1949, Kim Chŏng-suk was the first lady of North Korea. Major General N.G. Lebedev, executive officer of the Soviet occupation forces in North Korea, remembered her as a vivacious and generous lady who always cooked enormous amounts of food for the hungry Soviet generals when they visited Kim's home.[37] A statue was erected and a museum was built in her home town in Hoeryŏng after her son Kim Jong Il became prominent in North Korea in the late 1970s, but this tribute to her is in commemoration of the contribution to the Korean revolution as a partisan and not as wife of Kim Il Sung or mother of Kim Jong Il.

Given his personal background and the circumstances in Korea and Manchuria during the latter part of the Japanese occupation, Kim's record of anti-Japanese guerrilla activities is commendable. For a young man who had no family life to speak of and deprived of basic support from his family and friends, Kim did well to join a subversive, Communist group to fight for his country. Even if the United Army was a Chinese guerrilla force, he fought against the Japanese for the cause of communism in China and Korea. He suffered many defeats, but he also scored some impressive victories and made a name for himself — indeed, he became the most wanted guerrilla leader in Manchuria. He persisted in the hopeless fight without much support, but he endured and did not surrender or submit to the Japanese. He also preached to his men the cause of Korean independence and the need for communism and fostered anti-Japanese spirit in the darkest days of the Korean independence movement. He did not win many converts, and he had to resort to taking hostages to prolong his guerrilla activities, but he did fight to the end. When the Japanese expeditionary force crushed the guerrillas in Manchuria, he fled to the Soviet Union, where he was trained by the local Soviet authorities. He returned to North Korea when his country was liberated.

In an effort to denigrate his past records, South Korean sources consider him a fake, denying him his past revolutionary activities. But Kim is not a fake. To be sure, there were countless patriots who attained majority at the time of the fall of the Korean kingdom in 1910 and fought the Japanese throughout their adult lives, returning to Korea at the end of thirty-five years of Japanese occupation. There were many who perished, fighting for freedom in

Korea during the period. Compared to these men, Kim's period of struggle is indeed brief, and his contribution may not be considered significant as that of others, but his record is a solid one and deserving of recognition even if it was under the United Army of the Chinese Communists.

A more serious difficulty comes from his attempt to build a towering Korean image of himself by denying any of his Chinese and Soviet connections. North Koreans have manufactured evidence to prove that Kim was a Korean revolutionary who fought solely for Korean liberation, claiming nonexistent records and denying the contribution of others to the cause of Korean independence. Evidence of his close relationship with the Chinese guerrillas is overwhelming, however, and his persistent denial of such records does not improve his image as a Korean revolutionary. Many Koreans fought against the Japanese alongside whoever supported their cause. Even the Korean Nationalists who despised communism asked for assistance from the Soviet Union in the First Congress of the Toilers of the Far East and the Comintern in the 1920s.

Kim's image-building campaign is indeed extreme in many respects. His show of filial piety, for example, does not seem to be simple reverence of his parents, who in fact did little for Kim in his boyhood. His purpose, rather, seems to be more self-serving: an effort to build his own image as a pious Korean son from a revolutionary Korean family. As an uneducated Korean youth who spent most of his young life fighting what he considered to be his enemy, the Japanese, Kim's record is commendable, and his less-than-adequate knowledge of the tenets of communism is nothing to be ashamed of. His insistence that he taught fourth graders dialectical materialism when in fact he was expelled from school in the eighth grade does not make him a good Marxist.

To refute Kim's claims is not difficult. But more important than the false claims is his effort to build the tradition of Korean communism and Korean revolutionary spirit upon such fallacious foundations. His Chinese and Soviet connections were fortunate for his future in the northern half of liberated Korea, but the suppression of such records to show that he accomplished all for Korea in the name of Korea does not bring about the intended result. His partisan activities with the Chinese were not ever-victorious; in fact, they ended in defeat. It is his persistence and obstinate will, characteristics of many successful revolutionaries elsewhere, that deserve recognition. It was also his political good fortune to have had Chinese and Soviet connections that distinguished him from other Korean revolutionaries.

II

CONSOLIDATION OF
POLITICAL POWER

The Koreans greeted their liberators in 1945 with uncommon enthusiasm — not so much because they approved or disapproved the disparate political ideologies of the Soviets and the Americans but primarily because their military occupations brought an end to the harsh Japanese rule under which they had suffered so long. But they soon learned the consequences of the liberation their own revolutionaries did not bring home. The United States instituted direct military rule in the South and the Soviet Union virtually dictated its wishes in the North. The so-called temporary division of the country was to last longer than the entire period of the Japanese occupation. Numerous efforts at peaceful reunification of the country have failed, and the North Korean military attempt to reunify the country brought even more unwanted non-Korean military forces into Korea and killed more Koreans, yet left the country still divided. The flames of the Korean revolutionary spirit have died without truly attaining the ultimate objective: an independent and unified Korea.

There were many organized Korean independence groups outside of Korea, but none of their military units entered the country with the liberators. There was not even a contingent of an organized Korean group operating in either the United States or the Soviet forces that occupied Korea. The only organized group of any consequence, the Korean Provisional Government with its military unit, was with the Chinese Nationalists in China, but it was not the Chinese Nationalists that came and occupied Korea. The American occupation forces immediately dismissed the Korean Provisional Government as well as all other political groups when they returned to Korea. The long and sometimes grueling activities of the Korean Communists ended without any formal ties or official relationship with the Soviet Union and its occupation forces. Kim Il Sung's unit that was defeated by the Japanese and retreated to the Soviet Union came closest to being a Korean armed unit operating with the occupation forces. His unit was small and without foundation in Korea, but none of the others had any political roots or organized base in the North because the Japanese had succeeded in extirpating all organized resistance groups within Korea.

When compared with other, more popular Korean revolutionaries and their groups, Kim had two crucial elements on his side: one was the support of the Soviet occupation forces, the other was the division of Korea itself. The Soviet Union recognized no political groups in the North, nor had they prepared a leader in Moscow for Korea. Not knowing the past records of the Korean Communists, the Soviet military unit that occupied the North supported one of their own number. The division of Korea lured most of the prominent revolutionaries to Seoul, the capital of Korea in the South, leaving the North free for Kim to maneuver. It was in the South that major leaders fought each other for political hegemony, not realizing that they were fighting for the southern half only.

In retrospect, it was fortunate for Kim Il Sung to have fought with the Chinese in Manchuria and to have received training in the Soviet Union. His association with the Soviet military units there, although it lasted less than five years, was more than any Korean revolutionary group had ever had in the Soviet Union in more than three decades under the Japanese. During the Soviet occupation of three years and four months from August 1945, Kim faithfully carried out Soviet directives, putting himself in a leadership position and managing to control his opposition. He created a new party, a new army, and a new government, all patterned after the Soviet Communist system. Less than five years after he returned to Korea, Kim Il Sung tried to unify the country militarily with his newly trained soldiers. This effort failed just as surely as his partisan struggles in Manchuria, but in the process Kim had begun to lay the groundwork for his power. He used the failure in the Korean War to suppress his opposition and consolidate his power, just as he had used the defeat in Manchuria to his advantage in regrouping his partisans in the Soviet Union.

4

The Soviet Occupation
of North Korea

General Ivan M. Chistiakov, who commanded the 25th Division of the Soviet army that liberated and occupied North Korea after World War II, related that he was stationed in the Soviet Far East from 1935 to 1941.[1] He left the area for the German front in 1941 and led the 21st Division of the Red Army in the Stalingrad campaign,[2] but he returned to the Soviet Far East at the order of Marshal Stalin on June 24, 1945. The top generals of the 25th Division, P.F. Lagutin, V.A. Penkovsky, B.A. Makarov, V.C. Cherenkov, and N.P. Boroviagin, had all served in the Primori region and knew well the activities of the Chinese and Korean guerrilla groups. Major General Nikolai G. Lebedev, for example, had been in the area since 1941 until he led the assault into Korea in August 1945.

The extent of Kim Il Sung's relationship with these generals is not known. General Chistiakov later recalled that he had heard about the partisan activities of Kim Il Sung in Manchuria in the late 1930s, but if there was any meaningful relationship between Kim and Chistiakov, it was only from June to August 1945. Kim had not followed General Chistiakov to the German front, for when he fled Manchuria into the Soviet Union Chistiakov had already left the area. Furthermore, Kim denied participating on the German front many times after he returned to Korea.[3]

Major General Lebedev said that he himself did not meet Kim until after the war. When he first met him in Pyongyang, however, Kim was in a Soviet uniform wearing the insignia of a Soviet army captain. Lebedev said that Kim's men numbered about forty and were all in Soviet army uniform.[4] While the major thrust of the Soviet occupation forces of 40,000 men under General Chistiakov came into Korea by sea, landing in Unggi, Najin, Ch'ŏngjin, and Wŏnsan, the advance party came through Manchuria. Major General B.G. Sapozhnikov related that his advance troops came through Harbin, Mudanjiang, and Tumen and entered Korea through Kyŏngwŏn, Hoeryŏng, and Ch'ŏngjin.[5] He also said that when he came into Manchuria he looked for a Korean partisan group led by Pak In-ch'ŏl, whom he had helped earlier and returned to Manchuria. He found the group, but he learned that Pak In-ch'ŏl had been killed by the Japanese in August 1937.[6]

The Liberation of Korea

Kim claims that he returned to Korea triumphantly waging a joint operation of his own army with Soviet forces to defeat the fleeing Japanese. The Soviet generals who liberated Korea related that the main Soviet assault forces landed from the sea along the eastern coast from Unggi and Ch'ŏngjin in early August and marched throughout Kangwŏndo and Hwanghaedo, eventually arriving in Pyongyang on August 26, 1945. Kim Il Sung returned to Korea with his fellow guerrila leaders in the 88th Division of the international unit from the Soviet Union on September 19, 1945,[7] a day before Ch'usŏk, a Korean holiday. They arrived in Wŏnsan harbor long after Japan had surrendered, and the Soviet occupation forces completed the report of the 25th Division's combat operation to the commander-in-chief of the Soviet army in the Far East on August 27, 1945.[8]

There are many eyewitness reports of the events in the North shortly after the liberation, but most of them are vituperative accounts by defectors from the North to the South, berating the Communists and Kim Il Sung.[9] Korean leaders knew about Kim and his record of guerrilla activities in Manchuria because he fought primarily with the Chinese Communist guerrilla groups. During the first month after his arrival, Kim made several visits to local North Korean leaders such as Cho Man-sik, but he seems to have impressed no one.

Among so many committees, political parties, or governments that sprang up in both North and South Korea after the liberation, none listed Kim among their leaders. The Communists certainly did not include him, for he had not participated in any Korean Communist activities. It took a herculean effort on the part of the Soviet occupation authorities to introduce him to the people as a Korean patriot. Even then few believed he was really what he claimed to be — partly because he was so young, only thirty-three years old then, and partly because he claimed so many patriotic and Communist revolutionary activities that the people knew nothing about. Many considered him a fake, thinking that the real Kim Il Sung was a much older man. When the cold war between the Soviet Union and the United States became more pronounced, most Koreans in the South subscribed to the idea that he was indeed a fake put up by the Soviet Union to turn the northern half of their country into a Communist state. Kim may have had the support of the Soviet Union and the loyal following of his partisans from Manchuria, but his political future in Korea was an uphill fight.

The Soviet occupation authorities in North Korea followed closely the pattern of sovietization used in Eastern Europe.[10] The occupation was headed by an able and trusted Soviet army general, Ivan M. Chistiakov, and his chief-of-staff, Lt. General Valentine A. Penkovsky. His chief executive officer was Major General Nikolai G. Lebedev, who handled the political affairs of the occupation. His political advisor was Gerasim M. Balasanov, who had worked in Japan and spoke Japanese. Later in 1946 Anatolii I. Shabshin, who worked in the Soviet consulate in Seoul as deputy consul, joined them in the North. The military affairs of the 25th Division were handled by Major General G. I. Shanin, and the civil administration of the North was headed by an expert organization officer, Major General Andrei Alekseevich Romanenko. It was Romanenko who was chief civilian administrator of the occupation authorities and who handled the Koreans and political leaders in the North shortly after the liberation. General Terentii F. Shtykov, who negotiated with American forces in Seoul, did not arrive until February 1946, but he stayed in the North to oversee the civilian administration of the 25th Division. When the Soviet troops withdrew from the North, he was appointed by Stalin as first ambassador of the Soviet Union to North Korea.

General Chistiakov related that Major General Romanenko was an experienced organization officer formerly associated with the 35th Army who had prepared himself for the North Korean occupation in the Primori region. There are many critical accounts by defectors of the role played by Major General Romanenko, but General Chistiakov contends that he was a fair man who assembled several groups of experts and brought them along to the North. There were, for example, Colonel G. R. Lazarev on communication, Colonel A. T. Ilatovsk on finance, Major I. I. Kadishev on agriculture, Major A. I. Rotblyut on public health, and Colonel N. I. Dolgikh on army and civilian relations.[11] The most important of them all, perhaps, was Colonel Alexandre Mateevich Ignatiev for civil administration.

It was Colonel Ignatiev, under the direction of Major General Romanenko, who dealt with all Korean political leaders and the process of the sovietization in the North. Colonel Ignatiev was the key person who maneuvered Kim Il Sung into power, sustained him there, and supported him in the North. Ignatiev stayed long after Romanenko had left Korea. In fact, most of the generals and the occupation forces left Korea rather early; for example, General Chistiakov left the North as early as March 1947, and 30,000 soldiers of the Soviet occupation forces left within a year. General G. P. Korotkov succeeded him and commanded the remaining occupation forces, 10,000 strong, for another year. There was a further reduction of the occupation forces when Korotkov was replaced in May 1948 by General Merkulov, who commanded a small force until the entire army withdrew on December 24, 1948. But Colonel Ignatiev remained. When the Soviet embassy was established in October 1948 after the Democratic People's Republic of Korea was proclaimed, Ignatiev was retained in the Soviet embassy in Pyongyang as an adviser to Ambassador Shtykov.

General Lebedev related that Ignatiev had a good personal relationship with Koreans and handled civilian affairs well. He was in his mid-forties and was benevolent, restrained, and hardworking. Indeed, at times he used to work through the night to discuss setting up administrative machinery with Korean political leaders. Ignatiev was the chief architect of the sovietization of North Korea, and it was Ignatiev, together with Major General Romanenko, who engineered Kim Il Sung into the supreme power position.

The choice of Kim as leader of the liberated northern half of Korea should not be understood as a complicated procedure. The Soviet Union was more concerned with their occupation of Eastern Europe, and Kim Il Sung was not what Boleslaw Bierut was for Poland, nor was he for Korea what Wilhelm Pieck or Walter Ulbricht were for East Germany. The Soviet Union came into Korea not knowing any revolutionary leader or revolutionary organization. Their preparation for the occupation of Korea was made in the Primori region by the 25th Division, and it seemed to be truly an ad hoc preparation for military occupation. Stalin chose his military commander for the task only in June 1945, and General Chistiakov's major concern was a military operation against the Japanese army first and the sovietization of the North second. The Soviet Union needed no Korean assistance for the first objective, and it needed only a Korean figurehead for the second.

There was no prominent Korean Communist operating in Moscow who had a link to underground Communist organizations in Korea. Even after the Soviet occupation began, in fact, the indigenous Korean Communists who were known to the people in Korea for their past revolutionary activities did not actively seek cooperation with the Soviet authorities. The Soviet Union seemed to have chosen a fellow in the region where they were preparing for their campaigns against the Japanese. Kim was a young Korean Communist leader whom they trained, who wore their uniform of his own volition, and whose anti-Japanese guerrilla record they knew. They may not have been as confident on him as they might have been with someone groomed and dispatched from Moscow by Stalin. They might have preferred a national hero known to all Koreans, but once they had decided on Kim, they promoted and popularized

*Kim Il Sung in 1947, chairman of the North Korean
Provisional People's Committee*

*Soviet generals of the 25th Division who liberated North Korea
Left to right: S. G. Chiplenkov, G. I. Shanin, I.M. Chistiakov (commanding
general), N.G. Lebedev, I.M. Sokolov, P. F. Lagutin*

Officers of the Soviet occupation that implanted communism in North Korea, Pyongyang, 1947

him. In the absence of any competing Communist groups and leaders in the North, it was not a difficult task. Kim's obscure past and lack of popularity mattered little. The only alternative to Kim the Soviet authorities encountered after their arrival in the North was a Nationalist leader, a deacon of a Presbyterian church, Cho Mansik.[12] More prominent Korean political leaders, Nationalists and Communists alike, were all in the South, trying to negotiate with the Americans.

When they arrived in Pyongyang on August 26, 1945, the Soviet occupation authorities announced in their first declaration that the Korean people were liberated and their future happiness was in their own hands. Independence was given to Korea; the Koreans must bring about their own happiness. The authorities also proclaimed that the Soviet Union would help in every way it could in this Korean endeavor.[13] This declaration was quite a contrast to the proclamation issued to the people of Korea by General MacArthur on September 7, 1945, which stated in its first article that all powers of government over the territory and the people in the South would be exercised "under my authority."[14] For the Korean revolutionaries who read both documents, the difference seemed profound.

In reality, however, the contrast was not as great as the declarations seemed to suggest. Despite the American proclamation, most of the revolutionaries returned to the South, and there was a constant flow of refugees from North to South. American occupation authorities, of course, denied the legitimacy of any group — including the People's Republic of Korea, hastily put together by the Preparatory Committee for Korean Independence; the Korean Provisional Government, which returned to Seoul from Zhongqing after twenty-six years of continuous operation in China; and Syngman Rhee and his group from the United States.

The Sovietization of North Korea

The Soviet occupation forces accomplished the sovietization of the North in three stages in a relatively short time: the first stage of "genuine cooperation" from August 1945 to January 1946, the second stage of what may be called a "bogus coalition" from February 1946 to early 1948, and the final stage of establishing a monolithic regime from February to September 1948, when the Communist state was formally proclaimed.

Local leaders in the North organized a branch of the Preparatory Committee for Korean Independence in P'yŏngan namdo, where Pyongyang is located, and three representatives of this group were in the Pyongyang railroad station to welcome the Soviet army on August 26, 1945. This group presented, within a few days after their arrival, a roster of a fifteen-man Interim People's Committee of that province to Major General Romanenko and Colonel Ignatiev, but they were told to double its membership by adding fifteen Communists. Two women were added later, one each from the Communist and the Nationalist camps, to bring the administration staff to a total of thirty-two members. This was the first group organized to handle the day-to-day activities of P'yŏngan namdo, and similar groups, commonly known as the Interim People's Committee, were organized in all five provinces of the North.

On October 8, 1945, Major General Romanenko and Colonel Ignatiev called for a congress of representatives of the Interim People's Committees of all five provinces to organize an administrative unit to govern the entire northern half of Korea. Some seventy-five delegates attended this congress, which was held for only one day, and adjourned in various committees to work on the proposed agendas of the congress.[15] It was not until November 19, 1945, that the results of the congress were announced. It was known as the Five-Province Administration Bureau (*Odo haengjŏngguk*), a simple organization of ten bureaus headed by Nationalist leader Cho Man-sik.[16] Kim Il Sung was not a delegate to this congress, nor was he elected or appointed to head any bureau. There seems to have been "genuine cooperation" by the occupation authorities to bring together various local elements, Nationalists as well as Communists.

However, this bureau did not last long. The coalition collapsed with the controversial issue of the trusteeship of Korea in December 1945. In an effort to resolve military occupation and bring reunification of Korea, the United States and the Soviet Union agreed in Moscow to a five-year trusteeship of Korea. Colonel Ignatiev tried without success to persuade the chairman, Cho Man-sik, and members of the bureau to endorse the proposed five-year trusteeship by the allied powers. The Communists agreed but the Nationalists refused, thus dividing the bureau into two camps. This was true also of the situation in the South. Except for the Communists, most of the Korean leaders opposed trusteeship for any length of time. The Soviet Union was able to force the Communists to accept trusteeship, but the American authorities relented to the persistent and earnest desire of the Korean people to be independent and abandoned the idea.[17]

Unlike East European countries, the Korean Nationalists in the North did not challenge the Soviet occupation authorities — not because they were not determined to force the issue but because they had the ready alternative of fleeing the North and going to the South, thus avoiding, for example, such incidents as the Katyn forest massacre in Poland and the bloodshed in Warsaw. General T. F. Shtykov, who negotiated with the Americans on the future of Korea, condemned the Nationalists and Cho Man-sik in no uncertain terms. Regarding Cho's defiance, Shtykov said that Cho was not the only leader, and the meaning of class struggle should be explained to these defiant Koreans.[18] Cho himself had several opportunities to flee, but he remained in the North. He was later arrested and interned and presumed executed shortly before or after the outbreak of the Korean War. The genuine effort of cooperation between the Nationalists and the Communists ended with the trusteeship question by early January 1946.

After the collapse of the Five-Province Administration Bureau, the Soviet occupation authorities established the North Korean Provisional People's Committee on February 8, 1946, and appointed Kim Il Sung as its head. Some Nationalists participated in the committee, but it was unmistakably a Communist-dominated body created by the Soviet occupation authorities — a good example of a "bogus coalition." With Kim Il Sung as its chairman, the committee instituted six major "democratic reforms" in rapid succession: the land reform that redistributed more than 50 percent of the arable land, the labor law that instituted an eight-hour work day, the nationalization of all heavy industry, institution of an agriculture tax-in-kind system, equality of the sexes, and the new election code. These reforms were completed in less than six months.[19]

In instituting these measures and reforms, occupation authorities maintained a broad popular front, recruiting people from various groups and organizations. Behind the facade of the "bogus coalition," however, there seems to have been a clear distinction between the position of prominence and the position of power. The Soviet occupation authorities used Koreans from the Soviet Union, the Soviet-Koreans, in positions of power and controlled the sovietization process during this period.[20] Kim's lack of training and the dearth of trained manpower were augmented by the second-and third-generation Soviet-Koreans who returned to Korea after World War II. The exact number of these Soviet-Koreans who returned to Korea is not known, but they did play an important role in North Korean politics during the first decade after the liberation.

The sovietization process was given credibility in February 1948 when the Soviet Union helped Kim Il Sung to create the Korean People's Army. Kim consolidated his power with his guerrilla group from Manchuria, and his partisans played a key role in the formation and operation of the Korean People's Army. The Soviet occupation authorities helped in this process by assuring Kim that no other Korean armed group challenged him and his partisans. Kim was successful in disarming the only military group that was capable of challenging him — the group returning to Korea from Yanan, China, the Korean Volunteer Corps under the command of Kim Wŏn-bong. It was reported that an estimated 2,000 members of the corps were disarmed by Kim and his group as they entered Korea at Sinŭiju from Andong across the Yalu River. Kim is said to have personally inspected the situation and followed the directives of the occupation authorities of October 12, 1945, and disarmed all men of the Korean Volunteer Corps before permitting them to cross the border into Korea.[21]

On the domestic front the Public Security Bureau was headed by a Soviet-Korean, Pang Hak-se, who was assisted by Kim's own partisan from Manchuria. Pang was for North Korea what Stanislaw Radkiewicz was for Poland. There were others, such as Nam Ch'ang-yong and Kim P'a, but these men were all under the direction of Colonel Zagruzin of the Soviet secret police. Kim's partisans dominated every security and police organization in the army. All senior officers of the Red Security Corps, the Peace Preservation Corps, the Border Constabulary, and the Railroad Guards that controlled the movement of the people were members of Kim's partisans.

These security and army groups backed up Kim's administration of the sovietization and enforced his pronouncements. The Soviet authorities may have appointed Kim to administer their programs, but Kim had no organizational roots in Korea; he may have controlled military and security sectors of the administration, but the Communist Party was beyond his reach. Major General Romanenko and Colonel Ignatiev completed the sovietization process when they helped Kim to create a mass party in North Korea.

The Korean Communist Party knew little about Kim Il Sung, and he certainly was not one of its members who shared the ordeal of two decades under Japanese police surveillance since its establishment in April 1925. The party was reestablished in Seoul shortly after the liberation of Korea under the leadership of Pak Hŏn-yŏng and was in the process of rebuilding its branches throughout North and South Korea. The person sent to Pyongyang to organize the North Korean Branch Bureau of the Korean Communist Party was Hyŏn Chun-hyŏk, a native of Pyongyang who was educated by the Japanese but worked against them during their occupation of Korea. Hyŏn had a good record well known to the Korean revolutionaries.[22] Similar to the effort by the Korean Communist Party that tried to work with the Nationalists and the American occupation authorities in the South, Hyŏn tried to work with Cho Man-sik and the Nationalists in the North.

Korean Communist leaders from the five provinces in the North began organizing a branch bureau in the North, and Hyŏn headed this effort. But in September 28, 1945, Hyŏn was assassinated on his way back from a meeting with Major General Romanenko. He was in the front seat of a truck with Cho Man-sik, but his assailant killed only Hyŏn. There is an elaborate account of his death implicating Kim Il Sung as the culprit. Kim had arrived in Wŏnsan on September 19, 1945, less than ten days before the shooting, and it is unlikely that he was involved in the plot to eliminate Hyŏn. It was reported that Kim had conspired with Chang Si-u, head of the Justice Department of P'yŏngnam Provincial Bureau, to have one of their henchmen murder Hyŏn.[23] Political assassination was common in both North and South Korea shortly after the liberation.

Kim Il Sung proceeded to organize the branch bureau that Hyŏn had originally planned with one important modification — that is, a Communist Party independent of the party in Seoul. The negotiations for such an organization seem to have coincided with the congress of the Interim People's Committee held in October. The North Koreans claim today that the meeting was held for four days, October 10–13, 1945, but their own publications at the time stated that only a decision to establish such a branch was made on October 13, 1945, in a one-day meeting.[24] The latter version seems more accurate because it was one day after the declaration of the occupation forces giving permission for local political groups to organize themselves.

On October 12, 1945, a five-point proclamation was issued in the name of Generals Chistiakov and Penkovsky that permitted Koreans to organize anti-Japanese democratic groups, to organize unions and other nonpolitical groups, to attend church services, to report the roster of officers and men as well as platforms and by-laws of all such organizations, and to disarm all military groups and establish a security force in the North.[25]

The official announcement of the formation of the North Korea Branch Bureau of the Korean Communist Party in Pyongyang was not made until October 20, 1945. However, Kim was not elected chairman of the bureau, but Kim Yong-bŏm, a relatively unknown figure, was chosen to succeed Hyŏn as leader. The bureau was established as a branch of the Korean Communist Party headquartered in Seoul. In fact, it was reported that permission for establishing such a branch in North Korea was granted by the central organization of the Korean Communist Party in Seoul on October 26, 1945. The plenum of the bureau was held on November 15, 1945, to form a united front of all political and semipolitical groups in the North. It was not until the third enlarged plenum, held on December 17–18, 1945, that Kim took over the chairmanship of the bureau. Kim Yong-bŏm died later during a simple operation on a stomach tumor.

When Kim did succeed in getting control of the bureau, he immediately began to detach it from the Korean Communist Party in Seoul, and he met considerable opposition. It took him six months, and during the seventh plenum of the bureau on June 22–23, 1946, the name of the bureau was changed to the North Korean Communist Party, thereby proclaiming its independence from the Korean Communist Party in Seoul. Kim followed closely the instructions of Colonel A. Ignatiev, who attended the plenums of the bureau and participated in every discussion of the meetings.[26]

For Colonel Ignatiev, the process was merely a preliminary step for the creation of a mass party by uniting this party with other political parties. At the eighth plenum of the North Korean Communist Party in July 1946, barely one month after they had detached themselves from the Korean Communist Party in Seoul, Kim was told to form a coalition of the North Korean Communist Party with the New Democratic Party (a political party of the returned Communist revolutionaries from China) to form a Workers' Party. The work of Colonel Ignatiev in forming this coalition is obvious, for Kim had neither the vision for such a party nor the ability to win support of those returned revolutionaries from Yanan without Soviet persuasion. In fact, the similarity of the Soviet occupation policy in coercive fusion of political parties to create a mass party is striking in the creation of the Socialist Unity Party in East Germany, the United Polish Workers' Party, and the Workers' Party of Korea.

As a guerrilla leader who fought the Japanese in Manchuria with the Chinese, Kim was unable to forge a united front organization or a mass party of this kind in Korea. Nor is it conceivable that

Korean revolutionaries from other regions would follow his leadership without the persuasion of the Soviet occupation authorities. General Romanenko and Colonel Ignatiev used Kim well in their effort to institute the Soviet system in the North. Kim Il Sung for his part served as a good agent of the Soviet occupation authorities in this process, following faithfully their instructions. Perhaps Kim followed more faithfully than any spirited Korean Nationalist leader or any leader of the Korean Communist Party would have done, because others tended to look more toward Moscow and the Soviet government for instruction than to the Soviet military officers stationed in Korea.

The Soviet occupation authorities accomplished sovietization in a short time, taking full advantage of the lack of resistance to their programs. They used Kim Il Sung in accomplishing their objectives of organizing a mass party, instituting Communist reforms, and creating a military unit to support the system they instituted. All administrative directives and decisions by the Soviet occupation authorities were executed through Kim, making him the pivotal link between the Korean people and the occupation forces. In this way, it was possible for the Soviet Union to disavow unequivocally any direct measure to administer militarily while still succeeding in implanting a Communist system in Korea.

For the Soviet Union, it was far more important to implant a Communist system in the North than to promote Kim, but in the process they succeeded in anointing him as leader of the Korean people and made serious efforts to promote him as a national hero. This endorsement of Kim Il Sung by the Soviet occupation forces was the most important advantage he had in his competition with political rivals. A ballad about his heroic deeds in Manchuria, which schoolchildren were forced to sing, eventually became the most popular song in the North. A university was named after him, and poets were mobilized to write poems and stories about his partisan activities against the Japanese.

Although Kim received the blessing of the Soviet occupation authorities, his relationship with rival Korean political groups was quite another matter. He had to deal with three groups. The first and most numerous was the group of indigenous Communists, known as the domestic group, who operated underground in Japan and Korea; the second group was the returned revolutionaries from

China that formed the New Democratic Party (*Sinmindang*), more commonly known as the Yanan group; and the third was the Soviet-Koreans who returned to Korea with the Soviet army but remained to participate in the political process after the Soviet forces withdrew.

Kim had fewer than two hundred regrouped partisans from Manchuria; though they were completely loyal to him, they were few in number. Many factors helped Kim in his quest for power. First and foremost, of course, were the Soviet occupation authorities and Colonel Ignatiev. The second was the division of Korea itself, which kept most of the well-known veteran Korean Communists in the South. Seoul was the capital of Korea, and all prominent Korean political leaders thought their political future was to be decided in Seoul and not in Pyongyang. The third reason was that other groups were not united in supporting a single political figure. Not all Korean Communists supported Pak Hŏn-yŏng; not all members of the Yanan group supported Kim Tu-bong; and the Soviet-Koreans did not even consider themselves as a group. In fact, many Soviet-Koreans supported Kim at first because he was the choice of the Soviet occupation army. And finally, Kim's control of military and security forces meant that no other group had any control or exercised any influence. Kim's partisans and those Soviet-Koreans who returned to Korea as regular members of the Soviet army were united in supporting him.

Kim did have to deal with the domestic group when the old Communist revolutionaries came to the North from the South, however, and he also had to maneuver the Yanan group, some of whom had fought with Chinese Communist forces on the China mainland. Kim also had to pacify returning Koreans from the Soviet Union who claimed to have more knowledge of communism and Communist organization than he had. Colonel Ignatiev was confident in what he had created, however, and Kim met the challenge head on. Nowhere was this struggle more obvious than in the two most important organizations: the party and the government.

5

The Workers' Party of Korea

North Korea claims that the Workers' Party of Korea was founded on October 10, 1945, under the wise leadership of the great leader Kim Il Sung and commemorates the day annually. It was first organized by uniting the New Democratic Party and the North Korean Communist Party at its founding congress, August 28–30, 1946, under the direction of the Soviet occupation authorities. It was then known as the Workers' Party of North Korea. A similar coalition of political parties was made in the South among the Korean Communist Party, the New Democratic Party, and the People's Party, November 23–24, 1946, in Seoul to found the Workers' Party of South Korea. The formal union of the Workers' Party of North and South Korea was not consummated until June 24, 1949, when the first joint plenum was held.

The "union" of the two parties was in truth an absorption of the party in the South by that in the North. Thus the founding congress of the Workers' Party of North Korea is considered as the first congress of the Workers' Party of Korea, and the second congress of the Workers' Party of North Korea, held March 27–30, 1948, before the union, is the second congress of the Workers' Party of Korea. The party congress held from April 23–29, 1956, is the third congress, and the party held three more congresses: the fourth congress, September 11–16, 1961, the fifth congress, November 2–13, 1970, and the sixth congress, October 10–14, 1980.

The first move to create a mass organization by the occupation authorities was not in the party but in the youth organization. Kim Il Sung was told by the occupation forces to dissolve the Young Communist League and create a mass youth organization known as the Democratic Youth League. This move met resistance from the indigenous and local party leaders, for it was a forced merger of all youth groups in the North. The new Democratic Youth League that absorbed the Young Communist League as well as other groups was announced as early as January 17, 1946.[1] The Democratic Youth League later absorbed the youth section of the trade unions, expanded its membership rapidly, and claimed 1.25 million members within a year of its creation.

When it came to the forced fusion of the political parties, the occupation authorities ordered the New Democratic Party to take the first step and propose the merger of the two parties. This was done on July 23, 1946, and a reply by the North Korean Communist Party was sent on the following day to express agreement, although the party's official decision was not made until the eighth plenum on July 27, 1946.[2] The founding congress was held one month after the decision.

The First Party Congress: 1946

It is worthwhile explaining the details of the first congress because such information has not been made public heretofore.[3] The founding congress was held in Pyongyang, August 28 to August 30, 1946, and 801 delegates representing 336,339 members were present. The meeting of the first day, presided over by Kim Il Sung, was a short session of less than three hours beginning at 2:30 in the afternoon. The first order of business was to elect various officers of the congress — including a thirty-one-member executive group, a five-member credentials committee, a four-member secretariat, a five-member editorial committee to compile the records of the congress, a five-member platform committee, and a five-member bylaws committee — and establish a six-point agenda of the congress.[4] At the suggestion of a delegate from Hamgyŏng pukto, Hŏ Kŭk-bong, the great Marshal Stalin was elected honorary chairman of the congress and an open letter to him from the founding congress was read, thanking him and the Red Army for the liberation of Korea and hoping for continued support for the establishment of a unified and independent government in Korea. The delegates heard congratulatory remarks from representatives of the trade unions, the youth league, the agricultural unions, and the Korean Democratic Party; then the first session was adjourned.

The second day was presided over by Kim Yong-bŏm, and the meeting lasted from nine in the morning to seven in the evening. Delegates heard an elaborate statistical report from Pak Il-u about the 801 delegates to the congress, and his recommendation to certify the credentials of all 801 delegates to the congress was adopted. The delegates were mostly young men in their thirties with high school educations and many were office workers. Delegates who had fought abroad and those who had worked within Korea were evenly divided; delegates who had not been imprisoned by the Japanese for their revolutionary activities outnumbered those who had been captured and jailed.[5]

The most important business was the two keynote addresses by Kim Il Sung, chairman of the North Korean Communist Party, and Kim Tu-bong, chairman of the New Democratic Party. Kim's speech was a stunning condemnation of Nationalist leaders in the South, including Kim Ku and Syngman Rhee, and general conditions in the South under the American occupation. He then outlined the reasons for creating the Workers' Party and said that the purpose was to unite the democratic strength of the working masses to build a state that would represent and protect the rights of the working people. He condemned those members of the North Korean Communist Party who opposed the merger with the New Democratic Party and said that these men were a small group of arrogant leftists who thought they were the only true Communists in Korea. Kim said that the united party should become a strong vanguard party, bring about ideological unity of the two parties, work for the interests of the workers, lead other social organizations, and pay serious attention to the education of new cadres.[6]

Kim Tu-bong, like Kim Il Sung, condemned those members of the New Democratic Party who voiced opposition to the merger of the two parties and pointed out that many had committed the error of right opportunism. Kim Tu-bong said that these men were misled when they said the Communists were a bunch of rough-necks compared with the trained intellectual revolutionaries of the New Democratic Party. Kim Tu-bong concluded his speech, like Kim Il Sung, by presenting a five-point task to the members to strengthen the new party by firmly supporting the merger.[7]

The two speeches were similar in many ways. Clearly there was considerable dissension over the merger among members of both parties. The chairmen of both parties criticized their own dissident members in support of the merger. Colonel Ignatiev, who ordered the merger, was present throughout the congress. Fifteen delegates discussed the two speeches, and Kim Il Sung made concluding remarks in support of the merger. A resolution was adopted to approve the merger, to have a single party for the working masses, and to name the new party the Workers' Party of North Korea. Ch'oe Ch'ang-ik, a leader of the New Democratic Party, proposed a thirteen-article platform for the party, and after a brief discussion the platform was adopted and the congress adjourned.

On the third day, the congress was presided over by Chu Yŏng-ha and draft bylaws of the party were introduced by Kim Yong-bŏm. There were brief discussions of the bylaws by several delegates before they were adopted. Then came a brief report on the publications work of the party by T'ae Sŏng-su, a Soviet-Korean, proposing the merger of two newspapers — *Chŏngno* (Correct Path) of the North Korean Communist Party and *Chŏnjin* (Forward) of the New Democratic Party — into a new organ of the Workers' Party, *Nodong sinmun* (Workers' Daily). This proposal was adopted.[8]

Ch'oe Ch'ang-ik delivered a short speech concerning the conditions prevailing in the South and the progress made in merging three political parties to found the Workers' Party of South Korea. He reported that six dissident elements in the Korean Communist Party in Seoul who were obstructing the merger had been expelled from the party.[9] Ch'oe recommended that the decision to expel these men be approved by the Workers' Party of North Korea, and it was so approved.

The last and perhaps the most important business of the congress was to elect the members of the Central Committee. A prepared list of forty-three candidates was introduced by Kim Il Sung, and since there were no other nominations, each nominee was introduced and voted upon. All forty-three members were unanimously approved.[10] Another slate for an eleven-member Inspection Committee was introduced by Kim Tu-bong, and it too was approved unanimously after each nominee was introduced.[11] The congress adjourned at six in the evening after issuing an open letter to the people of Korea.

Leaders of Other Groups

In the merger of the two parties to found a mass party, several things became evident. Most apparent is that the leadership of Kim Il Sung was forced upon the leaders of other groups. The Soviet support of Kim made it clear that to oppose Kim was to oppose the Soviet occupation authorities. Such popular leaders of the New Democratic Party as Kim Tu-bong, Mu Chŏng, and Ch'oe Ch'ang-ik, who were well known to the people for their revolutionary activities in China, were told to hail Kim and shout long live Kim Il Sung, something these old, self-righteous Korean Communist revolutionaries in their late fifties would never have done for a young man of thirty-three with a non-Korean revolutionary record without Soviet coercion. One of the first to comment on Kim's speech, Pak Pyŏng-sŏ, remarked that in order for the Koreans to rule their own country, they must have a Korean leader, and that leader was Kim Il Sung. He went on to say that Kim was "the only leader," and anyone who opposed him or refused to vote for him was a reactionary and a traitor.[12]

Pak Chŏng-ae, a woman delegate from P'yŏngnam, said that such a remark was abrasive and unnecessary because Kim was already recognized as the leader of the entire Korean people.[13] It was Kim Il Sung who presided over the congress, delivered the address to the congress, and presented the forty-three nominees for the Central Committee. The potential rivals acquiesced not because of Kim himself or his personal power, but because of the omnipresence of the Soviet occupation forces and the omniscience of Colonel Ignatiev about the Communist future of Korea.

The leader of the domestic Communist group after the assassination of Hyŏn Chun-hyŏk was O Ki-sŏp, but O played only a minor role in this congress. The leaders of the Yanan group who had returned from China remained silent for the most part. Only one partisan, Yim Ch'un-ch'u, and one Soviet-Korean, Han Il-mu, spoke out in this congress, but it was an uneasy coalition and a tense congress where Korean groups acquiesced to Kim Il Sung as an agent of the Soviet Union.

The merger may have seemed a sign of cooperation and consolidation of the two parties, but in reality it took place amid significant opposition and mutual suspicion. Neither side understood the concept of a mass party — and if they did, no Korean Communist leader wanted to organize such a party. There was serious resistance within the North Korean Communist Party to a merger without the consent of the party in Seoul. Many Communists in the provinces resisted even the creation of a Communist party independent of the central Communist party in Seoul, let alone the merger with the New Democratic Party. The New Democratic Party was more interested in enlisting the support of the socialists and intellectuals and considered the Communist group much too radical for their purpose. Both Kim Il Sung and Kim Tu-bong therefore used their addresses to the congress to dispel suspicion of the members of both parties. Many hard-core members of both sides were apprehensive of recruiting large numbers of untrained members into the party, and some even said that the party would become a common ruck of undisciplined mobs. Kim Il Sung cautioned against such remarks and urged the training of new recruits.[14]

Kim did recruit indiscriminately in his effort to build a support group of local people. Kim said there were 4,530 members in the North Korean Branch Bureau when he assumed the chairmanship at the third enlarged plenum on December 17, 1945, but by April 20, 1946, the party had expelled approximately 1,400 members.[15] By the time of the founding congress in August 1946, however, Kim said the combined membership of the new party was 336,339 with the New Democratic Party contributing only 60,000 members. One discussant reported that in Hamgyŏng pukto alone they had recruited 9,200 members in eleven days from July 9 to July 20, 1946.[16]

According to the bylaws of the party, the Central Committee was charged with electing the officers of the party, a chairman, two vice-chairmen, and five members of the Political Committee. The bylaws provided that the chairman must also be a member of the Political Committee. The delegates may have acknowledged Kim's leadership in the congress, but the secret ballot to elect the top leaders of the party was quite different. The forty-three members of the Central Committee were divided into four groups; 13 members were from the domestic group, 12 were from the Yanan group, 6 were Soviet-Koreans, 8 members' affiliation were not known, and there were only 4 in Kim's partisan group.[17]

The first session of the Central Committee, held on August 31, 1946, elected Kim Tu-bong[18] of the Yanan group, not Kim Il Sung, chairman of the party. Kim Il Sung and Chu Yŏng-ha[19] of the domestic group were elected vice-chairmen of the party. Hŏ Ka-i, a Soviet-Korean, and Ch'oe Ch'ang-ik, a Yanan group leader, were elected members of the Political Committee.

The election of the top officers may be interpreted in two ways. One is that Kim had made a tactical arrangement with the leaders of the Yanan group prior to the congress and yielded the chairmanship of the party to the more popular Kim Tu-bong as the price for the Yanan group's initial cooperation in merging the two parties. Another is that Kim was defeated in the election. Since the election process in the plenums of the Central Committee was not made public, it is difficult to assess whether a secret ballot did in fact take place and Kim did lose in the balloting or whether the election was merely a pro forma approval of a predetermined slate of officers. Colonel Ignatiev might have operated under the assumption that it was wiser to work with a non-Communist figurehead under Communist control within the party.

One South Korean account relates that Kim was defeated in a fair election. This source states that various nominations were made and that after judging that Kim might not be elected chairman, Colonel Ignatiev had intervened and announced that there was no reason why Kim Il Sung had to be the chairman of the party.[20] However, this source seems to be in error, for it relates that the chairman was elected by the delegates of the congress and that the nomination of Kim Il Sung was made during the party congress

Kim Tu-bong, chairman

Kim Il Sung, vice-chairman

Ch'oe Ch'ang-ik, leader of the Yanan group

Hŏ Ka-i, the Soviet-Korean

by Pak Pyŏng-sŏ, a delegate from P'yŏngan pukto. The election of the top officers took place in the first plenum of the Central Committee, not in the party congress, and Pak was not elected to the Central Committee and thus was incapable of nominating a chairman of the party.

Whatever the interpretation, Kim was not elected chairman. In the Political Committee, two members represented the Yanan group (Kim Tu-bong and Ch'oe Ch'ang-ik); Kim Il Sung and Hŏ Ka-i, a Soviet-Korean, represented the Soviet occupation authorities; and one member, Chu Yŏng-ha, represented the domestic group. In his defeat, if it was indeed a defeat, Kim had succeeded in separating the local old Korean Communists from their headquarters in Seoul and, with the help of the Yanan group, forced the old Communists in Seoul to organize a similar mass party in the South. Within three months of the founding congress of the Workers' Party in the North, a similar coalition took place in the South among three leftist parties, November 23-34, 1946, and the Workers' Party of South Korea was founded.[21] Many old Communists stayed away from this coalition, dividing and debilitating the strength of the old Communists in the South. They were also under constant pressure and suppression from the American occupation authorities. These developments contributed much to the eventual consolidation of power by Kim Il Sung in the North.

The Second Party Congress: 1948

It was not until the Second Party Congress, March 27–30, 1948, that Kim made public the details of his difficulties and the opposition to his effort after he returned to the North.[22] The second congress was presided over by Kim Tu-bong and Chu Yŏng-ha throughout the four-day meeting. Some 990 delegates representing 750,000 members were assembled for the second congress.[23] The first day was a short session that began at six in the evening and ended in less than two hours. As in the past, officers were elected to handle the business of the congress.[24] The great leader Marshal Stalin was again elected honorary chairman, and a message extolling his achievements was adopted and sent to him. A simple agenda of three items was adopted, and the delegates heard congratulatory messages from various organizations, including the Workers' Party of South Korea.[25]

On the second day the delegates heard a report by Kim Il Sung on the work of the Central Committee. Kim first reviewed the international situation and the struggle of the two camps in the bipolar world and its effect on the domestic situation. He then praised the work of the party in instituting democratic reforms and condemned the situation in the South under the American occupation. In the third part of his speech he reviewed the work of the Central Committee, pointing out shortcomings of the party that needed to be improved.[26]

In his report Kim Il Sung said that some members of the party were engaged in factional struggles and individual heroism and were not cooperating in the work of the party. It is clear from the ensuing discussion that when Kim tried to organize a separate unit of the Korean Communist Party in North Korea, most of the indigenous Communist leaders in the North opposed his effort and pledged their loyalty to the party in Seoul. Kim said that this point was discussed extensively at the fourth plenum of the North Korean Branch Bureau in February 1946, shortly after he took over the bureau at the third plenum in December 1945, but the leaders of the indigenous Communist groups refused to cooperate.

The titular head of the domestic group in the North, after the assassination of Hyŏn, was O Ki-sŏp. O, born in 1903, was nine years senior to Kim. He had engaged in Communist activity from about 1923. One of the few Koreans who graduated from KUTV in the Soviet Union, he returned to his native town of Hongwŏn, Hamgyŏng namdo, and established a Communist group. He was arrested and imprisoned for his role in organizing a Communist youth group in October 1934. When he was released he remained in Korea and engaged in underground Communist activities. O was well regarded by his fellow Communists as both theoretician and pragmatist. He was important enough to occupy the chairmanship of two bureaus (labor and propaganda) in the North Korean Provisional People's Committee shortly after the liberation of Korea. Accused with him by Kim Il Sung were other members of the domestic group, including Chŏng Tal-hyŏn, Ch'oe Yong-dal, Yi Sun-gŭn, Chang Si-u, and Chang Sun-myŏng.[27]

Leading the attack on these men after Kim Il Sung were Soviet-Koreans. Han Il-mu, opened the criticism of O Ki-sŏp, accusing him of individual heroism and demanding that O recant his mistakes before the congress.[28] He accused Chŏng Tal-hyŏn of engaging in factional activities in Wŏnsan when he was chairman of the Hamgyŏng namdo party committee. He also accused Ch'oe Yong-dal of conspiring with Yi Chu-ha, who fled to the South, and Cho Chung-hwa, who sent embezzled party funds to the party in Seoul. Ch'oe was also accused of conspiring with Yi Kang-guk to reinstate Cho in the party.[29]

Pak Ch'ang-ok, another Soviet-Korean,[30] attacked O Ki-sŏp for his article on the role of the trade union in the North, which appeared in *Nodong sinmun* on September 18, 1946. O Ki-sŏp maintained that the collective interests of the workers must be preserved even when major industries were nationalized. Pak pointed out that such an idea was a direct challenge to the state and a deliberate act to mislead the workers against the state.

Still another Soviet-Korean, Kim Yŏl,[31] condemned O Ki-sŏp and Chŏng Tal-hyŏn for their refusal to cooperate in creating the North Korean Communist Party independent from the party in the South. Kim said that these men had failed to understand new and favorable conditions prevailing in the North under the Soviet occupation and had looked to the party in Seoul under the American occupation for leadership. These men also failed to communicate the directives from the party in Pyongyang to Hamgyŏng namdo and engaged in building a regional party — conduct similar to that of a semifeudal petty bourgeois. Kim Yŏl also accused Chang Sun-myŏng for failure to perform his duty on the Inspection Committee.[32] He said that Chang was derelict because he inspected only party members and not party organizations in various localities.

The targets of these attacks by the Soviet-Koreans were all indigenous Communists. It was obvious that the Soviet-Koreans were helping Kim Il Sung in his struggle to consolidate power, and the members of the domestic group painfully realized the price they were paying for the liberation they themselves did not win for Korea. In the eyes of native Communists, Han Il-mu, Pak Ch'ang-ok, and Kim Yŏl were Soviet-Koreans, strangers, whose names they heard for the first time after the liberation, and they wondered what these men had to do with the Korean Communist revolution. They knew a great deal about the Communists from Yanan, but the Yanan group remained silent in this struggle. None of the Yanan group was criticized, nor did anyone in that group attack the members of either the domestic group or the Soviet-Koreans.

In his turn, O Ki-sŏp did admit his mistakes and said that he had indeed committed an error in supporting the party in Seoul. O said that when he was criticized by Kim Il Sung as early as the fourth plenum of the North Korean Bureau in February 1946, his acceptance of Kim's criticism was formalistic. In truth, he did not agree with Kim and withheld his support, thus committing the error of double dealing. O apologized fully for his errors before the delegates of the second congress. However, he did defend himself, and said that Pak Ch'ang-ok's criticism of his article on the trade union was incorrect. O said that he had become obsessed with defending the interests of the workers during the struggle against the Japanese and he was not now advocating special rights or privileges for the workers against the state. As head of the Labor Bureau he had rejected all collective bargaining aimed at increasing the affluence of the workers at the expense of the state's treasury, but he said that workers' interests must be defended even in a socialist state. Furthermore, O said that many points in Kim Yŏl's criticism were factually incorrect. Nevertheless, he apologized for the time spent in the congress on things he had done or failed to do for the party.[33]

Two others followed O in apologizing to the congress. Chang Si-u, who headed the Commerce Bureau, merely apologized for his mistakes and pledged his loyalty to Kim Il Sung without any rebuttal. Yi Sun-gŭn, who headed the Agriculture and Forestry Bureau, promised technical improvements in agriculture and vowed his support for Kim Il Sung. Yi Sun-gŭn did this even before anyone lodged a complaint against him.

Ch'oe Yong-dal also recanted, admitting his errors in recruiting members of the Justice Bureau without a thorough investigation of their qualifications. He said that if some of the new members had collaborated with the Japanese in the past, the mistakes would be corrected. Ch'oe presented elaborate statistics showing the number of judges assigned and the alarming increase in the number of crimes and criminals in the liberated North and said that as head of the Justice Bureau he would improve the work of the judiciary. But Ch'oe also defended himself by pointing out that the general criticism of his selection of judges was incorrect because many high-level judges were not appointed by him but elected. Therefore, many of those who criticized him, including Han Il-mu, should share the responsibility for electing such judges. Furthermore, Ch'oe said that to point out his errors in the Wŏnsan City Party Committee operation in dealing with Communists who defected to the South was one thing, but to accuse him of factional struggle in the region was quite something else and unjustified.[34]

When Ch'oe finished his discussion, there was a ten-minute break in the session. When the meeting resumed, Hŏ Ka-i,[35] one of the most influential Soviet-Koreans, delivered a stunning condemnation of these men. In fact, he had not been scheduled to speak, and the presiding officer had to change the order of discussion to accommodate him. Hŏ said that since all four who recanted had not fully admitted their mistakes, their apologies were mere formalities. He said that O Ki-sŏp and Ch'oe Yong-dal in particular were defending their own personal dignity at the expense of party progress. The party had often discussed with Ch'oe the problems of teaching new students at the Law Institute, for example, but he still maintained the institute as a reeducation center for those who had been educated by the Japanese. Hŏ said that the party wanted to educate new students and build new leaders of liberated Korea; it was not interested in reeducating intellectuals who had been taught Japanese law. Hŏ then attacked O for his contemptuous attitude toward the party and his individual heroism.

Chu Yŏng-ha, vice-chairman of the party and a member of the domestic group, explained that the position of these men, particularly O Ki-sŏp's position on the question of the trade union was a phenomenon of the transitional stage of the time, and these mistakes would be corrected in due course. However, the message was clear. When Chŏng Tal-hyŏn's turn came, he admitted everything without defense or rebuttal. Chŏng said that he was one of those who opposed the establishment of the Branch Bureau by Kim Il

Sung. He said that he had operated underground so long for the party in Seoul under the Japanese that he failed to recognize the rapidly changing international situation which was creating a more favorable condition in the North. He admitted that he was slow to learn from those who operated in advanced Communist countries abroad such as the Soviet Union. Even after the fourth plenum of the Branch Bureau when Kim Il Sung told him of the need for an independent party in place of the party in Seoul, he supported the party in Seoul. These were serious mistakes, he said, and he apologized and pledged his support for Kim Il Sung.[36]

Still another member of the domestic group, Chang Sun-myŏng, said that he had joined the Korean Communist Party in 1925 when it was first organized. However, he said his present party identification card recorded his admission date as August 25, 1945. He had not recognized the great difference between the past and the present party, and he had obstructed the work of Kim Il Sung. He admitted that he did not support Kim's effort to organize a mass youth organization by uniting all youth groups and dissolving the Young Communist League. He confessed that he had secretly organized and maintained a Young Communist League in Hamgyŏng namdo and that there were secret Communist youth groups in many provinces in the North. He said that he too had opposed the creation of the Branch Bureau by Kim Il Sung and looked to Seoul for leadership. Chang thought that such serious crimes might be cleansed only by death. He also admitted every criticism leveled against him in the work of the Inspection Committee. He said that 4,134 members were convicted and sentenced for violation of the party bylaws during the past year, and he alone was responsible for this. Chang even admitted things he was not accused of.

At the end of two days of discussion by thirty-two delegates, Kim Il Sung delivered his concluding remarks to the congress. Kim said there was no substance to the self-criticism of O Ki-sŏp, Ch'oe Yong-dal, and Chŏng Tal-hyŏn. O's article on the trade union was not written for the workers, Kim said, but for O himself. He also accused O of plagiarizing from Lenin's book on new economic policy and said that had O submitted such an important article to the Political Committee for perusal he could have avoided his serious mistake. O was pretentious and arrogant, Kim charged, and had opposed the Branch Bureau for no other reason than his own self-ishness. Had he been elected chairman of the Branch Bureau, he would have supported it; but since it was Kim Yong-bŏm who was elected, O opposed the Branch Bureau.[37] Chŏng Tal-hyŏn's opposition to the Branch Bureau was also purely personal, Kim said. Had Chŏng been elected chairman of the Hamgyŏng namdo provincial committee of the bureau, he would have supported it. Ch'oe Yong-dal was courting the former Japanese collaborators and reactionaries from the South, and he was wrong to protest Han Il-mu's constructive criticism of him. Kim concluded by saying that those who were toying with the idea of playing the party in the North against the party in the South were engaged in a dangerous game, because the two would eventually become one.

Control of the Party

In his first confrontation with his rivals in Korea, Kim used the Soviet-Koreans to attack the indigenous Communists. None of his partisans spoke in this congress. It was the Soviet-Koreans who lashed out at members of the domestic group. The Yanan group remained neutral in this clash. Kim Tu-bong and Ch'oe Ch'ang-ik refrained from discussing the subject. At one time, O Ki-sŏp accused Mu Chŏng, a member of the Yanan group, of individual heroism because he was popularly called "the great father" in Hwanghaedo. But Mu Chŏng did not reply, and Kim Il Sung condemned O for dragging Mu Chŏng into his troubles.

Kim's main weapon, of course, was the backing of the Soviet occupation authorities and the Soviet-Koreans, who were rootless in Korea. The indigenous Korean Communists had no reason to support Kim Il Sung and the Soviet-Koreans, of whom they knew nothing, in place of their own party in Seoul. They did oppose Kim Il Sung and Colonel Ignatiev, who dismantled the existing Communist party and youth groups in the North and forced the local Communists to support creation of a new party. Kim and the Soviet-Koreans argued that their tactics were more advanced, and their organization methods more Leninist, than those the local Communists had learned from the Japanese. The local Communists were not convinced, but at the same time it was difficult to argue against those who had come into Korea with the Soviet army, wearing the Soviet uniform and operating under the direction of the Soviet occupation authorities. Many local Communists were subjects of brutal personal attacks by Kim Il Sung and suffered the consequences of their failure to adjust to this new reality.

Kim used another weapon, as well — the elimination of everyone who had ever collaborated with the Japanese. This policy was carried out without exception, and the domestic group suffered most. Kim's partisans, the Soviet-Koreans, and the Yanan group had all returned home from abroad, but many of the local Communists had, under significant pressure, ultimately submitted to the Japanese. It was not that collaboration with the Japanese was justifiable in any way, but to sustain Communist activities under the Japanese occupation was not an easy task, a fact not fully appreciated by revolutionaries who operated abroad. Many indigenous Korean Communists were released shortly before the liberation of Korea with the promise that they would not return to underground Communist activity in Korea. In fact, Ch'oe Yong-dal, Chang Si-u, Hyŏn Chun-hyŏk, and many other Communists were unacceptable to the "pure and unmarked Communists" who had conducted their revolutionary activities abroad. Kim Il Sung used this weapon mercilessly at all levels of the North Korean political arena.

At the recommendation of Hŏ Ka-i, a slate of nominees for membership on the Central Committee was prepared by an eleven-member committee consisting of five members of the Political Committee and one chairman each from six Provincial Party Committees. Kim Il Sung announced sixty-three nominees for membership and twenty nominees for candidate membership. Kim said the committee was guided by four principles in selecting nominees. They were recruited, first, from outstanding cadres; second, from leaders of various social, military, government, and security organs and the provincial party committees; third, from new cadres; and fourth, from those who had been reprimanded by the party but were basically good Communists.

In order of nomination each candidate stated his personal history and was voted upon by the delegates. Everyone was voted in unanimously except O Ki-sŏp. O was nominated as the forty-second member of the Central Committee. He said that he was born in 1903 and began his Communist revolutionary activities from 1923 and became head of the Hamgyŏng namdo Party Provincial Committee. He then said that "when I heard Kim's remark about me yesterday, I was not convinced, but..." O was sharply interrupted and told to confine his remarks to his qualifications. O stopped and the vote was taken. There were 985 votes in favor and five votes against his election.[38] In selecting candidate members of the Central Committee, the same procedure was followed, and everyone was voted in unanimously except one, Kim Tu-yong,[39] who had 989 votes for and one vote against his election. There was also an election of a seven-man Central Auditing Committee. All those nominated were unanimously elected. Some who had been severely criticized in the congress, among them Ch'oe Yong-dal and Chŏng Tal-hyŏn, were not elected, but some, including O Ki-sŏp and Chang Sun-myŏng, were reelected.

Of the Central Committee's 67 members, 30 were returnees from the first Central Committee and 37 were new members. Four new partisans from Kim Il Sung's guerrillas were elected at this time (Kang Kŏn, Kim Kwang-hyŏp, Kim Kyŏng-sŏk, and Pak Kŭmch'ŏl) and at least 8 new Soviet-Koreans were added. Members of the domestic group were still the most numerous in the Central Committee.[40]

During the first session of the newly elected Central Committee, officers of the party were elected. Kim Tu-bong remained chairman and Kim Il Sung and Chu Yŏng-ha retained their posts as vice-chairmen of the party. All five members of the Political Committee were reelected, and two new members were added: Kim Ch'aek from the partisan group and Pak Il-u from the Yanan group.

By the time two separate governments were declared in Korea in 1948, many leaders of the old Korean Communists had fled from the South to the North. They were given important posts in the Communist government. The chairman of the Korean Communist Party, Pak Hŏn-yŏng, was appointed vice-premier and minister of foreign affairs in Kim Il Sung's first cabinet. Hŏ Hŏn, chairman of the Workers' Party of South Korea, was elected first chairman of the Supreme People's Assembly. Others followed their lead and joined the Communist regime in the North, but many were simply refugees from the South rather than leaders of the mainstream of the Korean Communist movement.

Pak Hŏn-yŏng was said to have fled to the North as early as October 1946, where he had established a temporary North Korean center of the Workers' Party of South Korea in Haeju, a town near the 38th parallel, to direct Communist activities in the South, where the Korean Communist Party was banned. Pak had rented a building in Haeju and brought many of his followers from the South, among them Yi Sŭng-yŏp, Kwŏn O-jik, Chŏng Chae-dal, Yi T'ae-jun, Pak Mun-gyu, Hŏ Sŏng-t'aek, Yi Pyŏng-nam, Kim O-sŏng, Pak Sŭng-wŏn, Yi Wŏn-jo, and Yim Hwa. When these men fled north, the party in Seoul was manned by those who refused to leave the South, such as Kim Sam-yong and Yi Chu-ha, who had earlier fled south from Wŏnsan.

In August 1948, shortly before the Communist republic was proclaimed in the North, the leaders of the Workers' Party of North Korea and these men organized a temporary central committee of the two parties known as the Joint Central Committee of the Workers' Parties of North and South Korea (*Nambuk nodongdang yŏnhap chungang wiwŏnhoe*).[41] Although it was reported that this body was headed by Kim Il Sung, the two parties remained separate. Even so, Kim and his Soviet-Koreans in the North were the hosts and the refugees from Seoul were the guests. Kim moved further to strengthen his control of the Workers' Party of North Korea.

At the third plenum of the second Central Committee, September 24–25, 1948, Chu Yŏng-ha, vice-chairman of the party, was replaced by Hŏ Ka-i. Another important decision made at this plenum was the establishment of an Organization Committee to control party operations; this committee was chaired by Kim Il Sung and included four Soviet-Koreans, Hŏ Ka-i, Kim Yŏl, Pak Ch'ang-ok, and Pak Yŏng-sŏn. The Inspection Committee was chaired by Hŏ Ka-i. It was not until after his return from his month-long first official visit to Moscow in March and April 1949 to express appreciation to the Soviet Union that Kim moved to wrest control of the party chairmanship.

The first joint plenum of the two Central Committees of the

Workers' Party of North and South Korea was convened on June 24, 1949. Entirely new officers of the Central Committee were elected without a party congress. It was at this joint plenum that the official name of the Workers' Party of Korea was adopted, and Kim was formally elected chairman. Pak Hŏn-yŏng, former chairman of the Korean Communist Party in Seoul, was elected first vice-chairman, and Hŏ Ka-i, a Soviet-Korean, was elected second vice-chairman. There were three secretaries. The first secretary was Hŏ Ka-i; the second was Yi Sŭng-yŏp, a key member of the Communists from the South; and the third was Kim Sam-yong, a South Korean Communist who remained in the South to direct underground Communist activity there. A nine-member Political Committee included all five of these men and four additional members: two from the Yanan group, Kim Tu-bong and Pak Il-u; one partisan, Kim Ch'aek; and one from the South, Hŏ Hŏn. The Organization Committee was expanded to eleven members including the nine mentioned above and one from the Yanan group, Ch'oe Ch'ang-ik, and a Soviet-Korean, Kim Yŏl.[42]

When the two parties were united, the challenge to Kim Il Sung was real — not only because there were many South Korean Communists in the North but also because his staunchest supporter and the backbone of his power, the Soviet occupation forces, had withdrawn from the North in December 1948. Some of the Soviet-Koreans left with the occupation forces, and only the handful who held high positions in the army, the party, and the government remained. Kim's partisans were still few in number and were ineffective in the party, concentrating most of their strength in the army and security affairs. Those indigenous Communists who were on the receiving end of the attacks from Kim Il Sung and the Soviet-Koreans strengthened their group somewhat with a large number of hard-core Communists from the South.

Kim Il Sung had more than a fair chance for successful competition with rival groups. He controlled the administration of the newly established republic. He was premier of the cabinet. He was chairman of the Workers' Party of Korea. His mentor, Colonel Ignatiev, remained in the North after the Soviet army's withdrawal as an advisor to the Soviet ambassador, Terentii F. Shtykov, and gave him valuable direction for the future of his government. The

Soviet-Koreans who decided to stay in the North remained loyal to Kim. The Yanan group also avoided direct confrontation with the Soviet-Koreans and Kim Il Sung's group. North Korea in 1949 was still under the heavy influence of what was then known as the "fatherland of the proletariat," the Soviet Union, and Kim Il Sung was its chosen agent to run the satellite.

6

The Republic and the Army

Kim Il Sung had fewer problems establishing the republic than in gaining control of the party. Kim used local leaders and returned revolutionaries at his discretion to implement the sovietization program, and so long as he was effective in this endeavor by following Soviet directives, his position was secure. Kim went through two preliminary administrative reorganizations before formal pronouncement of the Communist republic.

Establishment of the Republic

The first administrative unit Kim headed was an improved version of the original Five-Province Administration Bureau. It was organized on February 9, 1946, the second day of the two-day conference held to create a central administration unit, and was known as the North Korean Provisional People's Committee (*Puk Chosŏn imsi inmin wiwŏnhoe*). On the first day, Kim delivered a ten-point outline of the sovietization program and said that the first task of the committee was to institute democratic reforms. In the original version of this speech, Kim said that the initiation committee had re-

ceived permission from the Soviet occupation authorities to organize the Provisional People's Committee, but this statement was
later edited to read that the Soviet occupation authorities supported
his proposal, and in the latest revision of this speech the entire reference to the Soviet authorities was deleted.[1]

It was reported that Kim Il Sung was elected chairman of the
Provisional People's Committee, but it is not known who elected
him or how he was elected. Kim Tu-bong was chosen vice-
chairman and Kang Yang-uk secretary. There were eleven bureaus,
and the head of each bureau was appointed by Kim Il Sung. Only
one partisan, Ch'oe Yong-gŏn, who headed the Internal Security
Bureau, and one member of the Yanan group, Ch'oe Ch'ang-ik,
who headed the General Bureau, were appointed; the rest were
from the domestic group.[2] This group was expanded as the work-
load increased and included O Ki-sŏp, who served concurrently as
head of the Propaganda and Labor Bureaus, Yi Chu-yŏn, and
Chŏng Chin-t'ae, all members of the domestic group. This group
carried out Colonel Ignatiev's initial democratic reforms, including
land reform, agricultural tax-in-kind, nationalization of major industries, labor laws, laws governing equality of sexes, and election
laws.[3]

Under the new election law passed by this committee, the first
election was held on November 3, 1946, and a legislative body
known as the People's Assembly of North Korea with 1,159 representatives was convened February 17–20, 1947.[4] This representative
body elected Kim chairman of a new People's Committee. In this
reorganization, Kim retained most of the members of the Provisional People's Committee with one important change — the ap-
pointment of his fellow partisan Kim Ch'aek as vice-chairman, replacing Kim Tu-bong, who became chairman of the People's
Assembly. Kim Ch'aek was also appointed concurrently as head of
the National Defense Bureau.

A few from the Yanan group were appointed to head bureaus —
Pak Il-u to the Internal Security Bureau and Ch'oe Ch'ang-ik to
the People's Procurator's Office — but the majority of the People's
Committee still consisted of members of the domestic group.[5] Not
a single Soviet-Korean was appointed to head a bureau in the People's Committee. Many local leaders in the provinces did not coop-

erate with Kim, and those who were criticized by Kim at the party congresses, including Yi Sun-gŭn, Yi Pong-su, Ch'oe Yong-dal, and O Ki-sŏp, were replaced. Kim brought in such obscure, manageable, and non-party-affiliated people as Yi Mun-hwan and Hŏ Nam-hŭi. In this way, Kim was able to manipulate his rival groups and their leaders by using and discarding them at will.

The People's Assemby held five sessions from February 1947 to September 1948 when the Communist republic was formally declared, but the work of founding the new republic was completed long before the official announcement. The first session of the assembly elected a chief justice of the court and appointed a procurator-general, and by the third session in November 1947 a committee was appointed to draft a constitution of the republic. The fourth session of the assembly, February 6–7, 1948, decided to establish an armed force, and the following day, February 8, seven months before the formal announcement of the establishment of the republic, the Korean People's Army was founded. Even a new national anthem was composed and proclaimed as early as June 1947, and the groundwork for creating a separate Communist government in the North was more or less completed.[6]

Kim Il Sung was opposed to the establishment of two separate governments in Korea, and he waited until after the establishment of a government in the South to proclaim his republic in the North. However, had there been a single government in Korea, Kim would not have enjoyed the leadership position he held, even with Soviet assistance. Compared with more prominent Nationalist leaders in the South — Syngman Rhee, Kim Ku, and Kim Kyusik — Kim Il Sung was a junior revolutionary. There were many in South Korea who could easily match or surpass Kim's record of revolutionary activity. After negotiations between the United States and the Soviet Union failed to establish a unified governing body in Korea, the Soviet Union refused to allow the United Nations observer group to oversee a general election throughout Korea. An election was held only in the South on May 10, 1948, under UN supervision, and a government was established there. This was one keystone assuring Kim's leadership position in the North.

Many leaders feared the permanent division of Korea and refused to participate in any efforts to establish a government by either side. Some leaders in the south — Yŏ Un-hyŏng, Kim Ku, and Kim Kyu-sik — did go North to talk with Kim Il Sung, hoping to prevent the creation of a separate government. Kim emphatically agreed with them and vowed that he would not establish a separate government first in the North. Yŏ Un-hyŏng, who first organized the Korean People's Republic in the South after the liberation, had gone to see Kim Il Sung as early as the summer of 1946. Kim had shown his respect for Yŏ and had greeted him cordially.

Kim Ku and Kim Kyu-sik, president and vice-president of the defunct Korean Provisional Government, abstained from participating in the creation of a separate South Korean government and visited the North in 1948, but this meeting, held from April 19 to 23, turned out to be a political rally instigated by Kim Il Sung to oppose the UN-supervised election in the South. A four-point joint communiqué was issued at the end of the meeting calling for withdrawal of both occupation forces from Korea, prevention of civil war, establishment of a single government for Korea by Koreans, and rejection of any unilateral establishment of a separate government in the South.[7]

In all meetings, however, the older revolutionaries went to the North as individuals to meet with a leader who himself had completed the task of establishing a separate government. In the review of a parade on April 25 in their honor, Kim Ku had complained to Kim Il Sung about the North Korean people carrying a huge portrait of Stalin and shouting long live Marshal Stalin and the Soviet Union. Both Kim Ku and Kim Kyu-sik returned south on May 4, 1948, shortly before the May 10 election.

On September 9, 1948, less than a month after the Republic of Korea was established in the South, a separate Communist republic, the Democratic People's Republic of Korea, was proclaimed in the North. Both sides claimed jurisdiction over the entire territory of Korea. North Korea legitimized its claim by the alleged election of 360 out of 572 members of the Supreme People's Assembly from the South. The Supreme People's Assembly, meeting from September 2 to September 10, adopted a constitution, elected Kim premier and approved his first cabinet, elected a chief justice, appointed a procurator-general, and elected a twenty-one-member Standing Committee of the assembly.[8]

For Kim, however, the Supreme People's Assembly was merely a legitimizing organization and not a functioning legislative body. Many political, religious, and social organizations were represented in the assembly, but there was not a single partisan or Soviet-Korean on the twenty-one-member Standing Committee of the Supreme People's Assembly. The representatives were elected for four years but served from September 1948 to September 1957. During those years, the assembly rubber-stamped unanimously everything that the party and Kim asked. It was the party and Kim's cabinet, controlled by the Soviet authorities, not the Supreme People's Assembly or its Standing Committee, that exercised power in the North.

Kim's first cabinet had three partisans: Kim (premier), Kim Ch'aek (vice-premier and concurrently minister of industry), and Ch'oe Yong-gŏn (national defense). There were four from the Yanan group: Pak Il-u (interior), Kim Wŏn-bong (state control), Ch'oe Ch'ang-ik (finance), and Hŏ Chŏng-suk (culture and propaganda). Thirteen other members were from the domestic group. Most prominent where those who came from the South, headed by Pak Hŏn-yŏng, who was appointed to serve concurrently as vice-premier and minister of foreign affairs, Yi Sŭng-yŏp (justice), and Pak Mun-gyu (agriculture and forestry). Some of the domestic Communists of North Korean origin were kept, including Chu Yŏng-ha (transportation) and Chang Si-u (commerce); representatives of the People's Party of South Korea, Paek Nam-un (education); the Ch'ŏndogyo Young Friends Party, Kim Chŏng-ju (communication); and the Progressive Party (*Sinjindang*), Yi Yong (city management). There were only a few technocrats — Chŏng Chun-t'aek (state planning), Yi Pyŏng-nam (public health), and Hŏ Sŏng-t'aek (labor). A philologist, a long-time independence fighter who fled from the South to the North, Yi Kŭk-no, was appointed minister without portfolio.

Changes within the cabinet were frequent, and Kim used cabinet posts to recruit men loyal to him and purge those who stood in his way. By the time of the second cabinet in 1957, more than fifty persons had served as cabinet ministers, but only six other than

The First Cabinet, September 1948

Front row: Chŏng Chun-t'aek (State Planning), Kim Ch'aek (vice-premier and Industry), Hong Myŏng-hŭi (vice-premier), Kim Il Sung (premier), Pak Hŏng-yŏng (vice-premier and Foreign Affairs), Ch'oe Yong-gŏn (National Defense), Hŏ Chŏng-suk (Culture and Propaganda)
Middle row: Yi Pyŏng-nam (Public Health), Kim Wŏn-bong (State Control), Paek Nam-un (Education), Chu Yŏng-ha (Transportation), Chang Si-u (Commerce), Ch'oe Ch'ang-ik (Fianance), Pak Il-u (Interior)
Back row: Pak Mun-gyu (Agriculture and Forestry), Yi Kŭk-no (Without Portfolio), Yi Yong (City Management), Kim Chŏng-ju (Communication), Yi Sŭng-yŏp (Justice), Hŏ Sŏng-t'aek (Labor)

Kim himself were reappointed to the second cabinet. Only technocrats (Chŏng Chun-t'aek, Hŏ Sŏng-t'aek, and Yi Pyŏng-nam) who pledged complete loyalty to Kim and abstained from political struggles in the party were reappointed.[9]

There was not a single Soviet-Korean in Kim's first cabinet. A State Department study on the Soviet takeover alleged that Soviet-Koreans were appointed vice-ministers and controlled the ministers, but this was not true. Most of the Soviet-Koreans were concentrating on the operation of the party and army, and in many cases the Soviet-Koreans headed various departments of the party that set the policy for the cabinet to implement, but they themselves were not appointed as vice-ministers. More than ten vice-ministers out of seventeen ministries of the first cabinet were local Korean Communists. Soviet-Koreans also served as heads of various security groups, but not as vice-ministers.[10] Most of Kim's partisans and the Soviet-Koreans concentrated their efforts on building the military and security forces.

The Army and the Security Forces

The Soviet occupation authorities helped Kim fight the local opposition in creating the mass party and also helped him become leader of the newly established republic, but they went one step further and helped to create an armed unit to sustain him. In this endeavor Kim faced the least opposition, and he used his partisan comrades to firmly control the military and security forces. Kim's only potential opposition was the military unit of the Yanan group under Kim Wŏn-bong, Mu Chŏng, and Pak Il-u, but the Soviet authorities had helped Kim to disarm them when they returned from China. Furthermore, any reference to their military hero Mu Chŏng as a leader in the North was immediately denounced as promotion of individual heroism by the Soviet-Koreans and the occupation forces.[11]

Almost immediately after his return to Korea, Kim Il Sung began to organize a security unit. All military and internal security posts from the liberation to the establishment of the Korean People's Army were taken by Kim's partisans. The first military officers and political cadre training school was founded as early as November 1945. Called Pyongyang Institute (*P'yŏngyang hagwŏn*), it was headed by Kim Ch'aek, a guerrilla from the Second Route Army in Manchuria, who had with him a Soviet-Korean, Ki Sŏk-bok, as dean of the institute. Ki was educated at Leningrad State University and later became editor of the party organ, *Kŭlloja*.

When the first Provisional People's Committee was organized in February 1946, the head of the Security Bureau was another partisan, Ch'oe Yong-gŏn. By August 1946, the central security officers training school (*Chungang poan kanbu hakkyo*) in Pyongyang and all other cadre training centers were headed by partisans. By the end of 1946 the training centers in Kaech'ŏn (P'yŏngan namdo), Sinŭiju (P'yŏngan pukto), Nanam (Hamgyŏng pukto), and Wŏnsan (Hamgyŏng namdo) had produced enough officers to staff an army of approximately 20,000 men. They were divided into the Nanam Division, Chinnamp'o Brigade, Kanggye Artillery Regiment, Railroad Constabulary, Border Constabulary, Internal Security Bureau, and Secret Police. The headquarters of these units were in Pyongyang and they were commanded by An Kil, a partisan.[12]

In his speech to the first graduating class of the Central Security Officers School on October 26, 1947, Kim emphasized that the army had a special mission in the creation of the people's government in the North.[13] The army did in fact enjoy a special status, primarily because it was led by the partisans and Soviet-Koreans, the military phalanx of the party. Some of the early recruits were trained by the Soviet occupation forces, and approximately 10,000 men were sent to Siberia each year for training.

The first wave of the Soviet withdrawal from North Korea occurred as early as March 1947, and the second in less than a year. It was important for Kim Il Sung to build his own armed forces, and the Korean People's Army was formally established on February 8, 1948, nearly seven months before proclamation of the government in North Korea. When the government was established, the military and the security police were separated. The military was entrusted to the Ministry of National Defense while the security police were reorganized into the Interior Ministry. The minister of national defense was Ch'oe Yong-gŏn, the vice-minister was Kim Il, and the commander-in-chief of the North Korean armed forces was Kang Kŏn, all partisans.[14]

During the first year after the Communist republic was established approximately 40,000 men were conscripted into the army, and many were sent to the Soviet Union and Manchuria for training. Kim Il Sung also recruited heavily among the Koreans living in Manchuria who chose to remain even after the Korean liberation. These Koreans were also recruited into the Chinese Communist army to fight the Chinese Nationalists in Manchuria during the Chinese civil war. They were called the Yi Hong-gwang Unit in honor of the Korean political commissar Yi Hong-gwang (Li Hongguang) of the First Route Army under Yang Jingyu.

Some of the Korean leaders of the United Army who chose to remain in Manchuria participated in the Northeast (Manchuria) Interim People's Committee in China. For example, Kim Kwang-hyŏp, who helped train many Korean soldiers in China. Kim Kwang-hyŏp eventually returned to Korea with a Korean contingent of Chinese army units after the Chinese Communists won their civil war in Manchuria, and he became general of the Korean People's Army.[15] The North Korean army had approximately 60,000 men divided into three army divisions by 1949. The First Division was commanded by Ch'oe Kwang, the Second Division by Ch'oe Hyŏn, and the Third Division by Kim Kwang-hyŏp. These men were all guerrilla fighters from the United Army and were loyal to Kim Il Sung.

The Interior Ministry was headed by Pak Il-u, a member of the Yanan group, but many Soviet-Koreans and partisans worked in the ministry. There were 12,000 regular police, 3,000 political thought police, 5,000 secret police, and a few others. The secret police were headed by Pang Hak-se, a Soviet-Korean, but he was later succeeded by Chi Kyŏng-su, a partisan. The partisans also moved into many local security police organizations; for example, the head of the Hwanghaedo security police was Sŏk San, another partisan. In this way, Kim Il Sung and his partisans completely dominated the military and security forces in the North, and no other group was able to challenge him.

Shortly after they fled to North Korea from the South, the leaders of the domestic group established a cadre school of their own, known as the Kangdong Political Institute in Kandong county, P'yŏngan namdo, in September 1947. The officers and men trained in this institute remained loyal to Pak Hŏn-yŏng, the leader of the Korean Communist Party, but these men were trained for the purpose of Communist operation in South Korea. However, even in this Kangdong Political Institute, the military training was conducted under the direction of Sŏ Ch'ŏl, a partisan. The school was disbanded in 1949 after the so-called September offensive in which some 630 agents were sent to the South for an abortive guerrilla operation. The graduates of this institute often shouted "Long live Pak Hŏn-yŏng!" instead of the customary pledge of fealty to Kim Il Sung, but their primary goal was to win the South, not to challenge Kim. When the school was closed, Kim established a new guerrilla training school in Hoeryŏng, Hamgyŏng pukto, known as the Hoeryŏng Cadres School under the direction of still another partisan, O Chin-u.

Kim Il Sung claims today that the liberation of Korea was the culmination of his long and arduous revolutionary struggle for Korea and asserts that he and his partisans defeated the Japanese and brought home the liberation. From the late 1960s to the mid-1980s North Koreans have omitted any reference to the role played by the Soviet Union in the liberation of Korea. They claim that it was Kim who returned triumphantly and founded the Communist republic of the North. These assertions deserve no refutation.

Kim Il Sung did, however, show uncommon skill in his consolidation of political power in the North. As in his guerrilla days in Manchuria, when he survived while other guerrilla leaders perished under the Japanese punitive expedition, Kim not only survived but gained strength. What he accomplished during the Soviet occupation was far beyond what he himself might ever have dreamed.

Kim's consolidation of political power was the result of many contributing factors. Foremost was the Soviet support he received during the period immediately after the liberation, particularly from Major General Romanenko and Colonel Ignatiev. Kim served the Soviet Union well in their effort to institute a Communist system in the North, and the Soviet Union in turn supported him in his quest for power. For the Soviet Union, the sovietization of the North was more important than the promotion of a local leader, but the success of their programs depended on the effectiveness of their chosen agent. In a way, Kim earned his leadership position by faithfully executing Soviet directives.

Another factor was the perpetuation of what was then known as the temporary division of Korea. Kim was indeed a minor figure in the context of the entire Korean revolutionary movement. There were people like Syngman Rhee, Kim Ku, and Kim Kyu-sik in the political arena, and there were generals like Yi Ch'ŏng-ch'ŏn and Yi Pŏm-sŏk in the military. But these Korean leaders, Communists and Nationalists alike, were all in the southern half of

Korea, and the political vacuum that was created in the North helped Kim Il Sung to consolidate his political power.

He was sharply aware of his lack of a political base in Korea, and his guerrillas and comrades from Manchuria were untrained and uninformed in the politics of liberated Korea. Kim filled the ranks with any and all who supported him in combating his opposition, primarily by manipulating the Soviet-Koreans, who were rootless in Korea. He was also effective in neutralizing the Yanan group, thus preventing rival groups from uniting against him. Such unity had never been contemplated by his rivals, but even if they had united in opposing his takeover, Kim had the most important element on his side — control of the military and security forces. Kim's takeover of North Korea, in a sense, can be characterized as a military takeover under Soviet tutelage. His partisans and the Soviet-Koreans controlled every military and security unit in the North, and they supported Kim's consolidation of political power.

The local North Korean Communists who opposed Kim by professing their loyalty to the Korean Communist Party in Seoul were dealt severe blows, while the leaders of the party in the South were getting their share from the American occupation forces. By the time these leaders from the South fled north, their strength had suffered significant setbacks from many abortive coups. Kim did share party and administrative posts with members of various other groups, but in dealing with the local Communists from the domestic group, Kim used his strongest weapon to dispose of many potential rivals: the stigma of collaboration with the Japanese during their occupation of Korea. Except for those who had spent their entire lives away from Korea during the Japanese occupation, people like Kim Il Sung and Soviet-Koreans, many of the Korean revolutionaries who had remained had submitted to the relentless Japanese campaign of subjugation. Many leaders in the domestic group suffered in this purification campaign by Kim Il Sung, and Kim used this weapon too to consolidate his political power.

III

CHALLENGES TO
KIM'S LEADERSHIP

In his consolidation of political power, Kim showed the resilience
and resoluteness of a guerrilla fighter. He served the Soviet authorities well, and they in turn continued to support his drive for
power. Kim showed his resolve to sustain his advantageous position
even after the Soviet army withdrew from Korea, and even then a
large number of the Soviet advisors remained to assist him.[1]

By the time the Communist republic was established in 1948,
however, political group affiliation became more pronounced, and
each group began to readjust and assert its position. The most numerous were the members of the domestic group, but they had to
divide their energies between their operation in the North and
their underground operation in the southern half of Korea. The
Yanan group of returned revolutionaries from mainland China suffered much from the Soviet occupation of Korea. Kim's own partisans and the Soviet-Koreans were not distinguished as separate bod-
ies during the first decade after the liberation because they
supported each other under Soviet tutelage, but they were two dis-
tinctly separate groups.

It took Kim less than two years after he proclaimed the republic to build his military to launch an attack on the South. Studies on the Korean War often attribute the cause of the war to international rather than domestic factors. It is important to examine domestic factors, however, and Kim's foremost objective in the war was to unify the divided country by military means. His effort to reunify the country militarily grew into an international conflict involving the United Nations and many other countries. Kim realized that his "fatherland liberation war" turned out to be a war he could not himself fight to win or lose. Shortly after the Chinese volunteers entered the conflict, management of the war was taken away from him, and the ultimate cease-fire was agreed upon by the United States and China.

More important to Kim was the challenge to his leadership, coming from an unsuccessful conclusion of the war. During the Korean War and shortly thereafter each group challenged his leadership. Kim managed not only to meet these challenges but also used the opportunities to crush his opponents and firmly establish himself in a position of power. The domestic group challenged him during the war when it was obvious that the fighting was not going as planned. At the height of the de-Stalinization campaign, some members of the Yanan group and a few Soviet-Koreans challenged him, but he crushed them mercilessly.

Many key posts in the party, military, government, news media, and cadre training schools were occupied by the Soviet-Koreans; their challenge was not taken lightly. Hŏ Ka-i, perhaps the most influential Soviet-Korean, was the first secretary of the party, and Kim Sŭng-hwa, another Soviet-Korean, headed the central party school where all new party cadres were trained. The editors of the party organs, newspapers and journals, were also Soviet-Koreans, and they controlled the information networks in the North. Even at Kim Il Sung University, many professors came from the Soviet Union.[2] However, Soviet-Koreans lost much when the Soviet Union withdrew and did not return to fight for Korea during the Korean War.

The remaining members of the Yanan group were purged by the time the Chinese troops withdrew from Korea in 1958, and Kim did show a sign of his unique leadership quality. It took him more than a decade, but by the time the Fourth Party Congress convened in 1961, traces of all these groups save Kim's own partisans had disappeared. Only those who were unconditionally loyal to Kim remained. In this process, Kim elevated his comrades from the guerrilla days into positions of prominence, established his partisan struggle as the only correct revolutionary tradition in Korea, and began to mold a new Communist Man in the tradition of the partisans.

7

The Korean War and
Kim's Rivals

It is commonly alleged that the Soviet Union instigated Kim to wage a war of national liberation against the South to unify the country. The North Koreans, of course, accuse the United States and the South Koreans of aggression against the North. In a limited conflict such as the Korean War, where the hostilities ended with neither victory nor defeat, it is difficult to arrive at a version to which both sides are willing to subscribe. While there is overwhelming evidence that North Korea launched what they themselves have called the "fatherland liberation war," it is impossible to pinpoint the extent of Soviet instigation or Chinese persuasion.

Because Kim Il Sung and the North Koreans were so strongly influenced by the Soviet Union at the time and because so many foreign troops, including the United Nations, were involved in the war, most efforts to assess the origin of the war have concentrated on international rather than domestic factors. The war has always been analyzed from the cold war viewpoint: the confrontation of superpowers, a complex accusation of collusion among North Korea, the Soviet Union, and China, and the concept of aggression by persuasion. However, it has not been analyzed from the North Korean or Kim's point of view. The objective of the war for Kim was quite different. It was neither the development of the concept of limited war, nor was it the expansion or containment of communism in Asia. The war for Kim was primarily the function of his own political ambition, and his effort to resolve the question of Korea's division.[1]

Kim's reasons for the war should therefore be examined in terms of North Korean politics. The U.S. troop withdrawal, the success of the Chinese Communists in mainland China, the Acheson declaration regarding the U.S. defense perimeter in Asia, and the general cold war atmosphere that characterized the period after World War II may all have contributed to Kim's decision to attack, but the decision was his own. Since he was so closely supervised by his advisors in the Soviet embassy, including his mentor, Colonel Ignatiev, it is indeed inconceivable that the Soviet Union was unaware of Kim's plan to march south. Kim must have had at least their acquiescence, if not their approval. He might have received Stalin's permission, as Khruschshev remembered, but Kim's own reasons for launching the war are quite different, and they should be analyzed.

Domestic Causes of the Korean War

Three domestic causes of the Korean War are considered here: Kim's resolve to reunify the country militarily, his difficulty in the 1949–1950 two-year economic plan, and his precarious relationship with the Communists from the South. Kim Il Sung wanted to reunify his country, if and when the international political situation surrounding the Korean peninsula was suitable for such an undertaking. Kim considered military reunification to be the most efficient solution, and he was not alone in this line of thinking. Many Korean revolutionaries who returned from abroad thought that Korea should be reunified, and Syngman Rhee in the South made his intention "to march North" known to the people of Korea. The difference between Kim and Rhee was that Kim was able to implement his plan and prepare his army for the task. From the time he was installed as head of the Provisional People's Committee on February 8, 1946, to the outbreak of war in June 1950, Kim never advocated peaceful reunification of Korea. He thought that the only way to achieve national reunification was by force of arms.

That Kim with his military past should resort to such a solution is not surprising, particularly when South Korea was in political and military disarray. It is true that Kim had the Democratic Front for the Fatherland Unification (*Choguk t'ongil minju chuŭi chŏnsŏn*), consisting of many social leaders, propose a peaceful unification in June 1949, approximately one year before the hostilities, but Kim himself did not appeal to the leaders of the South for peaceful reunification. As early as 1947 in his New Year address Kim said that the united and democratic Korea to which all Koreans aspired could be had only by ultimate victory over the reactionary traitors in the South. In another New Year address in 1950, Kim emphasized that unification was possible only through strengthening the People's Army and the security forces.[2]

Furthermore, on January 19, 1950, at the Third Party Congress of the Ch'ŏndogyo Young Friends Party, Kim made an important speech on the unification question. He said that building and strengthening the revolutionary bases in the North for the purpose of unifying the country was not enough; the North Koreans must wipe out the traitors in the South. He said that the great task of national reunification must be accomplished quickly and by "ourselves." He cited the examples of the October Revolution in the Soviet Union and the recent success of the Communist forces in mainland China. Citing Malenkov's speech at the thirty-second anniversary of the October Revolution, Kim said that he was not afraid of a war; it was South Koreans who should be afraid of the people's war. If there should be a third world war, not just one or two capitalist states but all the reactionary capitalist states would be doomed. He emphasized that "we will be victorious, but victory does not come on its own; victory must be won."[3]

Kim's effort to build a strong army in the North was evident from the beginning. He took steps to assign all his partisans to this effort. One of the first factories he built was a munition plant to manufacture guns and ammunition. When the Korean People's Army was formally established, Kim symbolically posed for a picture with his partisans, Ch'oe Yong-gŏn, Kim Ch'aek, Kang Kŏn, and Kim Il, giving them the first weapons manufactured in the North.

Kim built an army that was much larger and stronger than that in the South. Kim had many units trained during the Chinese civil war in Manchuria, and he brought many combat troops from northeastern China into North Korea prior to the beginning of the war.[4] By the time of the Korean War in June 1950, the military balance in his favor became much more apparent. Kim had approximately 120,000 men in arms compared with slightly more than 60,000 troops in the South. The extent of his mobilization becomes clearer when it is recalled that the North had about half the population of the South. The Fatherland Defense Assistance Association (*Choguk powi huwŏnhoe*) was organized as early as July 15, 1949, by the youth and women's groups to strengthen the People's Army. Through this organization the North Koreans began to urge the people to contribute to the defense fund. A number of individuals and private corporations contributed airplanes and tanks through this organization.

In his interview with a reporter of the French Communist newspaper *L'Humanité* on July 17, 1950, when the war was going in his favor, Kim said that he envisioned a short war, and had it not been for the American intervention the war would have been over. Kim's timetable was to liberate the entire South by August 15, 1950, and to celebrate that day in Seoul. In his radio address on October 11, 1950, when the United Nations forces began to cross the 38th parallel and march North, Kim said for the first time that he knew about the South Korean plan to attack the North in early May, more than one and a half months before the outbreak of war, and therefore was able to prepare for the South Korean invasion.[5]

One cause of the war that has often been neglected is the economic situation in the North. Kim had completed two one-year economic plans for 1947 and 1948, which he claimed were resounding successes. By the time of the Korean War, he had instituted a two-year economic plan for 1949–1950 which was in considerable difficulty. In contrast with his earlier economic figures, which he gave in great detail, counting even the number of domestic animals, no detailed economic statistics were announced in 1949 and

First weapons made in North Korea
From left to right: Ch'oe Yon-gŏn, Kim Ch'aek, Kim Il, Kim Il Sung, and Kang Kŏn

The Yi Hong-gwang Company, Korean soldiers in Northeast China

Korean volunteers in Northeast China, September 1947

Korean volunteers marching in Northeast China

production figures were now given in percentages based on comparison with some imaginary figures for preliberation Korea in 1944, rather than accomplishment of the 1948 plan. Korea was not

*Graduation ceremony of North Korean air force pilots and technicians,
December 1949*

At Pak Hŏn-yŏng's wedding

*Ambassador T. F. Shtykov, Mrs. Kim Chŏng-suk (Kim Il Sung's wife), Kim
Il Sung, the bride (Pak's new wife), Pak Hŏn-yŏng, Kim Tu-bong (facing to the
right), and Hong Myŏng-hŭi*

Kim Il Sung and Pak Hŏn-yŏng in happier days

Ambassador and Mrs. T. F. Shtykov, Kim Il Sung and his wife, and Pak Hŏn-yŏng and his wife

divided in 1944, of course, and thus there was no separate North Korean figure in the 1944 statistics under Japanese colonial rule. The categories of economic achievement and goals were also different from those earlier announced in 1948. By February 1950, Kim admitted the failure of the two-year plan, pointing to a certain unforeseen expansion of basic industries.[6]

The primary purpose of Kim's first trip to the Soviet Union in March-April 1949 was to ask for economic assistance for his two-year economic plan and not, as commonly alleged, to discuss Stalin's plan to force a war. There was no mutual defense treaty concluded between North Korea and the Soviet Union; rather, a treaty for economic and cultural cooperation for the next ten years was signed. Kim led a seven-member delegation to visit Stalin. Those who accompanied him to the Soviet Union were Pak Hŏn-yŏng, vice-premier and foreign minister; Chŏng Chun-t'aek, chairman of the State Planning Commission; Chang Si-u, minister of industry; Hong Myŏng-hŭi, vice-premier; Paek Nam-un, minister of education; and Kim Chŏng-ju, minister of communication. From the composition of the delegation, it is clear that this was not a military delegation but an economic mission.[7]

In his report to the Supreme People's Assembly upon his return from the Soviet Union, Kim made repeated claims of Soviet assurance of economic aid, liberal loans, technical assistance, and expansion of Soviet-Korean trade. But even after one year of intensive effort, his projected goals of economic achievement were nowhere in sight. Kim may have been advised by his comrades of the futility of trying to develop an independent North Korean economy with only half the labor force of the South while military conquest of the South and economic plans for all Korea seemed so close at hand. Reunification may have been seen as a means to plan for economic development of the entire country. A draft of the land reform law for the South was announced by Pak Mun-gyu, minister of agriculture, as early as May 1949, more than one year before the beginning of the war. When the North Koreans occupied the South during the war, they used this law to redistribute the land.

Most important of the domestic causes of the war is the relationship between Kim Il Sung and the domestic group, headed by Pak Hŏn-yŏng. In April 1949, a new policy calling for unification of many political and social organizations of the North and South was adopted. Under this policy the Workers' Party of North Korea and the Workers' Party of South Korea were united to form the Workers' Party of Korea in June 1949, and the Democratic National Front of South Korea and the Democratic National Front of North Korea were united to form the Democratic Front for the Fatherland Unification (*Choguk t'ongil minju chuŭi chŏnsŏn*).

The Democratic Front was reported to represent as many as twenty-six political and social organizations from both North and South Korea, and it too was organized in June 1949. The seven-member chairman group of the front did not include either Kim Il Sung or Pak Hŏn-yŏng,[8] and the front suddenly issued a declaration for peaceful unification of Korea on July 2, 1949, sending a copy to UN Secretary-General Trygve Lie. On July 13, the front sent an open letter to all South Korean political and social organizations that were not members of the front, reiterating its position on peaceful unification and stating that there were only two alternatives to unification. One was colonial enslavement of the Korean people under American imperialism; the other was to unify the fatherland by rescuing the southern half of Korea from the traitors.

The Democratic Front issued a number of proposals for peaceful unification of Korea as late as June 7, 1950, although Kim himself admitted that he knew about the coming of war in early May 1950. The last North Korean proposal for peaceful unification before the war was by the Standing Committee of the Supreme People's Assembly on June 19, 1950, six days before the North's attack.[9]

For different reasons, perhaps, both Kim Il Sung and Pak Hŏn-yŏng seem to have advocated the military unification of Korea. The development of two separate regimes may have given Kim a leadership position in the northern half of Korea, but it was not the North Korean government that commanded more people and recognition. It was the government headed by Syngman Rhee in the South that received the blessing of the United Nations and won recognition from many countries throughout the world. In his effort to reunify the country and establish a Communist state in Korea, Kim pushed for a revolution in the South.

From September 1949 to March 1950, Communist guerrilla activities in the South were intensified, and two Communist leaders in the South, Kim Sam-yong and Yi Chu-ha, used guerrillas sent from the North. More than 3,000 guerrillas were sent south during the period, including more than 600 cadres who had graduated from the Kangdong Political Institute. However, these activities were not successful, and most of the guerrillas sent from the North were arrested. When Kim Sam-yong and Yi Chu-ha were arrested on March 27, 1950, any hope of inciting revolt by the guerrillas in the South disappeared.[10]

Pak Hŏn-yŏng would have preferred a popular uprising to a military conquest to reclaim his leadership in the South, but since his followers and his underground agents were all arrested in the South, Pak would have to agree to military action. For Pak, there was more than one reason to march south. Most of his organizational units and operational bases were in the South, and once the South was liberated and the party and government moved from Pyongyang to Seoul, he and his domestic group could improve their position over other rival groups.

Pak is alleged to have told Kim that once the Korean People's Army started a military action to liberate the South, some 200,000 loyal followers of his organizations in the South would rise up and overthrow the South Korean regime.[11] Kim lamented Pak's credulity long after the conclusion of the war. Recollecting the events of the war on February 8, 1963, at the fifteenth anniversary of the People's Army, he told officers of the army that Pak was a "liar" and there had not been even 1,000 members, let alone 200,000. He had pushed as far South as the Naktong River, a stone's throw from Taegu, as Pak said, but no one revolted.[12]

These domestic factors alone, of course, were not the entire cause of the Korean War, but for Kim Il Sung they were important. For Kim, the unification of Korea should have been won in a civil war, just as the Chinese Communists had won in mainland China. The goal of militarily unifying the country was within his reach, had the United States abstained from helping the South. As early as September 11, 1950, when the war was still going in his favor, Kim expressed apprehension about the criticism of his aggression and asked, "How could anyone call people who rose up to fight for the freedom and independence of their own fatherland aggressors?"[13] However, what Kim failed to comprehend, was that the situation in the two Koreas was quite different from that in China after World War II. Two separate governments were formally proclaimed in Korea, one at least under the auspices of the United Nations. What Kim had done was to commit an act of aggression by one state against another, certainly different from the Chinese civil war.

Confronted with an unforeseen and adverse turn of events, Kim panicked when the United Nations forces crossed the 38th parallel into the North and occupied Pyongyang. The Chinese volunteers pushed Kim aside and took over management of the war. Two weeks after Pyongyang was recaptured for him by the Chinese, the third joint plenum of the Central Committee was called on December 21, 1950, in Kanggye.[14]

In a lengthy speech Kim attacked almost everybody, most particularly his own partisans who had mismanaged the war. He admitted that the American intervention was an unexpected turn of events and that his forces had suffered greatly from the sudden retreat, but he said there was a general laxity in party discipline and lashed out at undisciplined conduct by generals, party cadres, and government officials. His original speech was censored in four different places and omitted the content of his condemnation of officials before the text was made public. The omitted passages dealt with the conduct of military personnel and troop movements, failures of the guerrillas in the South, internal public security groups, and incompetence in the ministries of transportation and propaganda.

More important officials were publicly admonished, the majority being his most loyal partisans and Soviet-Koreans, including Kim Il, Ch'oe Kwang, Yim Ch'un-ch'u, and Kim Yŏl. They were relieved of their positions and were expelled from the party. Kim Han-jung and Mu Chŏng from the Yanan group and Hŏ Sŏng-t'aek and Pak Kwang-hŭi, from the domestic group, were also among those attacked.[15] Kim's condemnation was made in haste and incipient panic; when the Chinese Volunteer Army had recovered most of the lost territory, these people were reinstated. Kim Il was quickly recalled and became the ranking member of the Political Committee; Ch'oe Kwang eventually became commander-in-chief of the army; Yim Ch'un-ch'u became secretary of the party and Kim Yŏl vice-minister of heavy industry.

Only Mu Chŏng was permanently expelled, not so much because he was a potential rival to Kim and a well-known military leader but because he had been relieved of his command of the Second Corps earlier for having executed retreating soldiers as though he were a "feudal warlord." Mu Chŏng was charged with defending Pyongyang, but when the UN forces approached the city he reportedly fled to China without fighting. Kim said that Mu Chŏng must face not only political censure but a legal verdict for his crimes.

Hŏ Ka-i's Confrontation

When the Chinese Volunteer Army stabilized the fighting front in 1951, Kim's panic subsided somewhat. His first confrontation with other groups came in September 1951 in a dispute with Hŏ Ka-i, the highest-ranking Soviet-Korean, over the question of how to reorganize the tattered party and how to handle party members who were not completely loyal. Hŏ was recognized as the organization expert by the Soviet occupation authorities. After the party was established Hŏ moved up in party ranks; he was ranked fifth in the first Central Committee and fourth in both the Political and Standing Committees. By the time of the Second Party Congress Hŏ ranked third behind party Chairman Kim Tu-bong and Vice-Chairman Kim Il Sung. He chaired the Inspection Committee and created what became one of the power centers of the party, the Organization Committee, and controlled its operation. Hŏ replaced Chu Yŏng-ha as vice-chairman of the party, and when the two parties of the North and South were merged in June 1949 Hŏ became first secretary of the party. Hŏ also took a new wife in the North.

The confrontation between Kim and Hŏ began with the vigorous speech Kim made in the third joint plenum. Kim said the war had distinguished the loyal from the disloyal members of the party, and appropriate measures should be taken to punish the disloyal irrespective of their rank in the party. But Kim cautioned that each case should be processed through proper legal channels and the party should be magnanimous in dealing with low-ranking members and avoid indiscriminate purges. This task was to be carried out by the Inspection Committee headed by Hŏ.[16]

During the one-year period from December 1950, when Kim ordered the investigation, to November 1, 1951, when the fourth joint plenum was held, Hŏ did exactly the opposite of what Kim had instructed — that is, he conducted indiscriminate purges of low-ranking party members. Hŏ had expelled and punished 450,000 of the party's 600,000 members.[17]

During the brief period when UN forces occupied the North, the South Korean security forces captured and questioned many North Koreans with party identification cards, and this led party members in the occupied areas to discard, burn, or bury their cards. Hŏ issued a new card to each member of the party, and all those who were unable to produce their old cards in exchange for the new ones were considered collaborators and punished. Kim said that 80 to 85 percent of the expulsions were due to failure to produce the old party identification cards. In an extreme case, 154 out of 164 members of the Sunch'ŏn county party in P'yŏngan pukto were expelled because they had lost their cards. Kim said he had cautioned Hŏ in the Organization Committee meeting on September 1, 1951, against such harsh measures, but Hŏ had refused to cooperate.[18]

On a related issue, Kim said that Hŏ had closed doors on many qualified applicants to the party. In an effort to preserve a proper balance of proletariat and peasants, Hŏ had refused to consider applications from peasants. Kim said that 80 percent of the North Koreans were peasants and Hŏ should not have spent his time looking for the handful of industrial workers in the country. Kim said that Pakch'ŏn county, P'yŏngan pukto, had set a quota of seventeen peasant members and had refused other qualified peasant applicants. Others were rejected on the grounds of their educational level, their former affiliation, and involuntary service to the enemy. Kim said that 77.4 percent of 212 applicants in Hyesan county, Hamgyŏng pukto, were refused because they could not recite the party platform.

The central issue in the confrontation between Hŏ and Kim was whether to build an elite Communist party in the style of the Soviet Union or a mass party, as the Soviet occupation authorities had taught Kim to do. Kim said later that Hŏ had argued for an elite Communist party of fewer than 60,000 members, consisting primarily of industrial workers. Kim argued that Korea must build a mass party in accordance with the country's unique characteristics, and Hŏ should not have been looking for nonexistent industrial workers while denying peasant majority participation in the party. Kim emphasized that to force unsuitable foreign methods on Korea mechanically was improper, bureaucratic, and formalistic and should be avoided.[19]

Kim ordered most of those expelled to be reinstated, and by the time the fifth joint plenum was held on December 15, 1952, approximately one year after the confrontation, 69.2 percent of the expulsion orders had been rescinded. The membership had grown to one million by then, but Kim admitted later that approximately half of the 450,000 new members recruited during the Korean War were uneducated and barely able to read simple Korean.[20] Hŏ was purged, of course, and more members were recruited fairly indiscriminately. Meanwhile the uneducated were trained. By the time of the Third Party Congress in April 1956 the party claimed a membership of 1,164,945, approximately 12 percent of the population — the highest ratio of members to population of any Communist party in the world. Kim said that 51.7 percent of the entire membership had been recruited after the Korean War.[21]

The war brought some basic changes to Kim. He still parroted the customary adulation of Stalin and was profuse in his thanks for the Soviet contribution in the Korean War. On the second anniversary of the treaty of economic and cultural cooperation on March 17, 1951, he expressed deep appreciation to Stalin and again on April 16, 1952, when the Soviet Union gave him 50,000 tons of grain, Kim repeated himself many times in salutation.[22] It was the Chinese and not the Soviet Union that had saved him from certain defeat, and the Chinese occupation of the North after the war brought a definite change in the domestic political scene. The group most directly affected was the Soviet-Korean. In general, the Soviet-Koreans were not looked upon as favorably now as during the Soviet occupation. Marshal Stalin was dead, Ambassador Shtykov had been replaced, and Colonel Ignatiev had died early in the Korean War in an American air raid.[23] Most of the other political advisors had returned and were replaced by technical experts, undermining the political clout of the Soviet-Koreans.

Kim quickly readjusted. Although the Chinese volunteers who came to Korea were not his old comrades from Manchuria, he felt at ease with the Chinese. He could at least converse with them freely, without the help of the interpreter he had needed in dealing with the Soviet authorities. He ridiculed Hŏ for his claim of erudition in matters pertaining to party organization, stigmatizing him as a "party doctor" who knew it all but who could not even speak proper Korean.[24] Kim said that Hŏ acted as though he were spokesman for all those who came from the Soviet Union and thus committed the crime of individual heroism. Hŏ was secretive about everything, Kim charged, including party work.

Kim accused Hŏ of many other crimes he would not have dared to mention if the original occupation team that put Kim in power had been directing affairs in the north.[25] He accused Hŏ of engaging in constant bickering with Pak Il-u, a member of the Yanan group, over the style of political work within the army. Hŏ had insisted on the Soviet style and Pak on the Chinese style. Kim said that this was an unnecessary exercise in wrangling during a national crisis. At the sixth joint plenum of the Central Committee on August 4, 1953, it was reported that Hŏ had committed suicide, and his cowardly act was condemned. Hŏ's encounter with Kim was a mere confrontation, but a direct challenge to Kim's leadership was made by the domestic group during the Korean War.

Pak Hŏn-yŏng's Challenge

When Hŏ was expelled from the party in November 1951, Kim ensured that his expulsion did not signal the purge of other Soviet-Koreans. To many high party posts Hŏ had held, Kim appointed other Soviet-Koreans: Pak Ch'ang-ok, editor of the party organ, was appointed secretary of the party, and Pak Yŏng-bin was appointed to the Organization Committee.[26] Hŏ's encounter with Kim was not an organized confrontation of the Soviet-Korean group with Kim or his partisans. It was in essence Hŏ's implementation of the policy he considered best for building a strong Communist party in Korea that ran counter to Kim's policy, and other members of the Soviet-Korean group understood it to be that and nothing more.

However, the challenge of the domestic group was quite different. It was an organized effort to overthrow Kim and replace him with their own leader, Pak Hŏn-yŏng. They had been prevented from trying this maneuver by the presence of the Soviet occupation forces and the Soviet-Koreans, but when the war altered the balance somewhat the South Korean Communists began their move. Unlike the Soviet occupation, the Chinese occupation forces refrained from interfering in domestic politics. Furthermore, the absence of direct Soviet military participation and Kim's failure to unify Korea militarily gave rise to a conviction that Kim was indeed a puppet who had falsely claimed the leadership of the Korean Communist movement.

Compared with Kim, Pak represented the mainstream of the Korean Communist revolution. Though the Communists were divided into several factions and their revolution had failed, Pak was the best-known Communist in Korea during the Japanese occupation and commanded the support of Communists in both North and South Korea after the liberation.[27] Pak was a founding member of the first Korean Communist Party in April 1925, and he was elected first chairman of the Korean Communist Youth Association. At the time of the first Korean Communist Party incident in November 1925, he was arrested and imprisoned, but after serving nearly three years in prison he was released in August 1929, feigning mental disorder. He fled to Shanghai via Manchuria and the Soviet Union and returned to Korea only to be arrested again in 1933. He served a six-year term, and when he was released in 1939 he disguised himself as a common laborer and worked to reestablish the Communist party in Korea. When Korea was liberated, he emerged from a brick factory in Kwangju, Chŏlla namdo, a haggard but undaunted worker. He had not submitted to the Japanese. Pak was now the undisputed leader of the Korean Communist movement.

Indeed, it was Pak who was chairman of the Korean Communist Party in Seoul to whom the North Korean Communists pledged their loyalty when Kim tried to take over the branch bureau of the party in the north. The American occupation authorities issued a warrant for his arrest on September 6, 1946, forcing him to flee from South Korea to the north, but he did not participate in North Korean politics until separate governments were established on each side of the parallel. Pak became vice-chairman of the party, vice-premier, and concurrently foreign minister of the first cabinet in North Korea. Like Hŏ Ka-i, Pak took a new wife in the North.

A direct challenge to Kim was made by twelve supporters of Pak led by his most loyal and trusted lieutenant, Yi Sŭng-yŏp,[28] who was also the minister of justice in the first cabinet. During the brief period from June to September 1950 when the North Koreans occupied the South, the South Korean Communists had returned south and immediately established their party organizations. The chief organizer of this task was Yi Sŭng-yŏp, who was also chairman of the Provisional People's Committee and mayor of the capital city of Seoul. Yi appointed South Korean teams who were supporters of Pak to head each provincial party committee in the South.[29]

They began immediately and implemented the land reform law on July 4, confiscating and redistributing lands in the South. They also instituted a tax-in-kind system on August 18, taking in 25 percent of all grains harvested. As early as July 1, the general conscription law was proclaimed and young men were picked up from the streets of South Korean cities to serve in the North Korean army. Imprisoned members of the Communist party in the South were released, and they revived the party organizations there. But all these measures were short-lived, as the North Korean army retreated when the UN forces marched north. Most of their newly revived party organizations went underground. When the Chinese Communists recaptured Seoul in January 1951, Yi returned and established the Seoul Political Institute, a center to train party cadres and leaders of the underground guerrillas in the South on January 27, 1951, but this effort too was short-lived.

By June 1951 the seesaw battle along the 38th parallel had stabilized somewhat. The Political Committee of the party, by its Decision 44 on August 31, 1951, established in Sohŭng county, Hwanghaedo, on the northern side of the battle line, a party cadre and military leader training school known as the Kŭmgang Political Institute (*Kŭmgang chŏngch'i hagwŏn*) for the purpose of directing the underground guerrillas in the South. The institute was located in a region shielded by mountains and allowing easy penetration into the South. This institute was dominated by Yi Sŭng-yŏp's group loyal to Pak, and they trained many men to form a military unit of the South Korean group. The institute was headed by Kim Ŭng-bin, director, and Song Ŭl-su, deputy director and former director of the Seoul Political Institute; all workers from instructors and staff to the kitchen help were from the South. There were approximately 1,500 students in the institute.[30]

At the party headquarters in Pyongyang, the special bureau that handled all operations, guerrillas, and other matters pertaining to the South was the South Korean Liaison Bureau, which was also controlled by the Communists from the South: Cho Il-myŏng, Pae Ch'ŏl, Pak Sŭng-wŏn, and Yun Sun-dal,[31] all close comrades of Yi Sŭng-yŏp and loyal to Pak Hŏn-yŏng. Some of these men headed various Provincial People's Committees when the South was temporarily liberated.

It was in September 1951 that Yi Sŭng-yŏp was said to have begun preparing for a military coup to unseat Kim. Yi reportedly discussed his plan with leaders of the Liaison Bureau in Pyongyang and officers of the Kŭmgang Political Institute. Various posts for the coup were decided at the first session in his office: Yi was to be supreme commander, Pak Sŭng-wŏn was to be commander-in-chief, Pae Ch'ŏl was to head the military organization, Kim Ŭng-bin was to lead the armed group, and Cho Il-myŏng and Yim Hwa were to take care of communication and propaganda affairs.[32] They were to mobilize the students and cadres of the Kŭmgang Political Institute, and after the initial screening of every member they moved them into a position in Taedong county, near Pyongyang.

In February 1952 the government had ordered the organization and training of a new guerrilla unit in Namyŏnbaek, and Yi had seized this opportunity to train additional guerrillas and form the tenth company of armed guerrillas, headed by his own trusted officer Maeng Chong-ho.[33] In March 1952, Yi moved Hong Hyŏng-gi and his company, stationed in Naegŭmgang, Kangwŏndo, to Chunghwa near Pyongyang to use them for the coup. It was reported that by November 1952, Yi had tried to put together a military force of nearly 4,000 men.[34] In an effort to secure favorable propaganda for their move, Yi had Yi Wŏn-jo work on Kim Nam-ch'ŏn and Yi T'ae-jun, writers from the South, to seize control of the literary and art union of the North.[35]

On the first Sunday of September 1952, Yi and his group met in the living room of Pak Hŏn-yŏng while Pak was away and organized a new government to be installed after the coup. As their leaders they had Pak Hŏn-yŏng, premier; Chu Yŏng-ha and Chang Si-u, vice-premiers; Pak Sŭng-wŏn, minister of interior; Yi Kang-guk, minister of foreign affairs; Kim Ŭng-bin, minister of armed forces; Cho Il-myŏng, minister of propaganda; Yim Hwa, minister of education; Pae Ch'ŏl, minister of labor; Yun Sun-dal, minister of commerce; and Yi Sŭng-yŏp was to become first secretary of a new Communist party that was to be created.[36]

Although the details of the military campaign to overthrow Kim's government with the forces deployed near Pyongyang were not made public, it was reported that the coup was attempted in early 1953 but failed.[37] The exact circumstances were kept secret, but all the conspirators were arrested by early 1953. The trial record indicated that Yun Sun-dal was arrested on March 16, 1953, and Yi Wŏn-jo on April 12. The North Koreans claim that after the fifth joint plenum in December 1952, when Kim urged the organizational and ideological consolidation of the party, a campaign was launched to study Kim's speeches. The Party made a strong appeal in the January 1953 letter to all members to combat the enemy forces through criticism and self-criticism sessions, and as a result of this campaign "the antiparty traitors" were uncovered and apprehended.[38]

The Trials

On July 30, 1953, three days after the conclusion of the Korean War, twelve conspirators were indicted in accordance with Article 25 of the criminal law for high treason. The trial was held from August 3–6, 1953, in the Supreme Court presided over by Chief Justice Kim Ik-sŏn.[39] The prosecution was led by Procurator-General Yi Song-un, a partisan.[40]

Those prosecuted were:

Yi Sŭng-yŏp	secretary of the Central Committee of the Workers' Party of Korea, minister of justice, chairman of the People's Inspection Committee, chairman of the Seoul Provisional People's Committee
Cho Il-myŏng	vice-minister of culture and propaganda
Yim Hwa	vice-chairman of the Central Committee of the Soviet-Korean Cultural Association
Pak Sŭng-wŏn	chairman of the Kyŏnggido People's Committee, vice-chairman of the Liaison Bureau of the Workers' Party of Korea
Yi Kang-guk[41]	president of the General Commodities Importing Company of the Ministry of Trade
Pae Ch'ŏl	chairman of the Liaison Bureau of the Central Committee of the Workers' Party of Korea
Yun Sun-dal	vice-chairman of the Liaison Bureau of the Central Committee of the Workers' Party of Korea
Yi Wŏn-jo	vice-chairman of the Propaganda and Agitation Section of the Central Committee of the Workers' Party of Korea
Paek Hyŏng-bok	former chief of the Central Division Investigation Section of the Security Bureau, Ministry of Interior of South Korea
Cho Yong-bok	senior inspector of the People's Inspection Committee
Maeng Chong-ho	commander, Tenth Company of the Guerrilla Unit of the Korean People's Army
Sŏl Chŏng-sik	member of the Seventh Section, General Political Bureau, Supreme Command of the Korean People's Army

These men were accused on three counts: espionage activities for the United States, indiscriminate destruction and slaughter of democratic forces and Communist revolutionaries in the South, and the attempted overthrow of the government of the republic by military force. It is interesting to examine the charges. Only the charge of attempting to overthrow the government seems credible, and that should have been more than sufficient grounds to put them away for treason. But the crimes of espionage and the destruction of democratic forces in the South were added.

The "American imperialists" prominently cited in the trial records were Harold Noble, a top political advisor to the commanding general of the U.S. occupation forces during the last few months of the occupation and later advisor to the U.S. ambassador to Korea; Lt. General John R. Hodge, commander of the U.S. occupation forces in Korea; Horace Underwood, Jr., missionary educator at Yŏnhŭi (Yonsei) University; Colonel John N. Robinson; a certain military police captain named Johnson; and 2nd Lt. Leonard Bertsch. It is difficult to substantiate the charges of the defendants' espionage activities for these "imperialists," and conversely it is difficult to surmise that these American officials were fortunate enough to have such high-powered Communists as their agents.

The evidence presented in the trial documents is hardly convincing. The trial record showed that Harold Noble had instructed An Yŏng-dal on June 26, 1950, as he was fleeing Seoul, to tell Yi Sŭng-yŏp to organize a people's resistance force against the Communists because the Americans would soon return to Seoul. This story is utterly false — Noble was not in Korea on June 26, 1950, but in Tokyo on vacation when the war broke out.[42] It was General Hodge who banned the Communist Party in the South, and it was under his command that warrants were issued for the arrest of many Communists including Pak Hŏn-yŏng. Furthermore, all the alleged contacts with these men occurred before the war and would have had little effect on their attempt to overthrow the regime in 1952–1953.

One charge went as far back as 1935. It was alleged that Yi Kang-guk, who was returning to Korea from Berlin after studying there for three years, was hired in New York as an American spy. To charge people with a crime of this sort is one thing, but to execute them on such false accusation is quite different.

With regard to the destruction of the democratic forces in the South, it was alleged that the two South Korean Communist leaders, Kim Sam-yong and Yi Chu-ha, were arrested and executed in March 1950 because Cho Yong-bok and Paek Hyŏng-bok, two defendants, and An Yŏng-dal,[43] a confidant of Yi Sŭng-yŏp, led the South Korean police in their arrest. According to this story, Paek

Hyŏng-bok, who was then a detective in the Investigation Department of the Security Bureau of the South Korean national police, arrested An Yŏng-dal. In an effort to obtain his release, An had led Paek to the arrest of Cho Yong-bok, which eventually led to the arrest of Kim Sam-yong and Yi Chu-ha. After the last two were arrested, An Yŏng-dal and Cho Yong-bok, together with Detective Paek, had fled north.

This is an incredible story and hardly convincing. The arrest of Kim Sam-yong and Yi Chu-ha is amply detailed in the South Korean police records.[44] Furthermore, these two leaders were both supporters of Pak Hŏn-yŏng and close comrades of Yi Sŭng-yŏp, who detested Kim Il Sung's rule in the North. Kim Sam-yong had chosen to remain in the South even after he was elected third secretary of the party following the union of the Workers' Parties of the North and South in June 1949, and Yi Chu-ha was already under attack from the North when he fled Wŏnsan in 1946. Yi Chu-ha had refused to return to the North. The North Korean concern for these two South Korean leaders is as unbelievable as the charge that members of Yi Sŭng-yŏp's group had given information to the South Korean police.

Another charge related to this account concerned Yi's organization of the Land Investigation Committee to implement land reform during North Korea's brief occupation of the South. The extent of Yi's atrocities in the South through the operation of this committee was not known, but Yi was carrying out the July 4, 1950, land reform decree of the Standing Committee of the Supreme People's Assembly.

Perhaps the only credible charge was attempting to overthrow the government with armed force and replace Kim Il Sung with Pak Hŏn-yŏng. At the cross-examination of Pae Ch'ŏl, the prosecutor sarcastically asked him whether he had had any military training for his undertaking and Pae testified that he had none. In fact, none of the conspirators were trained militarily to take on Kim's partisans.[45]

All defendants admitted everything they were charged with. They said they were American spies, as charged, had arranged for the arrest of Kim Sam-yong and Yi Chu-ha, had slaughtered many fellow Communists to weaken the progressive democratic forces in the South, had planned the overthrow of the government, and had prepared for a new party and a new government. They went further and admitted that they wanted to see Kim Il Sung replaced by their own leader, Pak Hŏn-yŏng. They said they had written poems in praise of their supreme leader Pak. Sŏl Chŏng-sik, the only American-educated defendant,[46] admitted that he had written a poem entitled "Go Away Red Army" and said he had written it because he was convinced that Korea had been divided because of the Red Army's presence in the North. One of the twelve defendants, Yim Hwa, attempted suicide during their confinement but was not successful.[47] Toward the end of the trial, Pak Sŭng-wŏn said that every revolutionary, however hideous his crimes, had a country that he could call his homeland, but he himself could claim none. He said that he could not call the capitalist South or the Communist North his fatherland.

Since they were tried in the Supreme Court, all proper legal procedures were followed. Five defense attorneys were assigned by the court, and thirteen witnesses testified in court.[48] There was no serious defense for any of them, however, and the defense questioning was a mere formality. All were sentenced exactly as the prosecution demanded.

The fate of the South Korean Communists was reminiscent of their struggle during the Japanese occupation with perhaps one exception. The Japanese seldom executed Korean Communists, but the North Koreans sentenced ten of them to death. Yun Sun-dal was sentenced to fifteen years, and Yi Wŏn-jo was sentenced to twelve years' imprisonment. All the properties of the defendants were confiscated by the government. It is not known when the defendants were executed. Some of them were kept alive for more than two years because they appeared later as witnesses when Pak Hŏn-yŏng was tried.

Pak Hŏn-yŏng was arrested and expelled from the party but was not tried with his supporters in the same court or at the same time. He was not even indicted until some two years and four months later on December 3, 1955, by the same Procurator-General Yi Song-un, a partisan. A special panel of five judges was appointed by a decree of the Standing Committee of the Supreme People's Assembly on December 15, 1955.[49] Pak's trial was a quick one. It began at ten in the morning on December 15, 1955, and he was sentenced at eight in the evening of the same day. Pak refused a defense lawyer, and the trial proceeded without one, but nine witnesses were called in to testify against him.[50] Pak was charged with the same three counts of espionage activities for the Americans, destruction of democratic forces in the South, and the overthrow of the government in the North.

The charges leveled against Pak were more ludicrous than those against his supporters. Pak was accused of being a lackey of the Americans as early as 1919. When he was arrested by the Japanese in November 1925, Pak was alleged to have provided information on his fellow Communists to secure his release, and he was said to have submitted to the Japanese in Taejŏn prison in 1939. After the liberation of Korea, Pak was supposed to have been elected chairman of the Korean Communist Party with the assistance of Horace Underwood, Jr., and to have pledged his loyalty to Lt. General John R. Hodge, commanding general of the U.S. occupation forces. Pak was supposed to have entered the North at the direction of General Hodge for the purpose of controlling the North Korean government, and he was accused of having arranged for Yi Sŭng-yŏp and other followers to come north and to assist him in his task.

Pak was also accused of inciting adventurous strikes and unnecessary riots in the South that cost the lives of many of the democratic forces. He was also accused of planting many of his agents in the government and the party from October 1946 to 1953 and of disrupting the political process in the North. Abusing his position as foreign minister, Pak was accused of staffing the embassies in Moscow and Peking so as to disrupt the foreign relations of the North. Pak was said to have incited his followers to plan and exercise the conspiracy to overthrow the government and create a new party and a new government in the North. Lastly, he was accused of enjoying an affluent life beyond his means and was said to have embezzled 870,000 *wŏn* of North Korean currency and 1,600 grams of gold that were found in his possession at the time of his arrest.[51]

Pak admitted everything. He said that he was the chief American spy, that he had ordered the indiscriminate killing of Communists in the South, and that while he himself was not privileged to be a party to the military overthrow of the government and thus was ignorant of the details of preparation, those who attempted the overthrow were his trusted comrades and he would therefore take full responsibility for their action.

In accordance with Article 76, paragraph 2, Article 65, paragraph 1, and Articles 50, 78, and 68 of the Criminal Code of the North, Pak was sentenced to death and his property was confiscated. The reason for the delay in the prosecution of Pak is not clear, and it is not known when the sentence was carried out, but it is presumed that he was executed shortly thereafter.

8

After the War

Throughout his guerrilla days in Manchuria, defeat was something Kim experienced often, and he had learned to use his setbacks to advantage. Survival was his trade. He survived the Korean War and renewed his campaign to rebuild the North, charging the war's unsuccessful conclusion to others, such as Hŏ's bureaucratic mismanagement and Pak's factional opposition to him. For Kim the war ended as early as October 1950 when the Chinese volunteers took over the fight. While the Chinese volunteers refrained from interfering in the internal squabbles of domestic politics, they also demanded that Kim stay clear of their management of the war. Peng Dehuai, who commanded the Chinese volunteers, was reported to have told Kim that he and not Kim was in charge of the war. Peng is alleged to have told Kim that the Korean War was a fight between himself and General MacArthur, and Kim had no part in it. When Peng was purged in China some years later, one of the charges brought against him was that he had exercised Big Power chauvinism over Kim during the Korean War.[1]

The Chinese takeover of the Korean War was so comprehensive that the United States dealt primarily with the Chinese and not with Kim Il Sung directly. At the time of the initial negotiation for a cease-fire in July 1951, the North Korean reply to the call for cease-fire talks was signed by both Peng Dehuai and Kim Il Sung, stating that "we are authorized" to begin negotiation. This wording was completely proper for Peng as commander of the Chinese volunteers, but Kim was the head of state and needed no authorization from anyone to negotiate.[2] It was the Chinese volunteers who took over the war and brought a cease-fire, but there is not a single picture in honor of the Chinese contribution to the Korean War in the great hall of the revolutionary museum in Pyongyang today, and Kim, of course, claims the victory in the war.

As early as August 14, 1952, when the cease-fire negotiations were in progress, Kim conceded that truce meant cessation of military operations by the belligerents of an equal footing with no victor or vanquished.[3] Whatever the basis for his claim of victory today, there was none on the fighting front. Even if his own reasons for Korean national reunification by military means were understandable, the war, for Kim, was a devastating experience. He was branded an aggressor in the war, and he was humiliated by the Chinese. Worst of all, he had mobilized Koreans to fight against Koreans, but the fate of Korea was once again decided by non-Koreans, while the country still remained divided.

Kim was successful in meeting the domestic challenge to his position. While the trial of Yi Sŭng-yŏp and his group was in progress, Kim held the sixth joint plenum of the Central Committee from August 4–6, 1953, and restructured his party. Kim had lost a number of his trusted partisans in the war — including Vice-President Kim Ch'aek; and his commander-in-chief, Kang Kŏn; Cho Chŏng-ch'ŏl; and Ch'oe Ch'un-guk. He quickly reinstated those partisans who were reprimanded and expelled during the first retreat, such as Kim Il, and realigned those Soviet-Koreans who pledged support for him, such as Kim Yŏl. One person who emerged prominently from the realignment was Pak Chŏng-ae,[4] who delivered a lengthy speech on organizational matters in the sixth joint plenum and announced Kim's decision on the expulsion of the unfaithful and recruitment of the trustworthy.

In this shuffle most of the South Korean Communists were expelled from the party,[5] including the ambassadors to both the Soviet Union, Chu Yŏng-ha, and the People's Republic of China, Kwŏn O-jik. The chairman and vice-chairman of the Inspection Committee, Chang Sun-myŏng and Yi Ki-sŏk, both members of the domestic group, were relieved of their posts and replaced with Kim Ŭng-gi. Kim also made changes in the structure of the party. Positions considered to be the creations of Hŏ Ka-i, the Soviet expert on party organization — such as the posts of the first, second, and third secretaries of the party and the Organization Committee, which wielded unrestrained power within the party — were abolished. In their places a number of vice-chairmen of the party were appointed and the Standing Committee of the Central Committee was revived. Kim also appointed a committee to revise the party bylaws to accommodate the restructured party organization.[6]

New top leaders of the party in support of Kim were Kim Tu-bong, Pak Chŏng-ae, Pak Ch'ang-ok, and Kim Il, and they constituted the new Political Committee of the Central Committee. But this was a period of readjustment and changes were frequent in the party hierarchy. From January to April 1954, there was a general party election to fill various positions in the local party organization, and in the March plenum of 1954 two members of the Political Committee, Pak Ch'ang-ok and Kim Il, were appointed vice-premiers and the Central Committee elected Pak Yŏng-bin, a Soviet-Korean, and Kim Ch'ang-man, a member of the Yanan group, as members of the Political Committee. Only a handful of the South Korean Communists who pledged absolute loyalty remained in leadership positions after the war, and Kim recruited a number of Soviet-Koreans to replace most of those purged. These Soviet-Koreans included Pak Ch'ang-ok, Pak Yŏng-bin, Yim Hae, Kim Sŭng-hwa, and Nam Il.

Rehabilitation and Reconstruction

When the truce was finally concluded and the war was over, Kim set out to rebuild the North Korean countryside and strengthen the party leadership. During the two years of half-negotiation and half-fighting, the North Korean cities and countryside were devastated by the constant American bombing.[7] His basic economic policy was to give priority to the development of heavy industry and simultaneously to develop agriculture and light industry, a strategy that most people did not understand. It was translated later to mean that production of consumer goods would be sacrificed to concentrate on the development of heavy industry.

Kim led a six-member delegation to visit the Soviet Union from September 10–29, 1953, with two purposes in mind: to meet the new leaders of the Soviet Union after the death of Stalin and to secure economic aid from them.[8] Kim received a loan of one billion rubles for reconstruction of the destroyed industrial facilities and building of new factories. The loan was to be paid back in two years; two-thirds in 1954 and the rest in 1955. Kim also received an extension on the payment of all previous loans from the Soviet Union. Kim met Malenkov, Stalin's successor, at a reception arranged for him, but the Soviet leadership was still in flux following the death of Stalin and Kim's main accomplishment was getting the much-needed economic assistance.

Kim also led an eight-member delegation to Beijing, November 12–27, 1953, and there he received a loan of eight trillion Chinese yuan to be paid in two installments, three trillion in 1954 and the rest in 1955–1957. The Chinese were more generous than the Soviet Union and canceled all North Korean debts to China, including materials supplied by the Chinese during the Korean War from 1950 to 1953.[9] Still another delegation consisting of ten members headed by Yi Chu-yŏn traveled for five months from June to November 1953 to East European countries to collect relief aid for reconstruction of the North.[10]

With the new three-year economic plan (1954–1956) and its emphasis on heavy industries, Kim accomplished a clean sweep in nationalization of all industries, including the light industries and most of the means of production. In the agrarian sector, however, most of the farmland was privately owned and approximately half of the farmers were classified as poor peasants. Kim launched experimental cooperatives in November 1954 and said that the ultimate goal was to transform all farms into cooperatives. As he outlined the process, it was to be carried out slowly and in three stages, beginning with mutual assistance work teams in which only the work was done collectively. The second stage was the semisocialist collectivization of land and labor with distribution made in accordance with the amount of work done and the size of the land collectivized. The third stage called for complete socialist cooperatives in which the land and the means of production were collectivized and the shares were distributed according to the amount of work done.[11]

There was considerable resistance to both the industrial and the agrarian policies. Much of the opposition to the industrial programs was not to nationalization itself but to the great emphasis on heavy industry that sacrified the essential needs of the people for consumer goods. The people were deprived of basic necessities and were driven to hard work in major industries.

Most of the middle- and high-income farmers were opposed to the cooperatives, and while Kim paid lip service to moderate speed in collectivization of farmland, the entire process was completed within two years. The North Koreans claimed that 97.5 percent of all farmland was in the third stage of collectivization by the end of 1956.[12] While Kim claimed all sorts of accomplishments in both the industrial and agrarian sectors, such as surpassing the goals of production in industries and self-sufficiency in agriculture, he had merely begun his campaign to restore the economy to the prewar level.

Strengthening the Party

On the second problem, the ideological strengthening of his party leadership, Kim confronted any and all who opposed him and his policy or showed even a sign of becoming a potential rival. After meeting the direct challenge of the domestic group, Kim tightened his control and promoted himself as the chief propagator and the defender of the Korean revolution. He asserted that his position was the true Korean stance and rejected any attempt to emulate or imitate others. At the April plenum of the Central Committee in 1955, Kim gave a stern warning to the leaders of various groups to refrain from factional struggle.

He cautioned all party officials to become disciplined fighters of the Korean revolution, even though their own revolutionary past may have been in the Soviet Union or in China. He said that more than half the party members had been recruited into the party after the war. He admitted for the first time that because of the nature of the Korean revolution, there were revolutionaries who came from the Soviet Union, China, and South Korea, but no one should use his past for the purpose of factional struggle.

Kim warned that the factionalist is like a mouse, scurrying around at night when everyone is asleep. He said that Pak Hŏn-yŏng was such a mouse and that Hŏ Ka-i had claimed such factional leadership among the Soviet-Koreans. Kim also said that among those who had returned from China, Pak Il-u acted in such a manner, proclaiming himself leader of the Yanan group.[13] Kim alleged that Pak Il-u had constantly complained that few from the Yanan group were recruited into positions of leadership. Pak had tried to bring under his wing such members of the group as Pang Ho-san, the most decorated officer of the Korean War, the double hero of the republic. Pak Il-u's mistake was to confide in Kim Ch'ang-dŏk, a partisan, and Pak was immediately arrested.[14]

Among those who survived the purge of the domestic group, Kang Mun-sŏk was singled out and accused of being a self-proclaimed leader of the South Korean Communists. Kang was reported to have advertised himself as the caretaker of everyone from the South, thus committing the crime of individual heroism. Kim also cautioned against local groups in the North and once again whipped the already dead horse, O Ki-sŏp. Kim used O as an example of those who attempted to form a local group and charged him with the crime of regionalism.[15]

In dealing with the challenges of the South Korean Communists and confronting individual leaders of groups, Kim counted on his old partisans, who still had firm control of the army. Even after the death of such important partisans as Kim Ch'aek and Kang Kŏn, the Korean People's Army was still held together by other partisans, Ch'oe Yong-gŏn, Ch'oe Hyŏn, and Kim Kwang-hyŏp. Those partisans who were temporarily purged, such as Kim Il, Ch'oe Kwang, and Yim Ch'un-ch'u, were quickly reinstated, and Kim supplemented them with others who supported him unconditionally irrespective of their group affiliation. He succeeded in crushing any coalition that might have challenged him by publicly downgrading the leaders of other groups and purging the dangerous ones in the military.

Kim's method in this effort was to castigate those who had conducted their revolutionary activities abroad and to claim his partisan struggle as the mainstream of the Korean Communist revolution. To be sure, his own revolution was more non-Korean than those of the Yanan group, which at least maintained a separate Korean identity in China. After purging the South Korean Communist leaders who represented the mainstream of the Korean Communist revolution, Kim saw the need to establish his own guerrilla activities as *the* tradition of Korean revolution. Kim tried hard to find his Korean self-identity, and he carried on irrational tirades condemning all things non-Korean. The group that suffered most in this turn of events was the Soviet-Koreans.

In the Soviet Union Marshal Stalin had died and was being downgraded by the new leaders of the Soviet Union, who were advocating peaceful coexistence with the west. These were dangerous developments for Kim. Not only did the de-Stalinization campaign directly threaten his effort to emulate Stalin in building his own authoritarian power in Korea, but the policy of peaceful coexistence with the west ran counter to the conditions prevailing in divided Korea. The Chinese Communist army was still in the North, and the Chinese Communists were seriously questioning the wisdom of the de-Stalinization campaign in the Soviet Union and the Soviet policy of peaceful coexistence.

It was under these circumstances that Kim had delivered, on December 28, 1955, his first speech about *chuch'e*, his effort to find Korean identity as a counterweight to Soviet influence. His main message was to eliminate dogmatism and formalism and establish self-identity in the ideological work of the party. Under this new direction, the primary target was the Soviet-Korean group. Kim condemned Pak Ch'ang-ok, a recent recruit and fourth highest member of the Political Committee, charging that Pak had failed to recognize the value of Korean proletarian literature. Kim accused Pak of belittling the contribution by the Korean Artist Proletarian Federation and progressive writers in Korea. He said that Pak praised such bourgeois and reactionary writers as Yi Kwang-su and Yi T'ae-jun but ignored the work of such true proletarian writers as Han Sŏl-ya and Yi Ki-yŏng.[16]

Kim ridiculed the pictures of the Siberian steppe hanging on the wall of a People's Army rest home and the portraits of Pushkin in elementary schools. He said that the North Korean imitation of the Soviet Union should be corrected. Kim also chided the Soviet-Korean editors of North Korean newspapers for merely reproducing the headlines of *Pravda*, and he criticized the work of Ki Sŏk-bok, a Soviet-Korean editor of the party organ.

He also condemned Pak Yŏng-bin, another Soviet-Korean he had recruited into a party leadership position shortly after the war, for advocating peaceful coexistence with the west. Pak Yŏng-bin had apparently visited the Soviet Union and returned to tell the party that there were significant changes in the Soviet leadership, that they were advocating peaceful competition with the United States, and that the North Koreans should therefore relax their anti-American stance and drop the vitriolic propaganda against the United States. Kim angrily retorted that the North Korean people who had suffered indiscriminate bombing and "mass murder" of innocent people during the Korean War could not relax the attack on the United States. He said that the Russians, who had not fought the Americans, might do so, but the North Koreans were painfully aware that American military forces were still occupying the southern half of the country. Kim also reiterated his attack on Hŏ Ka-i, who committed suicide, and other Soviet-Koreans such as Kim Chae-uk.[17]

Kim's first outburst on finding his self-identity began with this anti-Soviet, but not necessarily anti-foreign, movement. It was certainly not an anti-Chinese campaign. Indeed, Kim said that in order to strengthen party spirit among the members, the Koreans must follow the example of the Chinese rectification campaign, the *zhengfeng* movement. His past praise of the Soviet Union and its contribution to Korea was surpassed only by his quickness to condemn the Soviet-Koreans during the Chinese occupation of the North.

Later, when the Chinese occupation forces withdrew from North Korea in 1958, his first speech about *chuch'e* was revised to delete his remark about following the example of the Chinese rectification campaign. Kim had to be cautious toward China and the Soviet Union, and he did not refer to the idea of *chuch'e* for the next eight years, until 1963. The North Koreans consider *chuch'e* as

Kim's political ideology, but they seldom refer to this first speech, reflecting its anti-Soviet and pro-Chinese origin.[18]

The Third Party Congress: 1956

Kim's efforts to find Korean self-identity had two basic problems: his non-Korean revolutionary past, which made it difficult for him to relate his records to those of other groups, and the international pressure that still played a dominant role in the North's domestic politics. Kim met the first problem by continuing to downgrade the domestic group for their failures in the past and to belittle the records of the Yanan group and the Soviet-Koreans. He also began in earnest to promote his partisan activities in Manchuria as the mainstream of the Korean revolutionary tradition. On the international front Kim maintained his loyalty to the Soviet Union even when there were significant changes in Soviet policy, such as de-Stalinization and the problem of collective leadership, that adversely affected him in the North.

While the trial that sentenced Pak Hŏn-yŏng to death was in progress on December 3, 1955, the Central Committee held its December plenum to announce the plan to hold the Third Party Congress in April 1956, eight years after the second congress. It is important to note that the planned party congress was held some two months after the twentieth party congress of the Communist Party of the Soviet Union when important pronouncements about changes in Soviet party policy were made by Nikita S. Khrushchev.[19] Ch'oe Yong-gŏn, Kim's most trusted partisan after the death of Kim Ch'aek, led the North Korean delegation to participate in the congress.[20]

When the delegation returned and reported the new direction of the Soviet leadership in the de-Stalinization campaign and collective leadership, Kim reacted quickly. In his speech at the P'yŏngan pukto provincial party organization meeting on April 7, 1956, Kim said that collective leadership meant to discuss problems with the participation of all members of the leadership organ, relying on everyone's creative suggestions and thus avoiding the arbitrary discretion of a single leader.[21] Kim said the past leaders of the domestic group such as Pak Hŏn-yŏng and Yi Sŭng-yŏp had exercised individual heroism and failed to observe this important principle of collective leadership.

At this time Kim was both chairman of the party and premier of the government, and throughout the period when the issue of collective leadership (*chipch'ejŏk chido*) was discussed, Kim never once related the top leadership position of the party and the government to the idea of collective leadership. Similarly, Kim always avoided the issue of de-Stalinization and abstained from casting slurs on Stalin. In the case of other ousted Soviet party leaders, Kim did not hesitate to downgrade the activities of Malenkov, Kaganovich, Molotov, and Bulganin; but Kim did not criticize Stalin or his past.

When the Third Party Congress was held, April 23–29, 1956, many important visitors came to North Korea to participate. Leonid I. Brezhnev headed the Soviet delegation and said in his congratulatory speech to the delegates that some important changes had been made in the Soviet Union at its twentieth party congress and stressed that the Third Party Congress of the Workers' Party of Korea should help implement the Leninist principle of collective leadership in all party organization from top to bottom.[22] Nie Rongzhen, representing the Chinese Communist Party, congratulated the gallant efforts of the Korean people in the reconstruction of their country after the war.[23]

Kim delivered a lengthy speech. He spoke on the North Korean position in international relations, primarily attacking the United States. He elaborated on the economic progress of the past and on anticipated domestic accomplishments. He also repeated the usual condemnation of the antiparty reactionaries of the domestic group and urged the delegates to strengthen the party. He deliberately avoided the most pressing issues of the time: the question of collective leadership and the problem of de-Stalinization in the Soviet Union.

In a lengthy account of how hideous the leaders of the domestic group were, Kim said that the failure of the Communist revolution in the South was due not to the American presence but to the malicious sabotage of the leaders of the domestic group. In an effort to revive the self-identity of the Korean people, he reiterated his plea to study more Korean history and repeated the twisted logic linking the Korean tradition and his own non-Korean partisan activities in Manchuria. Kim said that such nationalists as Kim Ku and Kim Kyu-sik, whom he had once called traitors, were patriots.[24] He urged scholars to study his partisan activities along with the history of the Korean peasant struggle under the Japanese.

Other than his usual salutory remarks, Kim refrained from either attacking or praising the Soviet Union throughout his speech — not necessarily because of the presence of Brezhnev but perhaps because of his urgent need to get more assistance from the Soviet Union to launch the first five-year economic plan. There was much confusion in his report: His anti-Soviet stance was restrained by his needs, he was reluctant to comment on the subject of collective leadership, and he felt the difficulty of insisting that his partisan activities should be considered the mainstream of the Korean Communist tradition. This was perhaps one of the least impressive speeches he made, and it is the only speech he made in any party congress that was not selected for inclusion in the latest edition of his selected works.[25]

In answer to the call for a thorough study of Kim's partisan activities and their link with Korean history and tradition, Yi Ch'ŏng-wŏn, one of the leading historians of the North,[26] spoke at the congress in support of Kim. Within two to three years after this congress, many historical studies blending grossly exaggerated accounts of his partisan exploits with traditional Korean history began to appear.[27] To elaborate on Kim's condemnation of the leaders of the domestic group, Procurator-General Yi Song-un, who had just finished prosecuting Pak Hŏn-yŏng and his followers, reminded the delegates that there were still many members of the domestic group who had failed to recant and perform correct self-criticism and there were even some who tried to hide their past relationship with the group.[28]

Kim's confusion was reflected in the newly elected officers, members, and candidate members of the Central Committee, as well. Many Soviet-Koreans still remained in high party posts, including the leader of the Soviet-Korean group, Pak Ch'ang-ok, who had already been condemned by Kim on several occasions before the party congress. Many members of the Yanan group whose revolutionary activities had been ridiculed by Kim in the past were reelected to the Central Committee, and even a few former sup-porters of Pak Hŏn-yŏng, such as Hŏ Sŏng-t'aek and Pak Mun-gyu,[29] who were criticized by Kim, were reelected to the Central Committee.

Kim managed to more than double the number of partisans in the Central Committee. Eleven members and six candidate mem-bers of the committee were partisans, but more important, of the six highest-ranking members, four were partisans.[30] Out of the confusion, however, came a definite sign of the prominence of the partisan group in the party leadership in support of Kim. They were not yet a dominant force, but Kim began to recruit more and more from his old partisan colleagues as he tried to legitimize his partisan record as the true tradition of the Korean revolution.

Out of seventy-one members of the Central Committee, only twenty-eight were reelected members from the Central Commit-tee of the Second Party Congress, and forty-three were newly elected members. Out of these forty-three new members, only five were promoted from the candidate membership of the Second Party Congress, and more than half of the entire membership of the Central Committee, thirty-seven members, were completely new. Among the candidate members, only two out of twenty can-didate members of the Second Party Congress were reelected, and out of forty-five candidate members of the Third Party Congress forty-three were new candidate members. These were drastic changes, and they reflected much difficulty in the party. It was especially obvious, for example, in the Inspection Committee, where none of the officers of the second congress were reelected in the third congress.

There was a sweeping change in the party bylaws, as well. Pak Chŏng-ae, who presented the amendments (virtually new bylaws) of the party, gave three reasons for the change: to facilitate the building of new socialism in the North, to accommodate the growth of the party, and to adjust to the changes in the fraternal socialist and Communist countries. In her speech to the party con-gress, Pak said that the impact of the decision of the twentieth party congress of the Soviet Union was significant, but there was little in the new bylaws to reflect any relevance. Much of her pre-sentation dealt with the rights and duties of party members and candidate members, and she pointed out the errors committed by such officers as Kim Yŏl and Pak Sŏng-sam, who were alleged to have harassed members of the party. The new bylaws were designed to protect party members from abuse by their own officers. There was little in the bylaws to substantiate such protection. But by the Third Party Congress adherence to the bylaws was perfunctory. The intent of Kim and his partisans was more important.[31]

The party had indeed grown, and Kim reported that there were 1,164,945 members organized in 58,259 cells. He said the party had grown in spite of the Korean War, increasing by 439,183 members and 28,496 cells from the level at the time of the Second Party Congress in 1948. The party membership represented approximately 10 percent of the entire population in the North.[32]

The Challenge of the Yanan Group

Less than two months after the conclusion of the Third Party Congress, Kim led a ten-member delegation to visit nine nations from June 1 to July 19, 1956, to solicit support for his new five-year economic plan. It is interesting to note that Kim took with him representatives of the Korean Democratic Party and Ch'ŏndogyo Young Friends Party and two labor heroes in addition to such usual officers as the chairman of the State Planning Commission and Kim's foreign minister.[33]

This mission was not as successful as Kim's earlier visit shortly after the war. The most important aid came from the Soviet Union and was reported to be 300 million rubles. Compared with the one billion rubles Kim had received earlier for his three-year economic plan, when the total investment by the government was estimated at 81 billion *wŏn*, the amount of 300 million rubles was indeed paltry for a five-year economic plan in which the government's total investment was estimated at 180 billion *wŏn*.[34] Kim also visited other East European countries, including East Germany, Poland, and Romania, but he came back virtually empty-handed. He did visit a Korean orphanage in Romania and a young Korean girls' school in Hungary, but no significant aid was received from these countries.

It was during this trip abroad that leading members of the Yanan group led by Ch'oe Ch'ang-ik and the frequently criticized Soviet-Korean Pak Ch'ang-ok conspired to challenge Kim and his authoritarian rule in favor of a collective leadership and easing of the tightly controlled party machine.[35] There are elaborate accounts emanating from the South of a dramatic attempt to overthrow Kim and his partisans by mobilizing some of the military forces under the command of generals who were members of the Yanan group. It was alleged that members of the group had informed both the Korean ambassador in Moscow, Yi Sang-jo (another member), and the Soviet ambassador in Pyongyang about the overthrow and that Kim had to cut short his trip and return to Korea to deal with the conspirators.[36]

The South Korean accounts seem to have been designed more to discredit Kim by dramatizing his opposition than to reveal what really happened. It is not true, for example, that Kim had to cut short his trip to Moscow. Kim had spent ten days from June 6 to 15, 1956, in the Soviet Union and stopped at Ulan Bator, Mongolia, for another three days before returning to the North on July 19. The Soviet ambassador to the North, V. I. Ivanov, was not in Pyongyang at the time. He was in Moscow accompanying Kim Il Sung during his stay in the Soviet Union. Furthermore, it was not until the end of August that the August plenum of the Central Committee was held and the committee heard the report of Kim's trip abroad. It was at this plenum that the confrontation took place on August 30–31, 1956.

Although the details of the challenge to Kim were not made public, there are many references to conspiracy. It was related that Kim Il Sung felt that something was amiss when he saw the pale-faced Ch'oe Ch'ang-ik at Pyongyang airport upon his return.[37] Kim said that all those who conspired were former members of the New Democratic Party, the Yanan group. He said further that Ch'oe was an ambitious antiparty counterrevolutionary who had his cronies challenge the leadership of the party.

At the August plenum Sŏ Hwi, a member of the Yanan group who was chairman of the Korean Trade Union, was alleged to have said that the workers in the trade union should maintain political independence and reserve the right to strike when necessary to protect a basic subsistence level of living. This line of argument was very similar to the position of O Ki-sŏp. Kim said that Sŏ was a revisionist who insisted that the trade union was more important than the party.[38] Yun Kong-hŭm, another member of the Yanan group, was alleged to have criticized Kim for his personality cult and to have urged collective leadership in the North in view of what had transpired in the Soviet Union. Ch'oe had supported Yun's argument, and Kim's leadership was thus openly challenged.

Ch'oe was alleged to have said that difficulties in North Korea's economic development, particularly the overemphasis on heavy industry had resulted in unbearable hardship for the common workers. Kim later alleged that Ch'oe even called for abandoning the Communist system in the North and instituting a political system based on a neutral Korea.[39] Kim said that even within the army such members of the Yanan group as Kim Ŭl-gyu had challenged the tradition of the partisans and had said that the Korean People's Army should inherit the tradition of the hard-fought agrarian movement in northern Korea during the Japanese occupation and not some non-Korean partisan activities in Manchuria. Such important officers of the army as Ch'oe Wal-chong and Ch'oe Chong-hak, chief of the general political bureau of the Korean People's Army, had also conspired with Ch'oe. All were members of the Yanan group.[40]

It is not clear whether the Yanan group actually conspired to overthrow Kim militarily, but here again the South Korean accounts relate that General Chang P'yŏng-san, a member of the Yanan group who commanded the Fourth Army Corps, had planned to take over the government shortly after a demonstration leading to riots by college students in Pyongyang.

It was alleged that if the takeover were successful Ch'oe Ch'ang-ik was to become premier and Pak Ch'ang-ok, the Soviet-Korean, would become secretary of the party.[41] This is a highly speculative account. Kim did mention that Ch'oe and his factionalists conspired to incite riots, but he did not mention any military venture on the part of the Yanan group. By this time most of the generals in the Korean People's Army were partisans, and they were not only in firm control of the military but also had begun to move into the ranks of the party as members and candidate members of the Central Committee.

The South Korean accounts mistakenly identified Kim Kwang-hyŏp and Kim Ch'ang-dŏk as generals of the Yanan group. They were Kim's partisans. Kim Kwang-hyŏp, Ch'oe Hyŏn, Yu Kyŏng-su, Kim Kyŏng-sŏk, Yi Yŏng-ho, Kim Ch'ang-dŏk, O Chin-u, Ch'oe Kwang, Ch'oe Yong-jin, and Kim Ch'ang-bong were all partisan generals of the army and also members of the Central Committee. Any serious military move by any group other than the partisans would have been suicidal at that time.

In a sweeping condemnation of all Yanan group members, Kim also accused the leader of the Yanan group, Kim Tu-bong,[42] perhaps the most important figure and the first chairman of the Workers' Party of Korea under whom Kim served as vice-chairman. Kim said that while there was no evidence as yet that Kim Tu-bong and a few others who were not even members of the Yanan group, such as Pak Ŭi-wan and O Ki-sŏp, had participated in the riots of the Yanan group, they were not loyal to the party and were guilty just the same. Kim accused Kim Tu-bong of not being completely honest in his dealing with the party and of confiding only in Ch'oe Ch'ang-ik and Han Pin, another member of the Yanan group.

Kim said that Han Pin had already been condemned by the party, but Kim Tu-bong continued to confide in him. Whenever Kim Tu-bong visited Han, he came out with new and revisionist ideas. Kim said that the crimes Kim Tu-bong had committed were serious, and he charged Kim Tu-bong with advocating the importance of the Standing Committee of the Supreme People's Assembly, of which he was the chairman, over the party. Similarly Pak Ŭi-wan, a Soviet-Korean, had tried to destroy the party by expulsion of its leaders. As for O Ki-sŏp, the most frequently criticized member of the domestic group, Kim said that the party had given him ample time, but he had refused to be completely frank.[43] These men should be punished.

It took Kim more than a year to eliminate the antiparty elements and return to the affairs of state. Kim used Hŏ Ka-i's method that he had once so harshly condemned to control subversive elements in the party — that was to issue a new party identification card and examine everyone when the new card was issued. This procedure was carried out from late 1956 to early 1957. Unlike the case of the domestic group, conspirators were prosecuted but not executed. They were purged and expelled from the party and the government.

In September 1957, ten years after the first Supreme People's Assembly was convened, Kim called for a national election to convene the second assembly. Some 215 representatives representing nine provinces and two cities were elected.[44] The attrition rate was greater in the Supreme People's Assembly than in the party Central Committee. Out of 572 members of the first Supreme People's Assembly, only 75 were reelected to the Second Supreme People's Assembly, and the remaining 140 were newly elected members. The chairman of the Standing Committee of the assembly was Ch'oe Yong-gŏn, a partisan, and important positions in Kim's second cabinet were also occupied by partisans, such as Kim Il (vice-premier) and Kim Kwang-hyŏp (minister of national defense).

After he put his house in order, Kim traveled to the Soviet Union again, the second time in two years (November 4–21, 1957), leading a government and party delegation to the celebration of the fortieth anniversary of the October Revolution. Kim spoke highly of the Soviet Union, praising Soviet achievements and claiming the Soviet Union as his spiritual inspiration.[45] What Kim may have tried to ascertain here was the extent of the ever-widening rift between the Soviet Union and China, his two greatest benefactors. He appealed for unity and cooperation among the fraternal socialist countries. He praised the Soviet Union as the bulwark of the world revolutionary movement for the past forty years and proclaimed it the "sacred duty" of all socialist countries to support and protect her.

However, Kim also began to exert his own identity. He said that each country must creatively apply Marxism and Leninism in accordance with its own national characteristics. He said that he rejected nationalism: his love for his own country was not nationalism but socialistic patriotism. Kim was cautious in his dealings with the Soviet Union and tempered the suppression of the Soviet influence in Korean domestic affairs by keeping a close watch on trends in the Soviet Union.

Kim went to the Soviet Union often. In fact he led still another North Korean delegation to attend the twenty-first congress of the

Communist Party of the Soviet Union in February 1959 and personally observed the seriousness of the unfolding Sino-Soviet dispute. Indeed, Kim was busy. He went to Beijing in October 1959 to attend the tenth anniversary of the founding of the People's Republic of China and pledged his friendship to the Chinese people. Kim needed both the Soviet Union and China, and he wanted to be faithful to both. But when the Sino-Soviet dispute intensified, Kim was forced to be introspective and sought self-identity.

On February 8, 1958, in commemoration of the tenth anniversary of the founding of the Korean People's Army, Kim said for the first time that the People's Army was the successor of the tradition of anti-Japanese armed struggle of his partisans in Manchuria. He said that all Korean Nationalist and Communist armed struggles had failed except his partisans. He began to promote his partisans openly in all segments of operations. The following month, the first party conference was held (March 3–6, 1958) to launch the first five-year economic plan. At this time Kim made public certain details of the conspiracy of the Yanan group.[46] By the time the Chinese Volunteer Army left Korea on March 11, 1958, Kim and his partisans had more or less eliminated every group capable of challenging them.

Kim spoke with authority on any subject, and no one dared question anything he said. Kim spoke on the judicial policy of the party in April 1958, for example, and said that ideas that "the law must be impartial to everyone" and that "human rights must be protected" was pure nonsense.[47] He emphasized that the party must exercise complete dictatorship over the landlords and capitalists and protect the working people. He said those who had advocated such ideas in the judiciary in the past must be punished, and he purged a number of judicial workers, including two of his three former chief justices of the Supreme Court, Cho Sŏng-mo and Hwang Se-hwan.

Kim went on to criticize those workers in the judiciary who released political criminals in the name of human rights and cited the example of the release of a Christian named Yi Man-hwa. He also attacked such religion said that Buddhists sit and meditate but do nothing. Such lassitude may be good for Buddhism, but it is bad for the state. When he successfully met the challenges of various groups by the end of the 1950s, it seemed there was nothing Kim was not capable of doing in the North.

The Korean War was a devastating experience for Kim not only because it failed to bring about national reunification, but also because it brought destruction to the North and opened the door for leaders of other groups to challenge Kim's leadership. As to the war itself, all theories of international complicity notwithstanding, the domestic causes of the war deserve attention. The Korean War should be understood as a national liberation war Kim started to reunify his country, and had it not been for U.S. intervention he might have succeeded in his venture. For Koreans at the time, both North and South Koreans alike, the idea of reunifying their country militarily was not uncommon. It was certainly not an idea unique to Kim Il Sung. To disavow any such intent by Kim today is as ludicrous as his claim of victory in the war. The South Korean desire for a military solution was so intense that Syngman Rhee and the Republic of Korea even refused to sign the cease-fire agreement that ended that war.

For Kim, the Korean War turned out to be a conflict he started but could not finish. Kim himself led his soldiers in battle — he was even wounded in a battle near Hamhŭng[48] — but his own fighting was over in about four months when the Chinese volunteers came in October 1950. More important to him than the actual fighting was the change in North Korean politics that followed the war — the change in the Soviet and Chinese influences on North Korean politics and the challenges to his leadership. The war brought many changes, but one of the important was the end of the Soviet influence and their domination of North Korean domestic politics. The Soviet army that had maneuvered Kim into power did not return to fight for him during the war; it was the Chinese who came to save him. The Chinese occupied North Korea for eight years, from 1950 to 1958, much longer than the three years the Soviet army occupied the North from 1945 to 1948. The Chinese were indifferent to the internal politics in North Korea. They seem to have been more interested in stabilizing and concluding the hostilities in Korea than in meddling with the North's internal politics.

Those who challenged Kim's leadership might have succeeded had they combined their forces and planned the coup more carefully. Many generals of the Yanan group who were discredited by

Kim, such as Mu Chŏng and Pak Il-u, were comrades who had fought with the Chinese Communists in Yanan. Kim had also fought with the Chinese Communists, but in Manchuria, and most of his mentors and comrades had died there. It is true that the Yanan group's operation did not last long and their relationship with the leaders of the Chinese Communists was not intimate, but they fought with the Chinese Communists who succeeded in China and who came into Korea to save them from sure defeat. The leaders of the Yanan group did not ask for the assistance of the Chinese occupation forces, nor did the Chinese offer any help in the internal power struggle.

Fortunately for Kim, there was no coalition to mount a combined attack against him. When the leaders of the domestic group challenged Kim, the members of the Yanan group abstained, and the Soviet-Koreans were on Kim's side in suppressing the domestic group. When the Yanan group challenged Kim, none of the domestic group who had survived the purge joined them. The Soviet-Koreans were rootless in Korea, and they enjoyed privileged positions at Kim's pleasure once the Soviet occupation forces had withdrawn. In fact, all the challenges were haphazard schemes.

The Soviet-Koreans, for example, had no organization or even close ties among themselves. They came from various cities and villages in Central Asia, others came from the Russian Maritime Province. When Hŏ committed suicide, none of the Soviet-Koreans spoke against Kim in favor of Hŏ, and when Pak Ch'ang-ok and Pak Ŭi-wan were purged there was no sign of indignation on the part of the Soviet-Koreans. However, many Soviet-Koreans began to leave North Korea and returned whence they came. Only the most loyal, such as Nam Il, remained.

For the domestic Communists, the trial and execution of their leaders put an end to any organized challenge to Kim's leadership. The Korean War intensified South Korea's anti-Communist stance, and the South no longer provided sanctuary for Communists who opposed Kim. Few renounced communism and fled to the South; most of the domestic group simply abstained from politics and remained in the North.

In comparison, no other group was as strongly united behind its leader as the partisans were for Kim. To be sure, Kim was vulnerable to attack and his supporters were few in number. His Soviet supporters had left him, and he had to answer for the unsuccessful conclusion of the war. After the death of Stalin, Kim had to fend off demands to institute collective leadership in North Korea.

Kim Il Sung met all these challenges masterfully. Although he was not successful in his original intent to unify the country militarily, he was saved from sure defeat by the Chinese volunteers. Once the war became an international conflict involving many countries, Kim had to deal only with his domestic political rivals. He met these challenges one by one, and he used the absence of the Soviet military presence in North Korea to eliminate the Soviet-Koreans. He used his own partisans to crush the direct challenge to his leadership by the domestic group, and he exploited his past Chinese ties during the Chinese occupation of North Korea to strengthen his anti-Soviet stance.

It is true that his challengers were inefficient and unorganized, but Kim showed that he could survive even when he failed in the Korean War. He also showed that he no longer needed the Soviet army to sustain his leadership, and he quickly reminded his political rivals of his Chinese connection. The challenge of Kim's opponents was no match for his talent for survival, but Kim had also enjoyed the good fortune of Chinese intervention in the Korean War to save him and their noninterference in North Korean domestic politics. Had the Chinese decided to promote one of their own revolutionaries from Yanan, Kim would have had a difficult time. Kim had learned much from the war, and he came to appreciate the people who supported him.

IV

SEARCH FOR
KOREAN IDENTITY

In his efforts to meet the challenges of various rivals in the 1950s, Kim Il Sung relied heavily on the support of his partisans, but he did not fail to seek the support of the people. In one of his intimate conversations with the people, he said that when the leaders of factionalist groups challenged the government and the party with the support of non-Korean influences, he had no one but the people of Korea to fall back on. He visited workers in factories and farmers in cooperatives often and encouraged them to work harder for the reconstruction of their country. He devised a number of methods to mobilize the workers, recognizing their efforts with medals and special designations and urging them to be competitive in surpassing the goals set by the party. In the process he educated the people to work hard for love of country and not in expectation of material reward.

When the Fourth Party congress was held in September 1961, he was truly in a position to implement his plan to improve economic conditions. He had met his challengers and emerged triumphant. He had promoted most of the partisans who had been loyal to him to prominent positions in the party. A number of former members of other groups who survived the struggle remained, but they served only upon their pledge of absolute loyalty to him and often vilified the records of their former comrades.

Indeed Kim had succeeded in establishing absolute power by the Fourth Party Congress, and there were neither Soviet nor Chinese occupation forces in the North. The Fourth Party Congress was a festive occasion at which a large number of representatives from the fraternal socialist states and Communist parties were represented, and he was confident of the political situation at home. It was also at this time that Kim and his partisans promoted Kim's guerrilla tradition as the true history of Korean revolutionary activities and the true basis of Korean identity.

Kim's immediate problems of the 1960s were not at home but in his international relations in the Communist world. He was caught in the heat of the Sino-Soviet dispute. During the first half of the 1960s, the North Koreans maintained a virulent feud with the Soviet Union, and the second half was spent trying to fend off the attacks of the Chinese Red Guards. Through these unfortunate encounters with two of his benefactors, which often reached open vituperation, Kim was able, and to a large extent forced, to seek his Korean identity. His feuds with both China and the Soviet Union helped him to overcome his past mendicancy, but they also inflicted a lasting mark on his future relationship with them.

All during the Sino-Soviet dispute, Kim Il Sung was extremely careful to remain neutral, but for a country that shared borders with both countries and had seen them involved in its liberatioin and in the preservation of its system, strict neutrality was impossible. In the name of the unity of the socialist camp, Kim insisted without success on the solidarity of the international Communist movement.

In an effort to establish North Korea's self-identity, Kim Il Sung kept himself from personal involvement in the dispute. In North Korea's altercations with the Soviet Union, they chose academically safe and politically irrelevant subjects, such as the interpretation of Korean history and the dispute over holding the Asian economic seminar in Pyongyang. Even when the Chinese Red Guards hurled insults at Kim, the North Koreans kept him out of the quarrel. In the most serious dispute with the Chinese concerning their boundary, Kim seems to have ended the argument in his favor without compromising North Korea's self-identity.

In both cases, however, the North Koreans alleged that their difficulties with China and the Soviet Union were caused not by the Koreans themselves but by revisionism in the Soviet Union and dogmatism in China. Kim, on his part, was forced to broaden his range of international contacts beyond the confines of the divided Communist world. Indeed, during the 1960s, in the heat of the Sino-Soviet dispute he began to look for friends and allies in the Third World.

9

Mobilization Campaigns

Kim Il Sung was in his forties in the late 1950s, and he was a young and energetic leader. In the style of his guerrilla days, he mounted relentless attacks on every task he undertook. While meeting the challenges of his opponents and traveling abroad to solicit funds for his economic plans, he participated in most major conferences and meetings of social groups at home, including the League of Socialist Working Youth, the Democratic Women's Union, the Union of Agricultural Working People, and the General Federation of Trade Unions. He also participated in the provincial party conferences from Yanggando to Kangwŏndo and spoke at length, sometimes rambling on for hours at a time. He also visited factories, mines, fishing harbors, and steel mills to give on-the-spot guidance whenever he had time and urged the people to work harder building a new socialist state in the North.[1] Kim often repeated to party functionaries the old Korean adage of *ŭisin chakch'ŭk*, to set standards by one's own example, and he tried to practice it himself.

The Superhuman Drives

In fact, Kim demanded more from the people. What he demanded was maximum effort with minimum reward. He spoke often enough to convince the people that they did not work for money or profit but for love of country.[2] He wanted to remold each person into a New Communist who would work at his command and voluntarily make superhuman efforts for the state. He devised slogans and mottos and launched many different campaigns to goad the people onward.

One of the first slogans was "maximum production with evincing thrift," and the first campaign was the Ch'ŏllima movement,[3] started in December 1956 when Kim visited Kangsŏn steel mill to personally direct the work of steel production. Kim was said to have revealed frankly the difficulties the party was facing and to have told the workers that he could trust no one but them in this time of crisis. He said that only through their hard work and increased production could he solve the country's problems and overcome the challenges of the factionalists.

He said that some of the factionalists, particularly the Soviet-Koreans such as Pak Ch'ang-ok and Kim Sŭng-hwa, who headed the machine industry and construction ministries of the government, discouraged the building of machine factories, pointed to the futility of North Korean efforts to develop sophisticated machine industries, and advised the government to import machinery from the Soviet Union.[4] This campaign prompted the workers to surpass their assigned quotas and to devise more efficient working methods, such as the substitution of anthracite for coke, that would save foreign exchange and reduce smelting time.

Similar production campaigns spread throughout the North not only in industry but also in other segments of the society. Thereafter persons who surpassed their quotas were decorated with the banner of the Ch'ŏllima and were called Ch'ŏllima riders; a group of workers who surpassed their assigned quota were pinned as a Ch'ŏllima workteam. A steel worker in the Kangsŏn steel mill named Chin Ŭng-wŏn was credited with initiating the Ch'ŏllima workteam movement, which organized workers in groups for the explicit purpose of surpassing the quota assigned to them.[5] Many workteams were organized for this purpose and some were named Ch'ŏllima Workteams; a few were even honored as Double Ch'ŏllima Workteams.

To what extent quality was compromised by overproduction or what standard was used to set the quotas is not clear, but Kim succeeded in convincing the people that they had to make almost superhuman efforts to rebuild the country with minimum external assistance. Examples of such efforts were many. One worker is alleged to have worked twenty-nine hours continuously in a river to make 580 sand bags, each weighing seventy kilograms, to build a dam, and he was said to have finished the entire project scheduled for forty days in five days. In another instance, one railroad construction group is said to have excavated 880,000 cubic meters of earth and built over 5,600 square meters of retaining walls, several bridges, a number of railway stations, and various flood control measures, including the relocation of 200 housing units. This project was scheduled to be completed in three or four years but the group completed it in seventy-five days.[6]

With such results, Kim traveled often. He visited the Hwanghae iron works several times, the Sup'ung hydroelectric plant, a number of agricultural cooperatives, and an automobile manufacturing plant. Kim claimed that the workers assembled the first truck, named Victory 58, in October 1958 at the Tŏkch'ŏn plant. Subsequently they also assembled bulldozers named Red Star 58 as well as some excavators.

Such miraculous achievements were short-lived, and Kim began to complain about the quality of the products. He admitted that some goods were of inferior quality and unsalable in the international marketplace. He also complained about the resulting shortage of foreign exchange and urged the workers to improve the quality of work in all areas.[7]

A New Communist Man and More Campaigns

Kim had belatedly come to realize that in order to achieve the desired goals in production, mere enthusiasm was good only for a few miracles but was not enough for general economic development. In his lecture at the meeting of city and county party committee workers, Kim elaborated on Communist education in Korea. He said in essence that a new Korean Communist should be armed with his partisan tradition, fight individualism and self-ishness, learn the spirit of socialist patriotism and proletarian inter-nationalism, cultivate love for labor and be constantly innovative, continuously revolutionary, and loyal to party and state.[8] His New Communist was truly a superhuman working machine that owned nothing and worked constantly without complaint for minimum reward. All industries were nationalized and all arable land was col-lectivized by 1958,[9] but Kim had no systematic plan for training the masses.

The educational process was slow and Kim's increasing on-the-spot guidance and the workers' corresponding enthusiasm were in-sufficient to meet the goals of the economic plan. Kim began to send members of the Central Committee and government officials to local party organizations to involve themselves directly in pro-duction work and to conduct what was known as the intensive guidance program (*chipchung chido*).[10] In March 1959, for example, a number of leaders from the Central Committee were sent to the Hamgyŏng pukto party committee for approximately one month to concentrate on correcting the past mistakes of the provincial party committee.

This method was used not only to help the local production unit produce more efficiently and in greater quantity but also to imple-ment the policies of the party. It was also used to root out all shades of opposition to the party by the local party units and to institute direct control in the provincial and county party units by the Cen-tral Committee. Kim himself came to the region at the end of the intensive guidance period and denounced certain local leaders for their inability to carry out the directives of the Central Committee.[11]

It was not lack of enthusiasm for work on the part of the local leaders and the people, but the incredible demands made by Kim and the central party organs and the lack of technical skills and professional training that accounted for the discrepancies between production and goals. Nevertheless, Kim's demand for loyalty and his mechanism for controlling the people were strengthened through these campaigns. His frequent visit to various provinces not only helped him to control the local party organs but also brought the people closer to the instructions from the party.

Among the many campaigns Kim launched during the height of the intensive guidance programs, two were especially noteworthy. One was in the agrarian sector and known as the Ch'ŏngsalli method; the other was in the industrial sector and known as the Taean work system. In February 1960, Kim had gone to a cooperative farm known as Ch'ŏngsalli near the suburbs of Pyongyang. He stayed there for fifteen days and instructed party organizations from the lowest units of the *ri* and county to the provincial organs. He pointed out the shortcomings of the basic unit organizations and criticized their inadequate concentration of farm work, their lack of planning, the waste of manpower, and the defects in the implementation of the socialist principle of distribution. He touched upon many minute details from the scheduling of a soccer game that took young people away from the farm to the amount of work points each farmer and party functionary should receive.[12]

He then addressed the county party organization and instructed them in ways of improving agricultural production. He said that they should not use obscure jargon in directives to convey a simple message, should even reduce the number of messages, and, if necessary, should personally visit work places to show how the work should be done. When he returned to Pyongyang toward the end of that month he called a meeting of the Standing Committee of the Central Committee to correct deficient methods in agrarian management by the party.[13]

From February to October 1960, Kim returned to Ch'ŏngsalli no fewer than thirty-eight times to see that his directives were carried out. This lesson in direct guidance led to a nationwide drive for efficient management of farm cooperatives under the slogan of "Ch'ŏngsalli method and Ch'ŏngsalli spirit" and is said to have motivated party functionaries to more spirited implementation of party policies, thus increasing production.

The following year, in December 1961, Kim paid a visit to the Taean electric machine plant, where he gave similar on-the-spot guidance to industrial workers and the party functionaries in charge of managing industries. The directives in Taean were in essence intended to ensure collective management in the operation of factories, thus avoiding friction among manager, engineers, and workers; to effect a planned management system, planning every detail of the plant with the participation of factory workers; to improve technical assistance in order to ensure a comprehensive production process; and to guarantee an efficient supply of materials so that the workers' precious time would not be wasted waiting for materials to reach the factory.[14]

No factory manager should exercise arbitrary and bureaucratic control of his factory, but should understand the workers and help them to produce more. The impact of Kim's personal guidance, not merely the merit of what he prescribed, was strongly felt by workers in the industrial sector and helped them to make superhuman efforts to improve their industries.

Kim visited his workers often and urged them to work harder with little reward. He appealed to their sense of loyalty to the fatherland and called upon their socialist patriotism in building a new and independent Korea in lieu of materialistic reward for their toil. Kim reportedly made more than 1,300 visits throughout the North during the seven-year period from 1954 to 1961.[15] This figure is a gross exaggeration, however, for it averages out to more than one visit every other day, but the fact remains that Kim did make great efforts to wring the maximum out of the people. By the beginning of the 1960s, Kim was able to talk the North Korean people into virtually any project.

The Fourth Party Congress: 1961

The Fourth Party Congress was held for eight days from September 11 to 18, 1961. For Kim Il Sung this party congress was a watershed in his political life. His long struggle to consolidate power was complete; he had successfully met his challengers and had begun to build a socialist state on his own. It was a festive occasion for him because he had recovered from the war through the completion of the five-year economic plan and had put his own house in order by numerous campaigns to mobilize the people. There were no longer any factions to challenge his position, and for the first time no foreign armed forces were occupying the North. Compared to this situation in the North, the South was undergoing a difficult transitional period of student demonstrations and a military coup that toppled the government. Kim called the Fourth Party Congress the congress of victors. Indeed he was victorious in his fight to put away all dissidents and place himself in an absolute, unchallengeable position in the North.

The congress was attended by 1,157 voting delegates and 73 nonvoting delegates representing the 1,166,359 regular members and 145,204 probationary members of the party.[16] There were many foreign delegates representing 32 countries and Communist parties — by far the largest number ever in the history of the party. The dignitaries from the fraternal socialist countries were headed by Frol L. Kozlov of the Soviet Union and Deng Xiaoping of the People's Republic of China.[17]

Kim made a lengthy report reviewing the work of the Central Committee of the party and spoke for six hours. Unlike his report to the Third Party Congress in 1956, Kim was confident about his position and the party's future direction. He was proud of his past accomplishments and looked to a bright future of a prosperous socialist state in the North. Kim spoke on five general topics.[18]

He first reviewed accomplishments during the five-year period since the Third Party Congress, citing the complete collectivization of agriculture and nationalization of all industries, including small handicrafts. Kim said that the North had solved its grain problems and was rapidly becoming a modern industrial state in which 52 percent of the work force were industrial workers. There was no trace of exploitation in the North. He said that the basic transformation had begun with the Ch'ŏllima movement, and he claimed that as of August 1961 more than two million workers were participating in the movement. He said there were 4,958 Ch'ŏllima Workteams with 125,028 workers and that 55 workteams had won the designation of Double Ch'ŏllima Workteam.

The second topic was the new seven-year economic plan. It was an ambitious scheme, and there was little doubt that Kim was planning to drive the workers to even higher levels of mobilization and patriotic sacrifice. Kim emphasized industrialization, particularly the technological revolution, and repeated the same slogans of giving priority to the development of heavy industry and simultaneously developing agriculture and light industry. He also emphasized the task of proletarian literature to mold the people into true revolutionaries devoid of any bourgeois traits. The statistical details of the seven-year plan was presented to the congress on the sixth day, September 16, by Kim Il.[19]

Third, he spoke about the peaceful reunification of Korea and disparaged the student uprising and the military coup that toppled the South Korean government. Compared with the transitional turmoil in the South, the political situation in the North in 1961 was much more stable. Kim certainly had the upper hand, but he proposed no concrete plan for reunification and repeated the usual condemnation of the South Korean regime and the American presence in the South.

Fourth, he spoke about the party and cited the party's victory in meeting the challenges of the factionalists. He said the party had grown rapidly and he had paid special attention to educating new cadres, particularly those who were loyal to the party during the Korean War. He also said that the party should recruit young cadres into responsible positions. Kim was trying to encourage the recruiting of able and loyal young people from the League of Socialist Working Youth to fill the void created by the expulsion of the leaders of various factions. He spoke at length about the league's role and the training programs of new cadres.

On the last topic, international relations, Kim firmly pledged his friendship to both the Soviet Union and China. He emphasized the solidarity among the socialist states and repeated his customary condemnation of the United States. Kim said that the Soviet people were close friends of the Korean people, and the Chinese were comrades-in-arms who had endured difficult times together in Korea. Kim was confronted with the increasingly strained relationship between his two powerful neighbors and benefactors and chose to take the only logical and safe course — that is, to support both sides and insist on solidarity among the fraternal socialist states.

Unlike his other reports in previous party congresses, Kim did not single out anyone by name to criticize in his report. More than thirty delegates discussed Kim's report in the congress, but none of them revealed anything about the purged comrades of the Yanan group or the Soviet-Koreans. Everyone refrained from the criticism and self-criticism that had characterized previous party congresses. Most of the discussants shared their experiences of hard work in trying to carry out the party's directives. The Fourth Party Congress was indeed a watershed, leaving the past factional struggles behind and looking toward the building of a new socialist state under the sole leadership of Kim and his partisans.

Frol L. Kozlov, representing the Soviet Union, delivered a lengthy speech congratulating the achievements of the party. He boasted about the Soviet sputnik and reiterated the new Soviet policy on peaceful coexistence, citing the Soviet effort to normalize relations with West Germany. He expressed appreciation to the Workers' Party of Korea for supporting the Soviet position. Deng Xiaoping, representing the Chinese Communist Party, spoke only briefly after Kozlov and supported the Soviet policy of peaceful coexistence and agreed with the Soviet plan to normalize relations with West Germany. Deng did caution that in Asia the American imperialists were still operating in South Korea, South Vietnam, Laos, and Taiwan from military bases in Japan, and he said that it was the duty of each peace-loving nation in Asia to thwart American military aggression in Asia. There was no confrontation between the Soviet Union and China in the Fourth Party Congress.[20]

On the last day of the congress, September 18, a few amendments of the party bylaws were introduced and quickly adopted without much discussion. The only noteworthy amendments were two new chapters dealing with the League of Socialist Working Youth and the Korean People's Army in line with the policy to recruit new cadres from the ranks of these organizations.[21]

Rise of the Partisan Group

The extent of changes in the leadership organs of the party and the extent of Kim's consolidation of power and the role his partisans played in it were made unmistakably clear in the election of new members and officers of the Central Committee. The Fourth Party Congress elected 85 members of the Central Committee, an increase of only 14 from the 71-member Central Committee of the Third Party Congress. Out of 85 members only 28 were returning members reelected from the Third Party Congress, and a two-thirds majority of 57 were newly elected members. The reelected 28 members represented less than 40 percent of the Central Committee of the Third Party Congress; all partisans except one who had died, Yu Kyŏng-su, were reelected.[22]

Except for a few who had denounced their former ties and pledged absolute loyalty to Kim, such as Kim Ch'ang-man and Nam Il, no members of the Yanan group or Soviet-Koreans were reelected. Most startling was the fact that out of 57 new members, 25 were partisans and approximately 21 were newly recruited young cadres who had no former ties with any group, recruited mostly from the League of Socialist Working Youth and the Korean People's Army.[23]

In addition there were a few who were not partisans but who had direct family ties with the partisan group and thus were loyal to the partisans, such as Kim Yŏng-ju, brother of Kim Il Sung, and Yi Hyo-sun, elder brother of the late partisan Yi Che-sun. In this way the partisans, those trained by the partisans, and those with family ties to the partisans constituted more than 80 percent of the Central Committee. It had taken Kim fifteen years since the First Party Congress, but by the time of the Fourth Party Congress there was no other group in the party except the partisan group.

The figures were more startling in the candidate membership of the Central Committee. Out of 50 candidate members elected to the Central Committee of the Fourth Party Congress, only one, Yi Chi-ch'an, was a returning member, and 49 were new members. Out of 49 new members, 8 were partisans and 37 members were partisan-trained young recruits.[24]

The pattern was similar in the election of the officers of the Central Committee. The first plenum of the Central Committee, held on the last day of the congress, September 18, 1961, elected Kim Il Sung chairman and five vice-chairmen of the party, Ch'oe Yong-gŏn, Kim Il, Pak Kŭm-ch'ŏl, Kim Ch'ang-man, and Yi Hyo-sun. Only Kim Ch'ang-man, the only surviving member of the Yanan group, was not one of the partisan group.

Eleven were elected to the Standing Committee as regular members and four were elected candidate members; all were either partisan or partisan-related members except Kim Ch'ang-man and Nam Il, a Soviet-Korean. In all other committees of the Central

Committee, there were at least one or two partisans present as members, if not as chairman or vice-chairman. The Inspection Committee was headed by Kim Ik-sŏn, for example, but Kim Ch'ang-dŏk, a partisan, was vice-chairman.

The two nonpartisan members of the Standing Committee were Kim Ch'ang-man and Nam Il.[25] Nam was better known to the outside world as a chief North Korean negotiator at the military armistice commission after the Korean War and as the foreign minister of North Korea from 1953 to 1959. He served Kim in various capacities from vice-minister of education in 1948 to vice-premier and chairman of the Light Industry Commission in 1976. As foreign minister, Nam accompanied Kim on visits to many countries, including the Soviet Union, whence he came. Nam had completely dissociated himself from other Soviet-Koreans in the North and never once mentioned his Soviet-Korean past. He served Kim well and earned his place in Kim's cabinet. He was not as prominent at home in the party hierarchy as he was in the outside world. First elected to the Central Committee of the Second Party Congress as a candidate member, he became a member of the Central Committee at the Third Party Congress, reaching the Standing Committee in the fourth Party Congress. However, by the time of the Fourth Party Congress, he had been relieved of his post as foreign minister and was replaced by a partisan, Pak Sŏng-ch'ŏl.

More prominent than Nam was Kim Ch'ang-man,[26] who was not only the sole surviving member of the Yanan group but ranked fifth in the Standing Committee as well as being one of five vice-chairmen of the party. Kim Ch'ang-man began his political life early in the North. He was first elected to the Central Committee of the First Party Congress, but for some alleged misconduct in social life he was not reelected to the Central Committee of the Second Party Congress in 1948. He was reinstated during the Korean War after members of the domestic group were purged. He appeared in the armistice talks as a member of the North Korean negotiating team under the assumed name of Chang Ch'un-san and climbed steadily, becoming minister of education and vice-premier in Kim's cabinet.

He was an opportunist. In order to win favors from Kim and the partisans he frequently lashed out against his former comrades of the Yanan group. He often falsely accused others. For example, in 1947, shortly after he returned from China to the North, he wrote that Kim Ku, a noted nationalist and president of the Korean Provisional Government in China, was an agent of the Chinese Nationalist intelligence service and accused him of murdering many patriotic Korean revolutionaries in China. He also accused Kim Ku of having made compromising deals with foreign powers at the expense of the provisional government. While he was accusing Kim Ku and others of these alleged crimes, he showered Kim Il Sung and his partisans with lavish praise as early as 1947.[27]

Furthermore, when the unsuccessful challenge of his former comrades of the Yanan group was bared, Kim Ch'ang-man wrote a stunning article in the party organ, *Kŭlloja*, attacking a number of his former comrades from China. He said that Kim Tu-bong, Ch'oe Ch'ang-ik, and Han Pin were American spies who had been in collusion with the United States as early as the liberation of Korea. He also accused the leaders of the domestic group, Pak Hŏn-yŏng, O Ki-sŏp, and Chu Yŏng-ha, as spies and alleged that they had tried to sell the Korean Communist Party to the Americans. He even attacked Yi Ch'ŏng-wŏn, a noted historian who fell into disfavor after the Third Party Congress. He said that Yi was trying to fit Korean history into a form that was made by and for foreigners. Yi's style of historical study, Kim said, was a history written with scissors and glue, pasting relevant Korean facts into a non-Korean formula.[28] Kim Ch'ang-man was a rancorous man who did not last long even with all these overzealous expressions of loyalty to the partisans.

The Fourth Party Congress brought in the new era of Kim and his partisans. The study of their past partisan activities was no longer recommended but ordered. A team of enthusiasts, sent to retrace the former battlegrounds in Manchuria, wrote unbelievable stories of their past victories against the Japanese there.[29] Many partisans were asked to reminisce, and an accomplished writer was assigned to record grossly exaggerated accounts of their past. Twelve volumes of such stories were published.[30] A number of partisans expanded their stories and wrote books extolling the partisan activities of Kim Il Sung. Other heroes who died fighting in Manchuria were also remembered as pioneers of the Korean revolution.[31]

By the time of the Fourth Party Congress, Kim had no problem indoctrinating the people with his exaggerated claims. His problems in the 1960s were not domestic but international. He had problems with both the Soviet Union and China, trying to balance his position between the feuding Communist neighbors, both his benefactors. It was his maneuvering in the Sino-Soviet dispute that eventually pushed him to be self-reliant and openly declare the independence of the North.

10

The Sino-Soviet Dispute and Kim Il Sung

Both by necessity and for tactical reasons Kim wanted to remain neutral in the Sino-Soviet dispute from the very beginning. Kim had maintained that whatever may have been the differences between the fraternal socialist countries they should be solved in the name of proletarian internationalism and the socialist countries should unite against the capitalist states. From the twentieth congress of the Communist Party of the Soviet Union in 1956 to the twenty-second congress in 1961, the acrimonious quarrels between his two benefactors and neighbors burgeoned into international alarums and excursions involving virtually every Communist party. Major issues dividing the Soviet Union and China were explained to Kim in Pyongyang by no lesser notables than Zhou Enlai and Deng Xiaoping from China and Aleksei Kosygin and Frol Kozlov from the Soviet Union, and Kim himself had traveled to Moscow and Beijing and met with both Khrushchev and Mao. Kim was sharply aware that most of the major revisionist thoughts advocated by Khrushchev ran counter to his own interests and those of North Korea.[1]

For a divided country such as Korea, the idea of peaceful coexistence was an unthinkable heresy. Kim has never conceded that he would recognize the existence of the regime in the South and peacefully coexist with it. For Kim, who had just learned the lesson of a limited war, Khrushchev's peaceful coexistence was not a convincing argument at all. In fact, there is no word in the North Korean vocabulary that expresses the concept of peaceful coexistence. Furthermore, in his repeated insistence on the peaceful unification of Korea in all of his post-Korean War speeches he never once renounced the use of force as a means of unification.

Similarly the de-Stalinization campaign and the concept of collective leadership were for Kim disloyal to the late Stalin. Kim had been very fond of Stalin, and when he met him in person he must have fulfilled one of his boyhood dreams. There was no one in the world he would rather emulate than Stalin, and whenever Kim mentioned Stalin he always used honorific expressions and superlative modifiers to describe him. When Stalin told him that the Workers' Party of Korea was the "shock brigade" of the international workers' movement, Kim repeated it on a number of occasions and urged his party cadres to make sacrifices to honor Stalin's trust in them.[2] All during and after the de-Stalinization campaigns Kim never once mentioned Stalin in disrespectful terms.

Kim often said that all socialist and Communist parties should unite under Soviet leadership. For Kim such issues as the Albanian question, Khrushchev's public attack on the Albanian Party of Labor in October 1961, and the rapprochement of the Soviet Union with Tito of Yugoslavia were secondary problems, not yet directly affecting the North. Kim thought that these were minor problems that would be solved for Korea once the Communist Party of the Soviet Union were to reassert its leadership in the international Communist movement, and he refrained from publicly addressing these issues.

The domestic consumption of these issues was not difficult. Kim, in his own peculiar way, condemned those who opposed him as revisionists and purged as antiparty factionalists those who advocated peaceful coexistence with the South. The idea of collective leadership did not bother him much either, because he accepted it and applied it at all levels of the party hierarchy except the top.[3]

What was most important to Kim was his relationship with the

Soviet Union and China and not the issues in the Sino-Soviet dispute. His difficulty was in adjusting his position to the patently unacceptable ideas emanating from the Soviet Union and also to the growing adamancy of the Chinese toward the Soviet Union. He wanted to attain independence from external influence and win self-reliance for Korea but not in defiance of the Soviet Union. Nor was he interested in accepting blindly the revisionist thoughts of Khrushchev and thereby arousing the ire of the Chinese.[4]

During the initial phase of the dispute from the twentieth congress in 1956 to the twenty-second congress in 1961 of the Communist Party of the Soviet Union, Kim was extremely busy trying to ascertain the seriousness of the dispute and thus decide his course of action. He visited the Soviet Union no fewer than five times in the six years from 1956 to 1961. Kim personally led the North Korean delegation attending the Soviet Union's twentieth party congress in July 1956, the twenty-first congress in January–February 1959, and the twenty-second congress in October 1961. In addition, he participated in the fortieth anniversary of the October Revolution in November 1957 and visited Moscow twice in June and October 1961.

He also visited China in November 1958 for approximately a month from November 21 to December 17, and Mao Zedong was reported to have invited Kim's former commanders, Zhou Baozhong and Li Yenlu of the Northeast Anti-Japanese United Army, to a dinner in honor of Kim, reminding him of the unbreakable ties going back to Kim's revolutionary days and the Sino-Korean camaraderie that were sealed in blood by the Korean War. Such a gesture on China's part was indeed effective, and Kim dutifully acknowledged with all due respect his former commanders who now sat toward the end of the table in the presence of the heads of state of China and North Korea.[5] Kim was indeed busy, and he returned to China in less than a year to commemorate the tenth anniversary celebration of the founding of the People's Republic of China on October 1, 1959. For this occasion he had written an elaborate article in recognition of the long and unbreakable ties between the Chinese and Korean people.[6]

The urgency of his visits should not be minimized, because they were made at a time when he himself was holding his Fourth Party

Congress in September 1961. In fact, he returned from China and the Soviet Union in July, held his own party congress in September, and went back to Moscow again in October 1961. In addition Kim had sent a mission headed by Chŏng Il-yong and another headed by Kim Il to discuss economic cooperation, as well as a military mission headed by Kim Kwang-hyŏp in May 1958 and still another in April 1959 headed by Ch'oe Yong-gŏn.[7] These men were all top leaders of economic, military, and political affairs, and they were learning about the dispute at first hand.

Kim had invited Khrushchev to visit the North in August 1960, but Khrushchev did not come. After the military coup in the South in May 1961, the deputy premier, Aleksei Kosygin, visited Kim in Pyongyang on May 30. In July of the same year, Kim visited both the Soviet Union and China to conclude treaties of friendship, cooperation, and mutual assistance with each country.[8] In all these brisk diplomatic exchanges associated with his balancing act in the Sino-Soviet dispute, Kim made efforts to remain neutral, but the increasing severity of the quarrel forced him to take his position every time the Chinese clashed with the Soviet Union on subsequent issues.

The Soviet-Korean Dispute

When he returned from the twenty-second congress of the Communist Party of the Soviet Union, Kim made a lengthy report to the second plenum of the Central Committee on November 27, 1961, praising the accomplishments of the Soviet Union. He did touch upon the problems of the cult of personality, referring specifically to Stalin, but he said that Stalin had been a leader of the Soviet Union for a long time and had a significant influence on the international Communist movement. Kim emphasized, however, that the judgment of Stalin's role in the Soviet Union was an internal problem and he had no intention of meddling with that country's domestic problems. He said that the Workers' Party of Korea should abide by the principle of noninterference in domestic problems of fraternal parties. He also acknowledged, and regretted, the abnormal relationship between the Soviet Union and Albania and expressed hope that better relations would prevail between them.[9]

This speech was printed only in the party organs, *Nodong sinmun* and *Kŭlloja*, and was never reprinted. It was excluded from all collections of Kim's selected works. In fact, Kim never spoke on the subject again until after Khrushchev was removed from power. Even when Premier Kosygin visited the North in February 1965 and when he met the new Soviet leader Brezhnev in May 1965 in Vladivostok, Kim did not even once comment on the issues that divided the Soviet Union and China. All during the most heated period of the Soviet-Korean quarrel from 1962 to 1964, Kim said nothing about the Sino-Soviet dispute. The tasks of attacking the Soviet Union and supporting China were taken up by his deputies and the official media of the North.

The North Koreans were most careful in supporting both the Soviet Union and China at first. On the first anniversary of their treaties of friendship, cooperation, and mutual assistance with the Soviet Union and China, the official organ of the party carried a lengthy editorial reaffirming strong and eternal friendship among the Soviet Union, China, and North Korea.[10] On the question of the Cuban missile crisis, the North Koreans supported Cuba and condemned the United States without directly commenting on Khrushchev's capitulation. On the Sino-Indian border dispute, the North Koreans were indeed careful and expressed strong support for China but refrained from directly attacking the Soviet Union. They were firm in their support for China against India and reprinted the Chinese editorial of *Renmin ribao* and made public the content of Zhou Enlai's letter to Kim on November 15 regarding the border dispute.[11] The North Koreans were also careful in their support for the socialist camp as a whole at the time of the North Korean celebration of the forty-fifth anniversary of the October Revolution.[12]

These were preludes to an open dispute between the Soviet Union and North Korea, which began after the North Koreans were publicly humiliated in international meetings for supporting China. The North Koreans were known to the pro-Soviet East European countries for their support for China, and this was made clear by Yi Chu-yŏn,[13] chief North Korean delegate to the twelfth congress of the Czechoslovak Communist Party in December 1962. But in the following month, January 1963, the chief North Korean delegate, Yi Hyo-sun, was barred from delivering his prepared speech congratulating the East German party. Yi had submitted his remarks in writing, but the text of his speech was not distributed to the delegates of the congress. Infuriated by these developments, the North Koreans charged that while the revisionists from Yugoslavia were allowed to speak, the North Koreans, the Vietnamese, and the Indonesians were not given the opportunity.[14]

On January 30, 1962, the North Koreans proclaimed that it was the duty of all socialist countries to support the socialist camp headed by the Soviet Union and China, just as it had been the duty of Communists in the past to support the socialist camp headed by the Soviet Union. They said that since China had two-thirds of the entire population of the socialist camp, it was not possible to speak of its unity and strength without China. They said that members of the socialist camp should not commit the mistake of unilaterally attacking China. To the question of which side the North Koreans stood in the Sino-Soviet dispute, the North Koreans answered that they were on the side of the socialist camp.

North Korea's position was not so much against the Soviet Union as it was for China, but there were more than ample signs of the pro-Chinese and anti-Soviet stance of the North. There were frequent visits to China by top-level government officials, including Pak Kŭm-ch'ŏl in June 1962 and Ch'oe Yong-gŏn in June 1963, which were reciprocated by the visit of Liu Xiaoqi in July 1963.[15] The North Koreans also insisted on a self-sustaining economy and adopted the Chinese motto *Zili gensheng* (self-resuscitation) signaling the end of Soviet economic aid to the North.[16] Moreover, Chinese daily editorials pointing out the difference between the Soviet Union and China were frequently reprinted.

When open attacks against the Soviet Union were begun by the North Koreans, however, they were on quite different subjects. One attack, in September 1963, centered on the Soviet interpretation of Korean history, and another concerned the international economic seminar held in Pyongyang in June 1964.

On the History of Korea. Three North Korean historians, Kim Sŏk-hyŏng, Kim Hŭi-il, and Son Yŏng-jong,[17] led the attack on the study of Korean history by the Academy of Sciences of the USSR.

This study of world history, *Vsemirnaia istoriia*, was published as a continuing series beginning in 1955, and the thirteenth volume was added in 1983.[18] The timing of the outbreak of the Soviet-Korean dispute in September 1963 was more political than scholarly. The North Korean scholars were attacking a Soviet study that had appeared long before 1963. The dispute began at a time when an official Chinese delegation headed by Liu Xiaoqi was visiting the North. The historical facts were clear but insignificant to the dispute between the two countries, and it seems that the North Koreans merely chose to vent their frustration against the Soviet Union on a topic on which they had an absolute upper hand. There was little doubt about the inadequate understanding of Soviet scholars on the subject, and there was no question about the North Korean historians' mastery of their own history, but here again the use of contemptuous language to point out scholarly errors was more noteworthy than the inaccuracies.[19]

The substance of the attack was divided into four parts: ancient history, the Three Kingdoms period, modern history, and miscellaneous errors. On the ancient history section, it was charged that the Russians had omitted four or five centuries of Korean history by stating that Korea was founded by Wiman in the second century B.C. The North Korean scholars said that had the Soviet scholars been able to read Chinese history books, such as *Guanze*, they would have known there was a record of trade between Korea and the Chinese kingdom of Qi as early as the seventh century B.C. Furthermore, Korea as a state was recorded in *Shiji* and *Weilue* with a succession of kings as early as the fourth and fifth centuries B.C., and it was reported that they had slaves and armies. On the theory of the coming of Kija from the country of Yin to settle in southern Manchuria and the adjacent peninsula, they claimed that this account had been advanced by flunkies of the past and the Soviet scholars had merely copied it.[20]

On the Three Kingdoms period, they accused the Soviet scholars of omitting several hundred years of Korean history. The Soviets said that the kingdom of Koguryŏ was founded in A.D. 313, Paekche in A.D. 346, and Silla in A.D. 356. It was not difficult to refute these dates because in the years the Soviet scholars listed as the founding dates, Koguryŏ was ruled by its fifteenth king,

Paekche by its thirteenth king, and Silla by its seventeenth king. The North Korean historians said that even the Japanese historians who had tried hard to slander the Koreans and their tradition during their occupation of Korea did not omit more than several decades, but the Soviet scholars were omitting nearly ten centuries. In fact, they said, some of the Soviet accounts of Korean history were copied from erroneous Japanese accounts — for example, in their treatment of Mimana to which Japanese soldiers were alleged to have been dispatched in support of Paekche during her conflict with Silla in *A.D.* 600. This was an invention of modern Japanese historians to justify their aggression into Korea because the Japanese at this time had not even unified all of Honshū, the major island of Japan, let alone sending her forces to Korea.[21]

On the modern period, the North Korean historians refuted the indiscriminate branding by Soviet scholars of the leaders of the Kapsin coup in 1884 as running dogs of Japanese imperialism. They argued that U Chŏng-gyu, for example, established a system whereby landless peasants worked in the mines of rich merchants. They also argued that such reformers as Yu Tae-ch'i and O Kyŏng-sŏk were not henchmen of the Japanese, and even such notables as Kim Ok-kyun and Hong Yŏng-sik were bourgeois reformers but not the running dogs of the Japanese.[22]

Among the miscellaneous items in contemporary history, they accused the Soviet scholars of minimizing the impact of the October Revolution on the March First Movement of 1919, criticizing them for giving credit to bourgeois turncoats. They also maintained that the Soviet scholars neglected the labor movement of the 1920s and 1930s in Korea under the Japanese.[23] The North Korean historians contended that much of what the Soviet scholars had done stemmed from indiscriminate use of Korean history books written by the Japanese. It may not have seemed important to the Soviet scholars, but for Koreans it was a serious charge to equate someone with the Japanese imperialists. It should be pointed out that while the North Korean historians were correct in their assessment of reformers and other historical facts, the Soviet scholars should not be faulted for failing to mention the accomplishments of such an obscure reformer as U Chŏng-gyu in a Soviet world history book. As to the substance of the history, there was no controversy. The Koreans knew their history and the Soviet scholars were not about to rewrite the work. The attacks were political; the North Koreans seem to have done what they set out to accomplish, and the Soviet Union did not challenge them.

From this point on, the North Koreans made several serious accusations against the Soviet Union. In a lengthy article on October 28, 1963, entitled "Let Us Defend the Socialist Camp," the North Koreans condemned the Soviet campaign to isolate China. They began to accuse the Soviet Union of racial bias and disputed the alleged Soviet claim of ethnic superiority. They also accused the Soviet Union of manipulating their economic aid to interfere with the affairs of Asian countries. The North Koreans recognized the ideological differences between the Soviet Union and Asian countries, but argued that these differences should not be allowed to affect the relationship among the socialist countries. They said also that the Soviet Union should stop imposing the issue of the cult of personality on other parties and maintained that the new party program and platform of the Communist Party of the Soviet Union should be confined to the Soviet Union.[24]

On more specific points of their relationship with the Soviet Union, they said that the Soviet Union in the past had ridiculed their five-year economic plan, calling it a fantasy; had laughed at the speed with which the North Koreans had collectivized their agriculture, calling it a collectivization without farm machinery; had discouraged the building of machine industries; and had interfered with the foreign languages taught in North Korean schools. They said that the Soviet Union had even scrutinized the kind of foreign movies shown in North Korean theatres. The Soviet Union should stop the pretense of benevolence in asserting that their advanced military technology was the only guarantee of the peace and security of socialist countries. Citing liberally from the works of Lenin and Stalin, the North Koreans stressed that the experience of the Soviet citizens under the leadership of Lenin and Stalin should be a great asset to the people of the Soviet Union. To deny it was to follow the revisionist road of Yugoslavia, and the Koreans were resolutely opposed to revisionism.

On November 3, 1963, the North Koreans reprinted a Chinese editorial exposing the collusion between the leaders of the Soviet

Union and India in opposition to China, and on the forty-sixth anniversary of the October Revolution, Pak Kŭm-ch'ŏl delivered a carping criticism of the Soviet Union in support of China. Pak said that the Soviet Union had used economic aid to pressure the North and denied the Soviet claim that North Korean development was the result of Soviet aid. Pak said that the Soviet Union at times even claimed the trade between the two countries was aid from the Soviet Union to the North.[25]

In two subsequent editorials the North Koreans supported the national liberation movement and proclaimed that they were strongly opposed to Soviet efforts to isolate China and Albania. They said further that the Soviet Union should stop forcing such mistaken ideas as peaceful transition and the cult of personality on the Asian people, and they renewed their attack on the alleged Soviet bias against the Asian people. In July 1964 they lashed out once again at the Soviet policy of splitting and destroying the Japanese Communist Party. They congratulated the Japanese Communists for exposing the revisionist group led by Shiga Yoshio and Suzuki Ichizō.[26] The most serious charge, however, came when the Soviet Union deliberately belittled the second seminar on Asian economy held in Pyongyang.

The Seminar on Asian Economy. The second international seminar on Asian economy was held in Pyongyang from June 16 to 23, 1964, and some two months later the Soviet Union carried an article in *Pravda* questioning the propriety of convening such a seminar in Pyongyang.[27] The *Pravda* article claimed that the seminar was to have been held in Nicosia, but the Chinese had conspired to move the site to Pyongyang. It said that the seminar was so hastily summoned that many countries received invitations to attend on the day it was convened. In fact, Mongolia and six other countries were not able to participate because they had no time to prepare themselves for the seminar.

The article also said that the Chinese had dominated the seminar, since their fourteen-member delegation constituted more than one-third of the participants at the conference.[28] It claimed that the seminar had nothing to do with Asian economy because the delegates had no knowledge of Asian economy. It charged that the

Chinese propaganda machine had suggested that Soviet aid was a sure way to compromise a recipient's national sovereignty. It also charged that the Chinese brand of national economy based on the principle of self-resuscitation was a schismatic, exclusivist, and isolationist tactic that contributed nothing to economic development.

To these charges the North Koreans replied that the voice of *Pravda* had a familiar tone that greatly resembled the Voice of America, but in essence it was worse. The North Koreans argued that their effort to build a self-reliant economy was a life-and-death struggle for their future. Taking the Korean example, they admitted that North Korea had received economic aid and technical assistance from the Soviet Union after the war and that the Soviet Union had helped to rebuild the Pyongyang textile mill and reconstruct portions of the Hŭngnam fertilizer plant. For these efforts the North Koreans were grateful. However, they revealed that the Soviet Union had sold the building materials and sundry Soviet goods at a price much higher than the prevailing international market price and in return carted away from Korea tons of gold bullion and a large quantity of nonferrous metals at a price much lower than the international market price.

On the question of delegates' ignorance of economic theory and development economics, the North Koreans listed the names of some of the leading participants, remarking that these were people knowledgeable about the developing economy and that the Soviet Union did not have a monopoly on theories of economic development, particularly not those of the Asian economy.[29] In fact, one delegate reported that as a result of Soviet economic aid, his country's economy had been exploited, its domestic affairs interfered with, and its government subjected to an attempted overthrow by the Soviet Union. To the question of who benefited from the seminar, the North Koreans answered that the seminar was for the benefit of the Asian people's struggle against the imperialists and colonialists and for the peace and national liberation of the Asian, African, and Latin American peoples.

No more was said about the seminar by the Soviet Union, and this was perhaps the harshest language the North Koreans ever used to denounce the Soviet Union. The third anniversary of the conclusion of the treaty of friendship, cooperation, and mutual assistance between North Korea and China was celebrated in July 1964, but the anniversary of the same treaty with the Soviet Union was ignored. There were other overt manifestations of the strengthening of Chinese and Korean ties, such as the participation by Ch'oe Yong-gŏn and Pak Kŭm-ch'ŏl in the fifteenth anniversary of the founding of the People's Republic of China. The North Koreans published a lengthy article on December 21, 1964, to commemorate the eighty-fifth birthday of Stalin together with his photograph, extolling him as a great Marxist and Leninist and an exceptional leader of the international Communist movement.[30]

The Soviet-Korean dispute had a profound impact on Kim Il Sung and North Korea. Kim was spared from engaging in any direct verbal exchanges of unpleasantries with the Soviet Union, and when the problem of the cult of personality was made clear to the North Koreans, they shielded him from the Soviet attack. They also kept him from making frequent public appearances. Indeed, Kim seldom appeared in public during the Soviet-Korean dispute from 1962 to the end of 1964. Except for visiting heads of state, such as Modibo Keita of Mali and Sukarno of Indonesia, most party and government delegations and other important visitors were greeted by Ch'oe Yong-gŏn, chairman of the Standing Committee of the Supreme People's Assembly. Many speeches normally made by Kim on special anniversaries were delivered by other party officials, such as Pak Kŭm-ch'ŏl and Kim Il, both vice-chairmen of the Central Committee of the party. Even the term "cult of personality" was translated into Korean to mean quite different: *kaein misin* (literally "individual superstition"). The Soviet Union may have put Kim in power, but they were not able to remove him.

On the question of peaceful transition in the Sino-Soviet dispute, the North Koreans imputed racial bias to the Soviet Union — discrimination against Asians and in favor of Europeans. They argued that the revisionists' ideas of peaceful transition or peaceful coexistence were, to the divided Asian countries of China, Vietnam, and North Korea, a purely heretical innovation to thwart the national liberation movement. They accused the Soviet Union of belittling Asian countries, and while admitting that they had received Soviet aid and technological assistance they insisted that Asians were capable of rebuilding their economies without assistance from the Soviet Union. (The North Koreans had a bitter experience building tractors without Soviet blueprints — the machine moved only backward for a while, but they eventually figured out how to make it go forward.) They said that there were old parties and new parties, large parties and small parties, developed countries and developing countries, but there were no superior or inferior parties in a hierarchical order among the fraternal socialist countries. Every party, however small, had a great deal to contribute to the international Communist movement.

In the dispute, the Soviet Union did not engage the North Koreans in a running controversy on any subject similar to the controversies between the Soviet Union and China. Each time the North Koreans attacked, the Soviet Union would drop the subject. This reaction only infuriated the North Koreans, but they did not capitulate, accusing the Soviet Union of ignorance on things Korean and of a hypocritical attitude toward helping the Koreans.

The Sino-Korean Dispute

In many respects, the Sino-Korean dispute was quite different in style and content from the Soviet-Korean quarrel. When the North Koreans had their differences with the Soviet Union, they at least expressed their dissent in print and aired their recriminations in public. They were silent, however, about their difficulties with the Chinese. Nor did the Chinese attack the North Koreans in their official publications. Both sides refrained from directly identifying the other or being specific about any issue in dispute, always airing their disparate views in the midst of ambiguous and wearying polemics about their relations with the Soviet Union. The North Koreans were articulate and to the point when they answered the Soviet charges, but they countered the Chinese with inscrutable smiles, hurling no insults while maintaining their unalterable position.

The content of the Sino-Korean dispute was, however, far more serious than that of the feud with the Soviet Union. In all their unpleasant encounters, the Soviet Union never once attacked Kim Il Sung or any of his deputies by name or anything to do with his person. By contrast, the Chinese Red Guards during the Cultural

Revolution made personal attacks on Kim in wall posters and resur-
rected a perennial problem on the China-Korea boundary by re-
claiming disputed territory. These were more substantive issues
that required a great deal of attention, but the two sides dealt with
the problems without publicly disagreeing on anything.

Contrary to the common view that the North Korean pendulum
swung back and forth in the Sino-Soviet dispute, the North Koreans viewed their position as firm as they tried to maintain their
independence between Soviet revisionism and Chinese dogmatism.
Indeed, they maintained their position during the rampageous
swing of Khrushchev's revisionist politics and tried to readjust
their relationship with the Soviet Union when Khrushchev fell.
They viewed their differences with the Chinese as due primarily
to the wild and unruly Red Guards during the Cultural Revolution.
The North Koreans maintained that they had never sided with one
against the other for whatever benefit they might accrue from such
a balancing act. Rather, it was the domestic difficulties of the Soviet Union and China that affected their position, and they simply
tried to maintain Korea's autonomy.

After the fall of Khrushchev in October 1964, the North Koreans
did try to readjust their relationship with the Soviet Union, irrespective of the persistent Chinese difficulties with the new leadership of Brezhnev and Kosygin. The North Koreans were not
happy with Khrushchevism without Khrushchev, but they explored the possibilities of readjusting their relations with the Soviet
Union. They were extremely cautious, however, and the new
Soviet-Korean relationship was not a restoration of the old, but
rather an adjustment to the new situation.

A North Korean delegation headed by Kim Il and Kim Ch'ang-
man participated in the forty-seventh anniversary of the October
Revolution in Moscow on November 7, 1964, but when they returned they clarified their position by stating that the revisionists
of the past were embellishing imperialism and all Communists
should support the national liberation movement and defend the
unity of the international Communist movement. Many important
visitors came from the Soviet Union: new Premier Kosygin in February 1965, Alexandr N. Shelepin in August 1965, and Vladimir
Novikov in May 1967, to mention only a few. Moreover, a number

of important North Korean officials went to the Soviet Union, including a military delegation headed by Ch'oe Kwang in May 1965 and a government delegation headed by Ch'oe Yong-gŏn in March 1966. These exchanges may have signified normalized relations between the two, but at the same time the North Koreans maintained their autonomy by refusing to participate in the Moscow meeting of international Communist parties in March 1965.

For the North Koreans, the normalized relationship with the Soviet Union was to their advantage, and a number of reasons may have compelled them to capitalize on the fall of Khrushchev. Foremost was the growth in the South of a strong and militant anti-Communist group that had strengthened its ties with the United States by sending South Korean troops to Vietnam in January 1965. Another reason was the normalization of South Korea's relations with Japan, and with it the South Korean economy took off for rapid and real growth. North Koreans, in contrast, were suffering from their ambitious seven-year economic plan, which they had to extend for three more years due in part to their altercation with the Soviet Union.

The difficulties between China and North Korea stemmed not so much from the Korean effort to normalize relations with the Soviet Union, which did raise the ire of the Chinese, as from the radical Red Guard movement of the Cultural Revolution. The eccentricities of the Red Guards reached the point where any party that was neutral or pro-Russian was considered to be anti-Chinese. The Soviet Union came to understand the independent position of the North, and they were happy that the North Koreans were not swept into the irrational campaigns of the Chinese. The Chinese, on the other hand, were unhappy about the North Korean rapprochement with the Soviet Union and condemned the North Koreans during the height of the Cultural Revolution. From 1967 to 1969, the Sino-Korean dispute centered on two subjects: one was the attack by the Red Guards on Kim Il Sung; the other was the Chinese territorial claim in the Chinese-Korean border area.

The Chinese Denunciation of Kim. The Red Guards in China began to put up wall posters denouncing Kim from 1967 and spread rumors about sensitive domestic political issues involving Kim's high-level deputies. Since they were wall posters, they appeared and disappeared quickly, leaving only allegations and scathing condemnation of Kim and his deputies. The first appeared on January 20, 1967, and alleged that General Kim Kwang-hyŏp, a partisan who was also vice-premier and the sixth-ranked member of the Political Committee, had been arrested by Ch'oe Yong-gŏn, also a partisan and the second highest member who, as chairman of the Standing Committee of the Supreme People's Assembly, was titular head of the North.[31]

This was but a rumor, for Kim Kwang-hyŏp was reappointed vice-premier of the cabinet at the fourth Supreme People's Assembly in December 1967. The Korean Central News Agency was reported to have issued a statement refuting the rumor as propaganda of the capitalist countries that should not be repeated. It said that the unfounded rumor was intolerable slander of the party, the government, the army, and the people of Korea. Nevertheless, the posters may have reflected internal dissension in the North because Kim Kwang-hyŏp was purged the following year.

The rumors persisted, and on February 4, 1967, the wall posters of the Red Guards reported that Kim Il Sung had been arrested by generals of the Korean People's Army without mentioning the names of the generals. Here again, subsequent developments in North Korean domestic politics in 1968–1969 might give some credence to the rumors. A number of generals, all partisans and high-ranking members of the Political Committee and the Central Committee, including Ch'oe Kwang, Hŏ Pong-hak, Kim Ch'ang-bong, Kim Ch'ang-dŏk, and Sŏk San, were purged.

Another poster, this time signed by the Chinese veterans of the Korean War, accused Kim of being a "revisionist and a disciple of Khrushchev." Kim was accused of sabotaging the just struggle of the Vietnamese people by refusing to send North Korean volunteers to the Vietnamese conflict.[32] The Chinese also accused the North Koreans of ignoring the Cultural Revolution in China. Indeed, the North Koreans were silent about the rampage of the Red Guards all during the Cultural Revolution. They neither praised it nor condemned it; they simply ignored it. Like the de-Stalinization campaign, it was distasteful to Korea but considered an internal affair of China.

Still another poster, put up this time by Beijing high school students who had returned from a visit to the North, depicted Kim as a revisionist indulging in materialistic pleasures and neglecting the revolutionary fervor of the time. It said that Kim slandered the works of the Cultural Revolution and defamed the good name of Chairman Mao. Any visitor going from China to the North might get such an impression not because Kim was actually defaming Mao or slandering the Cultural Revolution but because the North Koreans neglected to acknowledge the campaigns of the Red Guards. Not a single copy of the Little Red Book, the quotations of Chairman Mao, was circulated in Korea, for example. In fact, the North Koreans were busy revising their own selected works of Kim once again, and they put out the first volume of Kim's work (the third edition), the *Chŏjak sŏnjip*, in April 1967.

Through their foreign legations in Algiers, Jakarta, New Delhi, and Havana, the Korean Central News Agency was reported to have denied these charges and to have countered them with the statement that the Chinese were jealous of North Korea's economic development and should not question the independent line of the North Koreans. It was also reported that the North Koreans warned the Chinese to be fully responsible for the consequences of such unfriendly acts.[33]

The deterioration was serious enough to prompt the recall of the ambassadors to Beijing and Pyongyang. The embassies were manned by chargés d'affaires, and the Chinese delegation to the Armistice Commission withdrew from Korea. There were also rumors that the Chinese armed forces were regrouping near the North Korean border, and North Korean loudspeakers were blasting anti-Chinese propaganda across the border. Perhaps the most serious criticism appeared in an article circulated by the Guangzhou Red Guard in February 1968 in their journal *Wenge tongxun* (News of the Cultural Revolution) entitled "Jinri chaoxiu jituan" (The Korean revisionist clique of today).[34]

The article said that Kim Il Sung was a counterrevolutionary revisionist and a millionaire, an aristocrat, and a capitalist. It said that his residence in Pyongyang was set in a most scenic location near Moranbong, overlooking both the rivers Taedong and Po-t'ong, and his estate covered nearly ten acres of choice urban land surrounded by high walls with sentries all around. It also reported that there were five or six great gates to reach the central court-yard, reminiscent of the palaces of the emperors. The article charged that Kim had palaces built in many choice locations throughout the country; the first was in the Songnim district in a suburb of Pyongyang, the second near scenic Kŭmgang mountain, the third in Chuŭl hot springs, the fourth in Sinŭiju near the mouth of the Yalu River, facing the Yellow Sea, and the fifth in Ch'ŏngjin, a northeastern town on the coast of the East Sea. These villas were built on a grand scale, and while Kim would stay in these lavish places only briefly, his visit demanded the services of a huge staff and a number of armed force units and security person-nel to guard him.

The article also reported on Kim's show of filial piety to his grandparents and parents. Their cemeteries were decorated with flowers and plants and guarded by a special staff. Among the cadres of the Korean revisionists, the report continued, bribery was prac-ticed and lavish gifts were exchanged at gala dinner affairs. It cited one such example at the sixtieth birthday in 1965 of a certain minis-ter of communication, a man named Pak,[35] and described the ex-tent of decadence the North Koreans had reached in their corrupt bourgeois life.

As in the old adage, "Where there is smoke, there is fire," there was enough smoke to suggest fire, but most of these charges were difficult to substantiate. While it is impossible to verify all of Kim's summer and winter villas in the choice spots mentioned in the arti-cle, Kim certainly had a use for one or two such villas. It was never made public in the North, but Kim was married in the early 1960s, probably in the summer of 1963, to Kim Sŏng-ae, his present wife. No information about her personal background was ever made public. It was alleged that she was the secretary to Kim's security guards at his residence. She was a member and later chairman of the Sunan branch (P'yŏngan namdo) of the Democratic Women's Union and did not make a public appearance until long after her marriage to Kim.[36] She was introduced to the public as the vice-chairman of the Democratic Women's Union under the chairman-ship of Kim Ok-sun, a partisan, in 1965. She later became a member of the Central Committee of the party as well as a member of

Kim Il Sung and his second wife,
Kim Sŏng-ae, 1975

With Josip Broz Tito and his wife, 1975

Kim Sŏng-ae, second wife of Kim Il sung, 1975

Kim Il Sung on top of Mt. Paektu near Lake Ch'ŏnji, 1963

Kim Il Sung receives an honorary doctorate from the University of Indonesia, April 1965

the Standing Committee of the Supreme People's Assembly in 1971–1972.

In the style of the Red Guards' idolization of Mao during the Cultural Revolution, the North Koreans began to idolize Kim about this time. It was during the latter half of the 1960s that the North Koreans began to use a long and adulatory prefix to his name — he was called the leader of not only the people of North Korea, but also the forty million people of both North and South Korea. He was referred to as *suryŏng* (supreme leader), an appellation thus far reserved only for such notables as Lenin and Stalin. The allegation about his filial piety was correct. It was in 1967 that the North Koreans began to canonize his mother and father as saints of the Korean revolution and began to build monuments and museums for their alleged revolutionary activities.

As to the lavish life-styles of the partisans, this was nothing new to the leaders of the North. From the time when the Soviet-Koreans were prominent political leaders in the North, many were dismissed from their positions for opulent settings and immoral parties. The partisan tradition was promoted in the 1960s, and the partisans were few in number. Since Pak was perhaps one of the first partisans to reach the ripe old age of sixty in 1965, such extravagant feasts were understandable.

The Sino-Korean Territorial Dispute. More important than these insults was the controversy over the China-Korea boundary, involving what Kim and his partisans call their sacred mountain, Paektusan, the symbol of their revolution. The Koreans share their longest border, approximately 880 miles, with China, and it is generally known that two rivers, the Yalu and Tumen, mark the boundary of China and Korea. Between these two rivers, however, stands the tallest mountain, 2,744 meters, in both Korea and Northeast China. It is known as Paektusan (White Head Mountain) in Korea and Changbaishan (Ever-White or Long White Mountain) in China.[37] The two rivers trace their headwaters to this mountain, and it was the demarcation of approximately twenty miles of this mountain and a volcanic lake on top of the mountain, *Ch'ŏnji* (Heavenly Lake) or *Tianchi* in Chinese, that were in dispute.

The area near the mountain on both sides is inhospitable and uninhabited. Neither the Chinese nor the Koreans have assayed the mountain or explored the region for economic purposes, therefore, and the value of the mountain to both the Chinese and Koreans is more symbolic than material. Chinese legends claim the mountain as the origin of many kingdoms, including the Qing dynasty and its founder Nurhachi; Korean mythology similarly claims it for the kingdom of Korea. More pertinent to the North Koreans, however, is the fact that Kim and his partisans conducted their anti-Japanese guerrilla activities in the vicinity of this mountain and consider it holy ground for their revolution. In fact, the ballad of Kim Il Sung begins with this mountain, *Changbaeksan*, the Korean pronunciation of Changbaishan. Even the national anthem of South Korea mentions the mountain in its first stanza, and all Koreans regard it as a Korean mountain.

There were numerous controversies over the mountain, and a number of efforts were made to define the boundary between China and Korea. One such attempt was made as early as 1712.[38] It was reported that the Chinese notified the Koreans of the need to define the boundary around the mountain in February 1712, and the Chinese governor of Jilin province, Mukedeng, and a Korean envoy, Pak Kwŏn, met in May 1712. These two envoys and their assistants were to climb the mountain and place a marker stating that the boundary was from the mountain "to the west the Yalu River and to the east the Tumen River."[39]

The records of the Chosŏn dynasty show that Pak Kwŏn and his deputy, Yi Sŏn-bu, were too old to climb the mountain and were replaced by a lower-ranking military officer attached to the delegation, Yi Ŭi-bok, and the marker was placed somewhere around the foot of the mountain on the Korean side and not on top of the mountain, as had been directed. Dissension between the Chinese and Korean delegates was also reported. Apparently the Chinese delegation had a cartography staff and the Koreans did not, and the Chinese were extremely contemptuous of the Koreans and refused to show them their maps. When the Koreans asked for a map of the mountain, the Chinese delegate replied that since the mountain was in Korea, they did not have a map of it; the Koreans took this to mean that the mountain was on the Korean side.[40] On a number of old Korean maps, however, the boundary marker was located on the Korean slope of the mountain, putting the mountain clearly on the Chinese side.[41]

Considerable controversy emanated from this boundary marker, particularly on the eastern side of the mountain. After the Japanese assumed control of the foreign relations of Korea, they concluded an agreement with the Chinese on the boundary, recognizing the River Tumen as the boundary between China and Korea. Article 1 of this agreement, signed on September 4, 1909, stated that "the Governments of Japan and China declare that the River Tumen is recognized as forming the boundary between China and Korea, and that in the region of the source of that river the boundary line shall start from the boundary monument and hence follow the course of the stream Shihyishwei (Shiyishui)."[42] The Chinese and the Japanese maps differed as to the location of this stream Shiyishui (Sŏgülsu in Korean, Sekiotsusui in Japanese). While the Japanese maps show the stream going to the mountain, the Ting atlas of 1934 and other Chinese maps as late as 1943 connect the small stream with the Yalu River and bypass the mountain completely, placing the entire mountain on the Chinese side. (See map of the China-Korea border.)

After the People's Republic of China was proclaimed in October 1949, the Chinese established a Korean autonomous *zhou* (prefecture) on each side of the mountain — one, the Changbai Korean Autonomous *zhou*, bordering the Yalu River and the other, the Yanbian Korean Autonomous *zhou*, bordering the Tumen River. The first sign of concern about the mountain came in November 1961 when *Renmin huabao* featured a number of photographs of the mountain with an article about the Changbai mountain range on the Northeast China–Korea border. The text stated that the mountain was located in Jilin province and its main peak, Baitoushan (Paektusan in Korean), was more than 2,700 meters above sea level, making it the highest mountain in Northeast China. On this peak, it said, was a volcanic lake, approximately fourteen kilometers in circumference and two or three hundred meters in depth with deep blue waters, called Tianchi.[43]

The North Koreans, in turn, published a map in 1962 showing the entire mountain on their side and claiming the entire lake. In the boundary section it said that "the Tuman and Amnok rivers

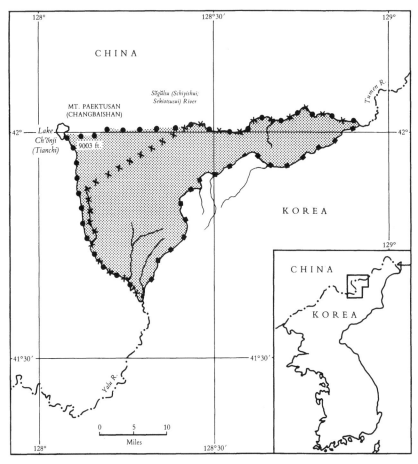

International boundary where Chinese, Japanese, and Korean maps agree.

● ● ●   Boundary generally used on Japanese maps and on most maps published in the United States. It follows the stream Sŏgŭlsu mentioned in the treaty of September 4, 1909, between Japan and China.

X X X   Boundary shown in the Ting atlas, 1934 (also follows the Sŏgŭlsu but connection with the Yalu differs from Japanese interpretation).

■ ■ ■   Approximate alignment shown on Chinese Communist maps.

Approximately 600 square miles. Area in dispute.

Source: Modified from the map in *China–Korea Boundary* by the Geographer of the U.S.A., Department of State.

The China-Korea Border

(the Tumen River and the Yalu River) and Mount Paektu (Paektusan) separate the country from its northern neighbors, the Maritime Province of the USSR and the northeastern region of the People's Republic of China."[44] The section on topography said that Korea is a mountainous country, with a number of high mountains, including Paektusan (2,744 meters).

Kim personally scaled the mountain in 1963, but no more was said about the boundary because the relationship between China and North Korea was most cordial at the time. From 1965, however, it was rumored that the Chinese were claiming the disputed territory. It was alleged that the North Korean embassy in Moscow made public the Chinese claim to approximately one hundred square miles of Korean territory.[45] The North Koreans seem not to have engaged the Chinese in the territorial dispute and stood their ground all during the difficult period of the Sino-Korean dispute from 1967 to 1969. There was no report that any agreement on the boundary problem was ever reached between the two, and there was no formal announcement from either side.

Suddenly, in 1969, a photograph of Kim Il Sung standing on top of Paektusan near Lake Ch'ŏnji was widely circulated in the North. The picture was prominently displayed in a number of publications, and a full-page photograph appeared right after Kim's portrait in the Korean Central Yearbook of 1969. There was a report from Taiwan in 1970 that the Chinese Communists and North Koreans had reached an agreement on the boundary question at the time of the ninth session of the meetings concerning the joint navigation committee of the Yalu and Tumen rivers held in Shenyang from December 29, 1969, to January 29, 1970.[46]

The Dictionary of History, published by the History Research Center of the Academy of Sciences of the Democratic People's Republic of Korea in 1971, stated that "Paektusan is located in Samjiyŏn county, Yanggang province, of Korea, and it is the highest mountain in *our country*." It said that Paektusan was the sacred mountain of their great leader Kim Il Sung's revolution and symbolized the spirit of Koreans from past to present. It said further that Kim Il Sung had instructed the North Koreans to construct railways to the mountain and build roads to the top and to Lake Ch'ŏnji and that this has been done. Many North Korean people were visiting the magnificent scenery of the mountain and appreciating the great care of Kim Il Sung. Kim had also instructed them to explore the rich minerals of the mountain and to build monuments to mark the revolutionary sites of Kim's partisans nearby.

An English information book published by the North Koreans in 1974 featured a picture of Kim standing on top of the mountain on the first page, even before the national emblem and national flag, and identified the mountain as being in Korea and as a sacred mountain associated with the revolutionary struggle of Kim Il Sung.[47] It is assumed that the North Koreans and the Chinese reached a satisfactory agreement by the time Zhou Enlai visited the North in April 1970. It should be pointed out, however, that the agreement, whatever its nature, may not be accepted by the South Korean authorities, just as the Koreans did not accept agreements between China and Japan on behalf of Korea during the Japanese occupation.

Several factors affected the restoration of normal relations between China and North Korea, but most important was the change within China. When the ninth congress of the Chinese Communist Party was held in April 1969, the intense campaign of the Cultural Revolution was relaxed somewhat and the Chinese renewed their cordial relationship with the North. On the twentieth anniversary of the founding of the People's Republic of China, a North Korean government delegation headed by Ch'oe Yong-gŏn participated in the celebration, and by March 1970 both the Chinese and the North Korean ambassadors had returned to their posts. Soon thereafter the Chinese delegation to the Armistice Commission reappeared, signifying the return of normal relations.

The rapidly changing political relations among South Korea, the United States, and Japan accelerated the normalization process between China and Korea. The signs of the gradual U.S. withdrawal and the exertion of greater influence by the Japanese in Asia evidenced by the Nixon-Satō joint communiqué in November 1969 brought Zhou Enlai to the North in April 1970. As in the case of the Soviet Union, the relaxation of tension between China and Korea was brought on by changes in China, and the North Koreans maintained their independent position without capitulating to Chinese pressure. It is commendable that the North Koreans restored their relations with the Chinese and the Soviet Union without compromising their desire for an independent and self-reliant Korea.

Kim's Declaration of Independence

All during the Soviet-Korean and Sino-Korean disputes Kim avoided personal participation in the disagreements and did not use any derogatory terms to deal with either the Soviet or the Chinese leaders. He did respond to Zhou Enlai's letters in August 1963 and October 1964 and supported the Chinese position and indirectly opposed the Soviet Union on the Anglo-American and Soviet nuclear test ban treaty. He also detested the adverse effects felt in Korea of the Chinese Cultural Revolution and the Red Guards, but in both cases Kim avoided direct involvement in the dispute. By the time friendly relations were restored with China and the Soviet Union, Kim had already turned his attention to the Third World. He wanted to expand his contacts with the nonaligned countries and tried to minimize his involvement with China and the Soviet Union.

For the first time in four years after his busy trips to and from Moscow and Beijing, Kim visited Indonesia in April 1965.[48] This was also his first trip after he married, but traveled alone. The timing was such that he celebrated his fifty-third birthday in Jakarta, but he was rewarded handsomely by his hosts Sukarno and Dipa N. Aidit, chairman of the Indonesian Community Party (PKI). Kim was awarded an honorary doctorate in technology at Indonesian University. For an eighth-grade expellee to receive an honorary doctorate was indeed an honor. His visit also coincided with the festivities of the tenth anniversary of the Bandung Conference, and he met with a number of leaders of the nonaligned nations.

In a goodwill gesture, a delegation from the Soviet Union came in August 1965 to participate in the gala celebration of the twentieth anniversary of the liberation of Korea from Japan. The delegation was headed by Alexandr N. Shelepin, a member of the Presidium and vice-chairman of the Council of Ministers of the USSR. He was accompanied by General Ivan M. Chistiakov, former commander of the 25th Division of the Red Army that liberated

Korea, his chief executive officer, Major General Nikolai G. Lebedev, and Kim's advisor who maneuvered him into power, Major General Alexandr A. Romanenko. They had come to reminisce about the old days and to renew old ties.[49] In a separate ceremony, all these veterans of the Korean liberation were decorated by Kim.

No sooner was this done in August 1965 than a Chinese delegation came in October 1965 to celebrate the fifteenth anniversary of the Chinese participation in the Korean War. This delegation was headed by General Yang Yong, former commander of the Chinese Volunteer Army from 1954 to 1958 and deputy chief of the General Staff of the People's Liberation Army of China. He was accompanied by several former deputy commanders of the Chinese Volunteer Army who collected their share of medals from Kim.[50]

Kim had to pay his debts to these men, but this was during the middle of the renewed Sino-Soviet dispute, and Kim wanted to turn away from the quarrel and look toward the Third World. Kim's reaction was swift; 1965 was the last time the North Koreans celebrated both national liberation day (August 15) and the anniversary of the Chinese participation in the Korean War (October 25). As time progressed, they even ignored the Soviet liberation of North Korea and the Chinese contribution to the Korean War.

Thereafter, the North Koreans observed only Korean national days: Kim Il Sung's birthday (April 15) and the anniversaries of the founding of the army (February 8), the state (September 9), and the party (October 10). The only international day they continued to observe was May Day, and in most cases they observed their national days by themselves and did not invite foreign guests. On May Day in 1967, the North Koreans invited guests from eighty nonaligned countries, including such leaders as Anwar Sadat, and minimized the Sino-Soviet influence in Korea.

In a lengthy article in August 1966 entitled "Let Us Defend Independence," the North Koreans stated their desire to be independent and vowed to remain neutral in the Sino-Soviet dispute.[51] They emphasized eight points: to oppose flunkyism and think for themselves, to rely on their own strength, to devise their own theory to lead their party under the general principle of Marxism and Leninism, to reject any mechanical application of non-Korean experiences to the Koreans, to reject national nihilism and cultivate confidence in themselves, to build the national economy on their own with external assistance of their own choice, to respect their independence, and to strengthen the joint anti-imperialist struggle with other socialist countries but at the same time to defend their own independence.

At the time of the Second Party Conference in October 1966 Kim broke his silence on foreign affairs and spoke about the independent position of the North Korean people in the international Communist movement.[52] After a lengthy condemnation of American imperialism, Kim touched upon the potential menace of Japanese militarism in Asia and West German militarism in Europe. He also clarified his position on the problem of Vietnam and said that the Vietnamese people were the masters of their fate. The fraternal socialist states were duty bound to offer aid, and the Vietnamese people were entitled to receive such aid. Kim said that he stood ready to send volunteers to help the Vietnamese people if requested. He proposed that an international force consisting of volunteers from the fraternal socialist countries should be sent to help the Vietnamese struggle against the American imperialists.[53]

After a brief comment on the need to support the struggles of all Asian, African, and Latin American countries, Kim said that the international Communist movement was experiencing trials and tribulations because of modern revisionism and dogmatism. Under the pretext of creative development, he said, modern revisionism tended to reject class struggle. He also attacked dogmatism and said that under no circumstances should one party impose its views upon others. Citing the example of Big Power chauvinism in interference in the internal affairs of the Japanese Communist Party,[54] he said that the relationship of the fraternal parties should be based on the principles of equality, independence, and mutual respect.

He said that the Koreans had in the past experienced Big Power chauvinism and harbored bitter memories of the interference. He said there were people who accused the Koreans of eclecticism and opportunism, of taking the road of unprincipled compromise and straddling two chairs. This was nonsense, he said. The Koreans had their own chair and need not sit uncomfortably straddling two non-Korean chairs. Those who accused the Koreans of straddling two chairs were themselves sitting on a chair leaning to the left or to the right.

Every party has its own point of view, he said, and it should be respected. Every party is also capable of judging things for itself and distinguishing right from wrong. The Big Powers tend to be suspicious of others and pressure others to take sides. Kim said that the Koreans took no sides except the side of Marxism and Leninism. He said that the policies of the fraternal socialist parties were not uniform because the conditions prevailing in each country were different. The international Communist movement should not preclude diversity in the policies of constituent members. He said that Big Power chauvinism should be checked and each party should be independent. He said that the conditions prevailing in the international Communist movement compelled him to remain vigilant in establishing and maintaining independence.

Kim also said that the Koreans would never dance to the tune of others. However, this did not mean that they had forsaken the principle of proletarian internationalism. He said that the Korean Communists categorically rejected isolationism and nationalism and worked for cooperation among the fraternal countries, but such cooperation should be based on the equality and independence of each member.

He went on to speak about two other subjects, the strengthening of the revolutionary base in the North and the situation in South Korea, but this speech was primarily on North Korean foreign policy. With this speech Kim indeed declared his independence, particularly from the Soviet Union and China. It came more than twenty years after the liberation of Korea, but the important fact is that Kim was able to take such an independent position. The persistent and acrimonious dispute between the Soviet Union and China brought the level of their toleration to the point where Kim was able to make such a declaration, but Kim should be credited for capitalizing on the opportunity to find his place in the polycentric Communist world and to exert Korean identity.

Subsequent to this speech, Kim did follow his independent policy and supported the Soviet Union in its intervention in Czechoslovakia in 1968, but the North withdrew from a Soviet-Korean joint oceanographic expedition in the Sea of Japan because of the Soviets' unilateral decision to include Japanese scientists in the project in 1970. It was the Chinese and not the Koreans who initiated "Sino-Korean Friendship" week in China, July 9–15, 1970, and Kim was able to shrug off even the Sino-American rapprochement in 1971. By the end of the 1960s, both the Soviet Union and China had come to respect Korea's independent position and to recognize Kim's self-reliant Korean identity.

By the time of the Fourth Party Congress in September 1961, Kim was in full control of the domestic political scene. He had successfully purged all his political rivals and their organizations and maneuvered his old guerrillas into important political positions. He had also mobilized the people for superhuman drives to build a strong and economically sound socialist state in the North. He tried to create a New Communist in North Korea who would make maximum efforts with minimum reward, work for the love of country and not for material gain, and be completely loyal to Kim and accept Kim's guerrilla record as the true Korean revolutionary tradition.

Kim was not an idle man; he traveled throughout the country to prod the people to work hard for him. He visited collective farms, factories, and steel mills to encourage the people, and he launched numerous campaigns to drive the people to the production line. In all these campaigns, such as the Ch'ŏllima, Ch'ŏngsalli, and Taean production drives, Kim was successful in mobilizing the people for the socialist construction of North Korea. His difficulties of the 1960s came not from his domestic politics but from his relation with China and the Soviet Union, particularly from the Sino-Soviet dispute.

Kim's basic foreign policy objectives during the 1960s were to remain neutral in the Sino-Soviet dispute by advocating the solidarity of the international Communist movement and to explore his own brand of diplomatic relations with the Third World. The theme he propagated was the equality and independence of every nation, and he won considerable support by constantly attacking the most hated enemy of all, the United States. His encounters with the Soviet Union and China during the 1960s were serious, and his contribution to the resolution of the problems he faced should not be minimized. From the time when he himself had to shuttle back and forth to Moscow and Beijing to comprehend the problems related to the Sino-Soviet dispute to the time when he could declare his independence from his two quarreling benefactors, Kim had steered his country well without capitulating.

He not only withstood the pressures from both sides but also upheld his convictions, always advocating the unity of the Communist world. Kim may have sought an independent Korean position, but the issues were also forced upon him. The emergence of Khrushchev and his revisionism in the Soviet Union and, similarly, the Chinese Cultural Revolution and the dogmatic and reckless Red Guards forced him to be self-reliant; but the course he took was such that he did not suffer the consequences of Albania, nor did his Chinese relations deteriorate beyond the point of recovery. There was no show of Chinese military force in the style of the Chinese confrontation with India in that border dispute. If he did, in fact, secure the "Korean mountain" from the Chinese as the North Koreans claim, his contribution to Korea should be praised.

While his dealings with the Soviet Union and China may have given him confidence, his domestic problems mounted during the 1960s. He suffered from the lack of Soviet and Chinese assistance for economic development and the modernization of his military forces. Thus he came to realize the perils of independence and suffered the consequences. There was also a significant political confrontation within the partisan groups that resulted in the purges of his most trusted generals. Perhaps worst of all was his conscious effort to promote himself to the people and have them revere him, his family, his revolution, and everything else related to him. This campaign began at the end of the 1960s.

V

PROBLEMS IN KIM'S INDEPENDENCE

Kim's ambitious seven-year economic plan was in trouble almost immediately after it was launched because of the unsettling international situation of the 1960s. After announcing to the world that the Soviet Union had used its economic aid to meddle in domestic affairs, the North Koreans for the first time had to develop a self-sustaining economy without economic aid or technical assistance from the Soviet Union. It cost them dearly. They had to extend their seven-year plan three more years to make it an unprecedented ten-year plan. Intermittent and uncertain Soviet military assistance forced them to devote more resources to their self-defense forces, and their military outlays increased steadily during the 1960s, undermining the projected economic development. Kim did much to preach his own political program of self-reliance in the 1960s, but he also experienced the hardships and problems of his independence.

His problems were compounded by a military coup in the South that brought in a new and more efficient political regime. Kim had had no competition from South Korea in the 1950s, but the new government in the South was serious about its anti-Communist stance. It normalized relations with Japan and began to show signs of serious economic growth. It also strengthened its military posture by sending troops to Vietnam and by training and modernizing military personnel and equipment.

Kim, for his part, did have more generals in the higher echelons of the party and the government after the Fourth Party Congress when more of his partisans attained high position, but their unchecked political and military prominence in the heightened campaign to upgrade the partisan tradition brought serious difficulties. An attempt was made on the life of the South Korean president, and the American ship *Pueblo* and its crew were captured in a dramatic encounter. A diversionary strategy of this sort in the Korean peninsula to counterbalance South Korea's participation in the Vietnamese conflict was dangerous for Kim. This was not a demonstration of North Korea's military preparedness but a foolish adventure when they were suffering strained relations with both the Soviet Union and China. Kim had to purge a large number of able partisan generals, something he was always reluctant to do because so few were left.

All during the difficulties with the Chinese and the Soviet Union as well as the United States, Kim benefited a great deal from the restraint exercised by the Big Powers. Kim was quick to turn these benefits to his credit, and when he survived these difficulties he was idolized by the people. By the time the Fifth Party Congress was held in 1970 he virtually commanded reverence for his leadership from the people. He had expanded his horizon from the North to the South and on to the Third World, and the North Koreans had mounted a campaign to project him as the leader of the Third World.

11

The Rise of
the Military

After the Fourth Party Congress when Kim consolidated his political power beyond challenge, his partisans occupied important positions in both the party and the government. The prominence the partisans won was responsible for two subsequent developments in the 1960s. One was the emergence of technocrats to augment the lack of managerial and technical skills of the partisans; the other was the rise of the military, because partisans mostly served in the military. It was easy to detect from the new cabinet in October 1962, the third cabinet, that only partisans and technocrats, only ten out of some thirty ministers, were reappointed from the second cabinet; and more than twenty newly recruited ministers of the third cabinet were either partisan political appointees or technocrats. Except for important political posts such as national defense (Kim Ch'ang-bong), public security (Sŏk San), and foreign affairs (Pak Sŏng-ch'ŏl), which were occupied by partisans, the functional ministries were in general manned by experts in the field. With the ambitious seven-year economic plan after the Fourth Party Congress and a new team of partisans and managerial and technical experts after the third Supreme People's Assembly, Kim launched a serious effort to develop his economy and refine his system.

He urged many leaders of factories and mines as well as the local party organizations to recruit without hesitation young cadres and assign them to more responsible positions.[1] The technocrats did bring out innovations, such as the County Cooperative Farm Management Committee to make the county the basic unit for both industrial and agrarian management, the rural industrial centers to bridge the growing urban-rural gap, and the institution of an independent accounting system for each county. Kim took up these suggestions and made long and frequent speeches on these topics.[2]

In his New Year address in 1962, Kim emphasized the conquering of six "highlands": 5 million tons of grain, 250 million meters of textiles, 800,000 tons of fishery products, 200,000 units of new housing, 1.2 million tons of steel, and 15 million tons of coal. He resorted to his old tactics of urging the people to work hard by appealing to their patriotism and by visiting a number of local factories and giving on-the-spot guidance. When these tactics did not produce the expected results, he launched campaigns — for example, the 120-day campaign that began on August 30, 1962, prodding the workers and reminding them that there were only 120 days left in the year to meet the required goal. He also handed out enough medals and citations to the workers to dilute much of their value. By employing such tactics and maintaining such a sweatshop style of operation on a national scale, Kim said that within a few years every North Korean would be wrapped in silk, live in a house with a tile roof, and enjoy three meals of rice and beef broth every day.[3]

A serious effect of the partisan prominence stemmed from the fact that a majority of them were generals on active duty or retired military professionals. They insisted on strengthening national defense by modernizing the armed forces. They knew their military capabilities because the North Korean military establishment was their domain from the very beginning. The Soviet-Korean dispute was deeply felt in the economic sector when the Soviet Union withdrew its technicians and aid, but it had still greater impact on military preparedness. When the Soviet Union began to curtail its military assistance, the North Koreans suffered. Fuel supplies, parts for sophisticated military machinery, and other technical assistance were as yet beyond the reach of North Korea's scientists. When Khrushchev capitulated in the Cuban missile crisis, the partisan generals were shocked. A North Korean military delegation headed by General Kim Kwang-hyŏp, who was vice-chairman of the party as well as vice-premier, visited the Soviet Union on November 29, 1962, only to return empty-handed on December 5, 1962, and the partisans had to seriously consider building their own defense facilities in the North.[4]

Arms and Hammer and Sickle

The partisan generals moved quickly, and during the fifth plenum of the Central Committee,[5] held December 10–14, 1962, they reassessed their priorities and decided to build up the military on their own. Kim himself did not make any public pronouncement or report on this important change in policy at the time. He did preside over the meeting and directed the discussion, but the crucial change of policy was made by the partisan generals. The record of the plenum revealed the famous slogan, "arms on the one hand and hammer and sickle on the other," that was to become the guiding principle of the North during the 1960s. It stated that all party members and the workers must build socialism more effectively by "protecting our streets and villages and our homeland from our enemies with arms on the one hand and hammer and sickle on the other."[6]

After carefully reviewing the record of the American encroachments in Cuba, Vietnam, and South Korea, the partisan generals decided to strengthen their military capabilities and fight to maintain, and not to beg for, peace. The decision of the plenum emphasized the determination of the partisan generals to strengthen their military capabilities even at the cost of compromising and limiting economic development.

It was also at this plenum that the partisan generals revealed the four basic military policies of the party: to arm the entire populace, to fortify the entire country, to train every soldier to become cadre, and to modernize military weapons and equipment. When he broke his silence on North Korean relations with fraternal socialist countries in October 1966 at the Second Party Conference, Kim elaborated on the four military policies.[7] Kim said that the policy of arming the entire populace meant building a flawless defense system both in the front and in the rear by arming not only the soldiers but also the workers, the peasants, and the entire people. This policy reorganized and reinforced what was known as the Worker-Peasant Red Guards (*Nonong chŏgwidae*), more than 1.5 million strong, and eventually created the Red Young Guards (*Pulgŭn ch'ŏngnyŏn kŭnwidae*) with 700,000 members. Under this policy the people were given military drills and lessons in military maneuvers in each factory and on every cooperative farm. Young children from seven or eight years old to old people in their late sixties were taught to shoot and handle guns, and members of the Red Young Guards were given as much as five hundred hours of military training per year.[8]

On the fortification of the entire country, the second policy, Kim elaborated that the outcome of modern warfare depended much on the endurance of manpower and the storage of material to sustain a protracted war. He also pointed out the need to strengthen the rear and fortify the strategic areas where supplies were stored. In addition he said that preparations should be made to facilitate the transformation of all North Korean industries into wartime production. Under this policy, the North Koreans dug underground shelters, built underground storage facilities, and dispersed the people from urban to rural areas. They began to build a number of underground factories and even built several underground arsenals.

Kim also elaborated on the third policy. What was meant by the policy to train every soldier to become cadre? Everyone from enlisted man to ranking officer should be trained to meet not only the duties assigned to them but also the duties of the person immediately above them. This policy had two objectives: to upgrade the morale of the soldiers and to prepare the regular army for expansion in case of emergency. Kim later said there would be a large number of new recruits in case of emergency and all members of the regular army would become cadres; the army would be expanded in such a way as to transform each regiment into an army corps, each battalion into a regiment, each company into a battalion, and so forth.[9] He emphasized that neither the soldiers nor the people should fall into lassitude but should sharpen their vigilance. Kim said that he did not want war, but he was not afraid of it, and his officers and men should be able to counter a surprise attack without the slightest confusion.

On the fourth policy, modernization of the armed forces, Kim said that since the enemy was armed to the teeth with modern weapons, the North Koreans should modernize their weapons whenever possible. Kim acknowledged the pace of international weapons development and the arms trade and stressed that his soldiers should be equipped with the most advanced weapons available to them. Kim cautioned, however, that such modernization efforts should be made in accord with the mountainous terrain, the long curvature of the Korean coastline, and other needs peculiar to the Korean People's Army. Kim said that the lessons of the Korean War should not be forgotten and the proper balance should be maintained between modern and conventional weapons. It was not until after 1965 when North Korea and the Soviet Union restored normal relations that North Koreans were able to import advanced modern weapons, but they did begin, from December 1962, to concentrate on the development of machine industries to produce conventional weapons at great sacrifice of national economic development.

In addition to these pronouncements to the soldiers and the people, the plenum revived the military organization that was established shortly after the Korean War, the Military Committee (*kunsa wiwŏnhoe*).[10] No details of this committee were made public, and although its existence was felt, its operations and membership were not revealed. The original Military Committee during the Korean War was established by the Supreme People's Assembly as its organ, but it was revived this time as a new organization under the supervision of the Central Committee of the party. It was not until after the Fifth Party congress in 1970 that the committee was incorporated into the party bylaws. Article 27 stated that the Military Committee discusses and decides military policy and the methods of its execution, organizes and strengthens the military industries, and directs the military forces.[11]

Kim had made it a policy to speak to the officers and men of the People's Army on every fifth anniversary of its founding. The only exception was during the Korean War when he visited them more often. On the fifteenth anniversary, on February 8, 1963, Kim spoke to the army officers above the level of deputy regimental commanders for political affairs and to other party and government functionaries.[12] In his effort to boost the morale of the soldiers and upgrade their class consciousness, Kim said that many new recruits had neither experienced life under harsh capitalist landowners nor fought against the Japanese colonialists during the liberation struggle or against the American imperialists during the Korean War.

Kim said that some of these young recruits were full of disdain for military training and contemptuous of vigilance and hard work. They even hated war movies and wanted to enjoy life without sacrifice. Some students who went to study abroad even began to resent the fact that they were born Korean. Kim said it was the duty of every army officer to straighten out these ungrateful brats and give them proper Communist training.

On the other hand, Kim said there were some old landlords whose land had been confiscated some seventeen years earlier who still tenaciously held on to the old documents of land ownership, reminded their grandchildren of the boundaries of their old landholdings, and urged them to recover the land when they attained majority. He cited an example of a stubborn old man of seventy-two in Pyongyang who had two of his sons educated in colleges at state expense and still openly opposed the Communist system. Kim warned that the ways of the capitalists do not change, and he asked how the Communists could forget the landlords when the landlords still remembered their land. Kim said that everyone, from the indolent young to the obstinate old, should be indoctrinated and armed with the spirit of class struggle.

As to the content of this class education, Kim said they should be taught to hate imperialists and the corruption of the capitalists and should be armed with socialistic patriotism and Communist moral rectitude. He elaborated on the use of literature and art to accomplish such indoctrination and told the army officers that it was the army's duty to strengthen the class consciousness of not only the soldiers but also the entire population. He admitted that the North Koreans already had the largest army among the socialist countries in proportion to their population, but he intended to arm the entire people and fortify the entire country.[13]

At the commencement address of the seventh graduating class of Kim Il Sung Military Academy in October 1963, Kim said that the graduates' uniforms were all made in North Korea with fabric produced by North Koreans. As late as 1960, uniforms had had to be imported. Similarly, Kim said that formerly they had imported approximately 500,000 tons of food every year to feed the soldiers but were now self-sufficient. With regard to arms and military equipment, Kim emphasized that the North Koreans should become self-reliant, but to become self-reliant in this field did not mean the exclusion of all military assistance from other countries. It meant that the North Koreans should be able to go it alone even when there was no assistance.[14]

Confronted with the temporary suspension of military aid from the Soviet Union during the Soviet-Korean dispute, Kim reiterated the need to arm the soldiers not only with the most advanced weapons but also with the most stringent revolutionary thought and hatred toward the enemy. On the arming of the entire people, Kim said that the North Korean economy had reached a stage where it could produce enough arms to equip everyone with a rifle. In line with the policy of fortifying the entire country, Kim urged the digging of tunnels near the front and the building of factories in underground shelters. Should hostilities begin, the entire nation should serve military objectives and take orders from the military.

At the time when their relationship with the Soviet Union was worsening, such heavy emphasis on a military buildup on their own was costly to the North Koreans in terms of economic development. Although their policy called for the simultaneous development of economic construction and military buildup, the two were mutually exclusive goals in the case of North Korea because their level of economic development rarely complemented their sophisticated military arsenals supplied by the Soviet Union. Indeed, there was evidence that such emphasis on the military sector retarded economic development. During the dispute with the Soviet Union from 1962 to 1964, the North Korean military establishment suffered considerable setbacks in its capabilities. Kim may have succeeded in arming the entire people and fortifying the entire country, but he lost ground both in economic development and in military strength.

When the military policy was first announced at the fifth plenum in December 1962, the party gave the people ten tasks in economic development, impossible goals to fulfill even with superhuman effort.[15] In his New Year address in 1963, Kim frankly admitted that some of the economic goals he had set for the past year were not met — for example, in such important areas as production of steel and coal.[16] To counter such setbacks, Kim said there were serious defects in manpower administration and ordered the mobilization of one million women into the labor force.[17] He also said that since the workers were not strictly observing the eight-hour workday, he was instituting a 480-minute workday instead.[18] He then divided the day into three segments: work eight hours, study eight hours, and rest eight hours. Under such a system, what gave way was the workers' rest hours.

In an effort to counterbalance the dwindling supply of foreign exchange resulting from the worsening relationship with the fraternal socialist countries, particularly the Soviet Union and Eastern Europe, Kim asked the mine workers to produce more precious metals. At one point he gave a blanket order to produce enough in the mining sector to earn approximately $100 million in foreign exchange.[19] He also gave a stern warning to the slothful and even suggested that workers should not drink excessively after work so they could conserve energy for the next day. He encouraged the workers by naming campaigns in honor of their sacrifices,[20] but as time passed there were more restrictions than the workers could follow. Kim at one point even set a quota of what each farm household was allowed to have — for example, one lamb, one or two pigs, about thirty chickens, and no cow.[21]

Kim himself seems to have made an honest effort to boost the morale of the people by using his personal charm to the limit. He toured various factories, cooperative farms, and schools and colleges, and wrote a number of directives, theses, and instructions to help the workers, but the response was slow and disappointing. He mobilized the North Korean intellectuals to bring about technical revolution with innovation in every economic endeavor, but such an upsurge in technology was not to be gained overnight. There was no immediate groundswell of devotion among the people to a total effort in the name of socialist patriotism.[22] Even nature was not cooperating. A tornado and inclement weather in 1964 reduced agricultural production below the level of 1963.[23]

It was domestic difficulty in both the military and economic sectors that prompted the North Koreans to react swiftly to the Soviet Union after the fall of Khrushchev in 1964. Not until they had restored a more amicable relationship with the Soviet Union were they able to make simultaneous progress in both economic development and military strength. Immediately after the fall of Khrushchev, Kim Il and Kim Ch'ang-man went to Moscow to help celebrate the forty-seventh anniversary of the October Revolution, and shortly after Premier Kosygin's visit to the North in 1965, a military delegation headed by Ch'oe Kwang, North Korean chief of staff, went to Moscow in May 1965 to help celebrate the twentieth anniversary of the Soviet victory over Germany.

Soviet technicians returned, trade volume increased, and a number of agreements on technical assistance programs were signed. In March 1966 Ch'oe Yong-gŏn headed the North Korean government delegation to the twenty-third congress of the Communist Party of the Soviet Union, and the following year Kim Il returned to Moscow to sign another agreement in March with K. T. Mazurov, the first vice-chairman of the Council of Ministers, on economic, scientific and technical cooperation. The mutual visits were frequent, and they resulted in a number of agreements. In May 1967 Vladimir Novikov visited Pyongyang, and North Korean vice-premier Yi Chu-yŏn visited Moscow in October 1967, establishing an economic, scientific, and technical consultative commission.[24]

Kim may have regained some lost ground by the renewed trade with the Soviet Union and may also have updated his military equipment by getting both needed parts and replacements, but the problems related to the policy of simultaneous emphasis on economic development and the strengthening of military capabilities were affecting the basic growth of national strength. The military outlay in the national budget jumped from about 2.6 percent in 1961 to 5.8 percent in 1964, reaching 10 percent by 1966. The following year it tripled to 30.4 percent and remained in the 30 percent range until 1971.

Kim indicated as early as 1965 that the pace of economic development was retarded because of increased military expenditures, and the goals of the seven-year economic plan would not be met on schedule.[25] But Kim kept up relentless pressure to achieve the goals set for the plan. He even outlined the methods that should be used to achieve balanced, unified, and detailed planning of the national economy,[26] but no matter what sort of plan was devised, the people began to show signs of exhaustion. The arms in one hand and the hammer and sickle in the other were too heavy for the North Korean worker, and the hand that held the hammer and sickle gradually began to sink.

The Second Party Conference: 1966

According to the party bylaws, party conferences are to be convened between party congresses to discuss and decide urgent problems of policy and strategy. These conferences are empowered to recall members and candidate members of the Central Committee and elect their replacements.[27] At the thirteenth plenum of the Central Committee in March and April 1966, Kim Kwang-hyŏp announced the convocation of the Second Party Conference in October 1966. The conference was to serve three purposes. The first was to announce the extension of the seven-year economic plan for an additional three years. Kim Il, the first vice-premier, reported that the extension had become necessary because of the heavy burden the nation had to bear in defense expenditures. The second purpose was for Kim Il Sung to break his long silence about North Korean relations with the fraternal socialist countries, particularly North Korea's position in the Sino-Soviet dispute. Moreover, Kim Il Sung made comments on the acceleration of socialist construction and the conditions for revolution in South Korea. The third purpose was to replace a number of demoted and purged members and candidate members of the Central Committee since the Fourth Party Congress in 1961.

On the first subject, the extension of the economic plan for another three years to 1970 was made official, but there was no change in the policy of simultaneously fulfilling the goals of the economic plan and strengthening military capabilities. With the normalization of relations with the Soviet Union, much was expended to equip the military but at great expense to economic development. On the second subject, Kim made a strong statement about North Korea's independence from both the Soviet Union and China and dissociated himself from the Sino-Soviet dispute. He also made a number of important statements on the South Korean revolution, and the conference adopted a declaration regarding the North Korean position on the situation developing in Vietnam.[28]

It was the third purpose of the conference that revealed the significant change that had taken place in the party hierarchy and leadership. The party conference did not publicize the new members and candidate members of the Central Committee, but from the composition of the executive group of the conference it was clear that more than one-fifth of the members of the Central Committee were replaced, and there were numerous partisans and generals in the new lineup. The conference elected new officers of the Central Committee whose names were made public. Out of eleven members of the Political Committee, five who were not partisans were removed: Kim Ch'ang-man, Pak Chŏng-ae, Chŏng Il-yong, Nam Il, and Yi Chong-ok.

Kim Ch'ang-man was the only remaining member of the Yanan group who turned against his fellow members to serve the partisans, but he was rumored to have been purged for championing the Chinese cause during the Soviet-Korean dispute. He may have been responsible for writing the criticism of the Soviet Union because he was one of the most experienced in casting aspersions on the integrity of others. He accompanied Kim Il on a visit to the Soviet Union in November 1964 shortly after the fall of Khrushchev, and he may have maintained a strong anti-Soviet and pro-Chinese attitude contrary to the need of the party. He was also responsible for directing the work of intellectuals and scientists, and he spoke on the subject of revising higher education and improving the quality of scientific research projects as late as July 1, 1965, at the eleventh plenum of the Central Committee, but the work of the intellectual community in the North fell far short of meeting the party's needs in both the economic and military sectors.[29]

Pak Chŏng-ae was once the most powerful woman in the North, but she was not a partisan. She had earlier relinquished her chairmanship of the Democratic Women's Union to Kim Ok-sun, a partisan. Contrary to some accounts she was not purged at this time, for she was later elected to the fourth Supreme People's Assembly as well as to its Standing Committee. She may have been purged shortly thereafter, however, for there was no further news about her from the North.[30]

Similarly Nam Il, the last remaining member of the Soviet-Korean group, was removed to make room for partisans in the Political Committee. He was earlier relieved of his post in the Foreign Ministry but was kept in other posts in the cabinet.[31] In addition, two technocrats, Chŏng Il-yong and Yi Chong-ok, were relieved of their places on the Political Committee. These men were not purged. They were recruited into the fourth cabinet in 1967 as minister of building materials industry and vice-premier of the cabinet, respectively, and Yi Chong-ok was made premier at the sixth Supreme People's Assembly in 1977.

The six remaining members were partisans or partisan-related: Kim Il Sung, Ch'oe Yong-gŏn, Kim Il, Pak Kŭm-ch'ŏl, Kim Kwang-hyŏp, and Yi Hyo-sun. The five new members elected at the Second Party Conference were all partisans except Kim Ik-sŏn, who was promoted from candidate membership of the Political Committee to full membership. Kim Ik-sŏn was also chairman of the Inspection Committee. Those newly elected were Kim Ch'ang-bong, Pak Sŏng-ch'ŏl, Ch'oe Hyŏn, and Yi Yŏng-ho. Not only was the Political Committee now without technocrats and completely dominated by partisans and partisan-related persons, but nearly all its members had professional military backgrounds; some, such as Kim Kwang-hyŏp, Kim Ch'ang-bong, Ch'oe Hyŏn, and Yi Yŏng-ho, were generals and admirals on active duty.

A similar pattern can be observed in the candidate membership of the Political Committee. The number of candidate members was increased from four to nine at the Second Party Conference. Except for Kim Ik-sŏn, who became a regular member of the Political Committee, the remaining three nonpartisan members (Yi Chu-yŏn, Ha Ang-ch'ŏn, and Han Sang-du) were replaced by partisan generals. The nine new candidate members were, in rank order, four partisan generals on active military duty (Sŏk San, Hŏ Pong-hak, Ch'oe Kwang, and O Chin-u), two partisans (Yim Ch'un-ch'u and Kim Tong-gyu), and three partisan-related candidate members (Kim Yŏng-ju, who was Kim Il Sung's younger brother, and Pak Yong-guk and Chŏng Kyŏng-bok, both known to be sons of deceased partisans).

The party conference also made one important structural change in the party organization by replacing the offices of chairman and vice-chairmen of the Central Committee with a secretariat staffed by one general secretary and ten secretaries. Kim Il Sung was elected general secretary, and the ten secretaries were, with one exception, partisan generals who were members and candidate members of the Political Committee. The exception was Kim To-man, who was reported to be a communication expert.[32] According to the party bylaws, revealed after the Fifth Party Congress in 1970, the members of the secretariat were elected by the Central Committee and decided on problems related to cadres and the internal affairs of the party.

The rise of the partisans was felt by all at the time of the Fourth Party Congress in 1961, but the emphasis on the military buildup in the North from 1962 to 1966 brought the partisan generals and partisan-related people to political prominence. This process also excluded technocrats and replaced them with partisan generals who were on active duty. This phenomenon resembled somewhat the trend in Japan in the 1930s when fanatic military officers controlled politics.

When fanatic military men, however patriotic or whatever their cause, dominate a political system and attain unchecked prominence, the system tends to overreact to the slightest provocation. Indeed, at times such a system tends to *initiate* incidents that cannot be controlled. When such overmilitarization occurred at the end of 1966, the North Koreans attempted a number of unprovoked incidents against South Korea and the United States.

12

The South Korean Revolution

North Korea's emphasis on strengthening military capability might have come from a fear of isolation, for what concerned them most was their security. But when they restored normal relations with the Soviet Union, they used their newfound military strength to back up their independent course of action. They began to participate more in the affairs of nonaligned nations, and a number of heads of state visited from faraway countries — among them Modibo Keita of Mali in 1964, Massamba Deba of Congo (Brazzaville) in 1965, and Mokto Ould Daddah of Mauritania in 1967. Most Koreans could not even pronounce their names let alone know whence they came.

Kim's primary concern, however, was an increasingly militant South Korea. The development in the South after the fall of two republics was something he could not overlook. Due primarily to his own difficulties at the beginning of the Sino-Soviet dispute, shuttling back and forth from Moscow to Beijing, Kim lost the opportunity to exploit the vulnerable political situation of the South in the early 1960s. Two governments fell in rapid succession in Seoul, one toppled by students and the other by soldiers. Kim remarked that South Korean politics were so corrupt that it mattered little whether the country was ruled by Syngman Rhee, Syngman Chang, or Syngman Park.[1]

The real development after the military revolution of May 1961 was something quite different, however, and Kim had to pay close attention — not so much because he recognized the potential the young generals later demonstrated in modernizing the country, but because the new regime in the South was about to consolidate political power by strengthening its ties with Japan through normalizing relations for the first time since the end of Japanese colonial rule in Korea. Furthermore the young military group in the South was contemplating sending Korean troops to participate in the Vietnam War on the American side, the first time in history that Koreans had ever sent troops outside their country.

In view of the help the South Koreans had received from the United Nations during the Korean War, there was little resistance to sending troops to defend South Vietnam from the "Communist menace" but considerable opposition to the conclusion of a normalization treaty with Japan. It was this opportunity that the North Koreans were trying to exploit in order to implant a viable revolutionary organization of their own in the South.

Kim's Unification Policy

Kim had always claimed that unification was the foremost goal of his government and the party, but from the conclusion of the Korean War to 1964 he had not once devoted an entire speech to the question of reunification. He had always managed to mention the problem at the end of speeches on various anniversaries or party congresses. Even on these occasions, the only time he consistently spoke about unification was when talking to soldiers on the anniversaries of the People's Army.[2] It was the eighth plenum of the fourth Central Committee in February 1964 that seriously discussed the question of unification by helping to foster a revolution in South Korea. One of the items on the agenda of the plenum was a discussion of conditions in South Korea and the party's task in unification.[3]

On the last day of the plenum, February 27, 1964, Kim spoke at length about the party's policy on the unification of Korea.[4] Kim said that the strengthening of three revolutionary forces was needed to bring about reunification of the fatherland: the revolutionary force of the North, the revolutionary force of the South, and the international revolutionary force. Kim repeated the usual slogans about strengthening North Korea's political, economic, and military capabilities, but on the South Korean revolution he cited an alleged rise in the suicide rate among the desperate people in the South and urged them to organize a party deeply rooted among the masses. He emphasized that all small revolutionary organizations in the South should form a united front against the counterrevolutionary forces. Kim said that the North Korean people were willing to help them, and he urged that South Korean defectors to the North be trained and returned for revolutionary work in the South.

On the strengthening of the international revolutionary forces, Kim departed from his usual reliance on the Soviet Union and China and urged close ties with the nonaligned Third World countries in order to isolate the "American imperialists." He went on to speak in detail about methods of implementing these policies, but the text of this portion of the speech was kept secret.[5] The reports of the eighth plenum stressed that liberating the people of the South was the most pressing revolutionary task of the party.[6]

In the South, the young generals who had successfully carried out the military coup in May 1961 were ensconced firmly in a new third republic and pushed their policy of normalizing relations with Japan. In spite of massive student demonstrations in major universities in Seoul, the normalization treaty was concluded in June 1965.[7] The North Korean reaction was a swiftly mounted propaganda campaign to nullify the treaty.[8]

What infuriated Kim and his generals even more was the agreement between the United States and Korea to send South Korean troops to Vietnam. The first noncombat troops left Korea in January 1965. Shortly thereafter, in February 1965, the United States began to bomb North Vietnamese targets. Kim on numerous occasions condemned South Korea's decision to send soldiers and said he stood ready to send North Korean troops to Vietnam.[9] What Kim really wanted was to form an international army of the socialist and Communist countries to aid Vietnam, but such cooperation in the midst of the Sino-Soviet dispute was not feasible. Kim was reluctant to face South Korean soldiers in the jungle of Vietnam. He clearly preferred to face them in Korea, but he was suffering from strained relations with the Soviet Union during the first half of the 1960s and from the worsening relationship with the Chinese in the second half.

His relationship with the Soviet Union after he declared his independence was not the same as when he had been the faithful chief of a Soviet satellite country. Even then Kim well remembered that it was the Chinese and not the Soviet Union who had helped him when he was thrown back to the Yalu River during the Korean War. However, during the second half of the 1960s, the Chinese did not hesitate in casting aspersions on Kim for fawning on the Russians. Eventually Kim chose to incite a revolution in the South and create diversionary actions in Korea.

Kim's effort to create a revolutionary force to incite antigovernment activities in the South was not as easy as he and his partisans first thought. When they purged the South Korean Communists under Pak Hŏn-yŏng, the North Koreans lost most of their supporters in the South and successive governments in the South uprooted organized Communist activities after the Korean War. The foremost concern of the third republic in the South was to institute an anti-Communist system and establish a tough intelligence system to enforce anti-Communist laws.

Kim admitted that the struggle of the revolutionary forces in the South was an arduous task undertaken by a small group of people, but he urged the South Korean people to oppose the reentry of Japanese militarism in Korea by fighting against the normalization treaty.[10] What Kim failed to distinguish was opposition to the normalization treaty and support for the cause of communism in Korea. Those South Korean opposition leaders who opposed the government and the treaty were as anti-Communist as the government, if not more so, and Kim refused to recognize this fact. Kim often repeated his basic policy of creating a revolutionary party, winning over the core leaders of the opposition, and uniting the working masses around that party. He said that the small South Korean revolutionary force should be saved from brutal suppression and expanded in preparation for the decisive hour of revolution, but these were tasks easier said than done.[11]

Within the party an unofficial organ called the Liaison Bureau directed the South Korean operation. It had been created by Communists from South Korea who directed the old underground operation there, but after the purge of the South Korean Communists in the North it had been taken over by Soviet-Koreans such as Pak Il-yŏng and Yim Hae, who knew nothing about the situation in the South. The bureau's operation has always remained secret, but under the Soviet-Koreans even its existence was not mentioned. When the partisans took over the bureau at the time of the Fourth Party Congress in 1961, Yi Hyo-sun was appointed director. Yi, perhaps the most prominent party official ever to direct the bureau, was a partisan and vice-chairman of the Central Committee. He served the bureau from 1961 to 1967.

Under Yi's direction, there were a few isolated incidents in which North Korean agents infiltrated the South. Yi knew better than anyone else how difficult it was to penetrate the anti-Communist front; and he knew that organizing a revolutionary force, selecting its core leaders, and forming a united front of the masses was a nearly impossible assignment. But during the fifteenth and sixteenth plenums of the Central Committee, held in May, June, and July 1967, Kim and his partisan generals decided to force the issue of the South Korean revolution.[12]

During these two plenums, Kim and his partisan generals removed two of the most powerful nonmilitary partisans, Pak Kŭmch'ŏl and Yi Hyo-sun, the fourth and fifth-ranking members of the Political Committee and secretaries of the party. They had been reelected to their prominent positions in the party less than a year earlier at the Second Party Conference in October 1966. Moreover, a number of partisan and partisan-related members of the Central Committee engaged in propaganda and ideological work were purged, including Hŏ Sŏk-sŏn, Kim To-man, and Ko Hyŏk.[13]

Yi was removed from the Liaison Bureau for failure to carry out more actively the party's policy on South Korean revolution. Pak Kŭm-ch'ŏl was accused of being unenthusiastic about the party's military policy. Hŏ Sŏk-sŏn was chief editor of the party organ,

Nodong sinmun, and was also chairman of the Korean Journalists Union and the Social Science Department of the Academy of Sciences. Kim To-man was in charge of the propaganda and agitation section of the Central Committee, Ko Hyŏk was chairman of the culture and arts section of the Central Committee as well as vice-premier of the cabinet in September 1966. In his lecture to party cadres on October 11, 1969, Kim Il Sung said that a number of "bad fellows" who had been in charge of ideological work had failed to propagate the party's great achievements and had not taught young cadres the great successes the people had achieved. He said that it was only after the fifteenth plenum of the fourth Central Committee that the party's ideological and propaganda work had been correctly carried out.[14]

While the details and exact circumstances surrounding the purges of these high-ranking partisans were not made public, this was the first time members of the partisan group had been purged. Kim himself did not mention any of these men disparagingly. In the absence of factual evidence, the reasons for the downfall of these prominent partisans can only be conjectured. Several factors may have contributed. One might have been the split between the military and nonmilitary partisans. Neither Yi Hyo-sun nor Pak Kŭmch'ŏl was a fighting soldier during the anti-Japanese partisan days; both had been arrested early and spent most of the Japanese occupation period in jail. Nor had they ever been members of the North Korean military establishment. These men might have resisted the fanatic enthusiasm of the partisan generals for setting unrealistic goals for the party. They might also have resisted the growing political prominence of an unusually large number of generals on active duty.

Another factor might have been the role of Yi and Pak in the Soviet-Korean dispute. All the purged men, including the editors of *Nodong sinmun,* the chairman of the propaganda and agitation section of the Central Committee, and the head of the culture and arts section of the party, might have contributed significantly to the denigration of the Soviet Union during the Soviet-Korean dispute — to the great displeasure of the generals, who needed sophisticated military weapons from the Soviet Union. Furthermore, when the relationship between the Soviet Union and North Korea was normalized in the latter half of the 1960s, they might have wanted to replace these men who had championed anti-Soviet sentiment in the propaganda and agitation section.

Perhaps the most immediate cause for the dismissal may have been differences over the strategy of the South Korean revolution. Yi, who had been in charge of the Liaison Bureau, might have revealed the reality of the difficulties in the underground operations in the South, giving the details of past failures. The partisan generals might have interpreted these to mean a lack of tactical guerrilla skills among nonmilitary partisans. They might have thought that an outright guerrilla operation in the South should replace the tactics of political subversion.

Whatever the reason, Yi was replaced by a partisan general, Hŏ Pong-hak.[15] After the sixteenth plenum of the Central Committee in July 1967, the attention of all the North Korean leaders was directed toward the South, and the unchecked fervor of the partisan generals added fuel to the desire to unify the country. Kim himself emphasized the importance of liberating the southern half of the country during his own generation, and he warned that they should not bequeath a divided fatherland to the next generation.[16]

In his speech at the fourth Supreme People's Assembly on December 16, 1967, when he revealed his ten-point task of the government, Kim said that one of the government's immediate concerns was to help the revolutionary forces in the South and to bring about the liberation of the South Korean people "as soon as possible."[17] In this speech Kim even mentioned a small affair known as the Kim Tae-su Spy Incident, involving a professor of Kyŏngbuk University. Kim said that this sort of activity was the beginning of a fierce revolutionary struggle by the South Korean people and had not been instigated by North Korean espionage agents. He said that no amount of brutal repression could dampen the indomitable spirit of these revolutionaries and that the northern brethren had a duty to support these activities vigorously. In fact, the Kim Tae-su incident was instigated by his defector brother, Kim Hyŏng-su, who was sent back to the South to organize revolutionary groups.[18]

In his speech Kim went a step further than in any speech he had ever made on the South Korean revolution and said that "the present situation requires us to conduct all our work in a more active, more revolutionary manner and subordinate everything to the struggle to accomplish the South Korean revolution by giving them support in their struggle and to reunify our country."[19] It was this call and the rise of the partisan generals that brought about two subsequent disturbances of significant proportions in the South. One was a daring attempt by North Korean commandos on the life of the South Korean president, Park Chung Hee; the other was the sacrifices involving the establishment of the Revolutionary Party for Reunification in the South. The rise of the generals to political prominence and the programs of arming the entire people and fortifying the entire nation eventually led to dangerous adventures in the seizing of the *Pueblo* and the downing of the American EC-121 spy plane.

The Commando Raids

The partisan generals began to implement the policy of South Korean revolution from late 1967, and the method they chose was to send a small guerrilla unit to the South for a limited purpose. This might have been a logical alternative for the partisan generals because they needed quick and spectacular results to show for their takeover of the South Korean operation. Perhaps the most daring was the attempt to assassinate South Korean President Park Chung Hee in conjunction with the celebration of the twentieth anniversary of the founding of the Korean People's Army on February 8, 1968.

In anticipation of the twentieth anniversary celebration, many activities were planned and there was an unusually large number of articles in newspapers and magazines linking the People's Army and the South Korean revolution.[20] There were lengthy editorials in *Nodong sinmun* on January 6 and 10, 1968, and a political opinion on Kim's militant leadership on January 6. Ch'oe Hyŏn, the old partisan general who had seldom written in the past, presented a lengthy article on the role of the People's Army in *Nodong sinmun* on January 18.[21]

The commando squad of thirty-one armed guerrillas left Pyongyang on January 16, 1968, and crossed the 38th parallel near Kaesŏng two days later. They spent the first night in the South on the mountain near Pŏbwŏlli but were immediately detected by a pair of villagers. It was reported that the squad debated whether to silence the villagers by killing them or to release them with a stern warning not to report the squad to the authorities. They chose the latter, and the villagers, of course, reported them. Nevertheless, they reached Seoul and approached within five hundred meters of the presidential residence on the night of January 21. After a brief skirmish, twenty-seven commandos were killed on the spot, three escaped, and one was captured alive.[22]

The survivor, Kim Sin-jo, revealed that the assassination squad was organized in July 1967 as a special unit of the 124th Division, located in Yŏnbaek county, Hwanghae pukto, and was trained to infiltrate the presidential residence in Seoul and assassinate President Park. He also confessed that there were a number of other armed guerrilla units trained for infiltration into the South. A number of small units consisting of three to five armed espionage agents were reported in various coastal areas. Some 120 guerrillas were reported to have landed from October to November 1968 in the eastern coastal areas near Ulsan, Kyŏngsang pukto, for example, but none of these high-risk guerrilla activities was successful. The South Korean police and intelligence forces stepped up their vigil and captured most of the North Korean armed guerrillas after the attack on the presidential residence.

The North Koreans, on their side, reported that a number of South Korean armed guerrillas spontaneously rose up to fight against the dictatorial regime and reported the attack on the presidential residence in detail as early as the following morning. From January 23 on, *Nodong sinmun* reported daily the armed guerrilla activities in other regions such as Koyang county and P'aju county of Kyŏnggido. The continuous reporting by the North Korean papers of small incidents involving only a few armed guerrillas in remote villages suggested strongly the execution of a plan devised to incite unrest in the South. They reported that armed guerrilla activities during 1967 numbered fewer than one hundred, but they then increased sharply and by October 1968 more than two hundred such incidents had been reported in the South. Kim Il Sung himself urged the South Koreans to rise up and said they were fighting a do-or-die battle to overturn colonial rule in the South.[23]

These were the usual inflated statistics from North Korea. In truth, the North Korean armed guerrillas and the commando raids all ended in defeat, and none accomplished its objective. What really saved the failures of the wild adventures toward the South was the seizure of the American intelligence vessel *Pueblo*. From all indications on the North Korean side, the capture of the *Pueblo* was an accident, not a planned action methodically executed. Irrespective of the legality of the ship's location, whether within territorial waters or on the high seas, the seizure of the vessel was an unexpected prize, caught with minimum effort and no preparation. Indeed, it was their good fortune to have dared an American navy commander who would surrender without fighting. Analysis of the domestic North Korean scene makes it clear that Kim Il Sung and his partisan generals were concentrating their energies on the South Korean revolution. It would have been unthinkable for them to seek a direct confrontation with the United States while they were nursing strained relations with China and barely recovering from a sharp confrontation with the Soviet Union.[24]

When the United States carrier *Enterprise* was positioned in the Sea of Japan, Kim panicked and mobilized the entire armed forces. Kim had been reciting his self-reliance theme too long and too often to expect any help from his usual sources of assistance, and his newly acquired friends in the nonaligned nations were no friends at all in this situation. Furthermore, he was not really ready to test his self-defense theory, not with such a formidable enemy in any case. All festivities planned for the twentieth anniversary of the founding of the Korean People's Army were canceled, and even the report he made on February 8, 1968, at a small ceremony in the evening was the shortest speech he had ever made on such an anniversary.[25] It was indeed the great restraint exercised by the United States, suffering abject humiliation to avoid the expansion of military involvement in Asia beyond Vietnam, that gave Kim comfort and cause for jubilation.

In answer to rumors circulated at the time that the North Korean commando attempt on the South Korean president's life and the capture of the *Pueblo* were closely coordinated with the Tet offensive of the Vietcong, Kim frankly said there was no such coordination.[26] Kim's contributions to the cause of the Vietnamese people were, first, to employ diversionary tactics in South Korea to pressure the South Koreans not to go to Vietnam and, second, to give North Vietnam the material assistance it needed.[27] But to confront the Americans in Korea was neither planned nor contemplated. The seizure of the *Pueblo* was a by-product of the heightened militarization of the North. Although Kim congratulated the officers and men of the 661st Army Unit and the 2423rd unit of the North Korean Coast Guard for their capture of the *Pueblo*, Kim and his partisan generals knew the price they had paid for such military adventurism.[28] After the *Pueblo*, Kim was called an ever-victorious, iron-willed genius, but few understood how fortunate he was to have avoided a direct confrontation.

The Revolutionary Party for Reunification

While the armed guerrilla and commando operations were conducted for a limited and short-range objective, a more serious effort was made to implant a revolutionary party in the South. A number of spies and agents were caught by the South Korean authorities trying to establish a foothold in the South. Some of these efforts were made directly from North Korea to South Korea, others were made through Japan, and still others through Europe.[29] One of the most famous cases involved an organization in the South known as the Revolutionary Party for Reunification (*T'ongil hyŏngmyŏng tang*).

The Revolutionary Party for Reunification (RPR) was an underground organization founded by South Korean Communist named Kim Chong-t'ae together with North Korean espionage agents.[30] After finishing two years of college at Tongguk University in Seoul, Kim Chong-t'ae returned to his native province of Kyŏngsang pukto and taught at a number of high schools, among them Andong Normal School and P'ohang High School. He once served as personal secretary to his elder brother, Kim Sang-do, a member of the National Assembly from 1954 to 1958. He managed a small store in Taegu when he was approached by a North Korean agent named Kim Mu-sam in March 1964 to organize an antigovernment revolutionary party.

He left Taegu to meet the chief North Korean agent in the South, Ch'oe Yŏng-do, at Imjado, an island off the southwest coast of Korea in Chŏlla namdo. There he met Ch'oe and was taken to North Korea by boat, arriving at Namp'o, a west coast port near Pyongyang, on March 19, 1964. He stayed in Pyongyang less than a week, returning to Ch'oe in Imjado by March 24. Through this route, he traveled to the North again in April 1964, July 1966, and May 1968, receiving instructions and funds for clandestine operations in the South.

While he was in the North, he was trained and instructed to organize a basic underground organization by recruiting former members of the Workers' Party of South Korea, to publish secret journals, to train cadres from among the students of Seoul National University, to organize a vanguard unit together with small groups of intellectuals, students, and young men, to secure an operational base where guerrillas could be trained, to form a united front of all antigovernment organizations in South Korea, and to prepare for an ultimate armed uprising in Seoul.

Kim Chong-t'ae did carry out some of these directives. The North Koreans claim that Kim and Ch'oe Yŏng-do, who later died of illness, organized the RPR on March 15, 1964, as the central underground organization for the South Korean revolution and pledged to Kim Il Sung that the South Korean revolution would be carried out by South Koreans like himself. He also published a journal, *Hyŏngmyŏng chŏnsŏn* (Revolutionary front), and a magazine, *Ch'ŏngmaek* (The blue ridge), and recruited a graduate of Seoul National University, Yi Mun-gyu, to edit the magazine. Yi too was taken to North Korea for indoctrination and training in May 1967 for approximately three weeks.[31]

The North Koreans claim that Kim Chong-t'ae organized nine separate organizations such as *Sae munhwa yŏn'guhoe* (New Culture Research Association) for students of the College of Arts and Science of Seoul National University, *Pulgyo ch'ŏngnyŏnhoe* (Buddhist Young Men's Association) for the students of Songgyun'gwan University, *Minjok chuŭi yŏn'guhoe* (Nationalism Research Association) for Tongguk University students, *Ch'ŏng-maek hoe* (Blue Ridge Association) for Ewha Women's University students, and others.[32]

The total number of people involved in these and other organizations reached approximately 150.

After the unsuccessful North Korean commando raid to assassinate President Park in January 1968, the search for North Korean agents and Communist sympathizers was intensified by the South Korean intelligence organization. It was not too long thereafter that Kim Chong-t'ae was arrested on July 4, 1968, and his accomplice, Yi Mun-gyu, was arrested on July 24. The South Korean authorities virtually wiped out the entire operation of the Revolutionary Party for Reunification and arrested a total of 158 people related to this organization. Kim Chong-t'ae was quickly prosecuted, convicted, and sentenced to death. The death sentence was carried out on January 24, 1969.[33]

Kim Il Sung's grand design to implant a revolutionary force in the South ended with this incident. There were no spontaneous uprisings and no massive outcry of the South Korean people in response to Kim's call for revolution. In fact, his commando attempt on the life of President Park and the effort to organize a party stiffened the anti-Communist stance of both the government and the people of the South. South Koreans who had experienced the cruelty of communism during the Korean War reacted strongly against armed guerrillas and any attempt to implant a revolutionary organization in the South.

In North Korea, Kim Chong-t'ae was a hero who had followed the instructions of Kim Il Sung. A number of tributes were paid to him. A resolution was passed by the Political Committee of the Central Committee of the party to commemorate him, the Standing Committee of the Supreme People's Assembly awarded him posthumously the title of Hero of the Republic, and the week of July 13 to 19 was observed as a memorial week for Kim Chong-t'ae. Furthermore, the Pyongyang electric locomotive factory was renamed in honor of Kim Chong-t'ae and Haeju Normal College was renamed Kim Chong-t'ae Normal College.[34]

It was only after the execution of Kim Chong-t'ae that the North Koreans made public several documents of the RPR, such as the declaration and twelve-point platform, in August 1969.[35] They also claimed that Kim Chong-t'ae was only the chairman of the Seoul Committee and the RPR continued to function in the

South. This sort of claim only intensified the South Korean vigil and did not serve the North's cause. In his speech at the twentieth anniversary of the founding of the North Korean republic Kim still insisted that the North was the only legitimate government in all Korea and still advocated armed struggle in South Korea.[36]

13

Disintegration of the Partisan Group

By the end of 1968, Kim had come to realize that the prominence of the partisan generals and the militarization of the North had drawbacks as well as advantages. The policy of arming all the people and fortifying the entire country may have prepared the North Koreans militarily, but the militarization cost him the extension of the economic plan and the efforts to arouse revolutionary fervor in the South had failed just as surely as all the efforts before them. In spite of support from the party and the government, the strategy of sending armed guerrillas into the South by the partisan generals was, in some ways, counterproductive — not because it failed but because such military action unified the people behind the government in the South. The seizure of the *Pueblo* might have given Kim the satisfaction of seeing the mighty Americans cowed, but he suffered more from panic over confronting the United States at a time when his allies were not behind him.

Furthermore, the prominence of the partisan generals had reached the stage where every soldier was indoctrinated to uphold the tradition of the anti-Japanese guerrillas in Manchuria, and their influence pervaded every aspect of North Korean politics. Almost everyone who had participated in the guerrilla activities, or was remotely connected to them, sought and occupied positions of influence. Statues were built for past heroes, books were written about them, plays were staged to glorify their past.[1]

The generals even began to give directives on nonmilitary affairs. For example, Kim Kwang-hyŏp, a leading partisan general who was vice-premier as well as secretary of the party, gave a long speech about the advantages of the small-unit management system in agriculture.[2] Furthermore, overconfidence in their own military strength after the *Pueblo* might have become a bit dangerous. While the seizure of the *Pueblo* was an unplanned encounter, the shooting down of the American EC-121 spy plane in 1969 was a deliberate attempt by the partisan generals to prove their military prowess. For Kim, however, the partisan generals were taking him to the brink too often and too recklessly. The overzealous generals were too domineering, and Kim may even have felt a certain threat from them.[3]

Fall of the Partisan Generals

There was no formal announcement of the fall of the partisan generals. Kim had learned to refrain from publicly condemning the purged political leaders of all factions in the early 1960s, and since these generals were partisans, Kim did not mention them at all. While the partisan tradition was being so intensely promoted, any such public denunciation of its prominent members was best avoided. Hŏ Pong-hak, director of the Liaison Bureau, who was responsible for the commando raids and the armed guerrillas sent to the South, was quietly replaced by Kim Chung-nin,[4] a nonmilitary man who was not a partisan but a member of the Standing Committee of the North Korean Red Cross.

In addition to Hŏ, approximately ten of the highest-ranking party generals were removed in 1969. These included Kim Kwang-hyŏp, vice-premier and one of the top partisan generals, secretary, and member of the Political Committee; Defense Minister Kim Ch'ang-bong; chief of staff of the North Korean armed forces, Ch'oe Kwang; Yi Yŏng-ho, admiral and member of the Political Committee; and Sŏk San, minister of public security and secretary of the party.

A South Korean account relates that the purge was ordered by Kim Il Sung in his concluding remarks at the eighteenth plenum of the Central Committee, November 11–16, 1968, but there is no record of such an order.[5] Another report suggests that the criticism of the partisan generals had taken place during the week of January 6–14, 1969, at the fourth plenary meeting of the Fourth Party Committee of the Korean People's Army, presided over by Kim Il Sung.[6]

At this meeting, Kim Il Sung was reported to have criticized the defense minister, Kim Ch'ang-bong, for advocating the use of only sophisticated and modern weapons and neglecting to balance military strength with both conventional and sophisticated weapons to suit the mountainous terrain of Korea. He was reported to have said that Kim Ch'ang-bong was interested only in fast, high-flying modern aircraft while the terrain of Korea called for slow, low-flying aircraft. Kim Ch'ang-bong was also accused of neglecting the fortification of the entire nation, of not securing weapons and equipment underground, and of belittling the importance of the Red Worker-Peasant Militia. He was alleged to have ignored the policy of arming the entire people and to have failed to establish a separate light infantry division to be used in mountainous regions, thus neglecting the joint operations of the regular army and the militia.

Serious conflict seems to have arisen between politically prominent partisans who advocated moderation and the partisan generals who advocated rapid modernization of their military arsenals. It was also alleged that O Chin-u, a partisan general who survived the purge to become the defense minister later, led the criticism session on January 13, 1969, and presented some thirteen items of misconduct by Kim Ch'ang-bong and his military group. These charges included, among others, nepotism in the military ranks, refusal to carry out instructions from the party, inadequate evaluation of the rank and file, the use of the armed forces in nonmilitary work, and waste of military supplies.

In the absence of original documents to substantiate these charges, the circumstances surrounding the purges of these generals are not clear. There is no doubt about their downfall, however, and from their past activities and subsequent developments the charges seem to have concentrated on four major topics. The first was the fact that the partisan generals had neglected the army's experiences during the Korean War and stressed only advanced weapons unsuitable for Korea; the second was the error they committed in carrying out the policy of fortifying the entire country by failing to dig tunnels and, at times, building underground bases in unsafe areas; the third was the allegation that they had wasted military supplies in some sectors and neglected to prepare parts and equipment adequately in others; and the fourth was the accusation that Kim Ch'ang-bong and the partisan generals had attempted to form their own clique within the military and had operated a number of regiments as though they were their own private army.

Kim was reported to have stressed the work of the party committees within the army and to have ordered more party cadres to each military unit. He was also alleged to have emphasized that the North Korean generals should not blindly follow the advice of the Soviet military experts but should adopt military strategies and tactics that fit the needs of the North Korean army. It was not disclosed exactly how many were involved in this round of purges, but many prominent and high-ranking generals were relieved of their positions. Apart from the already mentioned Vice-Premier Kim Kwang-hyŏp, Defense Minister Kim Ch'ang-bong, Chief of Staff Ch'oe Kwang, Admiral Yi Yŏng-ho, and Minister of Public Security Sŏk San, there were Ch'oe Min-ch'ŏl, Chŏng Pyŏng-gap, Kim Cha-rin, and Kim Ch'ang-dŏk, all partisans and all generals of the North Korean army.

Irrespective of the reasons for their dismissal, the fall of these generals signified several things. Foremost was the disintegration of the partisan group that had united behind Kim and supported him all their lives. By the end of the 1960s, Kim may have thought that his position was sufficiently firm, that the partisan group's support was no longer essential. The political prominence of any powerful military group, even his partisans, might have been uncomfortable for Kim, particularly when partisan records had been glorified as a matter of national policy.

The purge also signaled the end of the militant policy of the 1960s. With the restoration of normal relations with both China and the Soviet Union toward the end of the 1960s, Kim might have wanted to return to the neglected work of economic development and the refinement of his political system and thus might have taken this drastic measure to curb the generals. Also significant was the rise of technocrats and young leaders trained by the partisans in their tradition. Along with the emergence of new, young, partisan-trained party faithfuls, the prominence of Kim's immediate relatives was also detectable. Kim Yŏng-ju, Kim's younger brother, advanced to the fourth-ranking party post in the Political Committee, and Kim's wife, Kim Sŏng-ae, replaced Kim Ok-sun, wife of the purged partisan general Ch'oe Kwang, as chairman of the Democratic Women's Union of Korea. Others, including Pak Sŏng-ch'ŏl, Yang Hyŏng-sŏp, and Hŏ Tam, were reported to be related to Kim Il Sung.

The Fifth Party Congress: 1970

When the partisan generals were purged and military expenditures were checked, Kim returned to his old habits of visiting factories, farm cooperatives, mines, steel mills, and other production centers, urging the workers to meet the goals of the seven-year economic plan. In his speech to the eighteenth plenum of the fourth Central Committee on November 16, 1968, Kim revealed his dire need for more workers, explaining the acute manpower shortage to the party cadres. He had resorted to his old tricks to stir the people rather than rewarding them for their hard work. He emphasized political work to alleviate the manpower shortage and said that "most of our workers do not work for money, nor do they need any material incentive. They demand nothing more than the state's guarantee of their livelihood, and they work conscientiously. We must not put material incentives first. We must give priority to political incentives."[7]

Kim's political work was not entirely successful, for at the next plenum, the nineteenth, on June 30, 1969, he lashed out at those unpatriotic workers who coveted material things. He cited the example of a woman who sold eggs for profit after meeting her production quota, and her profit had almost equaled her monthly wage of 54 wŏn. Kim said it was unpatriotic of her to have kept the profit instead of presenting it to the state. He cited another example of a military officer's family that kept twenty to thirty pigs and sold some of them to buy Japanese-made household goods from the repatriated Koreans from Japan. There were even physicians who prescribed medicine for dead patients and then sold the medicine for personal gain.[8] Kim said that these were criminals of society who craved only material things and did not love their country.

In his effort to overcome the manpower shortage, Kim assigned discharged soldiers to a number of farm cooperatives and factories and also recruited more women to join the labor force by replacing men in light industries. He said that everyone must work and that soldiers, office workers, students, and all available workers should be mobilized to help the farmers in the countryside.[9] Kim had more problems. His emphasis on statistical goals compromised the quality of the products. He urged the workers in local industries to upgrade quality so they could export their products. Out of desperation Kim once said that they must improve quality even at the cost of importing machines and other means of production from abroad.[10]

His emphasis on strengthening the military took a heavy toll in the North's economic development, and his renewed emphasis on the hammer and sickle instead of arms on a strict diet of patriotism was not having the intended result. As early as December 1969 Kim claimed that he had reached the goals of the seven-year plan, and he decided to hold the Fifth Party Congress. The resolution at the twentieth plenum of the Central Committee stipulated that the Fifth Party Congress was to be held in October 1970, and it resolved to propose a new five-year economic plan.[11]

The Fifth Party Congress was delayed a month, however, and was held from November 2 to 13, 1970. A six-year economic plan, instead of the five-year economic plan announced in December 1969, was presented and adopted. Unlike the Fourth Party Congress, no foreign party delegations were invited, and in their place a number of Korean social organizations were present to offer congratulations. The most prominently featured was the delegation of the RPR, presumably coming from the South, headed by Yi Chong-hyŏk and two members, O Ch'ang-su and Yi Mun-u.[12] The other delegations included Korean residents in Japan and the Juvenile Corps. There was a mass rally in Pyongyang and 300,000 workers turned out to demonstrate their support for the party. The festivities were limited to such Korean activities as the display of calisthenic exercises and traditional dances, and foreign guests were limited to diplomats stationed in the North.

There were 1,871 delegates representing nearly two million members and 1,160 observers (all Korean) participating in the party congress. Kim Il Sung gave a long and comprehensive report on the work of the Central Committee.[13] On the domestic front, Kim said that North Korea had now completed the transformation from a developing nation into a socialist industrial state, and he supported his argument by citing the accomplishments in machine industries, the technological revolution in agriculture, the new nine-year compulsory education, the ideological unity, the defense system, and the socialist economic management system. He cited a number of statistics in all major industrial sectors comparing recent performance with past accomplishments.

In agriculture, Kim said that for the first time the North had become self-sufficient in grain production for food. On the question of national defense, Kim said that the 1960s were a difficult decade militarily. He supported the policy of arming the entire people and fortifying the entire nation, but he revealed that during this period the country's defense industries had heavily taxed economic development. Among many accomplishments cited in the economic management system, he said that the innovation of the County Cooperative Farm Management Committee was the most significant.

For the future development and consolidation of the socialist system, Kim revealed a new six-year economic plan. After enumerating a long list of goals, he relaxed and said that the technological revolution should be made to liberate the workers and particularly women from the burden of hard labor.[14] But he immediately added that the encroachment of corrupt bourgeois customs such as "Yankee culture" should be resolutely opposed. He still harped on the importance of socialist patriotism and preferred political incentives over material incentives.

On military policy, Kim reflected on some of the difficulties he had with his generals and said that North Korea was a mountainous country with many rivers and a long coastline. The development of military strength should follow closely the topographical conditions of the country, and random importation of sophisticated military arsenals irrespective of the conditions prevailing in the North should be avoided. Kim frankly admitted that North Korea was not an advanced country in military technology and was not able to compete with advanced countries — nor was there any need to compete, for modern warfare was not decided by weapons or military technology but by superiority in political and ideological consciousness of the soldiers. Kim said that he was not threatening anyone; his military capabilities were only for defense.

On the South Korean revolution, Kim repeated the role of the nonexistent RPR and pointed out the party's platform made public in August 1969. Kim outlined his unification policy at this time. He said that the withdrawal of U.S. troops from the South, the liquidation of the present South Korean "military fascist leaders," and the overturning of its government were prerequisites for the unity of the patriotic people of the South and the North and thus for the unification of Korea.

He also stressed cooperation of the international revolutionary forces to oppose the American imperialists and cited the progress he had made with Asian, African, and Latin American countries during the past decade. Last, Kim reemphasized the party work at all levels of every organization, especially the economic, youth, military, security, and judicial organizations.

Kim's report was a review of the 1960s without giving details of what had transpired during the period. His policy of simultaneous economic and military development had failed dismally. He had suffered the consequences of the rise of the partisan military, and he had come to realize that there was not even token, let alone overwhelming, support for him in the South. While he was being called leader of the forty million Korean people by his loyal subjects in the North, he knew his subjects were less than one-third of the entire Korean population. It was obvious that Kim was abandoning the policy of forcing arms on one hand and hammer and sickle on the other, but he still forced the people to work without adequate remuneration or material comfort.

On the second day, Kim Kuk-hun reported on the work of the Central Inspection Committee,[15] but the entire week was spent discussing Kim Il Sung's report. It was not until one week later on November 9 that Kim Il revealed the details of the new six-year plan.[16] Except for an extension of one year from the original five-year plan that was decided on less than a year earlier in December 1969, the plan was not ambitious.

On the last day, November 13, 1970, new officers and members of the Central Committee were elected, and the election revealed much about the changes in party leadership. Out of 117 elected members of the fifth Central Committee, only 31 were reelected members from the fourth Central Committee, and more than two-thirds, 86 members, were newly elected. Similarly in the candidate membership, out of 55 candidate members of the fifth Central Committee, only 7 were reelected from the fourth Central Committee, and the rest were new members.

As to the officers of the party, out of ten secretaries elected at the time of the Second Party Conference in October 1966, only three remained (Ch'oe Yong-gŏn, Kim Il, and Kim Yŏng-ju) and seven were replaced. It is important to note that the seven who were dropped from the secretariat were partisan generals and those who replaced them were partisan-trained technocrats and nonmilitary partisans such as Kim Tong-gyu, Han Ik-su, Kim Chung-nin, Hyŏn Mu-gwang, and Yang Hyŏng-sŏp. Only O Chin-u, who condemned other partisan generals for their militant policy, remained on active duty and a member of the secretariat.

Similarly in the Political Committee, of eleven members all except four (Kim Il Sung, Ch'oe Yong-gŏn, Kim Il, and Ch'oe Hyŏn) were replaced, and all the newly elected members except O Chin-u were nonmilitary partisans (Pak Sŏng-ch'ŏl, Kim Yŏng-ju, Kim Tong-gyu, Sŏ Ch'ŏl, Han Ik-su, and Kim Chung-nin). All candidate members of the Political Committee were replaced with nonmilitary party functionaries (Hyŏn Mu-gwang, Chŏng Chun-t'aek, Yang Hyŏng-sŏp, and Kim Man-gŭm).[17]

It was obvious from the new lineup of the party leadership that the militant policy of the party had changed to promote nonmilitary goals in the North. The only three durable partisans were Kim Il Sung, Ch'oe Yong-gŏn, and Kim Il, and their recruitment of nonmilitary partisans and technocrats was made clear in the choice of Pak Sŏng-ch'ŏl, Kim Tong-gyu, Kim Chung-nin,

Yang Hyŏng-sŏp, and Chŏng Chun-t'aek. The fifth party signaled the emergence of a new group of relatively unknown leaders who were not partisans but partisan-trained party functionaries. These young technocrats were loyal to Kim, and nearly 70 out of 117 members of the new Central Committee of the Fifth Party Congress were new and young leaders.

When Kim was the faithful chief of a Soviet satellite state, he often went to Stalin for direction and guidance. He renewed his old Chinese ties after the Korean War when the Chinese volunteers saved him from sure defeat, but when independence was forced upon him by the Sino-Soviet dispute, he was at a loss. He did not really know what to do with his freedom, nor was he able to cope with the attending problems. He sought a self-reliant and politically independent position, but he managed to engage in an acrimonious feud with both China and the Soviet Union in the process. When he proclaimed his independence from the influence of his longtime benefactors, he looked for new friends, giving elaborate welcomes and lavish gifts to African chiefs most Koreans had never heard of and collecting honorary degrees from Third World countries. The problems of his independence were far more complex than these mundane exercises in personal glory.

The lack of foreign technological assistance retarded the pace of the North's economic development, and Kim's quarrels with his two neighbors undermined the security he had taken for granted so long. He was therefore forced to concentrate on a costly military buildup, and with it came the prominence of the generals. The generals were his old comrades from the plains of Manchuria and fellow partisans, but they began to arm all the people and fortify the entire nation. They imported far more sophisticated military equipment than was needed for the North and at great sacrifice of the economy. The seven-year economic development plan was extended another three years to become an unprecedented ten-year economic plan.

In spite of the domestic difficulties, the generals were charting an adventurous course in dealing with South Korea, sending armed guerrillas and making commando raids into the South. Their efforts to create a diversionary action to keep the South Koreans from sending combat troops to Vietnam failed; and their effort to establish a foothold in the South, utilizing the popular dissent over South Korea's normalization of relations with Japan, also foundered. The South Koreans strengthened their position by strengthening their relations with both Japan and the United States while Kim was suffering from the heavy burden of standing alone and quarreling with both the Soviet Union and China.

Kim's generals became more and more adamant, eventually transforming their military prominence into political influence, and took Kim and the North to the brink of a precipice with the seizure of the *Pueblo* and the shooting down of the American EC-121 spy plane. Kim had to purge most of his loyal comrades in arms from the partisan days. By the time of the Fifth Party Congress, Kim had experienced the trials and tribulations of independence and returned to the normalcy of building a socialist state in the North.

VI

NORTH KOREA
UNDER KIM

Kim once remarked during the Korean War that Stalin had called the Workers' Party of Korea a "shock brigade" of the international workers' movement, and as a disciple of Stalin Kim had always championed the cause of the Communist camp in the cold war.[1] However, in the third and the fourth decades of his rule in the 1970s and the 1980s, there began to be definite signs of realignment in the old East-West confrontation. In addition to the Sino-Soviet dispute, there were the Sino-American rapprochement and the Soviet-Japanese and Sino-Japanese peace treaties. The cold war climate that had created the division of Korea was changing, to say the least, and Kim was forced to readjust his position to cope with the new developments. Kim took two steps in the hope that he could keep up with the rapidly developing international changes. One was to open a dialogue with the South Koreans to explore the possibilities of re-uniting the country; the other was to broaden and solidify his ties with the Third World. In both these endeavors, Kim was less than successful. He refused to adjust his attitude toward the South in the reunification negotiations, and his blatant self-promotion as leader of the Third World won him few friends.

In his dealings with the South, Kim's basic cold war attitude of winning the South over to the cause of communism had not changed, and he showed little respect for the South. The North Koreans maintained a hard line in both humanitarian and political negotiations, trying to bring the South to its knees and force agreement with Kim's conditions for unification. None of his South Korean compatriots was convinced of the sincerity he so often tried to project.

In dealing with the Third World, Kim was successful in having the North join the conference of nonaligned nations, and he was also successful in having many Third World countries endorse a pro–North Korean resolution in the United Nations. But he failed dismally in his foremost objective, projecting himself as leader of the Third World. Although he entertained lavishly, established centers in remote African countries to study his ideas, and hosted elaborate conferences to disseminate his brand of socialist patriotism at great expense to the North Korean people, he won few converts. Except for those he supported financially, none of the Third World leaders looked to him for inspiration. Nor were they convinced of his magic formula for success in North Korea while his international debts were mounting and his diplomats were being deported for unbecoming conduct.

In North Korea, where he commanded absolute respect, however, the situation was different. He succeeded in rewriting the constitution in 1972 and had himself elected president of the republic as well as chairman of the party. As he expanded his relations with Third World countries, his emphasis shifted from party to state. His political power shifted, for example, from use of the Political Committee and the Secretariat of the party to the Central People's Committee of the Supreme People's Assembly.

He greeted his sixtieth and seventieth birthdays with elaborate fanfare, building for himself the largest monuments ever seen in Korea. His absolute power surpassed that exercised by monarchs of the traditional Korean kingdom. He exalted the nonexistent revolutionary past of his parents only to prove himself a pious son, and he took steps to have his son succeed him. The rumor of a succession struggle swept the North in the mid-1970s, bringing down a few more loyal partisans in the process. By the Sixth Party Congress, however, it was clear that Kim's will prevailed.

Kim may have fulfilled his personal ambition and attained a position far beyond his wildest imagination, but what he built in the North resembled a personal domain more than a Communist or socialist state. His words were laws and his slightest whim was command. He may have crowned himself with personal glories and forced the people to cater to his every fancy, but his prescription of hard work on the strict diet of socialist patriotism and loyalty to him was less than adequate for North Korea's development in the rapidly changing world. He still emphasized overproduction in mining to earn foreign exchange and selling raw materials to import manufactured goods. Worst of all, his vast self-esteem suppressed the people, isolated them from the rest of the world, and denied them the power to chart their own future.

14

South Korea and the Third World

The Shanghai communique of February 27, 1972, issued by the United States and China brought a number of diplomatic realignments in East Asia. Soviet Foreign Minister Andrei Gromyko visited Japan to arrange for a Soviet-Japanese peace treaty in 1972, and Japanese Prime Minister Tanaka visited Beijing for the Sino-Japanese peace treaty in September 1972. A number of important emissaries from both China and the Soviet Union came to the North to explain the changing relations, and numerous party and government delegations visited both Moscow and Beijing to ascertain the new developments.[1] Learning from his experience in the 1960s, Kim did not criticize either China or the Soviet Union in their new relationship with the United States and Japan, but he himself remained a warrior and condemned the United States, calling President Nixon's visit to China and the Soviet Union the great surrender of a defeated American.[2]

Dialogues with South Korea

Although Kim condemned the United States at every opportunity, he began to respond to the changing conditions of the 1970s. As early as the second plenum of the fifth Central Committee in April 1971, he began to discuss the problem of reunification seriously. The plenum emphasized the struggle against American imperialists, the Japanese militarists, and their agents in South Korea to bring about reunification of the fatherland. Similarly the third plenum, held in November 1971, reaffirmed the militant intention of the party to deal decisively with the "puppet regime" of the South.[3] Kim may have seriously considered the problems of unification, but he certainly did not change his basic attitude toward the South.

The North Koreans agreed to speak to South Korean representatives of the Red Cross in August 1971, but Kim's motive from the very beginning was influenced not by cooperation with the South Korean efforts but by condemnation of the South's leaders. Even before any substantive issues were taken up in the Red Cross, he personally accused the South Korean leaders of using delaying tactics. He then implied that they had been forced to comply with the North Korean proposal for talks because they could not contain the outcry of the people for dialogue with the North.[4] It seemed as though Kim was more interested in claiming credit for the initiation of talks than in the substance of the negotiations.

The initiative to convene the Red Cross talks, to be sure, came from the president of South Korean National Red Cross, Ch'oe Tu-sŏn, who, on August 12, 1971, proposed to exchange information and explore the possibilities of reuniting families dispersed in the North and South. The North Koreans agreed to this proposal on August 14, 1971. The North often cites the eight-point national reunification proposal announced at the fifth session of the fourth Supreme People's Assembly (April 12–14, 1971) and also refers to the proposal Kim made on August 6, 1961, as their initiative for the talks, but no such talks by the Red Cross were suggested in either proposal.[5]

More important than the Red Cross talks was Kim's apparent willingness to discuss the reunification question through political consultation. After two secret missions, one by the director of the South Korean Central Intelligence Agency, Yi Hu-rak, to Pyongyang, and another by Vice-Premier Pak Sŏng-ch'ŏl, representing Kim's younger brother Kim Yŏng-ju, to Seoul, a dramatic joint

communiqué was issued on July 4, 1972.[6] In addition to the communiqué, an agreement was reached on the same day to install a
direct telephone line between Pyongyang and Seoul to facilitate the
discussion.

After three separate preliminary meetings in subsequent months,
both sides came to agree on the establishment of the North-South
Coordinating Committee on November 4, 1972.[7] The committee
held three meetings: the first in Seoul from November 30 to December 2, 1972, the second in Pyongyang from March 14 to March
16, 1973, and the third in Seoul from June 12 to June 14, 1973. The
fourth meeting was scheduled to be held in Pyongyang on August
28, 1973, but the North Koreans declined to convene it.

The South Korean position was based upon recognition of the
disparate political system of the North and South, noninterference
in the internal affairs of each side, nonimposition of one system
upon the other, and the promotion of mutual cooperation transcending the systemic differences between them. The South Koreans also proposed a number of measures to begin modest cooperation in economic and sociocultural fields.[8]

The North Koreans, on the other hand, sought to settle military
questions first and proposed cessation of the military buildup, reduction of men in arms to fewer than 100,000, withdrawal of all
foreign troops, including those of the United States, from Korea,
cessation of importation of arms, and a peace treaty incorporating
these propositions. In answer to the South Korean proposition of
gradual and modest cooperation in economic and sociocultural
fields, the North Koreans countered with cooperation in five
major fields simultaneously: political, economic, military, cultural,
and diplomatic endeavors.[9]

The South Korean delegates who traveled to the North for the
meeting reported that Kim Il Sung was very much interested in
the talks in the beginning, but he soon lost interest and refused
even to greet the South Korean official delegates as early as the
second meeting held in Pyongyang in March 1973. When the
North Koreans came to Seoul in June 1973 for the third meeting,
the entire North Korean delegation merely repeated its earlier position and refused to participate in any scheduled activities.

During the meetings the South Koreans cautioned the North

Korean delegation about repeated violations of the spirit of the dialogue by pointing out the abusive language used in the radio broadcasts by the RPR alleged to exist in the South. The North Koreans did not entertain the complaint and merely stated that the RPR question was an internal problem of the South. The North Koreans, on the other hand, expressed their wish to discuss the problem of reunification with representatives of political and social organizations in the South, apart from the Coordinating Committee. The North Koreans made it official on August 28, 1973, when the delegation announced in the name of its chairman, Kim Yŏng-ju, that they were no longer interested in participating in the Coordinating Committee meetings, citing as their reason the kidnapping of Kim Dae Jung from Japan on August 8, 1973. The vice-chairmen of each side continued to meet at P'anmunjŏm in the demilitarized zone from December 1973 to March 1975, but the dialogue was all but suspended. Similarly, the Red Cross talks were suspended after seven regular meetings from August 1972 to July 1973.[10]

What was made clear through the dialogue was Kim's inflexible resolve to unify the country under the formula he had advanced — that is, to win the South Korean people over to the North Korean side. Kim proceeded with the dialogue in the belief that the three principles of unification outlined in the first article of the joint communiqué were his own policies and that the South Koreans had finally come to agree to them. When he found that the South Koreans had not been enlightened about his policies but in fact differed in their interpretation of the basic policy embodied in the joint communiqué, he was no longer interested in the dialogue.

Kim later explained what he really meant by the three principles in the first article of the joint communiqué. He said that the first principle, an independent solution without the interference of external forces, meant the withdrawal of U.S. troops from South Korea: "Frankly speaking, to reunify the country independently means to force the United States imperialists out of South Korea."[11] The second principle, peaceful reunification, meant the reduction of armed forces and the halt of military modernization in the South. The third principle, great national unity transcending ideological and systemic differences, meant the democratization and freedom of political dissidents in the South. Kim emphasized that such democratization and freedom demanded the repeal of the anti-Communist law in the South and freedom to organize and operate subversive political and revolutionary groups friendly to the North.[12]

There was no change in Kim's basic attitude, and the three principles he claimed for the dialogue were simply extensions of the three policies for unification he had proclaimed in the 1960s: to strengthen the revolutionary base in the North, to strengthen the revolutionary forces in the South, and to strengthen the international revolutionary ties. They meant in essence to reunify the country by overthrowing the South Korean government. What he wanted through the dialogue was perhaps to effect the U.S. troop withdrawal from the South and more importantly to win over the subversive elements who opposed the South Korean government to the cause of communism in the North. His insistence on meeting with representatives of various opposition political parties, social and cultural organizations, and student groups, apart from the Red Cross or the North-South Coordinating Committee, was a clear indication of his attempt to exploit the pluralistically inclined society in the South and recruit revolutionaries to undermine the South's existing government.

Recognizing the North's impossible demands in the dialogue, South Korean President Park announced, on June 23, 1973, his willingness to have both the North and South admitted to the United Nations as separate entities. On the same day, Kim issued a new five-point policy for national reunification, repeating essentially the same provisions of his past programs against the South. They were, first, to reduce the military confrontation by removing U.S. troops from the South; second, to institute multifaceted collaboration simultaneously in political, economic, military, cultural, and diplomatic affairs; third, to convene a meeting of all social, political, and student organization representatives; fourth, to unite the two systems under a Confederal Republic of Koryŏ; and fifth, to join the United Nations not as two separate countries but as one.[13] At the enlarged meeting of the Political Committee of the Central Committee two days after President Park had proposed the simultaneous entry into the United Nations by both North and South

Korea as separate entities, Kim condemned the proposal as a way of perpetuating the division of Korea.

It was clear to the South Koreans that Kim was not to be trusted and that the underlying motive in his proposals was to bring about a revolution in the South. Nevertheless, they argued that they would want to continue the dialogue by maintaining confrontation with dialogue, competition with dialogue, and coexistence with dialogue.[14] To make his cause more appealing to the leaders of the nonaligned nations, Kim often used choice words to counter the South Koreans, such as collaboration with dialogue, unity with dialogue, and reunification with dialogue.[15] This was merely an exercise in semantics, however. Kim was never serious about true collaboration; he hoped only for South Korean cooperation in order to advance his programs.

There were serious difficulties in what each side was trying to accomplish, and they were nowhere near resolving the problems that divided their country. Even the humanitarian efforts toward their own compatriots and relatives in the Red Cross talks, let alone the political issues in the Coordinating Committee, were contravened. Kim also came to realize that the effort to subvert the South Korean people through dialogue was not working. In fact, the dialogue may have backfired in the sense that North Koreans who had long been indoctrinated to view the South as a land of poverty and corruption now had the opportunity to see on their own the vivacious and fast-developing South.

After the dialogue, Kim returned to his old strategy of applying relentless pressure to oppose the leaders and government of the South. Less than a year after the break in the dialogue, another attempt was made through the North Korean front organization in Japan to assassinate South Korean President Park on August 15, 1974, this time claiming the life of the president's wife.[16] As though this were not convincing evidence of their tough stance, the North Koreans dug tunnels along the demilitarized zone for the purpose of infiltrating the South and ax-murdered two American soldiers in the joint security area in the P'anmunjŏm negotiation compound.[17]

It is doubtful that Kim ordered or personally authorized these sorties, but they were manifestations of his indoctrination of his subjects in the North and the result of the intense hatred he had instilled in them. As in the earlier adventures in the late 1960s, the ax murder incident at P'anmunjŏm on August 18, 1976, took him to the brink once again. Panic-stricken, he ordered the mobilization of the entire army, the Red Worker-Peasant Militia, and the Red Young Guards to prepare for retaliation.[18]

Passion for fellow countrymen across the parallel and an intense desire to reunify their country may have obfuscated the issues and compromised their scrutiny of each other's true intentions, but it should have been worthwhile for both sides to examine objectively what had transpired in the past and what could be expected of each other in the future before plunging into another round of talks and patent disillusionment. It would be worthwhile, for example, for the South Koreans in particular to consider what the North Koreans would do if the situation were reversed. What would Kim do if it were the South Koreans who had attacked the North to unify the country in the Korean War, had sent armed commandos to the North to assassinate him, had repeatedly propagated the existence in the North of a South Korean revolutionary party for unification that was opposed to him, had assassinated his wife by manipulating a Korean resident organization in the Northeast Chinese Korean Autonomous *zhou*, and had dug tunnels from South to North for the purpose of infiltration and constantly urged the North Korean people to overthrow him? Would Kim be as eager as the South Koreans to sit across the table to hear how North Korea should reduce its armed forces and permit its citizens and representatives of political, social, and student organizations to speak directly to the South Korean authorities to undermine his rule?

It is important to detect changes in Kim's attitude before seeking any meaningful dialogue with the North. Kim is a stubborn man. His obstinacy was rewarded when he dealt with the Soviet Union and China in the 1960s and even with the Americans in the *Pueblo* incident, but to deal with the South requires something else.

The Sino-American normalization treaty of January 1979 forced the two eager but hostile groups together only to repeat their exercise in futility. The South Koreans insisted on the resumption of the North-South Coordinating Committee meetings while the North Koreans curtly replied that the committee no longer existed in North Korea. The North repeated its demand for meetings with the representatives of political and social organizations, trying to undermine the political authority of the South. Today the problem is no longer the lack of a unification formula, principles, or methods. More than enough formulas and principles have been devised and advocated by both sides. The North Koreans repeated their position even after the death of President Park, but they showed few changes in the basic policy to reunify the country. Even the new proposal of the Democratic Confederal Republic of Korea formula and the South Korean proposal for direct summit talks show little change in the basic attitudes of either side. Without a noticeable change in Kim's basically militant attitude toward the South and without considerable changes in South Korea's anti-Communist stance, Korea will remain divided.[19]

The Nonaligned Movement

From the time he first traveled to Indonesia to collect his first honorary degree in 1965 to his next trip ten years later for a second honorary degree from Algeria,[20] Kim was busy advocating the cause of the nonaligned nations. His difficulties with both the Soviet Union and China in the 1960s might have forced him to be serious about his dealings with the Third World in the 1970s. He may also have opted for this course of action for two other reasons: to win the support of the Third World in mounting a more effective anti-American campaign, waging a diplomatic assault against South Korea in the international arena and promoting himself as the leader of the Third World.

When he realized the seriousness of the Sino-Soviet dispute and its impact on the North, Kim tried to ameliorate the situation in the name of the unity of the socialist and Communist countries. But when he conceded that his call for unity was going unheeded, the tune changed from unity of the socialist and Communist countries to unity of the nonaligned nations. The change was nowhere more clearly illustrated than in his dealings with Tito of Yugoslavia. When he was calling for the unity of the socialist and Communist countries, he castigated Tito as a fascist running dog of international reactionaries and a modern revisionist servant of capitalists

Kim Il Sung receives an honorary doctorate from Algiers University, May 1975

who should be resolutely opposed.[21] When he switched his tune and tried to cultivate his friends in the Third World, however, Kim visited Tito, warmly embraced him, and praised him as a fighter of the international socialist movement as well as the nonalignment movement. When Tito visited Pyongyang in August 1977, Kim called him his "close and intimate friend."[22]

As late as the Second Party Conference in October 1966, Kim supported the unity of thirteen socialist states, excluding Yugoslavia, but he gradually moved away from that unity and joined Tito. The Sino-Soviet dispute was harmful to the disputants as well as to the Communist camp and particularly to Kim because both countries were so deeply involved in the preservation of his rule in the North. Kim thought that his expansion into the Third World was not only the way out of his perennial balancing act between the two but also the most convenient way to escape servitude to his long-time masters.

In his effort to win support from the Third World, Kim expanded diplomatic relations radically. When the Communist republic was established in 1948, only seven countries recognized the North. Indeed, during the first decade of the republic only four more countries recognized the North, bringing the total to eleven countries by 1957.[23] During the next two decades or so, the North Koreans managed to establish diplomatic relations with ninety-nine additional countries, bringing the total to one hundred and ten.[24] This progress reflected signifcant strides by Kim, who explored every opportunity from formalizing relations with countries he had condemned in the past, such as Yugoslavia in September 1971, to establishing ties with one of the smallest nations in the world, the Republic of Seychelles in August 1976.

When Kim normalized his relationship with China at the end of the Cultural Revolution, he exploited what may be called a "China route" and mounted an "invitation diplomacy," bringing to the North many heads-of-state of Third World countries who had paid official state visits to China. From 1971 to the death of Mao in 1976, several heads-of-state visited him every year.[25] The flow of visitors subsided briefly after the death of Mao, but it was revived again and no fewer than ten heads-of-state visited him in 1978.[26]

Kim reciprocated by sending practically all of his top-ranking party and government officials to these countries for one mission or another, and in 1975 he himself took two trips abroad. Shortly after the fall of Vietnam in April 1975, he visited Mao for the first time in more than a decade, and it turned out to be his last visit before Mao died the following year. It was a hurriedly arranged visit two days after his sixty-third birthday to fit into Mao's schedule. While in Beijing, Kim said that if a revolution were to break out in South Korea, he "will not just look at it with folded arms but will strongly support the South Korean people," and if a war were to break out in Korea he "will only lose the military demarcation line and will gain the country's reunification."[27]

The following month, May 1975, he visited a number of East European and African countries, including Romania, Algeria, Mauritania, Bulgaria, and Yugoslavia. During this trip, he advocated an independent solution for the Korean problem, soliciting support for North Korea's admission to the conference of nonaligned nations and for North Korea's efforts in the United Nations.[28]

The mutual visitation diplomacy was not all. Kim granted liberal interviews to foreign correspondents during which he promoted his accomplishments, his ideas, and North Korea's position in support of nonalignment. He downgraded South Korea and the United States as well as the American military presence in the South. His efforts, at times, were serious; for example, he granted fourteen interviews in 1974 and twelve in 1975.[29]

What Kim accomplished through these diplomatic offensives was recognition of his legitimate rule of an independent nation in the North, something the South Koreans and the western countries had long denied him during the cold war days. In the 1970s, however, even the South Korean authorities implied tacit recognition of his legitimacy when President Park proposed simultaneous entry into the United Nations as a separate nation on June 23, 1973. But Kim adamantly opposed any such move and claimed all Korea. He refused, for example, any plan that would allow cross-recognition; recognition of the North by the United States and Japan, of South Korea by the Soviet Union and China.[30]

North Korea was admitted as a full-fledged member of a number of specialized agencies of the United Nations beginning with membership in the World Health Organization. Kim also succeeded in having the North admitted to the International Parliamentary Union in March 1973. With the replacement of the Republic of China in Taiwan by the People's Republic of China in the United Nations in 1971, Kim managed to gain a foothold in the United Nations as an observer, and he maneuvered for several years to have Algeria and other nonaligned nations introduce a resolution favorable to the North in the United Nations. He even succeeded in having one such resolution passed in 1975.

It was a significant stride from the time when the United Nations was refused entry into the North in 1948 to oversee a nationwide election to create a unified Korea. The United Nations had also branded North Korea the aggressor in the Korean War, and UN forces were mobilized to stem the tide of Communist aggression toward the South in 1950. Indeed, he could claim a diplomatic victory of a sort when he was also successful in having the North admitted to the organization of nonaligned nations at the foreign ministers' meeting in Lima, Peru, in 1975,[31] while a similar application by the South was rejected.

All his diplomatic feats were not without sacrifice, however. Kim had the citizenry of the North line the streets of Pyongyang monthly to welcome some African chief or illustrious president of an obscure island they had never heard of. Such names as Mobut Sese Seko Kuku Ngbendu Wa Za Banga were not necessarily Korean household words, and few knew in which continent such countries as Sao Tome and Principe or Seychelles were located. The effort to mobilize the people was minor, however, compared with the kind of adjustment Kim had to make on certain established principles — for example, about the United Nations.

In the past Kim had always condemned the UN's role in Korea, not only the military role during the Korean War but also any role the United Nations would play in the reunification of Korea. Kim said in 1962 and again in 1963 that the United Nations had no business in Korea. Why should the Koreans ask for the UN's help in solving the problem of unification of their own country? To do so, he said, is an insult to the nation.[32] As late as September 1971, Kim said he was not going to abide by any decision passed by the United Nations, for the UN was but a tool of the American imperialists. When his chances of having the General Assembly pass a resolution favorable to the North improved, however, he suddenly said, in January 1972, that he had always respected the United Nations and had never violated its charter. Later that year, on September 17, in an interview with Japanese reporters, Kim insisted that the United Nations *must* debate the Korean reunification question.[33]

After several years of intensive political maneuvering and diplomatic campaigns at home and abroad to solicit votes of the nonaligned nations, Kim did succeed in having the resolution favorable to the North passed in the United Nations, but so did the South.[34] A more crushing blow to his efforts came when two conflicting resolutions were passed simultaneously in the same session. To a Spartan and resolute leader such as Kim, who needed a decisive diplomatic victory to sustain his drive, this sort of lukewarm resolution was hard to take.

As he expanded the relationship with the Third World, he was also exposed to the political vicissitudes of the nonaligned nations. He experienced political turnovers in such countries as Kampuchea and Chile, where his diplomatic missions were exchanged for South Korean missions in rapid succession, and also had political problems with such loyal friends as Mauritania, where Kim had paid a state visit to Moktar Ould Daddah as late as 1975.[35] Less than two years after Kim's visit there, Mauritania expelled North Korean diplomats and announced the severing of diplomatic relations on June 7, 1977. The reason given was North Korea's recognition of the independence and self-determination of the former Spanish colony in Western Sahara.[36] One week later on June 14, 1977, Argentina notified North Korea that it was severing diplomatic ties because the entire North Korean embassy staff had been withdrawn from Buenos Aires without notifying the host government. Similar problems had occurred with Australia in October 1975.[37]

The fifth conference of nonaligned nations was held in Colombo, Sri Lanka, in August 1976, the first such meeting for Kim after North Korea's admission a year earlier. The North Koreans planned an elaborate propaganda campaign in anticipation of Kim's personal participation in the conference, trying to project him as leader of the Third World, but their great expectations ended in consternation.

Suspected of aiding antigovernment armed guerrillas in Colombo, the North Korean mission had been expelled from Sri Lanka on March 28, 1971, and while they restored diplomatic relations four years later, in March 1975, the North Koreans still had no mission in Colombo. They sailed in one of their ships, carrying the largest delegation of 120 members, but other members of the nonaligned nations, as well as the host country, were not about to tolerate Kim's demonstration of his political clout in the conference. North Koreans had to cancel their plan for Kim's personal participation, and they were closely watched by the authorities of the host country. Sri Lanka, for example, stopped direct short-wave communication from the North Korean ship docked in Colombo to Pyongyang because it violated the convention and the laws of the host country.

The conference did pass two resolutions on Korean problems favorable to the North, but it also made it palpably clear to the

North Koreans that the conference of nonaligned nations was not a suitable place for the demonstration of Kim's greatness. The rest of the nonaligned nations may not have been as aggressive as the North Koreans in promoting their own leaders, but they implied that the conference of nonaligned nations was full of great leaders.[38]

Unfamiliar with the standard of diplomatic conduct in his suddenly expanded international contacts, Kim suffered from a number of difficulties: a shortage of trained personnel, lack of foreign exchange, less than adequate proficiency in commonly accepted diplomatic languages, and ignorance of the standard of diplomatic conduct in sophisticated non-Communist countries. It was not long after the expansion of contacts that North Korean diplomats were expelled from such countries as Sweden, Norway, Finland, and Denmark for peddling tax-exempt goods, trafficking in illicit drugs, and generally abusing diplomatic immunity.[39]

Unable to find qualified staff for their missions abroad, most newly recruited diplomats were trained on the job, tarnishing the resplendent image Kim wanted to project abroad. At times, even their goodwill was misplaced as they offered expensive but inappropriate gifts to the uninitiated — for example, aged and potent domestic snake whiskey to a nondrinking Moslem. These were telling proofs of their long yeears of isolation and unfamiliarity with the conventions of diplomatic conduct. Often their intense campaigns and diplomatic offensives were self-defeating. It was a case of too much too soon to too many countries that were indifferent to their cause.

Apart from these official diplomatic contacts, the North Koreans mounted a vigorous cultural campaign by sending performing troupes and elaborate exhibitions to Third World countries. During the first half of 1975, for example, their performing art troupes visited Uganda, Burundi, Zaire, Equatorial Guinea, Sudan, Mali, Togo, Sierra Leone, Senegal, Mauritania, Yugoslavia, and Australia. During the same year, the North Koreans had thirty-one separate exhibitions in twenty-three countries in Asia, Africa, and Latin America.[40] These were efforts to win respect and friends in the Third World, but the methods employed were so crude and assertive that in many cases they were forcing respect and commanding friendship from these countries.

One of the North Koreans' most important appeals to the Third World was their unequivocally anti-American stance and condemnation of the U.S. military presence in the South. Their anti-imperialism and anti-colonialism may have found common ground, and their appeal for American troop withdrawal from Korea may even have won sympathy from nonaligned nations, but such expressions of hatred as murders of Americans won them few friends and converts.

To promote Kim's self-reliant political ideas, they financed the establishment of more than two hundred organizations in approximately fifty countries all over the world, including one in the United States, but none survived on its own when the North's financial support was terminated.[41] When the North Korean debts in the international marketplace mounted, few renewed their enthusiasm for Kim's political ideas. Kim hosted a number of expensive seminars on his political ideas, inviting people from the Third World. Not a single participant among more than eighty-nine official representatives from seventy-three different countries in five continents of the globe raised one solitary question or made one mildly critical remark about his self-reliant ideals in the seminar held in September 1977.[42]

Kim had to learn the hard way that he had neither the resources nor the charisma to appeal to the people of the Third World. Geographically, too, North Korea was located in the midst of superpowers, unlike African, Latin American, and South and Southeast Asian countries, where projection of one leader from a small country in the region can be pursued. Relentless self-promotion won him not respect and friends but derision, at times making him a target of international mockery at great cost to him and his people.

When Kim learned the limits of the nonaligned movement, he stopped his campaign and returned to care for his own unresolved problems. His attitude toward personal interviews, for example, changed drastically. He enjoyed the prestige when reporters from the Communist bloc and Third World countries flocked to his doorway to get a glimpse of him, asking him mutually agreeable questions praising his accomplishments. But when he expanded his contacts with the non-Communist world, a number of reporters from capitalist countries asked him hard, at times embarrassing, questions, he stopped the interviews.

Kim also came to realize that while the support of the non-aligned countries could be had, it was often at great cost to him and contributed little to the solution of his real problems. His flirtation with the nonalignment movement ended where it had begun — with no solution to his problems with the countries that mattered to him, the Soviet Union and China on the one hand, and the United States and Japan on the other. Nor was he better able to compete with South Korea through his improved relations with the nonaligned nations. What Kim and his economy needed was not to look with self-satisfaction on their status in comparison with other Third World countries but on their need to acquire advanced technology to produce more and better goods that could compete in the international market.

The nonalignment movement was not an alternative to his balancing act in the Sino-Soviet dispute. What he needed to compete with South Korea was to be found not in the voting power of the nonaligned countries in the United Nations but in the technological development of the advanced western and Communist countries. Kim began to appeal directly to the United States, trying to undermine South Korea, but was met with a stiff rebuff.

He greeted cordially the Soviet government delegation headed by D. A. Kunayev, a member of the Political Bureau and first secretary of the Kazakh Communist Party, and N. N. Tarasov, minister of light industry and chairman of the Soviet-Korean Friendship Society in January 1978. They promised economic cooperation but also brought him the Order of Lenin that has been awarded to him six years earlier in April 1972 at the time of his sixtieth birthday. Kim must have regretted the lost opportunities during the 1970s with the Soviet Union and the deterioration of their relationship to the extent that he could not go to Moscow personally to receive the award. Kim must also have come to the painful realization that the Order of Lenin bestowed upon him in Moscow would have meant much more to him and to North Korea than his second honorary doctorate from Algeria.

15

The Shift from
Party to State

The advent of direct negotiations between the North and South brought significant changes in the political systems of both sides, each strengthening and consolidating the existing but disparate systems. The expansion of diplomatic relations with the Third World brought further adjustments in the political system of the North. These changes included the elevation of Kim from premier of the cabinet to president of the republic, a new constitution, creation of several new organs, and sundry other arrangements. The most important, however, was the shift in emphasis from operation of the party to the affairs of state. There was nothing written to document such a shift, nor was the change readily discernible, but it nevertheless emerges as the principal adjustment.

Shortly after the opening of the dialogue in July 1972, both North and South Korea underwent drastic shifts in their political systems. None of these changes was conducive to the cause of unification for which the dialogue was held. In fact, it almost seemed that both had rejected unification and tried to perpetuate the division of the country. In the South, the government of the third republic that had ruled for a decade after the military coup prepared for another decade by introducing a revitalized constitution (*yusin hŏnbŏp*) in October 1972. The new arrangement in the South was designed not only to prolong the tenure of President Park but to stiffen the anti-Communist laws by proclaiming a number of emergency decrees to prepare the people against the Communist North.[1]

The New Constitution

Similarly, the North Koreans introduced a new constitution in December 1972 — the first such overhaul since the creation of the republic in September 1948 — and solidified the Communist government. Except for the demonstration that each Korea was firmly committed to its own system against the other, the almost simultaneous announcement of the respective changes was coincidental and the nature of the change quite different. In contrast to the launching of new programs under the revitalized reform in the South, Kim was trying to legalize the past practices of the government in a new constitution. Perpetuation of his rule virtually assured, Kim was in effect trying to domesticate communism in Korea.

The change was profound in the sense that the new constitution was the proclamation of transformation into an independent state from a satellite Communist party created and heavily manipulated by domineering Communist superpowers in the past. With increased diplomatic contacts with nonaligned nations, Kim needed to become a head of state in fact as well as in law, and a great distinction was made between the conduct of the state and the operation of the party.[2]

A number of sundry changes distinguished the new constitution from the old, such as lowering the voting age from eighteen to seventeen (Article 52) and the change of the capital from Seoul to Pyongyang (Article 149), but the most radical changes were in the substitution of Kim's political thought for Communist ideology, the establishment of his revolutionary tradition as the tradition of Korea, and the institution of the new office of president of the republic and the all-powerful administrative organ of the Central People's Committee. The two new central organizations effectively took over the functions of government and gradually undermined the political clout of the Political Committee and Central Committee of the party.[3]

The new president of the republic was the head of state, concurrently serving as commander of the armed forces and chairman of the National Defense Committee; he had power to issue edicts, grant pardons, and conclude and abrogate treaties. The newly created Central People's Committee took over such functions of the former cabinet and the Standing Committee of the Supreme People's Assembly as setting state policy in both domestic and foreign affairs, guiding national security, ensuring observance of the constitution, and appointing and removing members of the Administration Council, the diplomatic corps, and generals and admirals of the armed forces.

These arrangements reduced the Administration Council, the new cabinet, to a mere functional organ that would carry out the orders of the president and his Central People's Committee. The powers to promulgate decrees, to direct foreign relations, and to oversee the works of the army and local organizations had all been exercised by the cabinet in the past.

Furthermore, even the Central Court (formerly the Supreme Court) and the Central Procurator's Office were responsible in their work to the Central People's Committee. These judicial organs under the old constitution reported to the Supreme People's Assembly, thus enjoying relative independence from political influence. The extent of Kim's power under the new constitution can be seen in Article 76, which stipulated that the highest leadership organ of the state, the Central People's Committee, was to consist of members elected by the Supreme People's Assembly upon recommendation by the president of the republic.[4]

Although Kim was crowned president of the republic, he also remained chairman of the party. The shifting emphasis from party to state was not readily discernible at the beginning because every member of the Political Committee of the party's Central Committee was concurrently elected a member of the Central People's Committee,[5] but many of the party's policy-setting functions were taken up by the Central People's Committee.

As time progressed, the party Central Committee plenums be-

came infrequent, and what had been mere annual ceremonial sessions of the Supreme People's Assembly to approve the national
budget became more frequent. The agenda of the Supreme People's
Assembly sessions now included important discussions, such as the
questions of unification proposals and the ten-year compulsory education system (the second session, April 5–10, 1973), abolition of
the tax system (the third session, March 20–25, 1974), organizational
problems and election of important government officials (the
fourth session, November 27–30, 1974), and adoption of a new land
law (the seventh session, April 26–29, 1977).

Promulgation of the new constitution came only two years after
the Fifth Party Congress, but more important it came about without serious and lengthy discussion by the party Central Committee. The fifth plenum of the Central Committee, held October
23–26, 1972, did discuss the proposed constitution, but the text of
Kim's speech was not made public. The party in that plenum undertook the sinister task of reissuing identity cards to every
member of the party, usually signaling the tightening up of the
party's rank and file. The party plenum of the Central Committee,
which had been convened on the average more than three or four
times each year, had dwindled to only once in 1976. The twelfth
plenum was held October 11–14, 1976, almost a year after the eleventh plenum, November 19–21, 1975. Even then the plenum's agenda in 1976 centered on the discussion of farming.[6]

Furthermore, Kim concentrated on speaking more often on
strengthening the state system after he became president of the republic and markedly less on the party's role.[7] This change may
have been due in part to his increased activities greeting visitors
and visiting heads of state, granting interviews, and participating
in the conferences of nonaligned nations, but his absence in party
affairs was becoming more obvious in the mid-1970s. By the time
of the sixth Supreme People's Assembly in December 1977, the contrast was manifest. The second seven-year economic plan, for example, was launched without discussion and approval by the Central Committee of the party. In fact, it was the first time such an
important economic plan had been launched without a party
congress.

When the first seven-year economic plan was extended for three additional years, the party congress was also delayed the same length of time to the conclusion of the extended first seven-year economic plan in 1970. The six-year economic plan was launched with considerable discussion at the Fifth Party Congress, but the second seven-year economic plan (1978–1984) was launched without discussion by the Central Committee of the party. The extent of the party's demise may be seen in the way the second seven-year plan was taken up. Only two days before the sixth Supreme People's Assembly was to convene, the fifteenth plenum of the Central Committee was called to hear details of the plan from a government functionary, Hong Sŏng-yong, who was not even a member of the Central Committee. At the Supreme People's Assembly, however, Yi Chong-ok, premier of the Administration Council and a member of the Central People's Committee, presented the plan, and a lengthy discussion by prominent government officials followed his presentation. After adoption of the plan in the assembly, a simple open letter was issued encouraging all party members to support the plan.[8]

During the fifth Supreme People's Assembly, the Central People's Committee with twenty-five members was large enough to accommodate all the members of the Political Committee of the party, but by the time of the sixth Supreme People's Assembly in December 1977, membership of the Central People's Committee was drastically reduced from twenty-five to fifteen, and many members of the Political Committee were not elected to the Central People's Committee. Those not elected included such important partisans and technocrats as Kim Yŏng-ju, Kim Tong-gyu, Kim Chung-nin, Hyŏn Mu-gwang, and Yang Hyŏng-sŏp.

Further demise of the party Political Committee can be seen in the deterioration of its membership. Most of the Committee's original appointees had either died, such as Ch'oe Yong-gŏn, Chŏng Chun-t'aek, and Han Ik-su,[9] or had been demoted, such as Kim Tong-gyu and Kim Chung-nin, but no official replacements were announced. During the first year of the sixth Supreme People's Assembly in 1978, the North Koreans began to hold joint sessions of the Central People's Committee of the assembly and the Political Committee of the party. Such joint sessions, held twice in 1978 (July 12 and August 2), were unprecedented in party history.

The shift of emphasis from party to state did not mean that Kim had relaxed the secrecy surrounding the party or state operations. Several speeches he made in the Central Committee, although fewer in number than before, were not made public. In fact, during the height of his diplomatic maneuvers in 1974 the ninth plenum of the Central Committee, held sometime in the fall of 1974, was kept secret altogether — not even the date let alone the agenda was announced.[10] Perhaps most flagrant was the secrecy imposed on the election results of the sixth Supreme People's Assembly. The 579 electoral districts were announced, and 100 percent voter turnout was reported, but the roster of 579 representatives elected to the Supreme People's Assembly was not made public. The roster was kept secret even from the people who elected them. A North Korean voter knows only the representative from his own district because he voted for that person, but no other representative. Secrecy had reached ludicrous proportions in the North.

The shift from party to state can also be detected by comparing Kim's public speeches on the thirtieth anniversaries of the founding of the party in October 1975 and the founding of the republic in September 1978.[11] Far greater emphasis was placed on the work of the government than on the party's tasks, so often repeated in the past. More conspicuous was Kim's speech at the sixth Supreme People's Assembly entitled "Let Us Further Strengthen the People's Government."[12] He said it was the government of the republic that defended the democratic freedom and rights of the people, and it was the government that was the revolutionary banner for the country's independence and prosperity. He said that by strengthening the government, the people would become happier and more dignified and the country would prosper endlessly. He did not mention the party's role even once in his entire speech.

The shift in emphasis from party to state may be attributed to many factors. It may have begun ceremonially from the need to elevate Kim as head of state in the expanded relationship with the Third World, but reasons may also be found in domestic political developments. He needed the party organization to consolidate his power and to meet the challenges of other groups. When he attained what was considered an unchallengeable position, his need to keep up the vigil in the party was not as great in the 1970s as it had been in the 1950s and 1960s.

Furthermore, his basic core of support from his partisan days in the party had begun to disintegrate — as a result of natural attrition, purges of the partisan generals in the late 1960s, and outright political purges. The unity of the partisan group, his mainstay in winning and sustaining political power in the North, was no longer necessary for Kim. What he needed more urgently in the 1970s were young technocrats who knew how to manage the government.

The shift may also be attributed to the change in North Korea's status from a satellite Communist party in the monolithic Communist world dominated by the Soviet Union to an independent state trying to attain full-fledged membership in the family of nations and the polycentric Communist world. The process was gradual and not readily discernible till the mid-1970s.

Kim may also have felt it necessary to become president rather than remain premier of the cabinet in order to promote himself as leader of the nonaligned nations. He may have felt obliged to equalize his status with that of the president of South Korea when he began to deal with the South Koreans in the dialogue. The South Koreans had a president above the premier of the cabinet, and Kim's status as a mere premier, though as powerful as the president of the South, might have set him back in diplomatic negotiations or serious dialogues with the South. When he became president of the North under the new constitution, provision was also made for a premier of the cabinet (the Administration Council).

Kim may have succeeded in proclaiming independence and crowning himself president of the republic, but the problems he faced in the 1970s were not the potential challenge to his political power by any group or control of the people by manipulation of the party. Nor was it his dealings with the developing Third World countries. It was the helpless feeling of isolation from the technologically advanced countries, too proud to learn and too poor to buy from them. Kim succeeded in convincing his people that there was nothing in the world to envy, insisting on a peculiar style of self-reliance, but he also succeeded in accumulating embarrassing debts far beyond his means to pay.

He continued to apply relentless pressure to the people to work hard under all kinds of mottos, such as "Pyongyang speed" and

"Ch'ŏllima speed," but when he realized the limitations of his strategy, he admitted for the first time that the people should be given material incentives along with the usual brass medals and colored ribbons.[13] His enthusiastic guidance was already inappropriate for the younger generations of the 1970s and 1980s. In his speech to the League of Socialist Working Youth, for example, he urged the young to learn foreign languages, including English and Japanese, but he said they needed to learn only a few phrases such as "hands up" and "put down your guns and surrender."[14] What they really needed, of course, was advanced English, if not more sophisticated scientific jargon, to bridge the phenomenal gap in technology. The problem has not been lack of industry or devotion on the part of the North Korean people; Kim's best tutelage and their most enthusiastic patriotism are simply not good enough for the world of the 1980s.

The Sixth Party Congress: 1980

Kim Il Sung has ruled the North for four decades, and mere longevity of rule has legitimized many of his political actions. Time has been a good teacher for Kim. He has seen many great political leaders of big and small nations rise and fall during his tenure in office. He witnessed the great leader Joseph Stalin downgraded after his death, and he also noted Mao's difficulty in choosing a successor. Kim thought often of the problem of succession and took careful steps to deal with it, but his solution has not been universally popular.

His solution, of course, was to name his son successor. Kim had effectively eliminated all his rivals, and the remaining partisans he trusted were few in number and too old by the 1970s. Furthermore, it is not difficult to recognize Kim's reluctance in trying to find among the ranks of his own generation anyone worthy of carrying on the work he had started. He chose his son, who was thirty years his junior, and began to implement his idea in the early 1970s when junior Kim was about the same age as Kim himself was when he took over the reins in the North. Kim was not much concerned about his unpopular decision; if he pushed the idea long and hard enough, surely he would be able to convince the people. Furthermore, his choice of his son would complete the image of a revolutionary family tradition that Kim had tried to project to the people: Kim's father was built up to be a great revolutionary by Kim himself, of course, and Kim's own son should likewise honor his father. Kim is not a religious man, and he may not have worried about his life hereafter, but he is no doubt interested in preserving his place in Korean history.

In contrast to the open recognition of his parents' and relatives' alleged contributions to the Korean revolution, the designation of his son as successor was done in a clandestine manner. Kim decided to have his son take over operation of the party, just as he himself had done in the late 1940s and 1950s. He had shifted the emphasis from party to state and entrusted the party's operation to his son under his close supervision. The campaign to implement this decision was the Three-Revolution Team movement (*Samdae hyŏngmyŏng sojo undong*).[15] This campaign was proposed in February 1973 by the Political Committee, but the crucial decision to implement the campaign under the leadership of his son seems to have been made in the fall of 1974 at the ninth plenum of the Central Committee, which was held in secret.

Several developments shortly thereafter point to the ninth plenum as the turning point. The agenda of the tenth plenum of the Central Committee (February 11–17, 1975) included Kim's stern order to carry out the campaign of the Three-Revolution Team, but the text of his speech was kept secret. He spoke at length on the subject less than a month later on March 3, 1975, at the meeting of the activists in the industrial sector, tracing the development and the rationale behind the campaign of the Three-Revolution Team movement.[16] Still another campaign was launched in December 1975, the Three-Revolution Red Flag movement, and an elaborate propaganda effort was made to support the campaign.[17]

These campaigns were to dispatch many young people, mostly untrained college students, to factories and cooperative farms to boost the sagging economy. In his speech to the Three-Revolution Team Council for Agriculture, Kim deplored the indolent — particularly lazy farmers who did not meet production quotas. He said that the students of the Three-Revolution Team should remain in the farm cooperatives from spring until fall to help the farmers.

He acknowledged that their work from planting to harvest would hamper their education, but he said that such activity was a living education.[18] In another speech to the Political Committee, Kim encouraged the college students' work on the Three-Revolution Team and also instructed the farmers and party functionaries to co-operate with them.[19]

Kim also began to criticize the old faithfuls who were not equipped to lead the new technologically advanced factory work and urged the party functionaries to replace the old with young people. He said that the team should consist of twenty to thirty people for a small factory and approximately fifty people in a large factory and should boldly apply new technical innovations in all fields. He continued to stress the work of the young, urging them to get rid of their fear of technology and the old bureaucratic work methods. He often encouraged the young to take over the revolution and carry it forward "generation after generation."[20]

Kim spent an inordinate amount of time encouraging young people and the party officials to carry out the Three-Revolution Team movement. His foremost objective, of course, was to urge his people to recognize the leadership of his son, but there were other aims as well. Kim wanted to improve the sagging economy by pouring young people into factories and farms, to replace the old leaders with new ones, and to solve some of the technological difficulties in the factories, mines, and farm cooperatives. Beginning with the six-year plan, Kim realized that the old method of simply supplying more laborers to unproductive farms or factories was insufficient. Both his charisma and his mobilization had limits. He said that a mere increase in manpower was not sufficient and criticized what he termed "human wave tactics" in manpower administration.[21]

Except for the party functionaries and factory managers who were directly involved in promoting the Three-Revolution Team movement, few knew of Kim's intent to anoint his son successor, although a number of indications in the early 1970s pointed to that intent. In the fall of 1975, North Koreans began to use a mysterious term, "party center," to refer to Kim's son. In the past, the authority of the party was commonly referred to as the party, the Central Committee of the party, the Political Committee of the party, or even the plenum of the party but from late 1975 to 1976 the directives coming from the party were referred to as the authority of the *"party center."* It was common to find such references as "our great *suryŏng* and the *party center*," "the father *suryŏng* and the *party center*," and "the new, creative, and independent direction of the *party center*." In many articles and reports, the term *"party center"* was used to refer not to the inanimate object of the party's central organization but to the third person singular, such as the "affection of the *party center*" and "the appeal of the *party center*."[22]

There were other developments. A number of festivities by young people, such as the youth festival and the children's athletic meet that brought some 15,000 children and young men to Pyongyang stadium, were held on February 16, 1976, the thirty-fourth birthday of Kim's son. Others in factories and mines began to put up slogans calling for completion of their assigned work by February 16 as a gesture of loyalty to the father *suryŏng* and to the *"party center."*[23] Kim's son was reported to have concentrated a great deal of effort on the performing arts, and the artists began to use the term *"party center"* in articles published in the official party organ, *Kŭlloja.*[24]

Still another indication is the sudden promotional campaign for Kim Chŏng-suk, Kim's first wife and the mother of Kim Jong Il. She had long been dismissed simply as a partisan who fought with Kim, and although she was the first lady of the North during the first year of the republic she was not recognized as such. In September 1974, the North Koreans featured an elaborate reminiscence of an indomitable partisan, adding the phrase "one who served Kim Il Sung close to her body." *Kŭlloja* carried a feature article about the Communist revolutionary partisan Kim Chŏng-suk, who was faithful to the great leader Kim Il Sung.[25] A museum was erected for her in her hometown of Hoeryŏng, Hamgyŏng pukto. Furthermore, Kim's present wife, Kim Sŏng-ae, who is chairman of the Democratic Women's Union of Korea, began to single out Kim Chŏng-suk, about whom she had been silent all those years, and praised her as an indomitable Communist revolutionary and a great leader of the Korean women's movement.[26]

The first convincing confirmation of the succession was a booklet published by the North Korean front organization in Japan,

Chōsōren, or General Association of Korean Residents in Japan, in February 1977.[27] The booklet was the text of a special lecture series held February 2–3, 1977, for the cadres of the association. The session was convened to announce the decision of the party's Central Committee in Pyongyang that designated Kim Jong Il as the only successor to Kim. Members of the association were directed to support "the dear leader Kim Jong Il" and carry forward the uninterrupted revolution and the great revolutionary task of the fatherland generation after generation.

The text was divided into three parts, all advancing the son as the only heir to Kim Il Sung. The first part reaffirmed that Kim Jong Il was the faithful servant of the great *suryŏng*, the loyal propagator of his ideas, the promoter of revolutionary culture through his wise direction of the performing arts, and one who had inherited the great *suryŏng's* virtue and affection. The second part claimed that the new leadership of Kim Jong Il was the continuation of the leadership of the great *suryŏng* to complete the great revolutionary task laid out by the great *suryŏng*. It also claimed that the new leadership of Kim Jong Il was to carry on the ideological work in accordance with the wishes of the great *suryŏng*, generation after generation. The third part was a directive ordering all members to pledge loyalty to the "new dear leader," to support his absolute authority, and to obey unconditionally the directives of the great leader's successor, Kim Jong Il.

Kim's effort to anoint his son heir ran into a number of difficulties. As soon as the rumors ran rampant, the term *"party center"* disappeared abruptly. Despite a spirited campaign to promote the Three-Revolution Team and the Three-Revolution Red Flag movements, many workers resented laboring under the watchful eyes of young students who knew the statistics but nothing about the work itself. Two new medals known as the Three-Revolution Red Flag and the Three-Revolution Honor Badge, specifically designed to promote the movement, were instituted, but production failed to improve.

There must have been opposition to the effort to install the son heir from the ranks within the party. Moreover, the rank and file of the party who served the supreme leader faithfully must have felt anything but happy to be told they were unfit for the party leadership because they lacked technological skills. The extent of their dissatisfaction, if any, was not made public. It was reflected only in the debilitation of the party, the unimproved production rate, and the general indifference to appeals of the party. The older workers simply tried to meet the minimum quota and stay clear of any complication with the authorities.

The problem among the key party leaders was quite different. From the mid-1970s, a number of top party leaders were conspicuously absent from public functions: Kim Tong-gyu (the third highest member of the party behind Kim Il Sung and Kim Il) from about October 1977, Kim Chung-nin (member of the Political Committee, secretary) from about September 1977, Yang Hyŏng-sŏp (secretary, candidate member of the Political Committee) from about May 1977, and Yi Yong-mu (general, member of the Central Committee) from about September 1977. All these men were dropped from membership in the Central People's Committee in December 1977 at the time of the sixth Supreme People's Assembly. Some of the leaders reappeared briefly — Kim Chung-nin in November 1977 and Yang Hyŏng-sŏp in November 1978 — but others, for example, Kim Tong-gyu, had been purged.

By the time of the Sixth Congress of the Workers' Party of Korea in October 1980, Kim Il Sung seems to have cleared away all opposition to publicly designating his son heir. Kim Jong Il was named secretary of the party's Secretariat right after his father, who is general secretary of the party. He was also elected the fourth highest ranking member to the Politburo, the Presidium of the Politburo, and the Central Committee of the party. In the Military Commission of the party, he was the third highest ranking member behind his father and General O Chin-u.[28] No other North Korean political leader had achieved such prominence in the party during four decades of Kim's rule. It is clear that the takeover of the operational aspect of the party by Kim's son was completed by October 1980.

The pattern of change from the Fifth to the Sixth Party Congress remained the same. One hundred forty-five members were elected to the Central Committee of the Sixth Party Congress, but more than half, seventy-eight members, were newly elected. Similarly, an overwhelming majority of 103 candidate members except for twelve were newly elected. The most important change was in the ten-member Secretariat where all were new members except

Kim Il Sung and Kim Chung-nin. The Secretariat manages the party's daily operation, and it was filled with new faces, all supporters of Kim Jong Il. They were Kim Yŏng-nam, Kim Hwan, Yŏn Hyŏng-muk, Yun Ki-bok, Hong Si-hak, Hwang Chang-yŏp, and Pak Su-dong. All seven members of the Control Commission headed by Sŏ Ch'ŏl, a partisan who fought with Kim Il Sung, were newly elected. The party that began with approximately 4,530 members in December 1945 when Kim took over has grown into a huge body of more than three million members, amounting to approximately 17 percent of the population of North Korea, the largest proportion in the Communist world.

Kim Il Sung spoke more than five hours to deliver his report on the work of the Central Committee of the party, telling the delegates to the party congress to support his son. His report was divided into five parts: accomplishments in the Three-Revolution movement, the *chuch'e* idea, the reunification question, the nonalignment policy, and the future tasks of the party. The most important accomplishment of the Sixth Party Congress, however, was the designation of Kim Jong Il as heir.

Kim Jong Il: The Rising Son

Like his father's record, the true record of Kim Jong Il is hard to find because so many accomplishments have been attributed to him since he was designated successor. Kim Jong Il was born on February 16, 1942, in the Soviet Far East and returned to Korea when he was three with his mother, Kim Chŏng-suk, the first wife of Kim Il Sung. Kim Jong Il was the eldest of three children, two boys and a girl; he lost his brother in 1947 when he was five and lost his mother in 1949 when he was seven. During the Korean War (1950–1953) junior Kim and his sister, Kyŏng-hŭi, fled Korea into Northeast China in 1950. He began his schooling at the kindergarten of Namsan Elementary School in Pyongyang before the war and enrolled as a fourth grader at the Man'gyŏngdae School for Children of Revolutionaries on November 22, 1952, after he returned from China. He also studied briefly at Samsŏk Primary School before he was admitted as a fifth grader in No. 4 Pyongyang Primary School in 1953.

Kim Jong Il (Kim Chŏng-il), the Rising Son

During his middle school days, Kim Jong Il is reported to have visited various revolutionary sites of his father, such as Poch'ŏnbo and the region near Mount Paektu (Paektusan). Junior Kim often complained that he spent much of his boyhood years alone because his father was so busy. It was said that Kim Jong Il was sent abroad to study in East Germany and Romania during the latter part of his high school years, but he returned to Pyongyang to attend college. It is alleged that Kim Jong Il insisted on a Korean college education, turning down offers from well-known colleges and universities in more advanced Communist countries.

Even from his high school days, many stories are attributed to him in praise of various accomplishments, but none seem credible. Not only was he the honor student who corrected his teachers, but he is also reputed to have taken care of other students. He helped his father in the affairs of state while going to school, and he participated in construction work all over the country. Kim Jong Il entered Kim Il Sung University in September 1960 and studied political economy, graduating on May 18, 1964. He wrote his graduation thesis on the role of the county in building socialism, an analysis of his father's theses on the socialist rural question.[29]

After graduation, he was assigned to work in the Department of Organization and Guidance of the Central Committee of the party. Kim Jong Il is said to have devoted much of his time to filmmaking and the production of stage plays. Junior Kim is credited with the production of six major films and musicals in the early 1970s. *P'ibada* (Sea of Blood), *Han chawidaewŏn ŭi unmyŏng* (Fate of a Member of the Self-Defense Corps), *Millim a iyagihara* (Tell the Story, O Forest), *Kkot p'anŭn ch'ŏnyŏ* (Flower Girl), *Tang ŭi ch'amdoen ttal* (True Daughter of the Party), and *Kŭmgangsan ŭi norae* (The Song of Mount Kŭmgang). It is alleged that Kim Jong Il wrote the libretto of some of these musicals. In any case, he seems to have worked closely with North Korean artists and others engaged in the performing arts.

It is alleged that whatever Kim Jong Il has done has become an "immortal work," including his college thesis and these musicals and films. He is also credited with a strange concept called the "seed theory." In literature and art, according to junior Kim, the seed is the essence of the work. It constitutes the thought pattern of the life described and should contain the writer's message. Since junior Kim is "the seed" of the great leader, his father Kim Il Sung, it is difficult to give much credence to these contrived theories. Because of these improper attributions to junior Kim, it is difficult to assess his true ability.

In the early 1980s, North Koreans credited junior Kim with exposing a plot against his father in the fifteenth plenum of the Central Committee of the party in 1967.[30] The plenum was held in secret from May 4–8, 1967, and no agenda of the plenum was announced. Nor was any agenda announced for the sixteenth plenum, which was held from June 28 to July 3, 1967. What kind of plot was exposed is, of course, not known, but it was during the time that the partisan generals were pursuing a militant policy that resulted in the assassination attempt on South Korean President Park and the North Korean capture of the *Pueblo* in 1968. It was also at this time that Kim Il Sung was on the receiving end of an attack by the Chinese Red Guards.

It was also made public only in the 1980s, after junior Kim was designated heir, that he had been elected secretary of the Central Committee of the party as early as September 1973 and a member of the Political Committee of the Central Committee in February 1974. There is no way to verify these claims, since interim elections are not announced by the party. Junior Kim led the Three-Revolution team movement, and he was responsible for numerous "speed campaigns" such as the seventy-day battle inaugurated in 1974. Kim Jong Il is considered loyal to his father, and to prove both his loyalty and his filial piety he coordinated the construction of the Arch of Triumph, the Tower of *Chuch'e*, the Kim Il Sung Stadium, and a host of other monuments to commemorate his father's seventieth birthday in 1982.[31] It is also alleged that it was the junior Kim who coined the word "Kimilsungism" to denote his father's political thought as early as 1973. In the days of Kim Il Sung, Kim's thought was known as the *chuch'e* idea; in his son's generation it has come to be called "Kimilsungism."

Kim Jong Il's takeover of party operations should not be taken lightly. It has been nearly a decade since Kim Il Sung alerted his party faithfuls to support his plan to name his son successor, and today junior Kim seems to have assumed effective control of the party. Kim Jong Il's generation is taking over the government and the military, as well. The new premier of the Administration Council, Kang Sŏng-san, who replaced the former premier Yi Chong-ok, is a son of the late Kang Kŏn, former chief of the General Staff of the Korean People's Army during the Korean War and an old guerrilla comrade of Kim Il Sung in Manchuria. Kang Kŏn died during the Korean War on September 9, 1950, while fighting for Kim Il Sung. Another son of one of Kim's old guerrillas is the chief of the General Staff of the North Korean Army, General O Kŭk-yŏl, whose father was O Chung-hŭp, who died fighting for Kim Il Sung in Manchuria.[32] There are also the sons of Kim Ch'aek, and there must be many more children of guerrillas occupying important positions in the North. If the takeover of North Korea by Kim Jong Il means the takeover by these children of Kim's guerrillas and their generation, Kim's plan to have his son succeed him may indeed work.

Kim Jong Il is not only the eldest son of Kim Il Sung by his first wife; he is also a graduate of Kim Il Sung University. In April 1979, he was decorated with the First Order of Kim Il Sung, the highest honor any North Korean can receive, by the Central People's Committee of North Korea. Kim Jong Il is already acclaimed as "great thinker and theoretician, outstanding genius of leadership, boundlessly benevolent teacher of the people, and the great leader of the century."[33] The North Korean people claim that Kim Jong Il stands at the head of the Workers' Party of Korea and their revolution.

We know very little about Kim Jong Il, who is about to inherit North Korea from his father. It is said that he is married and has two children, making Kim Il Sung a grandfather.[34] He has a sister, Kyŏng-hŭi, about whom nothing is reported, and four stepbrothers and stepsisters from his stepmother, Kim Sŏng-ae, the second wife of Kim Il Sung.[35] The Korean kingdoms of the past were full of stories about power struggles among potential family rivals: a son undermining his stepmother, an uncle assassinating his nephew, brothers fighting for the crown, and sons and stepsons waiting for the father to die.

16

Semiretirement in
the New Era

The seventh Supreme People's Assembly was convened in April 1982, and at its first session on April 5, Kim Il Sung was reelected president of the republic for still another four-year term. This was a perfunctory exercise — not because there were no challengers for the position but because he was not bound by his term of office. The agenda of the fifth session of the seventh Supreme People's Assembly, held in April 1986, dealt with the environmental protection law and the state budget rather than the reelection of President Kim. No one doubted his ability to be reelected, but the question of his expiring term of office was not even raised.[1]

It is more important to note that the seventh Supreme People's Assembly was convened in time to celebrate his seventieth birthday on April 15, 1982, and there was indeed a great celebration, including the unveiling of the world's tallest stone monument, the *chuch'et'ap*, a North Korean Arch of Triumph, the Kim Il Sung stadium, and a host of other monuments. To celebrate the occasion of Kim's birthday, the North Korean government extended an invitation to more than 200 representatives from 118 countries.

Kim in Semiretirement

It has become obvious that Kim has gradually turned over the affairs of the state and the party to his son. His prodigious energy, if not his term of office, seems to have expired. While his political power has not been challenged, his harsh rule of his people seems to have given way to the needs of a new generation. At the time of the first session of the seventh Supreme People's Assembly, Kim still retained his old partisan comrades from the guerrilla days, but many of them began to die. Two of his three vice-presidents of the republic died within two years of their election to the post: Kang Yang-uk on January 9, 1983, at the age of eighty, and Kim Il on March 9, 1984, at the age of seventy-four.[2]

Kim is used to seeing his close comrades leave him, either by defection during the days of his guerrilla struggle or by natural causes during his political rule of the North, but since his seventieth birthday a host of his long-time comrades and close friends have died in rapid succession. In addition to Kim Il and Kang Yang-uk, the losses that affected him most were the deaths of Ch'oe Yong-gŏn, his partisan guerrilla and long-time vice-president, on September 19, 1976, at the age of seventy-six,[3] and Ch'oe Hyŏn, who died at the age of seventy-five on April 9, 1982, a few days before Kim's birthday celebration.[4] Ch'oe Hyŏn was truly Kim's comrade-in-arms. He fought with him in Manchuria and in the Korean War and helped in building and refining the North Korean army. Ch'oe served as vice-chairman of the Military Affairs Commission under the chairmanship of Kim, and he was known as the only person who could speak freely to Kim in private.

There were others: Chŏn Ch'ang-ch'ŏl, who died on March 8, 1982; O Paek-yong, who was Kim's trusted partisan general of the North Korean army and who died on April 6, 1984, at the age of seventy-one; and Kim Man-gŭm, a long-time cabinet minister who died on November 2, 1984. Only a handful of his partisan comrades are left now, such as Pak Sŏng-ch'ŏl and Yim Ch'un-ch'u, who became vice-president of the republic, but Pak, for example, had joined Kim's guerrilla force as a boy in the children's detachment, and Yim was once purged by Kim for less than adequate loyalty.

They are hardly comrades to whom Kim can confide the trials and tribulations of his old age.

There were visible signs of Kim's relaxation. He seldom made the on-the-spot guidance tours to the countryside that he had enjoyed so much in the past. His son, Kim Jong Il, took up the chores of making the rounds, increasing the number of such guidance tours each year. The junior Kim is reported to have made approximately ten guidance tours in 1982 and 1983, but the number more than doubled in 1984. The elder Kim also made fewer appearances at public gatherings and reduced the number of his speeches. Except for welcoming remarks at banquets entertaining visiting dignitaries, he seldom addressed the problems of domestic politics and international issues.

Since April 1982, Kim has made only three speeches that can be considered important, including the one he made at the time of his birthday celebration. On April 14, 1982, Kim made a speech outlining three policies designed to enhance the power of the people: by strengthening the ideological, technological, and cultural revolutions, developing socialist economic construction, and emphasizing the role of an independent government.[5] The second important address was his speech in June 1983 to a delegation from Peru reviewing the Korean people's struggle to apply the *chuch'e* idea.[6] The third was his lecture to the teaching staff and students of Kim Il Sung Higher Party School on May 31, 1986.[7] However, these speeches were more a review of his past accomplishments than an outline of what needs to be done in the future. Even the speech he delivered to commemorate the thirty-fifth anniversary of the founding of the republic on September 9, 1983, was a short speech reviewing his past achievements.[8]

There were still other signs. Kim was fond of granting numerous interviews to foreign correspondents — he granted fourteen interviews in 1974 and twelve in 1975 — but since April 1982 this number has dwindled to only a few per year. He granted only one interview in 1983, to a delegation of "Scinteia," an organ of the Central Committee of the Romanian Communist Party. In 1984 he gave only two: one to the Soviet news agency, Tass, on May 31, 1984, and another to the editor-in-chief of the *Review of International Affairs* of Yugoslavia on December 28, 1984. There were four interviews in 1985: Kim answered questions raised by the first secretary of the Young Communist League of Romania in March, by the managing editor of the Japanese magazine *Sekai* and the deputy director of *Granma*, the organ of the Communist Party of Cuba in June, and by the editor-in-chief of *Kommunist*, the organ of the League of Communists of Yugoslavia in October 1985.[9]

After his seventieth birthday, Kim Il Sung traveled to China, the Soviet Union and East European countries. Kim's visit to Beijing in September 1982 was in part to reciprocate the earlier visit by Hu Yaobang and Deng Xiaoping to Pyongyang in April at the time of Kim's seventieth birthday, but, more important, Kim seems to have restored friendly relations with China and healed the wounds he had suffered at the hands of the Red Guards during the Cultural Revolution. In his speech at the Chengdu mass rally to welcome him, Kim reiterated their firm friendship by stating that "Korea and China have an exceptional relationship. The relationship between the two countries is as inseparable as the lips and teeth in the true sense of the word, a relationship between revolutionary comrades-in-arms and a relationship of kith and kin sealed with blood."[10]

Kim acknowledged the Chinese assistance during the Korean War and said that the Korean people will always remember that aid. He even cited an obscure hero of the Chinese people's volunteers named Huang Qiguang who came from Sichuan province, and he thanked the people of Chengdu for their help. The North Korean newspaper echoed his sentiment in two editorials.[11]

Kim visited the Soviet Union and East European countries for nearly a month from late May to late June 1984. His trip to the Soviet Union was his first in more than two decades. (He had deliberately avoided going to the Soviet Union after the Soviet-Korean dispute in the early 1960s). It was a leisurely trip by train across Siberia from Ch'ŏngjin to Moscow, leading an entourage of more than 250 government officials. In his speech at the banquet hosted by the ailing Chernenko, Kim expressed his wish to renew traditional friendly relations between the two countries.[12]

He went on to visit Wojciech Jaruzelski in Poland and then toured East Berlin and Prague, meeting with Erich Honecker and Gustav Husak. He also visited Janos Kadar in Hungary and Veselin

Djuranovic in Yugoslavia and concluded a treaty of friendship and cooperation with Todor Zhivkov of Bulgaria. He renewed his friendship with Nicolae Ceausescu of Romania, and at a mass rally held in his honor in Bucharest, Kim expressed his warm feeling toward the Romanian people and their leader.

When he returned from his trip, Kim began wearing a western-style coat and tie, replacing the usual people's jacket he had worn since the republic was first established in 1948. This may have been a symbolic gesture, but there were visible signs that the people too were more relaxed. They began wearing more colorful clothing than the customary workers' uniforms they had worn for so long. At the same time, Kim appears to have reconciled whatever difficulties remained from his disputes with these countries. To Kim, the leaders of the Soviet Union and China, as well as the leaders of the socialist countries in Eastern Europe, were a new generation, and he may have paid a goodwill visit to announce the coming of a new generation of leaders in North Korea as well.

Because an amicable relationship with the Soviet Union had been restored, Kim Il Sung celebrated, on August 15, 1985, the fortieth anniversary of the Soviet liberation of North Korea. The Soviet Union sent a government and military delegation headed by G. A. Aliyev, a member of the Politburo and first vice-chairman of the Council of Ministers, and Marshal V. I. Petrov, the first deputy minister of defense. Similarly, the Chinese sent a delegation in October 1985 to commemorate the thirty-fifth anniversary of China's entry into the Korean War. The delegation was headed by Li Peng, a member of the Politburo of the Chinese Communist Party and a vice-premier. These celebrations were conducted for the first time in twenty years. It was 1965 when Kim suspended observation of the Chinese and Soviet contributions to Korea. He now seems to have restored good relations with these countries and has recognized their contribution to Korea by rebuilding, much larger this time, the monuments he had built some three or four decades ago.

Kim Il Sung made two additional visits: one to the Soviet Union in October 1986, and another to China in May 1987. Both trips were short and sudden, each lasting less than a week. His visit to the Soviet Union seems to have been a courtesy call to meet with the newly elected general secretary of the Communist Party of the So-

viet Union, Mikhail Gorbachev. The visit was announced suddenly, and came shortly after Gorbachev's return from the Reykjavik
summit with President Reagan. Before his trip to the Soviet
Union, Kim had conferred with Chinese president Li Xiannian,
who visited Kim in Pyongyang. Kim was accompanied by Hŏ Tam
and Kim Yŏng-nam, his former and current foreign ministers.

His visit to China in May 1987 lasted only five days, beginning
May 21.[13] He was accompanied again by his current and former
foreign ministers and his former premier Yi Chong-ok. In addition
to the goodwill visit to Beijing, Kim toured Tianjin New Port,
inspecting Chinese economic progress. When he returned to
North Korea, a meeting of the Political Bureau of the Central
Committee of the Workers' Party of Korea was convened on May
27, 1987, and the meeting discussed Kim's visit to China. It was
reported in the meeting that the Chinese leaders wished Kim and
the North Korean people success in fulfilling the goals of the
Third Seven-Year National Economic Plan. The true intent of
Kim's goodwill visits to both the Soviet Union and China seems
to be in soliciting support for North Korean economic development, but Kim no longer takes two hundred and fifty government
officials with him on his trips and does not seem to carry the kind
of influence he used to have in the past.

Changes in the New Era

Although not easily noticeable and difficult to document, important changes occurred in North Korea after Kim's seventieth birthday. With Kim in semiretirement, his son and his son's generation
seem to have initiated policies that can be distinguished from the
traditional policy stance in North Korea. Changes in the new era
can be detected in inter-Korean relations, the emergence of new
leaders among party and government officials, and in the way economic issues are handled.

When he granted an interview with a Japanese magazine editor
on June 9, 1985, Kim finally conceded the difficulties in his reunification policy. He hopes to achieve reunification in his generation,
he said, but if that is not possible the work should be carried on
in his son's era.[14] Kim's hard-line unification policy continued into

the early 1980s, and he tried to undermine the government of the fifth republic in South Korea. At the time of the Sixth Party Congress in 1980, he reiterated his affirmation of the Ten-Point Policy, essentially repeated his proposal to create a confederal republic known as the democratic Confederal Republic of Korea. He also had his Vice-President Kim Il propose a joint meeting of one hundred political leaders from North and South Korea by designating fifty South Korean political leaders, including many antigovernment dissidents in the South, who could participate.

In his effort to isolate South Korea, Kim had long tried to establish contact with the United States. He has not been successful, of course, and when the United States advised him that he should begin a direct dialogue with the South Korean authorities, Kim proposed in February 1983 to meet with the leaders of South Korea to discuss a single-item agenda — removal of U.S. troops from South Korea. The most telling manifestations of Kim's hard-line policy was the bombing incident in Rangoon on October 9, 1983, an attempt to assassinate South Korean President Chun Doo Hwan during his official state visit to Burma. The North Korean terrorists failed in their assassination attempt, but they succeeded in killing seventeen high government officials. Although Kim vigorously denied North Korean involvement in the bombing, the Burmese government, after an extensive investigation, found North Korea and its agents guilty and severed diplomatic relations with North Korea.

After the Rangoon terrorist incident, there were signs of change in North Korea's reunification policy. The first such sign was the announcement in September 1984 that the North Korean Red Cross Society would send relief goods to flood victims in the South. They delivered 50,000 sŏk of rice (approximately 7,200 tons), 500,000 meters of textiles, 100,000 tons of cement, and 759 cases of medical supplies. This was the first time since the division of the country nearly four decades before that such a goodwill offer was made and accepted by both sides.

Shortly thereafter, in November 1984, North Korean Vice-Premier Kim Hwan proposed bilateral economic talks, and the two sides have met and discussed various proposals. At the time of the fourth session of the seventh Supreme People's Assembly on April

9–10, 1985, Hŏ Tam proposed a meeting of representatives of the Supreme People's Assembly of the North and the National Assembly of the South, and the leaders of the legislatures of North and South Korea met to discuss political problems.[15] Two such meetings took place in 1985.

The most important development was the exchange of the 151-member delegation of separated families and performing artists in September 1985. The arrangement for the exchange was made by the Red Cross organization, and for the first time since the division of Korea the two sides exchanged nonpolitical personnel for humanitarian and cultural purposes. Nearly fifty separated families were briefly reunited. Although each side criticized the other harshly after the reunion, it was an important step toward lessening tension between the two, and there was a definite change in North Korea's reunification policy that can be called a significant modification of Kim's hard-line policy.

The leaders of the new era in the North seem to have changed even their strategy for South Korean revolution. In August 1985, North Korea announced that it was changing the name of the Revolutionary Party for Reunification, a fictitious organization set up to effect a South Korean revolution, to the Korean National Democratic Front, and the name of its propaganda radio station from Voice of the Revolutionary Party for Reunification to Voice of National Salvation.[16]

There have been more definite signs of change within the North Korean political leadership since the first session of the seventh Supreme People's Assembly in 1982. Each session after the first session of the Supreme People's Assembly dealt with what is known as the organization problem: replacing high-ranking party and government officials. Some of these changes came from the need to fill vacant positions caused by the death of Kim's partisan leaders, but the change can also be attributed to the recruitment of new leaders with whom Kim Jong Il wanted to consolidate his power.

After the first session of the seventh Supreme People's Assembly, Vice-Presidents Kim Il and Kang Yang-uk died. Yim Ch'un-ch'u, the secretary of the Central People's Committee, was elected vice-president at the second session in April 1983. Yi Yong-ik was appointed secretary of the Central People's Committee, and Ch'oe

Yong-nim was named a member of the committee. Top officers of the Supreme People's Assembly were also replaced: Chairman Hwang Chang-yŏp and Vice-Chairmen Hŏ Chŏng-suk and Hong Ki-mun were replaced by new Chairman Yang Hyŏng-sŏp and two new vice-chairmen, Son Sŏng-p'il and Yŏ Yŏn-gu. Kim Il-tae was elevated to membership in the Standing Committee of the Supreme People's Assembly.

At the time of the third session of the Supreme People's Assembly, which was held less than a year later from January 25–27, 1984, even more changes were made in top government positions. Premier Yi Chong-ok was promoted to vice-president and Kang Sŏng-san was appointed premier of the Administration Council. In place of Kim I-hun, Kim Pong-ju was appointed secretary of the Central People's Committee, and four members (Kim Man-gŭm, Chu Ch'ang-jun, Pak Su-dong, and Chi Ch'ang-ik) were newly elected to the Standing Committee of the Supreme People's Assembly. A number of vice-premiers were also appointed, among them Cho Se-ŭng, Kim Pok-sin, and Kim Ch'ang-ju. An Sŭng-hak replaced Kim Hwan as chairman of the Budget Committee, and Ch'ae Hŭi-jŏng replaced Yun Ki-bok as chairman of the Bills Committee.

There were more frequent changes within the Central Committee of the Workers' Party of Korea. Every plenary meeting since the seventh plenum of the Sixth Central Committee held in June 1983 to the eleventh plenum held in February 1986 took up the organization problem. At the eighth plenary meeting in December 1983, for example, former Foreign Minister Hŏ Tam was elected a member of the Politburo, and three men (An Sŭng-hak, Hong Sŏng-yong, and Kim Pok-sin) were elected alternate members of the Politburo. There were also changes in membership of the Central Committee.[17]

At the time of the joint meeting of the Politburo and Central Committee of the Workers' Party of Korea and the Central People's Committee of the Supreme People's Assembly in October 1985, there were still more changes. Yŏn Hyŏng-muk, An Sŭng-hak, and Kim Pok-sin were appointed vice-premiers of the Administration Council, while Ch'oe Yong-nim, Kong Chin-t'ae, and Kim Hwan were relieved from that post.[18] However, in less than six months, the eleventh plenum of the sixth Central Committee was held from February 5-8, 1986, and a number of top-level leaders recently appointed alternate members of the Politburo were removed, including Kong Chin-t'ae, Hong Sŏng-yong, and An Sŭng-hak. Some new and unknown leaders including Hong Si-hak and Hong Sŏng-nam, were recruited. Similarly such important members of the party secretariat as Yŏn Hyŏng-muk, An Sŭng-hak, and Kim Chung-nin were relieved as secretaries of the party and new ones elected, including Yi Kŭn-mo, Kim Hwan, and Kye Ŭng-t'ae.

Such rapid change in the high-level government and party leadership is unprecedented in North Korea and its true meaning is not known. But a change in the top leadership to accommodate the transition from Kim Il Sung to a new era under Kim Jong Il cannot be ruled out. It is difficult, if not impossible at this time, to identify those who are loyal supporters of Kim Jong Il and his generation of leaders in the North, but clearly a change is taking place in North Korean politics.

There are still other differences. When Kim was active in the affairs of state, he drove the people to make superhuman efforts by working 480 minutes instead of eight hours per day and devised five-, six-, and seven-year economic plans and various working methods to mobilize the people. He held party congresses to initiate or celebrate the completion of these economic plans, but when his second seven-year National Economic Plan (1978–1984) was completed a year later in 1985, a mere bureau of the government, the Central Statistical Bureau, reported the plan's completion, claiming that the goals of the plan had been surpassed. Furthermore, the third seven-year economic plan was not announced. Instead a modest one-year economic plan was proclaimed at the tenth plenum of the sixth Central Committee of the party in December 1984.[19]

Such a relaxed attitude about the nation's economic plan does not indicate that North Korea is no longer interested in economic development. Indeed, great attention has been paid to economic endeavors, perhaps because of a feeling that North Korea lags behind the South. Apparently the leaders of the new era believe that Kim Il Sung's style of economic planning is no longer useful and his style of mobilization has its limits. Kim used to indoctrinate his people by saying that life in the North was so much improved compared to the time of the Japanese occupation that North Korea had nothing in the world to envy. On September 8, 1984, North Korea announced a joint-venture law in an effort to attract foreign investment. The law, consisting of five chapters and twenty-six articles, is most generous to foreign investors in North Korea, but there have been few takers.[20]

Adoption of the joint-venture law is a far cry from the proud slogan proclaiming that North Koreans have nothing to envy. The change in the new era recognizes that there is much in the world that the North Korean people need and want, and the new leaders seem to be trying to meet those needs. Many leaders of the North have visited the Shenzhen Special Economic Zone in Guangdong, China, in an effort to establish something similar in North Korea.

Kim Il Sung was reelected president of the republic at the eighth Supreme People's Assembly in December 1986 and is still general secretary of the party. Yi Kŭn-mo replaced Kang Sŏng-san as new premier of the Administration Council. Kim still participates in important ceremonies, such as the completion of the Namp'o Barrage on June 24, 1986, and still greets visitors occasionally, but his visitors, while meeting Kim Il Sung, have also begun to bring gifts to Kim Jong Il.[21] The extent of the new premier's relationship with Kim Jong Il is not known, but a change is taking place in North Korea. In late 1985, Kim expanded the cemetery for Revolutionary Martyrs in Taesŏngsan, on the outskirts of Pyongyang, and enshrined more than one hundred of his most loyal partisans. He appears to spend more time now reviewing his past accomplishments and seems to enjoy himself in semiretirement. Kim Il Sung can still exercise absolute power in the North, but he did not even speak at the second session of the eighth Supreme People's Assembly in April 1987 when the third seven-year National Economic Plan was launched. A new era has dawned.

VII

CHUCH'E AND THE
REPUBLIC

Kim's political ideas have developed from his anti-Soviet and
pro-Chinese stance of the 1950s after the Korean War. Like Mao
Zedong, Kim claimed that his ideas are an adaptation of the universal truth of Marxism and Leninism to the conditions peculiar to
Korea, and that his ideas represented his efforts to domesticate
communism specifically for Korea. However, after he had successfully rejected Soviet domination and Chinese interference in affairs
Korean and established his independence, he began to preach his
ideas as the universal truth. There are numerous centers throughout the Third World, all financed by North Korea, to study what
is now known not simply as *chuch'e*, but as Kimilsungism.

The republic Kim has built in North Korea is full of tributes to
his accomplishments. It looks more like a kingdom, where the eldest son is succeeding to his father's throne, than a Communist or
socialist state that all Korean Communists have fought for. All the
tributes, in fact, do disservice to his true accomplishments.

17

On Kim's
Political Thought

The political thought of Kim Il Sung is known as *chuch'e* (*juche*).
It consists of two Korean words: *chu* means lord, master, owner,
ruler, the main, and so forth; *ch'e* means the body, the whole, the
essence, the substance, a style. In Korean, the word refers to the
basic object, the main constituent, or basis of action. It is often used
with the suffix *sŏng* — for example, *chuch'esŏng*, meaning to act in
accord with one's own judgment. *Chuch'e* is the most important
political idea with which Kim ruled the people. It signified the
end of political dependence and subservience to the Soviet Union
and China and the promotion of Kim himself as a leader and thinker to the nonaligned nations. Article 4 of the 1972 constitution states
that North Korea is guided in its activity by the *chuch'e* idea —
creative application of Marxism and Leninism to the condition peculiar to the country. It is alleged that Kim domesticated communism in the North with this idea, but close analysis reveals that
the idea of *chuch'e* is irrelevant to the tenets of communism or the
intellectual profundities of Marxism and Leninism.

The Idea of Chuch'e

In his explanation of the idea, Kim said that the basis of *chuch'e* is man. Man is the master, and he decides all matters. The master of socialist construction is the masses, and the power to effect revolution and construction rests with the people. The master of one's fate is oneself, and the power to control one's fate rests with oneself.[1] In carrying out revolution and socialist construction, the Korean people should creatively apply the general truth of Marxism and Leninism to the specific realities of Korea and take into account the historical and practical situations, their own capacity and tradition, and their level of consciousness.

To establish *chuch'e* means to approach the revolution and construction by oneself in a self-reliant manner, using one's own head, trusting in one's own strength, relying on one's own revolutionary spirit of self-reliance, and rejecting dependence on others. It also means to maintain a creative mind, oppose dogmatism, apply the universal principle of Marxism and Leninism and the experiences of other countries to suit the national characteristics of one's own country.[2]

He said that the Koreans should respect the experiences of other countries, but they also should analyze them critically and adopt only those that would benefit their cause. The adoption of foreign ideas should be made at their own pace and at their own convenience in view of the situation prevailing in their own country. One should be the master of one's own revolution. What was accomplished in the North, he said, was done independently by the Korean people under the general principle of Marxism and Leninism. But there were many problems of modern Korea for which Marxism and Leninism had no prescriptive direction, and these were solved by the Koreans themselves in a self-reliant manner. Kim said that *chuch'e* is the Korean revolution.[3]

Under this principle of self-reliance, Kim formulated what is known as the monolithic ideological system (*yuil sasang ch'egye*) for North Korea. This thought system encompassed the idea of *chuch'e* in ideology, the idea of *chaju* (independence) in political work, the idea of *charip* (self-sustenance) in economic endeavors, and the idea of *chawi* (self-defense) in military affairs.[4] A self-reliant posture is essential for implementation of the principles of political independence, economic self-sustenance, and military self-defense. Since the master of revolution in any country is the people, the people should be armed with self-reliant thought, solving problems on their own and creating a national consciousness unique to Korea. Only through such ideological preparation of the people is it possible to attain true ideological liberation from flunkyism, revisionism, national nihilism, and all forms of ideological oppression.

The idea of *chaju*, the principle of political independence, is indispensable if a state is to become master of its destiny. In relations among nation-states, every state has equal rights and the right of self-determination. Every state must have the right to chart its future in order to assure the freedom and prosperity of its people. The idea of *chaju* also demands complete equality and mutual respect among nations. It refuses subjugation by others and also opposes the enslavement of others. Political independence is the basic guarantee for economic self-sustenance and military self-defense.[5]

The idea of *charip*, the principle of economic self-sustenance, shows the direction and content of socialist economic construction. It demands a self-sustaining economy constructed by the workers of the country with the resources produced in their own country under the spirit of self-resuscitation. To rely on other countries economically is to compromise political independence. Until economic self-sustenance is achieved, no country can escape a situation similar to the colonial enslavement of the past. Only through the self-sustaining economy of each country can mutual cooperation and economic development be fostered among nation-states. Such a self-sustaining economy is the material guarantee for a nation's political independence and military self-defense.[6]

The idea of *chawi* is the principle of military self-defense. It means to defend the people and the state from the aggression of imperialists and protect the revolutionary achievements of the country from aggressors. The principle also governs the military construction and military preparedness of every socialist and Communist state against the imperialist countries. It demands that every state should build military forces on its own and not depend on the military forces of other countries. It also demands that each state should be prepared to meet aggressors with its own military strength. So long as there are imperialist countries, the military self-defense of each country is the only means to safeguard political independence and foster economic development of the socialist states.[7]

What Kim has advocated in this monolithic ideological system sounds very much like nationalism — indeed, very much like Jacobin nationalism — but he said that the idea of *chuch'e* is not nationalism. He said that its purpose is to construct on its own the Communist system in Korea, and by such construction the Koreans are fulfilling their national responsibility to the international socialist and Communist movement. The idea of *chuch'e*, he said, was not in conflict with proletarian internationalism; on the contrary, it strengthens it. Every independent and self-reliant socialist revolution is part of the world Communist revolution. The independent socialist construction in each country is not only the responsibility but the duty of each self-reliant member of the international revolutionary movement. True proletarian internationalism is closely related to socialist patriotism. One who is not interested in one's own fatherland cannot be faithful to internationalism, and one who is not faithful to internationalism cannot love the people and their country. A true patriot is an internationalist, and a true internationalist is a patriot.[8]

The essence of *chuch'e* is to apply the general principle of Marxism and Leninism creatively, to reject revisionism, to abstain from unconditional reliance on the Big Powers, to oppose national nihilism and exclusivism, and to warn against uncritical restoration of the past. By national nihilism, Kim meant the negative attitude of North Korea toward its own past and the giving of undue credit to things non-Korean. On the other hand, he warned against restorationism — that is, restoring only their own past and uncritically praising their tradition.[9]

Last, but perhaps most important, is the role of the supreme leader, *suryŏng*, in the idea of *chuch'e*. Each state should have its own *suryŏng*, and the workers and people of each state should be armed with the thought of their own *suryŏng* to establish unity of thought and action. The idea stresses the unity of the revolutionary ranks around the *suryŏng* — the source of the people's unlimited loyalty and confidence they will succeed in their every endeavor.[10]

Clearly, then, the idea of *chuch'e* is not the philosophical exposition of an abstract idea; rather it is firmly rooted in the experience of the North Korean people and Kim Il Sung. It is basically a North Korean effort to be self-reliant — a reaction to their past political subjugation, economic dependence, and need for military assistance from the Soviet Union and China. As such it is valuable to Kim and his subjects and explains their often uncompromising and at times completely irrational attitude toward others. Much of their puzzling behavior can be explained in terms of this xenophobia: the domestic regimentation, their isolation from the rest of the world, their abnormal relationship with both China and the Soviet Union, their fanatic propaganda campaigns to Third World countries about their self-reliant posture, reinterpretation of their tradition and history, and even justification of their fanaticism concerning their *suryŏng*, Kim Il Sung. As a political idea, however, it is an inadequate exposition of nationalism and has little relevance to the tenets of Marxism and Leninism.

The Development of Chuch'e

The North Koreans claim that Kim invented the idea of *chuch'e* in the 1930s, and they have begun to rewrite his revolutionary past by incorporating the word *chuch'e* here and there to substantiate their claim. Since about the beginning of the 1970s, they have also engaged in the work of inventing speeches and reports that Kim is alleged to have made during the 1930s. The earliest was a fictitious report he is supposed to have made in Gelun to a regional youth group on June 30, 1930, when he was only eighteen years of age.[11] This report was published for the first time in July 1978, and Kim is supposed to have said that the Korean revolution must be carried out by Korean revolutionaries.

There are approximately fifteen such speeches and reports Kim is supposed to have made during his guerrilla days, all published for the first time in the 1970s.[12] In general, they deal with his appeal for a self-reliant Korean revolution; for example, his alleged speech on September 15, 1943, is entitled "The Korean Revolutionaries Must Know Korea Well."[13] These are apocryphal tales that were written not in the 1930s or 1940s but in the 1970s. If he had

had such notions about self-reliance in the Korean revolutionary movement in the 1930s during his partisan days in Manchuria, it would be exceptionally difficult for him to justify his partisan guerrilla activities with the Chinese rather than with the Korean revolutionaries.

The truth of the matter is that he did not speak about the idea of *chuch'e* at all during his partisan days. Nor did he speak about the idea during the Soviet occupation period after the liberation of Korea. Kim did not even hint at such self-reliance during the Korean War when the Chinese were fighting for him, nor was he eager to apply the principle to the Chinese occupation forces stationed in Korea for eight years from 1950 to 1958. In fact, the idea was first announced while Chinese troops were still occupying the North and was aimed not at China but against the Soviet Union.

It was not until a decade after the liberation of Korea, on December 28, 1955, that Kim first spoke about the idea of *chuch'e* before the propaganda and agitation workers of the party. It was basically an anti-Soviet and pro-Chinese speech.[14] He ridiculed a picture of the Siberian steppe hanging on the wall of a People's Army rest home and portraits of Mayakovsky and Pushkin in elementary schools. He derided the North Korean practice of compiling contents at the end of a book, imitating the Soviet practice, and attacked members of the Soviet Korean group, such as Pak Ch'ang-ok, for criticizing the Korean proletarian literary movement, and Pak Yŏng-bin, for proposing to ease tension by dropping anti-American slogans as in the Soviet Union. He said that some members of the party's Propaganda Department tried to copy mechanically from the Soviet Union in all their work. Many comrades, he said, "swallow Marxism and Leninism raw" without digesting it. He also cited a tendency in North Korea to copy the headlines of *Pravda* blindly and print them in *Nodong sinmun* and condemned the former editor, Ki Sŏk-bok, still another Soviet-Korean. In the original speech, Kim emphasized the need in Korea to undertake the Chinese rectification campaign. This reference to copying Chinese practice was deleted from later editions of his work.[15]

He gave other examples, such as an incident during the Korean War when Hŏ Ka-i, a Soviet-Korean, and Pak Il-u, a member of the Yanan group, quarreled over a strategy, each proposing Soviet and Chinese tactics. But Kim said, this was a waste of energy because it was Korean tactics that were needed. He made a strong case for studying Korean history, citing the lack of attention paid to such revolutionary traditions as the June Tenth Movement and the Kwangju student incident. This marked the beginning of his drive to oust revolutionaries returned from the Soviet Union and other bases abroad and to seek out and upgrade the partisans who had fought with him in the Manchurian plain.

For the next eight years, from December 1955 to February 1963, Kim did not speak often about the idea of *chuch'e*. When he shuttled back and forth from Moscow to Beijing like a man without *chuch'e*, trying to ascertain his own place in the intensifying Sino-Soviet dispute, he was silent about the subject and anything concerning the self-reliance of his party or government. Even at the Fourth Party Congress in September 1961, the last time both the Chinese and the Soviet delegates were invited to a party congress, he refrained from saying anything about the idea of *chuch'e* or political independence from China and the Soviet Union.[16]

It was not until he clearly understood the implications of the Sino-Soviet dispute for North Korea and had chosen sides that he began to elaborate on the subject of *chuch'e*. More important, it was after the Soviet Union had stopped its economic and military assistance to the North that Kim began to speak about self-sustenance and self-defense. It was on February 8, 1963, the fifteenth anniversary of the founding of the Korean People's Army, that Kim spoke about *chaju* (political independence) and *charip* (economic self-sustenance) to the cadres above the level of deputy regimental commander for political affairs of the People's Army, party functionaries, and government leaders.[17] Kim instructed the cadres to arm new recruits with the idea of *chuch'e* and train them to become truly Korean soldiers unspoiled by the influence of the Soviet Union.

This was also the time when Kim had to increase his national defense budget due to the sharp curtailment of military and technical assistance from the Soviet Union. In his speech to the seventh graduating class of Kim Il Sung Military Academy on October 5, 1963, he announced for the first time the idea of *chawi*, military self-defense.[18] Kim said that the army equipped with the *chuch'e* idea was mightier than the army equipped with modern weapons. Kim also revealed that, until a few years earlier, his soldiers had worn uniforms made from imported fabrics and had been fed with imported grains. Now they were self-reliant in these areas.

Full disclosure of his monolithic ideological system was not made until April 1965 when he visited Indonesia. The speech Kim made to Ali Archam Academy of Social Sciences of Indonesia was his way of declaring political independence from China and the Soviet Union. It also earned him an honorary degree from Indonesia. It was this speech that expressed his resolution to sever the two-decades-long hierarchical relationship of "master and puppet" with the Soviet Union and to seek friends in the Third World.[19] During the latter half of the 1960s, his woes increased with the coming of the Chinese Cultural Revolution. The Chinese disowned him and branded him a revisionist, and it was through this Chinese push that he was finally able to justify the claim that he was self-reliant, the founder and subscriber of the great idea of *chuch'e*.

Since the proclamation of *chuch'e* in December 1955, Kim has devised various strategies to implement the idea, such as the Ch'ŏllima movement, the Ch'ŏngsalli method, and the Taean work system, all innovative programs designed to befit the pace and realities of Korea. The idea of *chuch'e* was in full bloom when Kim delivered his speech on the independent line of North Korean foreign policy at the Second Party Conference on October 5, 1966. The idea of a monolithic ideological system was further crystallized in his speech of December 16, 1967, at the fourth Supreme People's Assembly.[20] He emphasized it further at the Fifth Party Congress in November 1970, when he invited no foreign guests to the congress. It was codified in the 1972 constitution, and has become the basic creed of the people and the state.

Undoubtedly Kim has contributed in no small way to the formation of a self-reliant attitude in the North Korean people and has aroused their national consciousness to solve Korean problems by innovation and creativity. He may not have domesticated communism in the North, but he found himself independent in the polycentric Communist world. His choice of words like *chuch'e*, *chaju*, *charip*, and *chawi* can be traced to Korean thinkers of the past, but the ideological framework within which he expounded his thought is uniquely his own and he should be given credit for it.

In the course of establishing *chuch'e*, Kim had more than mild stimuli. The Sino-Soviet dispute contributed much to the development of the self-reliant idea. Its strength lies not in the idea itself but in the process of its development. The bitter experience of the Korean people, their resilience, and their self-respect are responsible for the *chuch'e* idea.

Critique

There are many difficulties with the idea of *chuch'e*, particularly its relevance to Marxism and Leninism, its application to policies at home and abroad, and its development into a fanatic creed. The main difficulty lies in its relevance to the universal principle of Marxism and Leninism. Except for the fact that Kim started with a Communist system built by the Soviet occupation forces, there is little to link the idea of *chuch'e* with communism. It was never explained what elements of Marxism and Leninism were domesticated to become part of the *chuch'e* idea or which aspects of Marxism or Leninism were creatively applied to conditions peculiar to Korea.

It is easier to relate the idea of *chuch'e* to nationalism, but Kim condemned nationalism, saying that it destroys the fraternal relationship among countries because of its element of exclusivism.[21] He said that the basis of *chuch'e* is not nationalism but socialist patriotism. He has failed, however, to explain the difference between patriotism in his socialist patriotism and patriotism in nationalism. Nor does he explain the socialist component of his patriotism. Perhaps it would be more accurate to say that his is merely patriotism practiced in a socialist country.

A North Korean scholar contends that there are three basic characteristics of socialist patriotism: to serve their own people, to be faithful to their own working class, and to be loyal to their own party.[22] No student of nationalism would quarrel with such patriotism, socialist or otherwise, but North Korean scholars have failed to elaborate what characteristics in socialist patriotism are different from nationalism. Moreover, there is no explanation why socialist patriotism should promote proletarian internationalism or fraternal relationship among socialist countries. Kim's socialist patriotism seems to contain what he detests most in nationalism: national exclusivism. Nor is there any explanation of the relationship between socialist countries and capitalist countries based on the idea of socialist patriotism.

In fact, the idea of *chuch'e* can be better explained as a normal and healthy reaction of the Korean people to the deprivation they suffered under foreign domination. Political independence — *chaju* — was the way to renounce the remnants of Soviet and Chinese influence in the North. The principle of economic self-sustenance was used to establish a viable economy when foreign aid was cut off. It should be remembered that it was not Kim who refused Soviet aid in order to launch a self-sustaining economy in the North; it was the Soviet Union that refused to give aid, thus prompting Kim to go it alone. Similarly, with regard to self-defense, Soviet military assistance was curtailed to the point where Kim felt vulnerable, and only then did he advocate the virtues of self-defense. Kim had to pay dearly for self-reliance. He nursed the wound of Soviet rejection, and he had to extend his first seven-year national economic plan for an additional three years. His defense budget grew from 3 percent in the early 1960s to 33 percent of the national budget by the late 1960s.

In all these developments, there is nothing uniquely Marxist or Leninist about these reactions except that they occurred in a self-proclaimed Communist system. Why should such a normal and healthy reaction of the Korean people be regarded as a creative application of Marxism and Leninism? The North Koreans have failed to provide a rationalization in terms of Marxism and Leninism for such uniquely North Korean innovations as the Ch'ŏllima movement, the Ch'ŏngsalli method, the Taean work system, and even the Three-Revolution Team movement. They failed to explain how the universal principle of Marxism was applied in the creation of the uniquely North Korean innovation known as the County Cooperative Farm Management Committee.

There are numerous difficulties in the practical application of *chuch'e* in the North. Kim claims to be independent in politics, self-sustaining in economy, and self-reliant in defending the country. Nevertheless he still relies heavily on China. When Hua Guofeng visited the North in 1978, Kim had his maidens line the streets of Pyongyang with flowers, bowing their heads to the passing motorcade.[23] The spectacle resembled more the old relationship under the tributary system than the new system of *chuch'e.*

North Korea's well-publicized debts in its economic dealings with other countries are hardly the sign of a self-sustaining economy. The North Koreans have suffered a great deal since they decided to go it alone, and their effort to be economically independent from both China and the Soviet Union and to compete on their own in the international marketplace has been a failure.

The extent of North Korea's self-defense cannot be verified since the North has not been attacked. Would the North Koreans fight alone under this principle against an overwhelmingly strong and combined Korean and non-Korean force? The last time around in the Korean War, they certainly did not subscribe to the principle of self-defense. If this principle means self-sufficiency in construction and manufacturing of munitions and weapons, why must the North Koreans still import most of their sophisticated weapons? Closer to reality than these larger issues, one sees North Korean soldiers briskly goose-stepping in uniforms and insignia similar to those of the Soviet Union. Moreover, the political commissars and party functionaries wear uniforms very similar to those of the Chinese, even though the Koreans have their own traditional style of clothes.

The argument against national nihilism was well taken in the idea of *chuch'e.* The Koreans have long looked abroad to find excellence and have downgraded things Korean, not necessarily out of modesty. They readily dismiss Korean history as a sycophantic record of subservience to alien domination and have succeeded in reinterpreting history. What stands out more, however, is not the Marxist interpretation of Korean history but the shift in emphasis from nearly four thousand years of Korean history to less than forty years of Kim's revolutionary activities. More than half of the new thirty-three-volume Korean history deals with only fifty years of Kim's revolutionary past and his rule in the North. His version of the self-reliant *chuch'e* history is replete with exaggeration, distortion, and personal gratification.

In his first speech about *chuch'e* in December 1955, Kim said that historians should study such much-neglected Korean revolutionary activities as the June Tenth and Kwangju student incidents. But they have compromised and study only Kim's revolutionary activity. Although the alleged founding of Kim's guerrilla group in 1932 is commemorated, North Koreans no longer celebrate the March First Movement, let alone study the June Tenth incident. Kim has argued against indiscriminate restorationism, but his selective restorationism has recast the history of his own partisan activities. Even there, scholars have deleted his affiliation with the Chinese guerrillas.

The *chuch'e* idea has developed along the anti-Soviet and pro-Chinese line, and critical reassessment of the Chinese influence has been less than adequate. Kim may have succeeded in denouncing the Soviet domination over Korea, but not that of the Chinese. The Chinese still exercise heavy influence on North Korea as well as on Kim himself. Kim is still engrossed with the idea of filial piety, for example, building shrines for his father and mother for alleged revolutionary activities, and he no doubt expects similar filial piety from his son.

There are abundant examples to show that Kim has been less than self-reliant, such as his endorsement of the five-year trusteeship of Korea shortly after the liberation. Why would a self-reliant *chuch'e*-oriented Korean *suryŏng* subject himself to a five-year trusteeship by occupation forces in liberated Korea? On the first anniversary of the liberation of Korea on August 15, 1946, Kim said that the Korean people "shall *never* forget the blood shed by the sons and daughters of the great Soviet people,"[24] but the passage was deleted in less than a decade. Similar praise of Soviet economic assistance, laudatory remarks about the accomplishments of the Soviet army under the great *suryŏng* Stalin, the liberator, the godfather, and Kim's personal adulation of Stalin's benevolence were all deleted from the earlier edition of his work.[25] Some of these deleted portions are interesting to note, to say the least. For example, Kim said that "only by learning the advanced culture and art of the Soviet Union can we build our own resplendent national culture.[26]

This sort of simple trick to eliminate Soviet influence was only the first step. The phobia has grown to unbelievable proportions.

It is no longer the Soviet Union that liberated Korea; it is their own *suryŏng* Kim. It is no longer the Chinese Volunteer Army that saved the North in the Korean War; it is their own *suryŏng* Kim. Perhaps most fanatic is his son's futile effort to pass on the idea of *chuch'e* as a universal principle, *Kimilsungism*,[27] and to promote the North Korean *suryŏng* Kim as leader of the Third World. Whatever the name and however elaborate his claim, Kim's *chuch'e* idea is nothing more than xenophobic nationalism that has little relevance to communism.

18

The Republic
by Kim

In an age when empires have disintegrated and states have come to honor individual human rights, Kim seems to have reversed the trend in North Korea. From a potentate manipulated by the Soviet Union to sovietize the northern half of Korea after the liberation, Kim has become a ruler who wields more power than the notorious monarchs of the old Korean kingdom. He has used the party to consolidate his power and has established a government to rule an isolated state, but what he has built during the past four decades resembles more his personal kingdom than a Communist state and the people he rules are more his loyal subjects than New Communists.

When he became president of the republic under the new constitution in 1972, there were many provisions to indicate that it had apotheosized his rule in the North. The forty-eight articles of the first three chapters on politics, economics, and culture incorporated his ideas as the guiding principle of the state and canonized his methods of economic development and his revolutionary tradition as the only cultural heritage of the people. It also gave a peculiar twist to individual freedom; while granting the usual freedom of religion, the same article stipulated emphatically the right to propagate against religion.[1]

The usurpation of legislative power was blatant. His every wish was legislated and there was no legislation that did not pass unanimously. Although he was elected for a four-year term (Article 75), no one questioned the legality when he served beyond his term. Article 75 stipulated also that the term of office may be extended to the time of the next election when "unavoidable circumstances" render the election impossible; accordingly the expiration of each of his terms has come amid "unavoidable circumstances," and no election has ever been held on time.[2]

His executive power was not checked by any constitutional provisions. The new constitution provided that no one could serve in the top government posts, including the vice-presidents, members of the Central Peopel's Committee, and the Administration Council, without the president's recommendation. Even the judiciary and the procuratorate were accountable for their work to him. While Article 140 stipulated that the court is independent in administering the law, the Central Court is accountable to the president of the republic two articles later (Article 142). It is bad enough that a constitution is written to serve one man's rule, but when its provisions are grossly ignored it ceases to be a constitution and becomes a "historic document," as Kim said.[3]

What is manifest in the constitution of 1972 should be considered trivia compared with what is being practiced in the North. Kim's self-esteem is satiated only by unbounded loyalty and absolute submission throughout his domain. His cult of personality has been said to eclipse those of such Communist leaders as Stalin and Mao in scope, magnitude, and fervor.[4] Indeed, his cult requires not only subjugation to him but also reverence for his parents and loyalty to his son. He practices not communism in the so-called socialist state but a peculiar brand of oriental despotism.

Tributes

Kim is rarely called president but is commonly referred to as *suryŏng* (supreme leader), an appellation reserved only for the greatest. Kim used to call Lenin "our great *saryŏng*" during the period

316 CHUCH'E AND THE REPUBLIC

of Soviet occupation.[5] While Stalin was alive, Kim used to call him
"our dear and respected *suryŏng*" and *suryŏng* of the "entire working
people of the world."[6] When he needed Stalin's help during the
Korean War, Kim even called him "the godfather of the Korean
people."[7] When help came from China, Kim called Mao *suryŏng*
of the Chinese people.[8] Kim began to call himself *suryŏng* from
1967 during the Sino-Korean dispute when he declared himself self-
reliant. A serious promotion campaign began in earnest when the
Chinese hurled personal insults at Kim during the Cultural Revolution, calling him a revisionist swine who lived like an emperor
of bygone days.

The North Koreans more than matched the long list of prefixes
that characterized the Chinese adulation of Mao. Kim was called
the great leader, the great *suryŏng*, peerless patriot, national hero,
ever-victorious iron-willed brilliant commander, an outstanding
leader of the international Communist movement, an ingenious
thinker, the sun of the nation, the red sun of the oppressed people
of the world, the greatest leader of our time, and on and on. He
seems to have been called by every honorary title imaginable.

It is perhaps understandable that a small country in search of
self-identity should launch a campaign to project an image of unity
and stability of its people and their political system abroad and promote their leader in the process, but the North Korean practice
has surpassed any other campaign anywhere by Communists or
non-Communists. Indeed, the magnitude of adulation often borders on fanaticism. His photograph is displayed ahead of the national flag and the national emblem; the song of Marshal Kim Il
Sung is played ahead of the national anthem; the best institution
of higher learning is named after him; the highest party school is
also named after him; and there are songs, poems, essays, stories,
and even a flower named after him.[9]

Perhaps the best example of this hysteria is the commemoration
of his sixtieth birthday in April 1972. For this occasion the North
Koreans unveiled a revolutionary museum built in marble and a
bronze statue of the *suryŏng* Kim painted in gold standing twenty
meters high (approximately sixty-six feet). The statue is the largest
ever built by Koreans for any leader, dead or alive, past or present.
These colossal monuments occupy 240,000 square meters of the

The great Suryŏng

choicest land in the most scenic spot on the high hill of Mansudae overlooking the River Taedong in Pyongyang. Ironically, it is the same spot where a shrine was erected during the Japanese occupation for worship of the deified Japanese emperors.

The museum was opened on April 25, 1972, with more than 300,000 of his subjects participating. It has ninety-two exhibition rooms with a length of 4,500 meters. It is divided into seven sec-

The Chuch'e Tower, 1982

The Arch of Triumph, 1982

tions; his anti-Japanese struggle period, the liberation of Korea, the Korean War period, the initial phase of socialist construction, the completion phase of socialist construction, the South Korean revolution, and his exploits in the international arena. Each room contains more than a hundred items — from his gloves, shoes, belts, and caps to painting and sculptures depicting his activities during his revolutionary days. Each item displayed is said to have had his personal approval.[10] There is nothing to indicate the efforts of the people or the achievements of the state, only the grossly exaggerated accounts of Kim's personal accomplishments from his cradle to his sixtieth birthday in 1972. The message that comes through clearest is not what he wanted to convey about his greatness but rather his insatiable craving for recognition and deference.

In addition to the museum and statue, many "historical" monuments in marble and granite have been erected. For example, his birthplace was rebuilt with markers for the place where he sat with his father, his fishing spot, his sledding hill, his swing site, his wrestling grounds, his favorite tree, his study spot, and on and on. He also built a statue for his father in Ponghwari, one for his mother in Ch'ilgol, one for his uncle in Hongwǒn, a museum each for them, and marker after marker commemorating more than thirty-three alleged sundry activities. For himself, there are twenty-three "historical" monuments in the Ponch'ǒnbo and Musan areas alone where he fought the Japanese during the late 1930s. For his on-the-spot guidance, the North Koreans unveiled sixty monuments in every province and every major city, factory, mine, and agricultural cooperative. They claim that in less than a thousand days he traveled 1,270,000 *ri* for the purpose of on-the-spot guidance, averaging 127 *ri* (approximately 32 miles) per day. These are incredible claims, to say the least.[11]

A few revelations were made by these monument-building activities. For example, a "historical" marker 2 meters wide and 1.2 meters in height erected on October 10, 1969, commemorates his personal guidance in the third joint plenum held December 21–23, 1950, during the Korean War. This was the panic meeting Kim held after he was chased out of Pyongyang by the United Nations forces, during which he indiscriminately purged some of his top generals. It was alleged that the plenum took place in a town known as

Pyŏrori, but in fact it was held in Kanggye, Chagang county, in Chagangdo near the Yalu River. The monument was erected in Hyanghari, near Kanggye.[12] Another important revelation is a "historical" marker erected on August 10, 1972, in commemoration of Kim's personal visit to Paektusan, the disputed mountain on the border between China and Korea. The inscription on the marker indicates that Kim personally climbed the mountain on August 10, 1963.[13] Here again, the marker is not to define the border between China and Korea but to honor his visit to the mountain.

Every conceivable activity to commemorate his sixtieth birthday was planned — from a songfest to serious lecture sessions by every group from the youth and women's organizations to the party and the government. Scholars were invited from all over the world to celebrate his birthday and pass a resolution praising him as the "red sun" of the oppressed of the world. Kim awarded himself a "double hero gold medal" of the republic and the "order of the national banner, first class," the highest honors of the North. He then established a number of awards in his name, such as the Kim Il Sung medal, the Kim Il Sung gold medal, and the Kim Il Sung youth award. These activities were not confined to 1972, the year of his sixtieth birthday, but continued into the 1980s, intensifying in fervor each year.

For his seventieth birthday in April 1982, an Arch of Triumph was built in front of Moranbong to commemorate Kim's victorious return and the first speech he made on October 14, 1945, after he was introduced to the Korean people as a Korean patriot by the Soviet occupation forces. The Arch of Triumph was built on the spot where he gave the speech. The arch is quite similar to the original in Paris but, of course, for Kim's triumph, bigger. The arch is 60 meters high and 52.5 meters wide, and on it are carved, in bas-relief, seventy Korean azaleas in commemoration of Kim's seventieth birthday.

This is not all. A Tower of *Chuch'e* was built on the banks of the Taedong River to commemorate his original thought in bringing out the *chuch'e* idea. The tower stands 150 meters high with a torch, 20 meters high, on top. The entire tower is 170 meters high, 1 meter higher than the Washington Monument, and the North Koreans claim that it is the highest stone tower in the world. It was built with 25,550 blocks of white granite, each stone symbolizing each day Kim lived until his seventieth birthday. And if the South Koreans can build a stadium big enough to hold the Olympic Games, Kim can do better. Kim Il Sung Stadium was built from the old Moranbong Stadium with a seating capacity of 100,000. The stadium building has a total area of 46,000 square meters, and the arena is 20,230 square meters. When the stadium was opened on Kim's seventieth birthday in April 1982, an international marathon was held with only six countries participating.

The Record

In the fourth decade of Kim's rule in the North, his usefulness as a Communist leader of the people has passed. His style of forced labor and 480-minute working days on a diet of loyalty to him are no longer relevant to the North's future development. His preaching of self-reliance does little more than keep his subjects in bondage. His effort to lure South Korean dissidents and the people of Korea into his domain in the name of the fatherland reunification is a splendid illusion. His campaign to promote himself abroad has been as unrewarding as it is unrealistic. He has succeeded in building a strong party to control the people, but this too has given way to the promotion of his self-esteem. When he was elected president of the republic, the power center shifted from the party to the state, and the state eventually turned into nothing less than his personal domain.

Curiously, Kim's intense craving for deference to his person may be his own admission that he has outlived his usefulness to the people of the North. He said that he wanted to be the servant of the people throughout his life,[14] but he no longer serves the people. It is the people who serve him and his son. Although there is no political force or individual capable of unseating him, it is not the twisted and sad ending of his long career that is at stake. Rather, it is the hardship of people who have nothing but monuments to show for their four decades of toil under his unforgiving rule. Meanwhile they must constantly remind themselves that there is nothing to envy in the world beyond.

The burden of Kim's political leadership in the North is perhaps not the longevity of his absolute and dictatorial rule or even the effort to have his son succeed him, but the suppression of the people. He is no longer interested in the affairs of the people or in building and refining a socialist state, but only in his personal self-esteem. In this sense, he has betrayed the Korean Communist revolution and the aspirations of every Korean Communist who served him, including those old Communists who perished under the Japanese for the cause of communism in Korea.

The campaign to glorify him — not the people he is supposed to have served nor the system the Korean Communists wanted to build — has surpassed fanatic religious fervor. The North Korean "sun of the nation" shines both day and night, and it is hard to escape his ubiquity. His domain glitters with his "historical" monuments, but the people may no longer look at them with awe. Bathed in constant praise, Kim himself has come to believe his sycophants, and nothing short of impetuous praise will satisfy him.

In truth, these tributes are unnecessary. Exaggeration and unsubstantiated claims not only obscure his true record but also do disservice to him, for his true record is impressive. Kim can claim a place in the annals of modern Korea for what he has achieved without fabricating spectacular feats. From the time of his guerrilla days, his persistence and resolve to fight to the end without submitting to the Japanese deserve far more recognition than his claim of having formed a fictitious revolutionary army and political organizations. The fact that he survived and fled to the Soviet Union was indeed fortunate for him, and when he was selected to head the interim governing body by the Soviet occupation authorities, he was given a unique opportunity. What deserves recognition is his ability to have transformed this opportunity into a real political power in the North and not his absurd claim of a victorious return to Korea ignoring the contribution of the United States and the Soviet Union in the Korean liberation.

This is also true in the case of the Korean War. Both the North and South Korean governments advocated a military solution to the Korean division after two separate regimes were established. Kim should attribute the war to the desire of the Korean people to be united and to his effort to reunify the country militarily rather than accuse the South and the United States for starting the conflict. He should also acknowledge the Chinese assistance that saved North Korea rather than claim victory in the war. Similarly, his accusation of attempting to overturn the government is sufficient to put his challengers away; his claim that they are agents of the United States is neither convincing nor relevant.

Kim devoted much time to the reconstruction of North Korea, and it is not difficult to see that he is an industrious man with an unusual amount of energy. He literally practiced his favorite axiom of *ŭisin chakch'ŭk* — setting the standard by his own example. His numerous on-the-spot guidance tours nearly drove the people to the limit of their endurance, but his exaggerated claim of traveling more than thirty-two miles a day for nearly ten years does little to enhance his image as a diligent leader. He was also careful in handling the Sino-Soviet dispute, eventually proclaiming independence and self-reliance. Kim was correct in maintaining that the Sino-Korean and Soviet-Korean disputes were not of his making but were due rather to revisionism in the Soviet Union and dogmatism in China. If Kim secured Korea's northern border with China near Mount Paektu, he should be remembered as the leader who resolved the century-old dispute between China and Korea. Neither North Korea nor China made their border agreement public, and only the monument to Kim Il Sung stands on top of the mountain.

His declaration of independence from both the Soviet Union and China can be considered a victory for him and North Korea, and it was a fortunate turn of events when Kim turned to the nonaligned movement. It took a strong will and courage to curb his militant generals and his old partisan comrades in order to steer the difficult road to nonalignment. But here again Kim failed to exploit his advantage by declaring independence from the Soviet Union and China: instead he used his independence to isolate his people from the rest of the world. He seldom compared the North Korean people to the people of industrialized countries; by using the standard of Third World countries, Kim told his people there was nothing to envy in the world. He spent more time promoting himself as leader of the nonalignment movement than exploiting international markets to benefit his people and enrich his country.

Where Kim failed completely, however, is in South Korea. His unification policy was not only impractical but was also despised by the people of South Korea. Kim has never abandoned his hard-line policy, and although it was not an attempt to unify the country militarily as was the case in the Korean War, he did want the South Korean people and government to subscribe to his policy for reunification. No matter what kind of organization he may have invented to arouse revolutionary fervor in South Korea, such as the Revolutionary Party for Reunification, the reunification of Korea is a goal beyond his reach. In fact, he has made the situation worse by allowing clandestine operations and irresponsible terrorist acts such as tunnels under the demilitarized zone and the bombing in Rangoon.

The idea of *chuch'e* was a logical development for a leader who wished to follow his own course of action. It is good that the Koreans are aware of their past subjugation to the Soviet Union and China, but the effort to promote the idea of *chuch'e* as pure ideology for the people of Third World countries has failed. In fact, such a promotion is a disservice to his valuable idea of self-reliance. *Kimilsungism* will not become a household word in the Third World.

Kim's biggest failure has been his inability to build and refine a socialist political system that will survive him. Instead, what he has built in the North is a political system to accommodate his personal rule, and he has had to appoint his son heir to prolong his republic. In this sense, Kim has betrayed the hopes of all those Koreans who fought to establish a Communist system of government in Korea and died for that cause.

In the darkest of his guerrilla fighting days, Kim was never afraid of the Japanese expeditionary force. What he feared more was the hunger, the cold, the snow, and the defection of his men. Today, in the last years of his life, Kim is not afraid of his political enemies at home or abroad. What he fears more than his enemies are old age, declining health, the growing though benign tumor in his neck, and loneliness as his aging comrades die.

Appendix 1. Partisans of the United Army in North Korean Politics

WPK: Workers' Party of Korea. (Numbers represent party congresses where one was a member or candidate member of the Central Committee.)

SPA: Supreme People's Assembly. (Numbers represent sessions of the assembly where one was a member.)

AC: Administration Council (Cabinet). M–minister; OP–other than ministerial rank post in the cabinet.

KPA: Korean People's Army. gen–generals from major general to marshal; sec–security and police officers; OMP–other military posts.

RAG: Contributed to *Reminiscences of Anti-Japanese Guerrillas*. (Numbers represent volume number where the article appears.)

Name	WPK	SPA	AC	KPA	RAG	Remarks
An Chŏng-suk				sec	4, 6	woman
An Kil	1			gen		died 1947 statue 1968
An Yŏng	4	3, 4		gen	9	diplomat
Chang Sang-yong		4			7	
Chi Kyŏng-su		5	M	sec/gen	1	died 1976
Chi Pyŏng-hak	4, 5	3-5	OP	gen	8, 11	died 1977
Cho Chŏng-ch'ŏl				OMP		died 1950 statue 1968
Cho Myŏng-sŏn	5,6				3, 6	

Cho Tong-uk			OP	sec	2, 3	
Ch'oe Ch'un-guk			OMP			died 1950 statue 1968
Ch'oe Hyŏn	3-6	2-5, 7	M	gen	1, 2 4-7, 10	vice-chairman, National Defense Commission; died 1982
Ch'oe In-dŏk	5, 6	4, 5, 7		gen	8-10	
Ch'oe Ki-ch'ŏl	4	3	OP	sec	1, 6, 7	
Ch'oe Kwang	3, 4, 6	1-4, 7	OP	gen	3, 5, 7	purged 1969 reinstated
Ch'oe Min-ch'ŏl	4	4	OP	gen	3, 6, 9	
Ch'oe Yong-gŏn	3-5	1-5	M	gen		died 1976 vice-president
Ch'oe Yong-jin	3-6	2-5	M	gen		vice-premier
Chŏn Ch'ang-ch'ŏl	4-6	3-5, 7			11, 12	diplomat died 1982
Chŏn Mun-sŏp	4-6	3-5, 7		gen	2, 7-9	
Chŏn Mun-uk	5, 6	4, 7		OMP	7	
Chŏng Pyŏng-gap	4	3, 4		gen	4	
Chu To-il	5, 6	3-5, 7		gen	1, 3	
Han Ik-su	4, 5	3-5	OP	gen	4	diplomat died 1978
Hŏ Ch'ang-suk	5, 6				4	wife of Kim Il
Hŏ Hak-song	3, 4	2, 3				
Hŏ Pong-hak	4	3, 4	OP	gen	1, 2, 4, 5, 9	purged 1969
Hŏ Sŏk-sŏn	4	3, 4				purged 1967
Hwang Sun-hŭi	4-6	3-5, 7			4, 5, 7	woman
Kang Kŏn	2	1	OP	gen		died 1950 statue 1968
Kang Sang-ho			OP	sec/gen		died 1969
Kim Cha-rin	4	4	OP	sec	2-5	
Kim Ch'aek	1, 2	1	M	gen		died 1951 statue 1968
Kim Ch'ang-bong	3, 4	3, 4	M	gen	5, 6	purged 1969
Kim Ch'ang-dŏk	3, 4	2-4		gen		purged 1969
Kim Ch'ŏl-man	5, 6	3-5	OP	gen	10	
Kim Chwa-hyŏk	4-6	3, 4	OP	gen	1, 3, 5, 6	
Kim Ik-hyŏn	5		OP	gen	12	

Name						
Kim Il	1-6	1-7	M	gen		vice-president of the republic; died 1984
Kim Il Sung	1-6	1-7	M	gen		president of the republic
Kim Kwang-hyŏp	2-4	2-4	M	gen		purged 1969
Kim Kyŏng-sŏk	2-4	2		OMP	10	died 1962
Kim Myŏng-jun		2			3	
Kim Myŏng-suk		4			2, 4, 5	woman
Kim Ok-sun	4	3-5			2, 7, 9	woman
Kim Pyŏng-sik	4	3-5	M		4, 9	
Kim Sŏng-guk	5	4		gen	3, 5, 6	diplomat
Kim Tae-hong	4, 5	3, 4	OP	gen	10	
Kim Tong-gyu	4, 5	3-5			3, 7-10	purged 1977
Kim Yang-ch'un		3, 4	OP	gen	7, 8	
Kim Yŏ-jung	3-5	3, 4			1	diplomat died 1978
Kim Yong-yŏn	5, 6	4, 7		gen	2, 4, 7, 8	
O Chae-wŏn	5, 6	4, 5, 7		gen	4, 5	
O Chin-u	3-6	3-5, 7	M	gen	5, 6	Joint Chief-of-Staff of KPA
O Peak-yong	4-6	3-5, 7	OP	gen	2-6, 8, 9	died 1984
Paek Hak-nim	4-6	4, 5, 7	OP	sec/gen	1-3, 6, 7	
Pak Kŭm-ch'ŏl	2-4	2, 3		gen		purged 1967
Pak Kwang-sŏn	4	3, 4	M	gen	7	diplomat
Pak Kyŏng-suk	4	3, 4			8	wife of Kang Kŏn
Pak Sŏng-ch'ŏl	4-6	3-5, 7	M	gen	1-3, 5-8	vice president of the Republic
Pak U-sŏp	4			gen	8	
Pak Yŏng-sun	4-6	3-5, 7	M	gen	1-8	
Sŏ Ch'ŏl	3-6	3-5, 7		gen	8	diplomat
Sŏk San	3, 4	3, 4	M	sec/gen	8	purged 1969
Son Chong-jun				sec	1, 2, 5, 6	
T'ae Pyŏng-yŏl	4-6	3-5, 7		gen	8	
Wang Ok-hwan	5, 6				4	wife of Ch'oe Yong-gŏn
Yi Kuk-chin	4	3, 4			8	former chief justice
Yi Pong-su	4		OP	gen	1, 9	died 1967
Yi Song-un	2-4	2	OP			former procurator-general; diplomat

Yi Tu-ch'an	6	5, 7			1, 5, 12	
Yi Tu-ik	5, 6	3-5, 7	OP	gen		
Yi Ŭl-sŏl	5, 6	3-5, 7		gen	9	
Yi Yong-gu		4			9, 10	former chief justice
Yi Yŏng-ho	3, 4	3, 4	OP	gen		diplomat
Yi Yŏng-suk		4, 5			4, 5	woman
Yim Ch'ŏl	4, 5	4, 5		gen	4-6	diplomat
Yim Ch'un-ch'u	4-6	3, 5, 7	M		1, 2	diplomat vice-president
Yim Hae	1-3	2	M	gen		diplomat
Yu Ch'ang-gwŏn	4	3, 4		gen	6	
Yu Kyŏng-su	3	2		gen		died 1958 statue 1968
Yun T'ae-hong	4	4		gen	1-4, 7, 8	former procur-ator- general

Appendix 2. Partisans of the United Army Not in North Korean Politics

These are mostly men and women who are illiterate, elderly, or physically handicapped.

Chang Chŏl-gu*
Cho To-ŏn*
Ch'oe Pong-ho
Ch'oe Pong-song
Ch'oe Sŏng-suk*
Chŏn Hŭi*
Chŏn Sun-hui*
Han Ch'ŏn-ch'u
Han T'ae-ryong
Hong Ch'un-su
Hwang Kŭm-ok*
Hyŏn Ch'ŏl
Kang Wi-ryong
Kim Chi-myŏng
Kim Ch'ŏl-ho*
Kim Chŏng-p'il
Kim Ch'ung-yol
Kim Myŏng-hwa*
Kim Yong-hwa*
Kim Yu-gil

Ko Hyŏn-suk*
Kong Chŏng-su
Nam Tong-su
O Chuk-sun*
Pak Chŏng-suk*
Pak Kyŏng-ok*
Pak Sŏng-u
Pak Tal
Pak Tu-gyŏng
Sŏk Tong-su
Song Sŭng-p'il
Yi Chŏng-in*
Yi Chong-san*
Yi Myŏng-sŏn
Yi O-song
Yi Pong-nok*
Yi Tu-su
Yu Kyŏng-hŭi*
Yu Myŏng-ok*
Yu Ŭng-sam

* Woman.

Appendix 3. Partisans Who Died Before the Liberation of Korea

Prominent Korean partisans who were Kim's superiors or comrades whom the North Koreans refuse to recognize

An Pong-hak	Fourth Division Commander, Second Army; surrendered September 30, 1936
Chŏn Kwang (alias O Sŏng-yun)	Political Commissar, First Route Army; surrendered January 30, 1941
Chu Chin (alias Chu Chin-su)	Commander, Second Army; arrested February 1935
Han Ho	First Division Commander, First Army; died 1937
Han In-hwa	Chief-of-Staff, First Army; died November 16, 1939
Kim Chae-bŏm	Company Commander, First Division, Second Army; arrested July 12, 1940
Kim Hwa	Division Commander, Eastern Command, Fifth Army; whereabouts unknown
Kim Kwang-hak	Company Commander, Second Army; arrested July 12, 1940
Kim Se-hyŏng	Deputy Comander, First Army; died in 1938
Pak Tŭk-bŏm	Chief-of-Staff, Third Directional Army; arrested September 27, 1940
Sŏ Pyŏng-san	Political Commissar, Seventh Army; whereabouts

	unknown
Yi Kwang-nim	Third Division Commander, Fifth Army; whereabouts unknown
Yi Sang-muk	Political Commissar, Second Army; whereabouts unknown
Yi Tong-il	Organization Chief, Southern Provincial Committee; surrendered

Prominent Korean partisans whose contribution the North Koreans recognize

An T'ae-bŏm	
Chŏng Il-gwŏn	
Hŏ Hyŏng-sik	Chief of Staff, Third Army; died August 3, 1942
Hŏ Song-hak	
Kang Ton	(1914-1938)
Kim Hak-sil	(1919-1938); woman
Kim Nak-ch'ŏn	(1907-1935)
Kim San-ho	(1911-1937)
Ma Tong-hŭi	(1912-1938)
Mun Pung-san	Company Commander, Second Army; died 1935
Nam Ch'ang-il	Detachment Commander, Second Army; died 1935
O Chung-hwa	
Pak Kil-song	(1917-1943); Detachment Commander, Second Army; executed August 12, 1943
Pak Nok-kŭm	(1915-1940); woman who participated in the Poch'ŏnbo raid
Pak Sun-il	Division Commander, Fifth Army; died 1937
Sin Kwang-sun	
Son Wŏn-gŭm	
Yi Hak-man	Commander, Seventh Army; died August 6, 1938
Yi Hong-gwang	Deputy Commander, First Army; died March 1935
Yi Kwŏn-haeng	(1921-1940)
Yi Kye-sun	(1916-1938); woman
Yi Tong-gwang	Company Commander, First Army; died July 1937

Korean guerrillas of the United Army whom the Chinese Communists recognize

Ch'a Yong-dŏk   O Ŭng-yong

Han Ho

Han In-hwa

Hŏ Hyŏng-sik

Hŏ Sŏng-suk*

Kim Chong-guk

Kim Kŭn

Kim Sun-hŭi*

Ma Tŏk-san

O Se-yong

Pae Sŏng-ch'un*

Pak Chin-u

Sŏ Kwang-hae

Yang Yim

Yi Hak-bok

Yi Il-p'yŏng

Yi Kwang-nim

Yi Tong-gwang

Yim Chong-ok*

* Woman

Appendix 4. Chronology of Kim Il Sung

1912	April 15	Born Kim Sŏng-ju as the eldest son of Kim Hyŏng-jik and Kang Pan-sŏk in Man'gyŏngdae near Pyongyang.
1919	Autumn	Kim goes to Manchuria and enters Badaogou Elementary School.
1923	April	Kim returns to Pyongyang and enters Ch'angdŏk Elementary School.
1925	January	Kim returns to Badaogou, Manchuria.
	Spring	Kim enters Fusong Elementary School in Manchuria.
1926	June 5	Kim's father, Kim Hyŏng-jik, dies.
	June	Kim enters Hwasŏng Middle School.
1927	January 17	Kim transfers to Yuwen Middle School in Jilin, Manchuria.
1929	Autumn	Kim is arrested and jailed for participating in a subversive organization.
1930	May	Kim is released from jail.
	July	Kim goes to Gelun to teach school and he is given the pseudonym of Kim Il Sung.
1932	April 25	Il Sung claims to have organized the first anti-Japanese guerrilla unit in Antu, Manchuria. (North Korea celebrates this day as the founding date of the Korean People's Army.)
	July 31	Kim's mother, Kang Pan-sŏk, dies.
1933		Kim participates in small-scale guerrilla

		operations led by Korean and Chinese revolutionaries in Manchuria.
	September 18	Yang Jingyu organizes a Chinese Communist guerrilla force, the Northeast People's Revolutionary Army.
1934	March	Chu Chin, a Korean guerrilla fighter, establishes the second army of the Northeast People's Revolutionary Army.
1935	February	The Daihuanggou meeting is held to deal with the *minsaengdan* problem.
1936	February	The Northeast Anti-Japanese United Army (NEAJUA) is established with Yang Jingyu as commander.
	June 10	The Korean Fatherland Restoration Association is founded by O Sŏng-yun.
	August	Kim fights in the region of Fusung prefecture.
1937	June 4	The Poch'ŏnbo raid by Kim Il Sung and his guerrillas.
	June 9	The musan raid by Ch'oe Hyŏn.
1938	April 26	The Liudaogou raid by Kim Il Sung.
	November	Kim becomes commmander of the Second Directional army of the NEAJUA.
1939	May 18	Kim reenters Korea to fight the Japanese police in border towns.
1940	February 23	Yang Jingyu is killed by Japanese expeditionary forces.
	March 13	Kim's guerrillas fight the Japanese police force headed by Maeda Takashi at Daimalugou in Helong prefecture in Manchuria.
1941	March 8	Wei Zhengmin is killed by the Japanese.
	March	Kim retreats into the Soviet Union and marries his long-time comrade Kim Chŏng-suk.
1942	February 16	Kim's first son, Kim Jong Il, is born in the Soviet Union.
1945	August 15	Korea is liberated by the United States and the Soviet Union, bringing the end of World War II.
	September 19	Kim returns to Korea from the Soviet Union via Wŏnsan by boat.

	October	Kim is introduced to the North Korean people as a hero of the Korean revolution by the Soviet occupation forces.
	December 17	Kim becomes chairman of the North Korean Branch Bureau of the Korean Communist Party at its third enlarged plenum.
1946	February 8	Kim becomes chairman of the North Korean Provisional People's Committee.
	August 28-30	At the founding congress of the North Korean Workers' Party, Kim is elected vice-chairman of the party.
	October 1	Kim Il Sung University is established.
	November 23-24	The South Korean Workers' Party is established.
1947	February 17-20	First Congress of the People's Assembly of North Korea.
	October 12	Mangyŏndae Revolutionary School is established for the children of Korean Communist revolutionaries.
1948	February 8	The Korean People's Army (KPA) is established.
	March 27-30	Second Congress of the North Korean Workers' Party.
	September 2	First Supreme People's Assembly (SPA).
	September 9	The Democratic People's Republic of Korea (DPRK) is founded and Kim becomes its first premier.
1949	June 26	The Democratic Front for the Fatherland Reunification is formed.
	June 30	The North Korean Workers' Party and the South Korean Workers' Party unite to form the Workers' Party of Korea (WPK). Kim becomes its chairman.
	September	Kim Chŏng-suk, Kim's wife, dies while delivering a stillborn baby.
1950	June 25	The Korean War breaks out.
	October 25	Chinese volunteers join the North Koreans and fight the UN forces.
1953	July 27	The cease-fire agreement is signed, bringing an end to the Korean War.

	August 3-6	Trials are held to indict twelve conspirators for high treason.
	September 10-29	Kim travels to the Soviet Union to seek aid.
	November 12-27	Kim travels to China to express appreciation for Chinese help in the Korean War and to seek aid.
1955	December 28	Kim delivers his speech on the *chuch'e* idea.
1956	April 23-29	Third Congress of the WPK.
	June-July	Kim visits the Soviet Union for the 20th Congress of the Communist Party of the Soviet Union (CPSU); he also visits East Germany, Romania, Hungary, Czechoslovakia, Bulgaria, Albania, and Mongolia.
	September 18	Second Supreme People's Assembly.
1957	November 14-19	Kim visits the Soviet Union on the fortieth anniversary of the October Revolution.
1958	March 3-6	First Conference of the WPK.
	November-December	Kim visits China and Vietnam.
1959	January-February	Kim visits the Soviet Union for the 21st Congress of the CPSU.
1960	February	Kim goes to Ch'ŏngsalli and devises the Ch'ŏngsalli method in agriculture.
1961	June-July	Kim visits the Soviet Union and China.
	September 11-18	Fourth Congress of the WPK; Kim is reelected chairman.
	October	Kim visits the Soviet Union to participate in the 22nd Congress of the CPSU.
1962	October 22	Third Supreme People's Assembly.
	November	Kim visits Taean electric factory and prescribes the Taean work method.
1963		Kim marries his second wife, Kim Sŏng-ae.
	August 10	Kim ascends Paektusan, the mountain that signifies the border dispute between China and North Korea.
1965	April 10-20	Kim visits Indonesia, delivers a lecture at Ali Archam Institute for Social Sciences, receives an honorary doctorate from Indonesian University.
1966	October 5-12	Second Conference of the WPK.
1967	December 14-16	Fourth Supreme People's Assembly.

1968	January 16	North Korean commandos attempt to assassinate South Korean president Park Chung Hee.
	January 23	North Korea captures the USS *Pueblo* in the Sea of Japan.
1969	August	North Korea's organization of the Revolutionary Party for Reunification (RPR) in South Korea is revealed.
1970	November 2-13	Fifth Congress of the WPK.
1972	April 14	On his sixtieth birthday, Kim is awarded the Order of Double Hero of the DPRK by the Standing Committee of the SPA.
	July 4	Kim declares the Joint Statement with the South stipulating three principles for national reunification.
	December 25-28	Fifth SPA; Kim is elected president of the DPRK.
	December 27	A new socialist constitution is proclaimed.
1973	June 25	Kim proclaims the Five-Point Policy for national reunification.
1974		Ninth plenum of the Central Committee of the WPK (held in secret).
1975	April 18-26	KIm visits Mao Zedong in China.
	May 22-June 9	Kim visits Romania, Algeria, Mauritania, Bulgaria, Yugoslavia. In Algeria he receives his second honorary doctorate.
1977	December 15	Sixth SPA; Kim is reelected president of the DPRK.
1980	May 7-12	Kim attends Tito's funeral service and visits Romania on his way back from Yugoslavia.
	October 10-14	Sixth Congress of the WPK; Kim is reelected general secretary of the party. His son Kim Jong Il is promoted to the second highest position in the party. Kim announces the ten point policy for national reunification, including the proposal to establish the Democratic Confederal Republic of Korea.
1982	April 5	Seventh SPA; Kim is reelected president of the DPRK.
	April 15	Kim's seventieth birthday is observed by

		unveiling the Arch of Triumph, the Tower of *Chuch'e*, and Kim Il Sung Stadium.
	September 15-25	Kim visits China and meets with Deng Xiaoping and Hu Yaobang.
1983	October 9	North Korean terrorists attempt to assassinate President Chun of South Korea in Rangoon. They fail to assassinate Chun but kill seventeen high-ranking South Korean government officials.
1984	January 10	Kim proposes a tripartite talk among North Korea, the United States, and South Korea.
	May 19-June 21	Kim visits the Soviet Union, Poland, East Germany, Czechoslovakia, Hungary, Yugoslavia, Bulgaria, and Romania.
	November 26-28	Kim makes an unofficial visit to China.
1985	April 9-10	Kim proposes that representatives from the National Assembly of South Korea and the Supreme People's Assembly of North Korea meet to discuss the question of national reunification.
	September	For the first time since Korea's division in 1945, 151-member delegations of North and South are exchanged, reuniting separated families and introducing performing arts troupes in Seoul and Pyongyang.
1986	March 8-11	Fidel Castro of Cuba visits Kim in Pyongyang.
	May 31	Kim delivers a lecture to the teaching staff and students of Kim Il Sung Higher Party School.

Notes

PART I. YOUNG KIM AND THE UNITED ARMY

1. The official account is in *Nodong sinmun*, supplement, April 10, 1952. This work was translated into Chinese and appeared in the Chinese weekly magazine *Shijie zhishi* in 1952 in four installments (May 17, 24, 31, and June 7). For earlier versions see, for example, Han Sŏl-ya, *Uri ŭi t'aeyang* and Yun Se-p'yŏng, "Kim Il Sung changgun ŭi hangil mujang t'ujaeng."

2. Yi Na-yŏng, *Chosŏn minjok haebang t'ujaengsa*, pp. 321-448. This version is no longer used by the North Koreans. Yi was purged and his writings are no longer cited in any of their publications.

3. I met Kim Ŭl-ch'ŏn during my visit to the Academy of Sciences of North Korea in 1974. We had extensive discussions on Kim Il Sung's early revolutionary activities. We agreed on some basic information but disagreed much on interpretation. See his writings in *Chosŏn kŭndae hyŏngmyŏng undongsa*, pp. 292-444.

4. Paek Pong is, of course, a pseudonym, and the identity of this person is not revealed. He is said to be a Korean literary writer residing in Japan who has done extensive research into the life of Kim. See Paek Pong, *Minjok ŭi t'aeyang Kim Il Sung changgun*. The original Korean version is in two volumes. Other versions appeared in three volumes. See the English version, Baik Bong, *Kim Il Sung, Biography*.

5. *Widaehan suryŏng Kim Il Sung tongji chŏn'gi*.

1. Background

1. There are many pamphlets about the place; see, among others, *Mangyongdae* and *The Magnolias of Mangyongdae*.

2. There are many propaganda pamphlets about Kim's father and his alleged revolutionary activities. See, among others, *Kim Hyong-jik*. For his mother see, among others, Mrs. *Kang Ban-sok, Mother of the Great Leader of Korea*.

3. For Kim Hyŏng-gwŏn, see *An Indomitable Revolutionary Fighter, Comrade Kim Hyong Gwon*.

4. Paek Pong, *Minjok ŭi t'aeyang Kim Il Sung changgun*, 1:75-76. For earlier claims of graduation see, among others, *Nodong sinmun*, April 10, 1952; Yi Na-yŏng, *Chosŏn minjok haebang t'ujaengsa*, pp. 336-338.

5. Kim is fluent in Chinese, and this fact was often emphasized by his fellow partisans. See, for example, *Hangil mujang t'ujaeng chŏnjŏkchi rŭl ch'ajŏsŏ*, p. 199.

6. It is interesting to compare the accounts of Kim's early life in Paek Pong with those by Yi Na-yŏng and Kim Ŭl-ch'ŏn. There was no Korean Communist Party in Manchuria in 1930; see my earlier study, *The Korean Communist Movement, 1918-1948*, pp. 261-268.

7. I was very happy to see this document displayed because I had found it and used it in my earlier study. The North Koreans told me they had located the document independently, but they acknowledged that they had also seen it in my study. The original document is available in the Japanese Foreign Ministry Archives "Zai Kirin sōryōjikan oyobi Tonka bunkan," reel SP86, frames 9640-9643. This is a part 12 of the History of the Ministry of Foreign Affairs Police, Manchuria, April 1876-December 1937. See the discussion of this incident in my earlier study, *The Korean Communist Movement, 1918-1948*, pp. 266-267.

8. Yi Kŭm-ch'ŏn, alias Yi Ki-ho, was from Kyŏngsang pukto and a member of the Tuesday Association. Both men were expelled from Manchuria on October 10, 1931, for three years by the Japanese gendarmes stationed in Jilin. See the details in the History of the Ministry of Foreign Affairs Police, Manchuria, April 1876-December 1937, "Zai Kirin sōryōjikan oyobi Tonka bunkan," reel SP86, frames 9994 and 10264.

9. For Wei Zhengmin, see Ji Yunlong, *Yang Jingyu huo kanglien diyilujun*; "Shinkyō kōtō kensatsu chōnai shisō jōsei," *Shisō geppō*, (November 1940), pp. 150-152; *Wei Manzhuoguoshi*, pp. 530-533.

10. I spent about three days in May 1974 in this revolutionary museum, a magnificent building with many exhibitions to glorify Kim's past activities. However, many of the valuable exhibitions suffer from unnecessary omission and displays of unauthentic items quite easy to detect. Many parts of authentic photographs from the guerrilla days and a few Japanese documents have been edited, leaving many blank spaces, and the huge paintings depicting him as an ever-victorious general, well equipped with binoculars and pistol and smartly dressed with leather boots and all, hardly match the haggard look in tattered partisan clothes, lugging an old Japanese rifle, in the original photographs. His biographers claim that Kim had a white horse; see the claim in Paek Pong, *Minjok ŭi t'aeyang Kim Il Sung changgun*, 1;114-115.

11. The North Korean claim of Chinese characters meaning "one star" seems to be stretching a point too far, because there were other revolutionaries who fought in Manchuria with that name. The currently used characters are "Il"

meaning sun or day and "Sung" meaning to complete or to become. The South Korean publication they cite is Ch'oe Hyŏng-u, *Haeoe Chosŏn hyŏngmyŏng undong sosa*, p. 31.

12. As late as 1974, one South Korean study still maintained that the North Korean President Kim Il Sung was a fake, but this is more a politically motivated effort than a scholarly study. See Yi Myŏng-yŏng, *Kim Il-sŏng yŏlchŏn*. This is an unfortunate study, for the author seems to have done considerable research, interviewing many people who knew Kim, including a few former Japanese army officers who fought Kim in Manchuria. However, the author seems to have gathered information only to substantiate his politically motivated conclusion that Kim is a fake, which he fails to prove. For more responsible studies see, among others, Kim Chun-yŏp and Kim Ch'ang-sun, *Chosŏn kongsan chuŭi undongsa*, 5:51-83; Tamaki Motoi, *Kin Nichisei no shisō to kōdō*, pp. 29-53. For clarification of his names and controversy surrounding his identity, see my earlier study, *The Korean Communist Movement, 1918-1948*, pp. 256-276.

13. For a Chinese account see, among others, Ma Yi, ed., *Chaoxian geming shihua*, pp. 49-50. For a Korean account published before the liberation of Korea, see an organ of the Korean revolutionary army in Zhongjing, *Chŏndo* [Forward path] (June 28, 1937), no. 18. This magazine briefly mentions Kim's activities in Manchuria.

14. These photographs, along with others, are in the Library of Congress. One appeared in Paek Pong's biography between pp. 218 and 219. For the Chinese reproduction of these photographs see *Dongbei huabao* [Northeast pictorial] (May 1946), 1(2):14-15.

15. Chosŏn minju chuŭi inmin konghwaguk sahoe kwahagwŏn yŏksa yŏn'guso, *Yŏksa sajŏn*, pp. 720-721.

16. Yim Ch'un-ch'u, *Hangil mujang t'ujaeng sigirŭl hoesang hayŏ*, pp. 22-24.

17. Yim Ch'un-ch'u, *Hangil mujang t'ujaeng chŏnjŏkchi rŭl ch'ajŏsŏ*, pp. 47-49; Yi Na-yŏng, *Chosŏn minjok haebang t'ujaengsa*, pp. 342-343.

18. For this change, see an editorial in *Nodong sinmun*, February 8, 1978. See also *Nodong sinmun*, April 25, 1978.

19. *Chosŏn kŭndae hyŏngmyŏng undongsa*, pp. 294-295; Yim Ch'un-ch'u, *Hangil mujang t'ujaeng sigirŭl hoesang hayŏ*, pp. 22-24.

20. Yang was born in 1896 and died in 1934. There are many records of Yang's activities in Manchuria. He was as old as Kim's father. For personal details of Yang see, among others, *Han'guk inmyŏng taesajŏn*, p. 453.

21. I have made several lists of Korean partisans, including those who returned to the North and recounted their activities. See appendixes 1, 2, and 3.

22. There are twelve volumes of *Hangil ppalchisan ch'amgajadŭl ŭi hoesanggi*. These are also reproduced in *Inmin ŭi chayu wa haebang ŭl wihayŏ*. This series has appeared in four volumes so far, and they have been published in another edition from Japan. There are many English pamphlets of individual stories taken from these books. Many of these stories appeared more than once in such magazines as *Korea Today* and newspapers including *Nodong sinmun*. The latest addition is a five-volume reminiscence by leading North Korean partisans, *Pulgŭn haebal arae*

hangil hyŏngmyŏng 20nyŏn.

23. *Saikin ni okeru Chōsen chian jōkyō* (1936), pp. 250-251; *Yŏksa sajŏn*, pp. 615-616. For his death, see Japanese Foreign Ministry Archives, reel SP86, frame 10704.

2. Kim and the Northeast Anti-Japanese United Army

1. There are a number of accounts of Yang's guerrilla activities in Manchuria: Ji Yunlong, *Yang Jingyu huo kanglien diyilujun*; Lei Ding, *Dongbei yiyongjun yundong shihua*; and his life stories in *Hongqi biao biao*, 5:119-123 and 124-131; 8:57-58.

2. Manshūkoku chianbu keimushi, *Manshūkoku keisatsushi*, pp. 533-542.

3. Yi Hong-gwang was a close comrade in arms of Yang Jingyu. He was born in 1910 in Tandong, Yongin-gun, Kyŏnggido, Korea, and went to Manchuria in 1926 with his parents. He fought gallantly, killing many Korean collaborators, such as Ko Sŏk-kap. During his fighting days, he was also known as Yi Hong-hae or Yi Ŭi-san, and his disguise was so effective at times that the Japanese mistook him for a woman. Yi died in May 1935 at the age of twenty-five. He is one of the very few guerrillas whom North Koreans recognize as a Korean fighter in Manchuria. During the Chinese civil war after the end of World War II, the Korean volunteer group that helped the Chinese Communists in Northeast China was known as the Yi Hong-gwang Company. For an account of Yi's life see, among others, Dongbei lieshi jinianguan, ed., *Dongbei kangri lieshichuan*, 1:69-82; *Xinghuo liaoyuan*, 4:378-388.

4. The Jiandao May 30 Communist Incident was a joint uprising by Chinese and Korean Communists on May 30, 1930. It was one of the rare uprisings that was successful. The insurrection was to commemorate the dissolution of Korean Communist organizations in Manchuria and encourage the Korean Communists to join the Chinese Communists. See the details in my earlier study, *The Korean Communist Movement, 1918-1948.*

5. For the Fourth Army, there is an excellent account written in 1936 and published in Paris: Sun Jie, *Dongbei kangri lianjun disijun.* This book was later translated into Russian; see Sun Tsze, *Partizanskaya bor'ba Man'chzhurii* [Partisan struggles in Manchuria] (Moscow, 1939).

6. Manshūkoku chianbu keimushi, *Manshūkoku keisatsushi*, pp. 536-537. Chinese Communist accounts today claim much larger numbers, but there is no way to verify their claims. For the Chinese account, see *Wei Manzhouguoshi*, p. 497.

7. For the text of the declaration and draft bylaws of the formation of the Northeast Anti-Japanese United Army, see Gunseibu gomonbu, *Manshū kyōsan hi no kenkyū.* 1:775-786.

8. There is much conflicting information from different sources. Recent Chinese Communist sources include *Wei Manzhouguoshi*, pp. 498-500; Dongbei lieshi jinianguan, ed.; *Dongbei kangri lieshichuan.* Earlier Chinese sources include Ji Yunlong, *Yang Jingyu huo kanglien diyilujun*, for the First Route Army and Sun Jie, *Dongbei kangri lianjun disijun* for the Fourth Army. Recent Japanese sources include Katō Toyotaka, *Manshūkoku keisatsu shoshi*; *Gendaishi shiryō*; Ranseikai, *Manshū kokugun*, pp. 287-292. For earlier Japanese sources, see Shihōshō, keiji-

kyoku, dai goka, *Manshū ni okeru kyōsan shugi undō*, Shisō kenkyū shiryō tokushū, dai 41-go, Shisō jōsei shisatsu hōkokusho, May 4 1938, p. 205; Gunseibu gomonbu, *Manshū kyōsan hi no kenkyū*, 1:162-762.

9. There were others too numerous to mention here. In the First Route Army, there were Pak Tŭk-bŏm, Han In-hwa, An Kwang-hun, Kim In-guk Kim Chae-bŏm, and others. In the Second Route Army, there were Kim Ch'ŏl-u, Kang Tong-su, Kang Sin-il, and Kang Sin-t'ae. In the Third Route Army, there were Kim Kang, Ch'oe Myŏng-gu, and Yi In-gŭn, and others, to mention only a few. Consult the partisan lists in appendixes 1 to 3.

10. Chu Chin, born in 1878, was also known as Chu Chin-su. He fled to Manchuria shortly after the Japanese annexation of Korea and participated in Korean Communist activities in both Russia and Manchuria. Today the North Koreans do not mention any of his anti-Japanese activities. Chu was executed by the Japanese shortly after his arrest. See the record of his arrest in the Japanese Foreign Ministry Archives, History of the Ministry of Foreign Affairs Police: Jiandao and Hunchun areas, May 1910-March 1938, pt. 8, "Kantō chihō heihi no bōdō to waga keisatsukan no katsudō oyobi kōgun no shutsudō," reel SP105, frame 9303. See the photographs in reel SP76, frame 3608.

11. Others mentioned include Yi Pong-su, who was vice-minister of the Ministry of defense until his death in the North in 1967; Ch'oe Hyŏn, who was the vice-chairman of the National Defense Commission; Nam Ch'ang-il, who died fighting the Japanese in Manchuria; and An Pong-hak, who surrendered to the Japanese on September 30, 1936. See *ibid*, reel SP105, frames 9390, 9396, 9402, 9408, 9412-13, 9418, 9420, and other frames in the series. Ranseikai, *Manshū kokugun*, p. 354. Here again the North Korean historians mention nothing of An's guerrilla activities.

12. The joint operation of the Second and Fifth Armies had four commands: Western, Central, Eastern, and Auxiliary. The entire force was under the command of Zhou Baozhong, and Kim was in the Central Command under Chai Shiying. For the entire roster see *ibid*., p. 289. It is also available in Gunseibu gomonbu, *Manshū kyōsan hi no kenkyū*, 1:176-177.

13. Ranseikai, *Manshū kokugun*, pp. 370-371.

14. For Nozoe's command, there are a number of sources that give division-by-division information. For the conference on October 1, 1939, attended by the commander of the *Kantōgun*, General Iimura, Minister Hoshino, and others, see *Manshūkokushi*, pp. 321-322; *Gendaishi shiryō*, pp. 456-471.

15. Ji Yunlong, *Yang Jingyu huo kanglien diyilujun*, pp. 62-89. There are some errors in dates and places in this book, but it is one of the most reliable records in Chinese. The author related that he had interviewed many participants in the United Army, including Kim Il Sung. There are many records of this final reorganization in Japanese sources. See, for example, Ranseikai, *Manshū kokugun*, pp. 401-402; *Manshūkokushi*, pp. 310-311.

16. Yang was invited to surrender, but he fought to the end; when he was killed, the police honored him with a samurai-style burial. Today there is a museum built in his honor and even a town named after him in Northeast China.

For the account of Yang's final battle, see Katō Toyotaka, *Manshūkoku keisatsu shoshi*, 3:31-41; Ranseikai, *Manshū kokugun*, pp. 415-417. For the Chinese source, see Dongbei lieshi jinianguan, ed., *Dongbei kangri lieshichuan*, 1:41-68.

17. See the record of Cao Yafan's death in *Gendaishi shiryō, p. 432. See the Chinese version in Dongbei lieshi jinianguan, ed., Dongbei kangri lieshichuan*, 2:59-65.

18. *Shisō ihō* (December 1940), no. 25, pp. 62-75; *Shisō geppō* (November 1940), no. 77, pp. 129-176.

19. For the record of Kim's retreat into the Soviet Union in March 1941, see, among others, *Manshūkokushi*, p. 325; Ranseikai, *Manshū kokugun*, p. 411; Katō Toyotaka, *Manshūkoku keisatusu shoshi*, 3:48-49. Here Katō believes that Kim entered the Soviet Union as early as July 1940, but there is ample evidence of Kim's activities into early 1941 in Manchuria.

20. Ranseikai, *Manshū kokugun*, pp. 413-417.

21. There are monthly statistics of "bandit appearances" from November 1934 to March 1940 in Ranseikai, *Manshū kokugun*, pp. 422-489. For the Chinese account, see *Wei Manzhouguoshi*, p. 497.

22. For a study of the Chinese Communist revolutionary struggle in Manchuria, see Chong-sik Lee, *Revolutionary Struggle in Manchuria: Chinese Communism and Soviet Interest, 1922-1945*. For Chinese sources see, among others, Zhou Baozhong, *Zhandou zai baishan heisui*, and the memoirs of Li Yen-lu. See also Suzuki Shōji, "Manshū kyōsan shugi undō kenkyū no gendankai."

3. Guerrilla Accomplishments

1. For others in this category, including Cao Yafan, Chen Hanzhang, and Ch'oe Hyŏn, see Ranseikai, *Manshū kokugun*, p. 402.

2. *Ibid.*, pp. 350, 371-373.

3. Paek Pong, *Minjok ŭi t'aeyang Kim Il Sung changgun*, 1:112-119.

4. For many informative statistics about the Koreans in Manchuria, see Gunseibu gomonbu, *Manshū kyōsan hi no kenkyū*, 1:139-146, 484-609.

5. There were other organizations that performed similar functions. The most commonly cited is a Nationalist group, *Yŏnbyŏn chach'i ch'okchinhoe*, headed by Chŏn Sŏng-ho. For details of Hyŏpchohoe, see Gunseibu gomonbu, *Manshū kyōsan hi no kenkyū*, 2:149-200; also in Ranseikai, *Manshū kokugun*, pp. 491-501.

6. Yi Sang-muk wrote an open letter decrying the unfair treatment of Korean partisans by the Chinese. A somewhat moderating Chinese attitude was expressed in a statement by the Chinese. See both documents in my earlier study, *Documents of Korean Communism*, pp. 452-454.

7. This information was the result of the internment and torture of a group of Korean partisans under Kim Hyŏn. See the report in Gunseibu gomonbu, *Manshū kyōsan hi no kenkyū*, 1:120-121.

8. The five Koreans from Tangyuan who reported Xia's inhumane activities to Zhao were Yi Man-sul, Kim Sŏng-gyo, Pae Kyo-jik, Sin Che-sŏp, and Hŏ Chŏng-bin. There are many stories of this nature. See the details in Gunseibu gomonbu, *Manshū kyōsan hi no kenkyū*, 1:755-756.

9. Paek Pong, *Minjok ŭi t'aeyang Kim Il Sung changgun*, pp. 160-162. For the earlier version, see *Chosŏn kŭndae hyŏngmyŏng undongsa*, pp. 229-330. For a complete list of those who participated in the meeting see Gunseibu gomonbu, *Manshū kyōsan hi no kenkyū*, 1:115.

10. Kin Seimei, *Chōsen dokuritsu undō, kyōsan shugi undō hen*, 5:441-468. This raid is also known as the Hyesanjin Incident. See *Gendaishi shiryō*, 30:257-323.

11. North Korean historians claim that the association was founded on May 5, 1936, and that the association had more than one hundred branches and more than 200,000 members. The ten-article platform of the association was widely circulated, but a heavily edited declaration of this association appeared for the first time only in June 1978 (*Nodong sinmun*, June 2, 1978). The original platform, declaration, and bylaws are available in *Shisō ihō* (March 1938), no. 14, pp. 60-64. The original documents were translated and appeared in my earlier study *Documents of Korean Communism*, pp. 455-467.

12. For O's activities, see *Tong-a ilbo*, March 30, March 31, April 1, and May 6, 1922. They are also recorded in Kuksa p'yŏnch'an wiwŏnhoe, *Ilche ch'imyak haŭi han'guk samsimyungnyŏnsa*, 6:744 and 782. See also a study of O's activities in Yi Myŏng-yŏng, "Tongman ŭi p'ung-un-a O Sŏng-yun." Yi has also written an interesting article on the Fatherland Restoration Association in *Sŏnggun'gwan taehakkyo nonmunjip* [Collection of essays of Sŏnggyun'gwan University], no. 17.

13. *Chosŏn ilbo*, October 7, 1936.

14. For other reports on Kim's banditry in Manchuria, see *Chŏson ilbo*, November 11, 20, 22, 24, 27, December 5, 22, 1936. There are many North Korean claims to various reporting of Kims's activities in *Tong-a ilbo* (August 17, 1936) and *Chŏson ilbo* (September 12, 1936), describing Kim's guerrilla forces of 5,000 strong, but no such article can be found. See the South Korean rebuttal of North Korean claims in *Kim Il Sung kwa Kim Sŏng-ju*, pp. 45-66.

15. Kim Il Sung claims that he killed 110 Japanese and took more than 60 prisoners. See Paek Pong, *Minjok ŭi t'aeyang Kim Il Sung changgun*, 1:252-254. For the Japanese account, see Ranseikai, *Manshū kokugun*, pp. 354-361. There are several Japanese maps of troop deployment against Kim's guerrillas. Another Japanese account is in *Gendaishi shiryō*, 30:344-346.

16. Kiuchi Tadao, "Kantō shōnai hizoku tōbatsu jōkyō ni kansuru ken" [Concerning suppression of bandits in Jiandao province], report of Japanese consul in Hunchun, April 19, 1940. For other activities, nearly a day to day account of the last days of the United Army, see *Gendaishi shiryō*, 30:222-728.

17. *Tong-a ilbo*, July 11 and 16, 1937; Gunseibu gomonbu, *Manshū kyōsan hi no kenkyū*, 1:196; *Gendaishi shiryō*, 30:409-413, 435.

18. There are three examples of threatening notes written by members of the Second Army in my earlier study, *Documents of Korean Communism*, pp. 449-451. For the originals and more examples, see Gunseibu gomonbu, *Manshū kyōsan hi no kenkyū*, 1:213-217, and 2:272-276.

19. *Saikin ni okeru Chōsen chian jōkyō* (1939), p. 415. See also Kin Seimei, *Chōsen dokuritsu undō*, 5:446-453. For Korean newspaper reports, see *Chosŏn ilbo*,

October 7, 23, 29, November 7, 22, and December 4, 5, 1936. There are others too numerous to cite here.

20. See Paek Pong, *Minjok ŭi t'aeyang Kim Il Sung changgun*, 1:240-242. There are many unbelievable stories in various accounts of those who participated in the guerrilla activities, so inflated that it is quite easy to distinguish fact from fiction. See among others the many stories in 12 volumes of *Hangil ppalchisan ch'amgajadŭl ŭi hoesanggi*.

21. Kiuchi Tadao, "Kin Nichisei hidan no naibu jōkyō ni kansuru ken" [Concerning the internal conditions of the Kim Il Sung Communist Bandit Group], by the consul of Hunchun, top secret no. 186, July 26, 1940.

22. This was revealed during the interrogation of a surrendered Korean partisan named Ch'oe Kwang-suk on December 14, 1935. For the acquisition of arms by Ch'oe Hyŏn, see Gunseibo gomonbu, *Manshū kyōsan hi no kenkyū*, 1:189-222.

23. There are many articles on this small bomb Pak invented. The model I saw in the revolutionary museum looked more like a grenade. Pak has written a book about this device, *Yŏn'gil p'okt'an* [Yanji bomb]; Yanji is the prefecture in eastern Manchuria where he was from.

24. There are many accounts of Yi Hak-man's purchase of arms from the Russian Maritime Province. See Gunseibu gomonbu, *Manshū kyōsan hi no kenkyū*, 1:808-809.

25. *Wei Manzhouguoshi*, pp. 555-557.

26. For Kim's retreat, see *Tokumu ihō* (May 1943), no. 4, pp. 5-60. For Zhou Baozhong, see Donald W. Klein and Ann B. Clark, *Biographic Dictionary of Chinese Communism*, 1:225-228; Mu Qing, "Dongbei kangri lienjun douzheng shilo" [Brief history of struggle of the Northeast Anti-Japanese United Army], in *Wei dongbei di heping minzhu er douzheng*, 1:62-79; *Manshūkokushi*, p. 325.

27. See the reference in Han Chae-dŏk, *Han'guk kongsan chuŭi wa pukhan ŭi yŏksa*, pp. 130-133. There is no way to verify this fact because that particular issue of *Minju Chosŏn* is not available.

28. B. G. Sapozhnikov, "Iz istorii sovetsko-koreiskoi druzvy," in *Osvobozhdenie Korei*, pp. 164-183.

29. Manshūkoku, chianbu, keimushi, tokumuka, *Tokumu ihō* (May 1943), no. 4, pp. 23-32. "Habarosuku yaei gakkō no jōkyō," *Gaiji geppō*.

30. *Gendaishi shiryō*, 30:694 and 733-767. See also excerpts from Zhou Baozhong's diary, "Zhou Baozhong 'Kanglien riji' zhaichao," *Shehui kexue zhanxian* (1984), no. 2, pp. 213-226.

31. *Gendaishi shiryō*, 30:708-720. The Soviet Union sent Korean agents into Manchuria to help Korean partisans there. See Japanese Foreign Ministry Archives, History of the Ministry of Foreign Affairs Police: Jiandao and Hunchun areas, pt. 7, "Manshū jihen oyobi sono igo," reel SP105, frames 9082-9087. See also an informative study of Kim's activities by Wada Haruki, "Kin Nichisei to Manshū no kōnichi busō tōsō."

32. One defector who met Kim several times in Pyongyang before he fled the North related in his memoir that Kim had told him a brief story of his partisan activities. The accounts of the defectors, including this one, are in most respects

unreliable. See O Yŏng-jin, *Hana ŭi chŭngŏn*, p. 176; "Soren busō Chōsen jin chōsha no sennai sennyū jiken," in *Tokkō gaiji geppō*; "Kin Nichisei no katsudō jōkyō," *Tokkō gaiji geppō*; B.G. Sapozhnikov, "Iz istorii sovetsko-koreiskoi druzvy," pp. 164-183.

33. For the interrogation report on Pak Kil-song, see top secret reports by Japanese consul Hiraoka Nin in Heihe consulate on January 12 (no. 7), January 18 (no. 13), February 17 (no. 53), March 20 (no. 76), March 26 (no. 82), and others of 1943. Reproductions of these reports are also available in *Gendaishi shiryō*, 30:694-731.

34. See the North Korean version of Kim Chŏng-suk in *Yŏksa sajŏn*, 1:251-254. For her guerrilla activities, see several articles mentioning her in *Hangil ppalchisan ch'amgajadŭl ŭi hoesanggi*, 2:140; 7:108; and 10:55; see also "Kin Nichisei hidan no naibu jōkyō ni kansuru ken," Report of Kimura Tadao, July 26, 1940.

35. There is a newspaper article of the capture of Kim's wife in *Chosŏn ilbo*, July 5, 1940. See also Yi Myŏng-yŏng, *Kim Il Sung yŏlchŏn*, pp. 318-320. In this book, Yi Myŏng-yŏng is trying to prove that Kim Il Sung is a fake, and the man named Kim Il Sung who fought in the Northeast Anti-Japanese United Army had died in Manchuria.

36. *Akahata*, September 28, 1949.

37. Interview with Major General N. G. Lebedev in Moscow on July 21, 1978.

PART II. CONSOLIDATION OF POLITICAL POWER

4. The Soviet Occupation of North Korea

1. I. M. Chistiakov, "Voevoi puti 25-i armii," pp. 11-60.

2. See the account of Generals Chistiakov and Romanenko in The Stalingrad campaign in A. I. Evemenko, *Stalingrad*, pp. 387-426; also in A. M. Samsonov, *Stalingradskaya bitva*, pp. 379-381 and 526-527.

3.There are many accounts of his denial. In answer to one direct question about whether he had fought on the German front, Kim is reported to have said that he himself had not, but some of his men were sent; O Yŏng-jin, *Hana ŭi chŭngŏn*, pp. 176-177.

4. My interview with General Nikolai G. Lebedev in Moscow on July 21, 1978. Many South Korean accounts relate that Kim was wearing the uniform of a Soviet army major, but there are other reports that he was wearing the insignia of a captain.

5. B. G. Sapozhnikov, "Iz istorii sovetsko-koreiskoi druzhvy," pp. 168-169.

6. I have not been able to identify the guerrilla leader known as Pak In-ch'ŏl. There are records of Paek Yŏng-ch'ŏl and Pak Ch'ŏl; both died about 1937.

7. Kim Il Sung is said to have returned with Ch'oe Yong-gŏn, Kang Kŏn, Ch'oe Hyŏn, Ch'oe Yong-jin, Yi Yŏng-ho, Ch'oe Kwang, Kim Kwang-hyŏp, Kim Kyŏng-sŏk, Cho Chŏng-ch'ŏl, Kim Ch'un-yŏk, Ch'oe Ch'un-guk, Yi Pong-su, and Yu Kyŏng-su. All these men came back on a boat with their wives. Kim did

not return to Korea fighting the Japanese; he simply returned home as many Korean revolutionaries had done after the close of World War II. For Kim's return, see Yim Ŭn, "Suryŏng ŭi ch'angsegi: Kim Il Sung ilsa." This manuscript was later translated into Japanese and English by South Korean authorities. Yim Ŭn is a Soviet-Korean who participated in North Korean politics and is known to North Korea as Hŏ Chin.

8. For the report of the 25th Division and its operation in North Korea, see Document 6, report of August 27, 1945, stating that the operation was completed the previous day. *Otnosheniia Sovetskogo Soiuza s narodnoi Koreei, 1945-1980: dokymentii i materialii*, pp. 9-10.

9. They are too numerous to mention in detail, but some informative accounts are by those who participated in the initial phase of the Russian occupation. Since these men are defectors, their views are biased and their criticism carping. See among others; Han Chae-dŏk, *Han'guk ŭi kongsan chuŭi wa pukhan ŭi yŏksa*; O Yŏng-jin, *Hana ŭi chŭngŏn*; Kim Ch'ang-sun, *Pukhan sibonyŏnsa*.

10. On the Sovietization of the North see my article "A Preconceived Formula for Sovietization: North Korea," pp. 473-489. See a South Korean analysis in Yang Ho-min, *Pukhan ŭi ideorogi wa chŏngch'i*, pp. 79-109. See another recent study in *Pukhan chŏngch'iron*, pp. 87-106.

11. B. V. Schetinin, "V Koree posle osvobozhdenia," pp. 244-249. See also I. M. Chistiakov, "Voevoi puti 25-i armii," p. 51-52.

12. Cho Man-sik led the initial Korean cooperation with the Soviet occupation authorities, but Cho was a man of principle who later opposed the Soviet plan to institute a trusteeship in Korea. He was later interned and presumed killed in the North shortly before the start of the Korean War. See Han Kŭn-jo, *Kodang, Cho Man-sik*.

13. For the Russian text of this declaration, see *Otnosheniia Sovetskogo Soiuza s narodnoi Koreei, 1945-1980: dokymentii i materialii*, pp. 6-7. For the Korean version, see *Chosŏn chungang yŏn'gam, 1949*, pp. 57-58.

14. *Documents on Korean-American Relations, 1943-1976*, pp. 28-29. Kim compared these two proclamations in his speech at the second party congress in March 1948. See the text in Kim Il Sung, "Puk Chosŏn nodongdang che ich'a chŏndang taehoe esŏ chinsul han tang chungang wiwŏnhoe saŏp kyŏlsan pogowa kyŏllon" [Report to the Second Congress of the Workers' Party of North Korea on the work of the Central Committee], *Kim Il Sung sŏnjip*, 2:38-39.

15. There were 31 delegates from P'yŏngan namdo, 15 from P'yŏngan pukto, 11 from Hwanghaedo, 11 from Hamgyŏng namdo, and 7 from Hamgyŏng pukto. The agenda included agricultural production and food supply, transformation of factories from military to civilian use, financial and banking problems, and reorganization of local administration. See *Chosŏn chungang yŏn'gam, 1950*, pp. 196-197.

16. *Haebang hu simnyŏn ilchi, 1945-1955*, p. 24. The ten bureaus were: Industry, Transportation, Agriculture and Forestry, Commerce, Communication, Finance, Education, Public Health, Justice, and Security.

17. For details of the negotiations and the issue of trusteeship, see U. S. Depart-

ment of State, *Foreign Relations of the United States, 1947*, 6:596-889. For documents relating to the trusteeship, see among others U. S. Department of State, *The Record on Korean Unification, 1943-1960*.

18. For Shtykov's comment on Cho Man-sik, see I. M. Chistiakov, "Voevoi puti 25-i armii," p. 56. General Shtykov's negotiating team consisted of Major General Lebedev, Minister G. I. Tounkin from the Soviet Foreign Office, and political advisor G. M. Balasanov, who spoke Japanese.

19. Ch'ian-guk t'ŭkbyŏl chŏngbogwa, *Pukhan kongsan koeroe chŏnggwŏn e taehan koch'al*, pp. 31-53.

20. U. S. Department of State, *North Korea: A Case Study in the Technique of Takeover*, pp. 100-105. This study claims that approximately 200 key positions were occupied by the Soviet-Koreans. See also Yi Hong-gŭn, *Ssoryŏn kunjŏng ŭi simal*, pp. 4-10.

21. Kim Ch'ang-sun, *Pukan sibonyŏnsa*, pp. 61-65.

22. Hyŏn Chun-hyŏk was born in Kaech'ŏn, P'yŏngan namdo, and was highly educated, graduating from Yŏnhŭi College (Yonsei University) and Keijō Imperial University (Seoul National University). He taught at Taegu Normal School and was imprisoned for six years for his participation in the antiwar movement, opposing the Japanese advance into China. He later submitted to the Japanese and was released.

23. There are many different accounts of Hyŏn's death, all from South Korea; see Kim Ch'ang-sun, *Yŏksa ŭi chŭngin*, pp. 20-40. See a Japanese account in Tsuboe Senji, *Hokusen no kaihō jūnen*, pp. 2-51. For a eulogy of Hyŏn, see *Haebang ilbo*, October 3, 1945.

24. *Haebanghu simnyŏn ilchi*, pp. 41-42. For the revised version of these dates, see *Chosŏn nodongdang i kŏrŏon yŏnggwang sŭrŏun kil*, pp. 73-74.

25. This proclamation is in *Chosŏn chungang yŏn'gam, 1949*, pp. 58-59.

26. For the date of changing the name, see *Haebanghu simnyŏn ilchi*. Han Chae-dŏk, a defector who participated in some of these early meetings, reported that Colonel Ignatiev was always present; see Han Chae-dŏk, *Han'guk ŭi kongsan chuŭi wa pukhan ŭi yŏksa*, pp. 198-199.

5. The Workers' Party of Korea

1. Kim Il Sung, *The Youth Must Take Over the Revolution and Carry It Forward*, pp. 1-4. Kim made a speech at this conference, but it appears only in the second edition of his selected works.

2. *Chŏngno*, July 31, 1946. *Chŏngno* was the official organ of the North Korean Communist Party.

3. The minutes of the congress were made known for the first time in 1977 in the Records Seized by United States Military Forces in Korea, Record Group 242, National Archives Collection of Foreign Records Seized, Shipping Advice 2008, Box 9, item 101: *Puk Chosŏn nodongdang ch'angnip taehoe hoeŭirok* [Minutes of the founding congress of the Workers' Party of North Korea]. Hereafter cited as *Minutes of the Founding Congress*.

4. *Minutes of the Founding Congress*, pp. 1-3.

5. There were 89 female delegates out of 801 delegates. There were 229 delegates in their twenties, 417 delegates in their thirties, 129 delegates in their forties, and 26 delegates in their fifties and above. As to occupation, 183 delegates were classified as workers, 157 were peasants, 385 were office workers, and there were 76 others. Some 228 delegates had only elementary school education, 359 delegates had high school education, and 214 delegates had college or above education. Only 291 delegates (36 percent) had a record of imprisonment by the Japanese, and 427 delegates (53 percent) were returnees from abroad. These statistics were made known in other publications, but the original list is available in the *Minutes of the Founding Congress*, pp. 14-15.

6. This speech is available in many sources. It can be found in its entirety in the minutes of the founding congress and in a published pamphlet of documents pertaining to the founding congress. See *Puk Chosŏn nodongdang ch'angnip taehoe, checharyo*, pp. 2-18. It also appeared in the first issue of the party organ, *Kŭlloja*, under the title "Modŭn kŏsŭn minju yŏngyang chunbi rŭl wihayŏ." A heavily edited version appears in all editions of Kim's selected works.

7. For the text of Kim Tu-bong's speech, see *Puk Chosŏn nodongdang ch'angnip taehoe, checharyo*, pp. 19-33. It also appeared in *Kŭlloja* (October 25, 1946), no. 1, pp. 19-30.

8. The first issue of *Chŏngno* was published on November 1, 1945. The *Nodong sinmun* began publication after the first party congress. A new journal named *Kŭlloja* was decided upon after the congress, and the first issue was published on October 25, 1946. It was not published as a monthly in the beginning. The second issue was published in December 1946, and the combined third and fourth issue was published in February 1947. The fifth issue was published in March 1947. It was not until the sixth issue, published in June 1947, that it became a monthly. The editor of the journal was T'ae Sŏng-su, and all editors during the occupation of the North were Soviet-Koreans. T'ae was succeeded by Pak Ch'ang-ok and then Ki Sŏk-bok.

9. These men were Kim Ch'ŏl-su, Kang Chin, Mun Kap-song, Yi Chŏng-yun, Sŏ Chung-sŏk, and Kim Kŭn. They were all members of the old Korean Communist Party with records of anti-Japanese Communist activity in Korea, Manchuria, and the Soviet Union. They vehemently opposed the merger of the Korean Communist Party from China and the People's Party in Korea. All remained in the South except Kang Chin, who grew up in the North. He was elected to the First Supreme People's Assembly but was purged soon thereafter.

10. The members of the Central Committee of the First Congress of the Workers' Party of Korea were Kim Tu-bong, Kim Il Sung, Chu Yŏng-ha, Ch'oe Ch'ang-ik, Hŏ Ka-i, Pak Ch'ang-sik, Kim Ch'ang-man, Hŏ Chŏng-suk, Kim Yong-t'ae, Pak Chŏng-ae, Kim Ch'aek, Mu Chŏng, Yi Ch'un-am, An Kil, Kim Ye-p'il, Kim Il, Pak Hyo-sam, Chang Sun-myŏng, Kim Yŏl, Kim Chae-uk, Yun Kong-hŭm, Han Il-mu, Kim Min-san, Pak Hun-il, Pak Il-u, T'ae Sŏng-su, Han Sŏl-ya, Ch'oe Kyŏng-dŏk, Kang Chin-gŏn, Chang Si-u, Chŏng Tu-hyŏn, Yim To-jun, Yim Hae, O Ki-sŏp, Kim Uk-chin, Yi Sun-gŭn, Kim Kyo-yŏng, Myŏng Hŭi-jo, Han Pin, Yi Chong-ik, Chin Sŏng-hwa, Kim Wŏl-sŏng, and Chang

Chong-sik. They are listed in rank order according to *Minutes of the Founding Congress*, p. 110. A slightly different rank order putting three men (Kim Min-san, Pak Hun-il, and Pak Il-u) at the end is in *Puk Chosŏn nodongdang ch'angnip taehoe, checharyo*, p. 72.

11. They were Kim Yong-bŏm, Chin Pan-su, Pang U-yong, Kim Sŭng-hŭm, Yi Tong-hwa, Kim Ch'an, Ch'oe Yong-dal, Kim Ch'ae-ryong, Pak Ch'un-sŏp, Yu Yŏng-gi, and Pak Ŭng-ik. *Ibid.*

12. Pak was a delegate from P'yŏngan pukto and unknown to most Koreans. See his discussion in *Minutes of the Founding Congress*, pp. 42-43.

13. Pak Chŏng-ae was generally known as the wife of Kim Yong-bŏm, but she seems to have been a common-law wife. After Kim died, she became one of the most powerful women in the North, supporting Kim Il Sung. See her discussion in *Minutes of the Founding Congress*, pp. 55-56.

14. *Puk Chosŏn nodongdang ch'angnip taehoe, checharyo*, pp. 34-35; also in *Minutes of the Founding Congress*, pp. 63-64.

15. Kim Il Sung, "Uridang i kŏrŏon kilgwa tangmyŏn han myŏtkaji kwaŏp e taehayŏ" [The path trodden by our party and several current tasks], *Kim Il Sung sŏnjip*, 1:80-88. This speech is available only in the second edition of his selected works.

16. *Minutes of the Founding Congress*, p. 46. For a slightly different number for party membership, see *Chosŏn nodongdang yŏksa kyojae*, p. 185.

17. They were Kim Il Sung, Kim Ch'aek, An Kil, and Kim Il. For details on various groups and their successes and failures within the Central Committee in subsequent elections see my earlier study, "Communist Party Leadership," in Dae-Sook Suh and Chae-Jin Lee, eds., *Political Leadership in Korea*, pp. 159-191.

18. Kim Tu-bong, also known as Kim Paek-yŏn, was born on March 16, 1889, in Kijang, Kyŏngsang namdo. Kim was a philologist by training and had published important works on the Korean language. He received a doctorate in linguistics in 1948 in the North. He first fled Korea in 1919 shortly after the March First Incident to Shanghai and engaged in Korean revolutionary activities in Zhongqing until 1942. He then went to Yanan where he organized and headed the Korean Independence League and fought the Japanese in North China on the side of the Chinese Communists. When he returned to Korea, the league was changed into the New Democratic Party. He held a number of important positions in the North, including the first chairmanships of the party, the Standing Committee of the Supreme People's Assembly, and the Democratic National United Front of the Fatherland. He was also president of Kim Il Sung University and held many other important positions until 1958, when he was purged.

19. Chu Yŏng-ha was educated in Seoul and studied at the Communist University of the Toilers of the East (KUTV). He had participated in Communist activities in his native province of Hamgyŏng namdo at the Hŭngnam Fertilizer Company in November 1930. In May 1935 he was arrested in P'yŏngan namdo with Kim Yong-bŏm and imprisoned. When Korea was liberated he became the first chairman of the People's Committee of Wŏnsan city in Hamgyŏng namdo. He was appointed first minister of transportation in Kim Il Sung's first cabinet in

September 1948, but he resigned to become the first North Korean ambassador to the Soviet Union. Chu was purged in 1953.

20. Kim Ch'ang-sun, *Pukhan sibonyŏnsa*, pp. 99-102. There are many reasons why this version is incorrect – such as the dates of the congress, the order of speakers, the alleged nomination of Kim by Pak, and the intervention of Colonel Ignatiev, which temporarily halted the proceedings of the congress. This book was written without benefit of a source that is now available, the minutes of the founding congress. As such, however, this source gives much information about the early politics of Kim.

21. For the Workers' Party of South Korea, see the comprehensive study by Kim Nam-sik, *Sillok, namnodang*, pp. 291-320.

22. Here again the minutes of the Second Party Congress were revealed for the first time in 1977 in the Records Seized by United States Military Forces in Korea, Record Group 242, National Archives Collection of Foreign Records Seized, Shipping Advice 2008, Box 9, item 100: *Puk Chosŏn nodongdang che ich'a chŏndang taehoe hoeŭirok* [Minutes of the Second Congress of the Workers' Party of North Korea], hereafter cited as *Minutes of the Second Congress*. There is a companion book, *Puk Chosŏn nodongdang chŏndang taehoe che chaeryojip*. Together with the materials on the founding congress, these two books are very valuable and not available for examination even in the North.

23. The elected delegates totaled 999, but 9 were absent. Of the 990 delegates only 96 were authorized by the Central Committee to speak in the congress. There is detailed statistical information on these delegates in *Minutes of the Second Congress*, pp. 84-87.

24. There was a 57-member executive group of the congress, a 9-member secretariat, a 7-member credentials committee, and a 15-member committee to draft the documents of the party. Names of members of all these committees are available in *Minutes of the Second Congress*, pp. 1-8. Names of members of the Central Committee and the agenda of the Central Committee and the party congresses from the first to the sixth are available in English in Dae-Sook Suh, *Korean Communism, 1945-1980*.

25. The message from the Workers' Party of South Korea was read by Hŏ Chŏng-suk, and others delivered congratulatory messages representing the workers, peasants, and other groups. Hŏ reported that there were 5,287 letters and 7,515 telegrams congratulating the congress.

26. The text of this speech is available in many places, including all editions of his selected works, but later versions are heavily edited. See the unedited original in Kim Il Sung, *Tang ŭi konggohwa rŭl wihayŏ*, pp. 105-212. The extent of revision and reinterpretation of this speech may be seen in the latest comment on the thirtieth anniversary of this speech in *Nodong sinmun*, March 29, 1978.

27. These men were all important native Korean Communists who had participated in some capacity in the administration of the North. For example, Ch'oe Yong-dal was head of the Justice Bureau, Yi Sun-gŭn was head of the Agriculture and Forestry Bureau, and Chang Si-u was head of the Commerce Bureau.

28. Han Il-mu was one of the first Soviet-Koreans to participate actively in

North Korean politics. He was born and raised in the Soviet Union and unknown to the Communists at home. Han served in the Soviet navy and contributed to the building of the North Korean navy, becoming its chief with the rank of admiral. He was the North Korean ambassador to Mongolia from 1958 but retired and returned to the Soviet Union in 1962.

29. Details of these affairs were not revealed, but important figures in the North were implicated. Yi Chu-ha, a prominent native Communist, fled South and was one of the key members of the Korean Communist Party in Seoul. Yi Kang-guk was head of the Foreign Affairs Bureau in the Provisional People's Committee. For his speech see *Minutes of the Second Congress*, pp. 84-89.

30. Pak Ch'ang-ok was another Soviet-Korean who was active in North Korean politics. Pak was born and educated in the Soviet Union and remained in the North. He became editor of the party journal, *Kŭlloja*, and climbed as high as vice-premier of the North in 1954, but he was purged by Kim Il Sung in 1956. For Pak's speech, see *Minutes of the Second Congress*, pp. 112-115.

31. Kim Yŏl, another Soviet-Korean who was born and raised in the Soviet Union, became head of the Hwanghae Provincial Party Committee in 1951 and also the vice-minister of heavy industry in 1952, but he too was purged in 1956. For Kim's speech, see *Minutes of the Second Congress*, pp. 126-130.

32. Chang Sun-myŏng was a member of the Central Committee of the First Party Congress, but he must have been appointed to the Inspection Committee after the party congress because he was not a member of the Inspection Committee at the time of the First Party Congress. He apparently replaced Kim Yong-bŏm when Kim died. In spite of the criticism, Chang was elected vice-chairman of the Inspection Committee at the Second Party Congress. See the list of Inspection Committee members in *Puk Chosŏn nodongdang che ich'a chŏndang taehoe che chaeryojip*, p. 132.

33. For O's speech see *Minutes of the Second Congress*, pp. 134-138.

34. Ch'oe was a leader of the old Korean Communist movement in the late 1930s. He was highly educated, graduated from Keijō Imperial University (Seoul National University), and taught at Posŏng College (Korea University). Arrested and imprisoned for his participation in the Wŏnsan Labor Union Incident, he was released on the pledge that he would not engage in Communist activities. He was the first head of the Justice Bureau of the North Korean Interim People's Committee. For Ch'oe's speech, see *Minutes of the Second Congress*, pp. 144-148.

35. Hŏ Ka-i was perhaps the highest-ranking Soviet-Korean in the North. He became vice-chairman of the party, replacing Chu Yŏng-ha, and later became first secretary of the party. He was vice-premier of the North, but he too was purged during the Korean War. Hŏ did much to support Kim's position and reorganized the party in support of him. Hŏ was born in 1904 in the Russian Maritime Province and was said to have held a local party post in the Possiet region. See Hŏ's condemnation in *Minutes of the Second Congress*, pp. 149-151.

36. Chŏng Tal-hyŏn was educated both in Korea and the Soviet Union. He was also a graduate of KUTV who returned to Korea and engaged in the labor union movement. He was arrested for his role in the famous Pyongyang Red

Labor Union Incident of February 1931 and was imprisoned for six years. He and O Ki-sŏp were perhaps the two most important Communist leaders in Hamgyŏng namdo after the liberation of Korea.

37. Most subsequent publications do not carry Kim's concluding remarks, though heavily edited versions are carried in some. See the original in *Minutes of the Second Congress*, pp. 171-179.

38. It was not known who cast the five negative votes. The voting record is in *Minutes of the Second Congress*, pp. 232-237.

39. It is not known who voted against Kim Tu-yong, but Kim Tu-yong was a well-known figure who devoted most of his revolutionary activities to Korean Communists in Japan. Kim was a graduate of Tokyo Imperial University and was arrested March 28, 1933, for his Communist activities in Japan. He organized leftist groups and published an underground journal called *Musanja*. After the end of World War II, Kim was vice-chairman of the Korean Communist group attached to the Japanese Communist Party. Kim is from Chŏlla namdo, and he too submitted to the Japanese before the end of the war. Perhaps that was the reason for the one negative vote.

40. For a detailed analysis of the composition of the Central Committee and changes in the committee, see my earlier study, *Korean Communism, 1945-1980*, pp. 273-278.

41. Kim Nam-sik, *Sillok, namnodang*, pp. 423-426; see the North Korean account in *Chosŏn nodongdang yŏksa kyojae*, pp. 227-228.

42. For the complete roster see my study, *Korean Communism, 1945-1980*, pp. 321-322.

6. The Republic and the Army

1. Compare the texts of this speech. The original version is in Kim Il Sung, *Chosŏn minju chuŭi inmin konghawaguk surip ŭi kil*, pp. 1-14. The revised version is in *Kim Il Sung sŏnjip*, 2d ed., 1:24-37. The latest revision is in *Kim Il Sung chŏjak sŏnjip*, 3d ed., 1:22-29.

2. The 24 members of the North Korean Provisional People's Committee chosen on February 9, 1946, were: chairman, Kim Il Sung; vice-chairman, Kim Tu-bong; secretary, Kang Yang-uk; Commerce Bureau, Han Tong-ch'an; Communication Bureau, Cho Yŏng-yŏl; Finance Bureau, Yi Pong-su; Education Bureau, Chang Chong-sik; Public Health Bureau, Yun Ki-yŏng; Justice Bureau, Ch'oe Yong-dal; Internal Security Bureau, Ch'oe Yong-gŏn. See *Chosŏn chungang yŏn'gam, 1950*, p. 197. For the Russian account of the People's Committee, see B. V. Shchetinin, "Vozniknovenie narodnykh komitetov v severnoi Koree."

3. Details of the work of this committee are in *Haebang hu simnyŏn ilchi*, pp. 17-41. See also a good analysis of these reforms in Ch'ian-guk t'ŭkpyŏl chŏngbogwa, *Pukhan kongsan koeroe chŏnggwŏn e taehan koch'al*, pp. 31-53.

4. In his speech on November 25, 1946, to report on the election results, Kim said that 4,401,813 (99.6 percent of the electorate) had voted and elected 3,459 representatives to the provincial, city, and county assemblies. Only 1,159 representatives were elected for the central People's Assembly. Details on the represent-

atives' affiliation, education, age, and other statistics are available in *Haebang hu simnyŏn ilchi*, p. 17, and in *Chosŏn chungang yŏn'gam, 1949*, pp. 83-84. For Kim's speech on the election, see Kim Il Sung, *Minju chuŭi inmin konghawaguk surip ŭl wihayŏ*, pp. 143-170.

5. There were two representing the Nationalist Democratic Party, Hong Ki-ju and Yi Tong-yŏng, and there were two who represented Ch'ŏndogyo Young Friends Party, Chu Hwang-sŏp and Kim Chŏng-ju. See the complete roster of the committee in *Puk Chosŏn inminhoeŭi che ilch'a hoeŭi hoeŭirok*, pp. 1-64.

6. All the details of the People's Assembly sessions are available in the minutes of the sessions. These documents were made public for the first time in the captured documents. See the minutes of the People's Assembly from the first to the fifth sessions in the Records Seized by United States Military Forces in Korea, Record group 242, Shipping Advice 2005, Box 5, Items 6-10: *Puk Chosŏn inminhoeŭi hoeŭirok*. Item 6 is the first session (64 pp.), item 7 is the second session (76 pp.), item 8 is the third session (172 pp.), item 9 is the fourth session (174 pp.), and item 10 is the fifth session (117 pp.). They were published by the Standing Committee of the North Korean People's Assembly; the first two sessions were published in 1947 and the rest were published in 1948. Many important source materials were made available in 1977 when the captured documents were declassified. There are detailed records, for example, *Puk Chosŏn inminhoeŭi t'ŭkpyŏl hoeŭi hoeŭirok*, Shipping Advice 2008, Box 9, item 93, 202 pp. There is also a bulletin of the Standing Committee of the People's Assembly, the first issue (49 pp.) in Shipping Advice 2008, Box 9, item 99.

7. For the details of the meeting between Kim Il Sung and Kim Ku, see Kim Nam-sik, *Sillok, namnodang*, pp. 370-386. For the North Korean account see Paek Pong, *Minjok ŭi t'aeyang Kim Il Sung changgun*, 2:172-181. See also *Nambuk Chosŏn che chŏngdang sahoe tanch'e taep'yoja yŏnsŏk hoeŭi chungyo charyojip*. This book is available in the Records Seized by United States Military Forces in Korea, Record group 242, Shipping Advice 2005, Box 2, item 51.

8. For the complete record of the first session of the Supreme People's Assembly, see *Chosŏn minju chuŭi inmin konghwaguk ch'oego inmin hoeŭi che ilch'a hoeŭirok*. This book is available in the captured documents in Shipping Advice 2005, Box 5, item 3. For Russian studies of the state structure, see B. Baianov and M. Shafir, *Gosudarstvennyi stroi Koreiskoi Narodno-Demokratichskoi Respubliki*, and another one by the same title by V. A. Kim in 1955.

9. The other three were Hong Myŏng-hŭi, who was reappointed vice-premier but died shortly thereafter from old age; Pak Mun-gyu, a Japanese-educated South Korean intellectual who completely abstained from the political struggles of the South Koreans in the North; and Hŏ Chŏng-suk, the only woman member of the cabinet, from the Yanan group. See the complete roster of cabinet members and members of the Supreme People's Assembly in Dae-Sook Suh, *Korean Communism, 1945-1980*, pp. 360-494.

10. *North Korea: A Case Study in the Techniques of Takeover*, pp. 15-16, 29-30, 100-104. This study was a report by the State Department Research Mission sent to Korea during the Korean War in October 1950; it was declassified in 1961 and

published by the U. S. State Department as publication 7118. It is an informative analytical study, but it suffers from incorrect information gathered from refugees in identifying Soviet-Koreans and distinguishing between the Soviet-Koreans and Kim's partisans. It should be added that the distinction among those returned revolutionaries from many foreign countries was difficult to make at the time.

11. Mu Chŏng was a native of Kyŏngsŏng, Hamgyŏng pukto, and went to China in the early 1920s. He graduated from Henan Military Academy and worked for Yan Xishan. He is said to have joined the Chinese Communist Party in 1926 in Shanghai and worked in the Ruijin Soviet in Jiangxi province. He is one of the few Koreans who participated in the Long March. He was an artillery officer of the Eighth Route Army. He worked in the Korean Independence League in Yanan and returned to Korea at the end of the war. He was widely acclaimed by Koreans as a genuine general from China, to the great displeasure of Kim Il Sung. Mu Chŏng was purged during the Korean War by Kim. For other Chinese connections of Mu Chŏng, see Chong-sik Lee, "Korean Communists and Yenan."

12. An, one of the closest comrades of Kim Il Sung from Manchuria, was also known as An Sang-gil. He was born on February 24, 1907, in Kyŏngwŏn, Hamgyŏng pukto, and participated in Kim's guerrilla forces all during the 1930s. He was known for his fluency in Chinese. An died on December 13, 1947, after a long illness. Kim Il Sung built a statue for him in 1968. For more information about An Kil, see *Yŏksa sajŏn*, pp. 1179-1181.

13. For Kim's speech, see *Kim Il Sung sŏnjip*, 1st ed., pp. 481-489. A slightly edited version is included in the 2d ed., pp. 371-377, but this speech was dropped in the 3d ed.

14. Kang succeeded An Kil as commander of the People's Army. He was also one of Kim's close comrades. Kang was born on June 23, 1918, in Sangju county, Kyŏngsang pukto, and was said to have joined Kim when he was only a teenager in 1933. He fought with Kim in Manchuria during the 1930s and fled Manchuria with Kim. Kang was commander of the North Korean army when the Korean War started and was one of the first casualties; he died on September 8, 1950. There is a military academy named after him, Kang Kŏn Military Academy, in the North, and Kim also built a statue for him in 1968. For his life story, see *Yŏksa sajŏn*, pp. 23-25.

15. For Kim Kwang-hyŏp's participation in the Northeast (Manchuria) Interim People's Committee, see Liu Baiyu, *Huanxing dongbei*, pp. 105-110; Zhou Erfu, *Dongbei hengduanmien*, pp. 129-132.

PART III. CHALLENGES TO KIM'S LEADERSHIP

1. A memorandum by the Central Intelligence Agency on June 19, 1950, reported that there were as many as 4,000 advisors in Pyongyang; U. S. Department of State, *Foreign Relations of the United States, 1950*, 7:111-112.

2. The record of the Liberal Arts Department of Kim Il Sung University revealed that many professors came from the Soviet Union – for example, Hŏ Ik,

formerly of the Leningrad State University, O Wan-muk, Kim Yong-sŏng, Pak Yŏng, and Yi Mun-il. There is a complete file of vitae of all members of the College of Liberal Arts of Kim Il Sung University in the Records Seized by the United States Military Forces in Korea, Record Group 242, National Archives Collection of Foreign Records Seized, Shipping Advice 2011, Box 7, item 35.

In his speech on March 17, 1950, to commemorate the first anniversary of the Soviet-Korean Economic and Cultural Agreement, Kim hailed the Soviet Union for assistance of all kinds, material as well as moral. Kim proudly said that more than 30 Russian scholars were in the North teaching the Koreans. This speech, of course, is no longer carried in any North Korean sourcebook. See Kim Il Sung, *Choguk ŭi t'ongil tongnip kwa minjuhwa rŭl wihayŏ*, 1:513-530. The chief editor of *Nodong sinmun* was Ki Sŏk-bok; the editor of *Kŭlloja* was T'ae Sŏng-su.

7. The Korean War and Kim's Rivals

1. There are many books and articles written on the Korean War, and it is not my purpose here to elaborate on sources available on the subject. For the official North Korean account, see their *History of the Just Fatherland Liberation War of the Korean People*. For the American decision to enter the war, see Glenn D. Paige, *The Korean Decision, June 24-30, 1950*. For the Chinese entry in the Korean War, see Allen S. Whiting, *China Crosses the Yalu*. For the study on the background leading to the war, see Bruce Cumings, *The Origins of the Korean War*.

2. For the New Year address of 1947, see Kim Il Sung, *Chosŏn minju chuŭi inmin konghwaguk surip ŭi kil*, pp. 158-165. For the New Year address of 1950, see Kim Il Sung, *Choguk ŭi t'ongil tongnip kwa minjuhwa rŭl wihayŏ*, 2:465-472.

3. This important speech appeared only in the first edition of Kim's selected works. See Kim Il Sung, *Kim Il Sung sŏnjip*, 1st ed., 2:485-496.

4. There are many reports of Chinese Communist units composed of soldiers of Korean descent coming into North Korea from Manchuria; they were amalgamated into the Korean People's Army units. In November 1949, approximately three thousand troops came into Nanam and Sinŭiju. See *Report of KMAG Liaison Officer, April 1. 1950*.

5. *Chosŏn chungang yŏn'gam, 1951-52*, pp. 21-23; Kim Il Sung, *Chayu wa tongnip ŭl wihan Chosŏn inmin ŭi chŏngŭi ŭi choguk haebang chŏnjaeng*, pp. 35-40.

6. This speech was delivered at the fifth session of the first Supreme People's Assembly on February 28, 1950. It was not selected for inclusion in the first edition and appeared only in the second edition of Kim's selected works. See Kim Il Sung, *Kim Il Sung sŏnjip*, 2d ed., 2:399-408.

7. A detailed report of his trip as well as the economic and cultural agreement, including some trade figures, are available in his report to the third session of the first Supreme People's Assembly on April 21, 1949. See Kim Il Sung, *Ssoryŏn ŭl pangmun han Chosŏn minju chuŭi inmin konghwaguk taep'yodan ŭi saŏp e taehayŏ, pp. 1-26*. See also Paek Nam-un, *Ssoryŏn insang*, pp. 2-342.

8. The seven-member chairman group of the Democratic Front included Kim Tu-bong and Hŏ Hŏn among others. There were no politically prominent South

Korean leaders in this group, and most were older revolutionaries known to the people of the South. This front was organized exactly one year before the outbreak of war. For details of this front, see *Choguk t'ongil minju chuŭi chŏnsŏn kyŏlsŏng taehoe munhŏnjip*, pp. 1-188.

9. See the text in *Chosŏn chungang yŏn'gam, 1951-1952*, pp. 80-81.

10. The South Korean guerrilla operation was commanded by Kim Tal-sam and Nam To-bu. An elaborate and detailed account of the arrest and prosecution of the guerrillas is in an eleven-volume report by the Public Security Bureau of the South Korean Prosecutor's Office. See *Chwaik sagŏn sillok*.

11. Kim Il Sung, *Namchosŏn hyŏngmyŏng kwa choguk t'ongil e taehayŏ*, p. 117. Many South Korean accounts ignore the fact that Pak had insisted on the war, charging Kim and the Soviet Union with starting the war. This line of argument comes from the defectors who were former underlings of Pak. They claim that Pak preferred popular uprising to an all-out war to unify the South. See, among others, *Han'guk e issŏsŏ ŭi kongsan chuŭi*, pp. 352-353.

12. Kim Il Sung, *Uri ŭi hyŏngmyŏng kwa inmin kundae ŭi kwaŏp e taehayŏ*, pp. 148-216. This speech is also available in English in his *Selected Works*, 3:316-325.

13. His radio address on September 11, 1950. The text appeared only in the first edition of his selected works: *Kim Il Sung sŏnjip*, 3:104-115.

14. The North Koreans claim that Pyongyang was recaptured on December 6, 1950, by the Chinese forces and the North Korean army entered the city on December 10. A mass rally to welcome the soldiers was held on December 11, and it was Kim Ch'aek and not Kim Il Sung who delivered the major speech. See *P'yŏngyangji*, pp. 472-473. Most South Korean accounts of the third joint plenum state that the meeting was held in a small town named Pyŏl-o-ri, but the North Korean account states that it was held in Kanggye, Chagangdo. See *History of the Just Fatherland Liberation War of the Korean People*, p. 162.

15. Kim Il was criticized for his defeatism and was relieved of the vice-minister's position in the Ministry of Defense. He was alleged to have said that the war was lost because of the lack of airplanes. Ch'oe Kwang and Kim Han-jung were busy taking care of themselves and neglected their duty, and they were relieved of their posts as division commanders. Mu Chŏng was charged with disobeying direct orders and with killing many retreating soldiers. Kim Yŏl failed to supply war materials from the rear to the front. Hŏ Sŏng-t'aek had failed to carry out the orders of the party in the guerrilla operation in the South. Others, such as Yim Ch'un-ch'u and Pak Kwang-hŭi, were accused of disobeying the orders of the committees. See the details in his speech, which appeared in the first edition of his selected works and the collection of documents relating to the war. After the war, it was suppressed and not reprinted. See the full text in *Kim Il Sung sŏnjip*, 1st ed., 3:122-173.

16. For Kim's caution, see *Kim Il Sung sŏnjip*, 3:166-172. See also Decree 42 of the Military Committee prohibiting indiscriminate purges in *Chosŏn chungang yŏn'gam, 1951-52*, p. 105. Hŏ's Russian first name was considered to be Alexandr; see Chong-sik Lee and Ki-wan Oh, "The Russian Faction in North Korea."

17. Kim said in his speech delivered on April 7, 1956, that on the average the party had expelled about 2,250 members each year from 1948 to 1956, approximately 15 percent of the entire membership of the provincial party. See Kim Il Sung, *P'yŏngan pukto tang tanch'e dŭl ŭi kwaŏp*, pp. 2-66.

18. Kim Il Sung, *Tang tanch'e dŭl ŭi chojik saŏp esŏ ŭi myŏtkaji kyŏlham dŭl ŭi taehayŏ*, pp. 3-85. This report was made at the fourth joint plenum of the Central Committee on November 1, 1951.

19. Kim Il Sung, *Sasang saŏp esŏ kyojo chuŭi wa hyŏngsik chuŭi rŭl t'oech'i hago chuch'e rŭl hwangnip halte taehayŏ*, pp. 9-29. This is one of the most famous speeches made by Kim, announcing his *Chuch'e* idea. The original version is important because it was edited many times in subsequent editions. The original version is also available in *Kim Il Sung sŏnjip*, 2d ed., 4:325-354.

20. Kim Il Sung, *Nodongdang ŭi chojikchŏk sasangjŏk kanghwa nŭn uri sŭngni ŭi kich'o*, pp. 2-73. This speech was delivered on December 15, 1952, at the fifth joint plenum of the Central Committee. There are many edited versions of this speech in subsequent publications. There is even a 20th-anniversary article on this speech written by Chang Yong-ch'ŏl in *Nodong sinmun*, December 15, 1972. It is important to read the original.

21. There are many edited versions of this report to the Third Party Congress, and this is the only report by Kim to the party congress that was not included in the third edition of his selected works. It is worthwhile to scrutinize the original. See Kim Il Sung's report in the second edition of his selected works, 4:433-571.

22. See his speech carried in *Nodong sinmun*, March 17, 1951, for the second anniversary and April 16, 1952, for the grain.

23. My interview with General Nikolai G. Lebedev in Moscow on July 21, 1978. General Lebedev said that Major General Romanenko had died some years before. Lebedev returned to North Korea several times as deputy head of the Soviet-Korean Friendship Association. He had passed by Colonel Ignatiev's grave near Pyongyang. See General Lebedev, "S Soznaniem ispolnennogo dolga," pp. 61-105.

24. See Kim's concluding remark at the eighth plenum of the Central Committee of the Third Party Congress on February 25, 1959. This speech appeared only in the second edition of the selected works and was not selected for the third edition. See *Kim Il Sung sŏnjip*, 2d ed., 6:269. See Kim's comment on Hŏ's ability to speak Korean in a speech at the enlarged plenum of the Standing Committee of the Central Committee on February 23, 1960, in Kim Il Sung, *Sahoe chuŭi kyŏngje kwalli munje e taehayŏ*, 1:342-383.

25. Kim's condemnation of Hŏ lasted more than a decade. In addition to those already cited, see Kim's speeches on April 4, 1955, April 7, 1956, April 23, 1956, March 7, 1958, November 20, 1958, February 26, 1959, February 23, 1960, January 23, 1961, October 18, 1966, and May 27, 1968. They appear in Kim's selected works, *Kim Il Sung sŏnjip*, 2d ed., 2:531; 3:7; 4:267, 335-336, 344, 385, 407, 409, 536; 5:85, 409.

26. Pak Ch'ang-ok and Pak Yŏng-bin were both Soviet-Koreans, and Hŏ's

chairmanship of the Inspection Committee was given to Kim Ŭng-gi, a member of the domestic group. There were many changes in various party posts during and shortly after the war. For example, Pak Chŏng-ae, chairman of the Democratic Women's Union, was appointed secretary in the party. See the details of the change in Dae-Sook Suh, *Korean Communism, 1945-1980*, pp. 315-336.

27. Pak Hŏn-yŏng was born in 1900 in Yesan, Ch'ungch'ŏng namdo. He graduated from Taehŭng Elementary School in his hometown, went to Seoul and graduated from the First High School, then learned English in the YMCA before going to Shanghai, where he continued his study in English. Pak went to the Soviet Union from there. He was a graduate of the Communist University of Toilers of the East (KUTV) and was arrested when he returned to Korea and served 18 months in jail. Upon his release he worked as a reporter for *Tong-a ilbo* in Seoul. He was also known at various times as Kim Sŏng-sam and Wang Yang-ok and was married to a well-known Communist revolutionary, Chu Se-juk of Hamhŭng.

28. Yi Sŭng-yŏp was born on February 8, 1905, in Puch'ŏn county, Kyŏnggi province. He entered the Korean Communist Party in September 1925 and was a reporter for *Chosŏn ilbo*. He was arrested in 1931, 1937, and 1940, each time serving approximately four years. He was arrested for printing and distributing antiwar handbills against the Japanese police and worked under Pak Hŏn-yŏng. When Korea was liberated, Yi became a member of the Central Committee of the Korean Communist Party and was editor of the party organ, *Haebang ilbo*.

29. They were Pak Kwang-hŭi for the Kyŏnggi Provincial Party Committee, Yi Sŏng-gyŏng for the Ch'ungch'ŏng pukto Provincial Party Committee, Pak U-hŏn for the Ch'ungch'ŏng namdo Provincial Party Committee, Pang Chung-p'yo for the Chŏlla pukto Provincial Party Committee, Pak Yŏng-bal for the Chŏlla namdo Provincial Party Committee, Pak Chong-gŭn for the Kyŏngsang pukto Provincial Party Committee, Nam Kyŏng-u for the Kyŏngsang namdo Provincial Party Committee, and Kim Ŭng-bin for the Seoul City Party Committee. See Kim Nam-sik, *Sillok, namnodang*, pp. 529-530.

30. There were other officers, such as Yi In-dong, who was the deputy director for rear operations, and Yim Ho for military training. There is a detailed account of the operation of the Kŭmgang Political Institute in Kim Nam-sik, *Sillok, namnodang*, pp. 555-556. Kim Nam-sik is a graduate of the institute and former member of the group in the North. See also *Pukhan koejip chŏnsul munhŏnjip*, pp. 425-458.

31. Cho Il-myŏng (alias Cho Tu-wŏn), born on December 1, 1903, in Yangyang county, Kangwŏndo, was a member of Pak Hŏn-yŏng's brain trust and was Pak's speech writer.

Pae Ch'ŏl was born on January 6, 1912, in Seoul. He graduated from Songdo High School and studied at Nippon University, majoring in sociology. He joined the Japanese Communist Party in 1932. After the liberation of Korea, he headed the organization section of the North Korean front organization, *Chōsōren*, before he returned to Seoul in January 1946. He became chairman of the Kyŏngsang pukto Provincial Party Committee in 1948 before he fled to the North.

Pak Sŭng-wŏn (alias Pak I-ch'ŏl) was born on February 28, 1913, in Yongju county, Kyŏngsang pukto. He was a political reporter for *Seoul sinmun* and also served as associate editor of *Kŭlloja*, the party organ, in 1949.

Yun Sun-dal was born on January 16, 1914, in Kangjin county, Chŏlla namdo. He worked underground with Kim Sam-yong in the Kwangju region in 1940. After the liberation of Korea he was chairman of the Kwangju City Party Committee. Yun was arrested by the South Korean police in August 1949 and was one of those Communists released by the North Korean armed forces when they occupied Seoul on June 28, 1950.

32. Yim Hwa was born on October 13, 1908, in Kangwŏndo but lived in Seoul. He graduated from Posŏng School and studied in Japan. He was a member of the Korean Proletarian Literary Association (KAPF) and became its chairman in 1932. He was arrested by the Japanese several times for his leftist writings and was one of the leading leftist literary writers of Korea. He was married to Chi Ha-yŏn.

33. Maeng Chong-ho (alias Hŏ Chong-il) was born on August 10, 1911, in Kyŏngsŏng county, Hamgyŏng pukto. Maeng served four years in prison before the liberation and was chairman of the Central District Party Committee in Seoul in 1946 before he fled to the North in 1947. He was trained as a guerrilla in the Kŭmgang Political Institute and became commander of its Tenth Division.

34. Information given here is based on the official document and trial records released by the North Korean authorities. The most comprehensive is the book entitled *Mijeguk chuŭi koyong kanch'ŏp Pak Hŏn-yŏng Yi Sŭng-yŏp todang ŭi Chosŏn minju chuŭi inmin konghwaguk chŏnggwŏn chŏnbok ŭmmo wa kanch'ŏp sagŏn kongp'an munhŏn*, pp. 153-160 (hereafter cited as *Trial Records*). Many sources carried the trial records, the indictment, the prosecution and defense questioning, testimony of the witnesses, and the sentence. All are available in the above-cited source. They appear also in *Minju Chosŏn* and *Nodong sinmun*, August 5, 6, 7, and 8, 1952.

35. Yi Wŏn-jo was born on June 2, 1919, in Andong county, Kyŏngsang pukto. He graduated from Hōsei University in Japan in 1935 and was a reporter for *Chosŏn ilbo*. He became editor of *Hyŏndae ilbo* in 1946 before he fled the South in 1947.

36. *Trial Records*, pp. 150-160.

37. *Chosŏn nodongdang yŏksa kyojae*, p. 297.

38. *Ibid.*, pp. 298-299. For Kim's speech on December 15, 1952, see *Nodongdang ŭi chojikchŏk sasangjŏk kanghwa nŭn uri sŭngni ŭi kich'o*, pp. 35-73.

39. Kim Ik-sŏn, the first chief justice of the North, was arrested in April 1938 for his participation in Communist activities in Korea. When released from prison he went to the Soviet Union and studied the Soviet legal system. Kim is a native of Hamgyŏng pukto. His associate judges for this trial were Pak Yong-suk and Pak Kyŏng-ho. The secretary for the court was Kim Yŏng-ju, brother of Kim Il Sung.

40. Yi Song-un was one of the few educated partisans. He had participated in guerrilla activities with Kim in the Hyesanjin incident, for which he was arrested. He later fled to the Soviet Union to study and returned to Korea after the libera-

tion. He was appointed procurator-general during the Korean War, succeeding Chang Hae-u, the first procurator-general.

41. Yi Kang-guk, a native of Seoul, was born on February 7, 1906. Yi was one of the leading intellectuals of Korea. He studied under Japanese leftist professor Miyake Shikanosuke at Keijō Imperial University (Seoul National University), graduating in 1930. He went to Germany and studied at Berlin University for three years, returning to Korea in 1935. He participated in a number of leftist activities, such as the Red Labor Union Incident in 1936, and was arrested several times. When he was finally released in 1941, he became a member of the Central Committee of the Korean Communist Party. Yi was ordered arrested by the American occupation authorities in September 1946. He fled the South in October 1946 and became the first head of the Foreign Affairs Bureau in Kim Il Sung's first People's Committee in the North. See his book, *Minju chuŭi Chosŏn ŭi kŏnsŏl*.

42. Harold Noble recorded details of his activities during the war in his memoirs, *Embassy at War*, pp. 43-64. See the charges in *Trial Records*.

43. Cho Yong-bok (alias Pak Sang-ok) was born on May 21, 1909, in Miryang county, Kyŏngsang namdo. Cho joined the Japanese Communist Party in 1932 and was employed as a clerk for the Korean Forwarding Company while working as a Communist. He worked under Kim Sam-yong in Seoul in 1949 and was arrested by the South Korean police in September 1949. He fled to the North in May 1950 after he was released.

Paek Hyŏng-bok was born on October 24, 1917, in Changhŭng county, Chŏlla namdo. Paek was a police officer from 1940 under the Japanese and was a detective assigned to the high criminal division of Chŏnju city before the liberation and became chief detective of the Central Investigation Division.

An Yŏng-dal was a comrade of Yi Sŭng-yŏp. An had worked with Yi in 1931 printing and distributing antiwar handbills to Japanese soldiers going to Manchuria. It was alleged that when Yi Sŭng-yŏp found out about An's role in the arrest of Kim Sam-yong and Yi Chu-ha, Yi had An sent to the fighting front during the war and had him shot.

44. The South Korean police records show that the arrest of An Yŏng-dal was the beginning of an intensive search for Kim Sam-yong and Yi Chu-ha. Information An provided was used for the arrest, but it was the work of the South Korean police. See the details in *Chwaik sagŏn sillok*, pp. 866-895; see also *Hyŏndaesa wa kongsan chuŭi*, pp. 212-226.

45. In general most South Korean accounts downplay all charges leveled against Yi Sŭng-yŏp and his group. One of the most logical defenses of these men can be found in the study of Pang In-hu, *Pukhan Chosŏn nodongdang ŭi hyŏngsŏnggwa palchŏn*, pp. 171-174.

46. Sŏl Chŏng-sik was born on September 18, 1912, in Tanch'ŏn, Hamgyŏng namdo. Sŏl was also one of the intellectuals who worked with the Communists. He graduated from Yŏnhŭi College (Yonsei University) and studied in the United States, graduating from Mt. Union College in Ohio and Columbia University. He worked in the Information Bureau of the American military occupation forces

and joined the Communist Party in September 1946. Sŏl was editor of *Seoul Times,* an English-language paper. He was the first North Korean interpreter at the initial cease-fire negotiations held in Kaesŏng in July 1951.

47. For a dramatic story about Yim Hwa and the fate of the South Korean Communists made into a novel, see Matsumoto Seichō, *Kita no shijin.* A similar book in Japanese about this incident is *Bokareta imbo.*

48. Only Yi Sŭng-yŏp was assigned an individual defense attorney, Chi Yong-dae. Other defense attorneys were Yi Kyu-hong, Kim Mun-p'yŏng, Chŏng Yŏng-hwa, and Kil Pyŏng-ok.

49. They were Ch'oe Yong-gŏn, Kim Ik-sŏn, Yim Hae, Pang Hak-se, and Cho Sŏng-mo.

50. The witnesses were Han Ch'ŏl, Ha P'il-wŏn, Kim Hae-gyun, Kim So-mok, Hyŏn Hyo-sŏm, Kwŏn O-jik, Yi Sun-gŭn, Yi Kang-guk, and Cho Il-myŏng. There is no doubt that these witnesses were forced to testify against Pak because all of them were Pak's loyal supporters and comrades from the 1930s. They had worked together against the Japanese and often shared prison cells, and it is most unlikely that they would have testified against Pak of their own free will.

51. Pak was accused of arranging positions for most of the twelve conspirators and other South Korean Communists in the North including Chu Yŏng-ha and Kwŏn O-jik as ambassadors to Moscow and Peking. All the names and positions are cited in *Trial Records,* pp. 111-122.

8. *After the War*

1. In exercising Big-Power chauvinism Peng was reported to have told Kim that "during the period of the war of resistance [World War II], I was the deputy commander-in-chief of the Eighth Route Army, while you were a division commander of the United Army in Manchuria." This sort of statement contributed to the strained Sino-Korean relations during the Korean War. Peng was also alleged to have said that the credit for the "Resist the U. S., Aid Korea" struggle was due to two persons, Gao Gang and Hong Xuejin. It was alleged that this sort of statement enabled Soviet revisionism to creep in and Zhou Enlai denounced Peng for Exercising Big-Power chauvinism. See "Wicked History of Peng Dehuai," *Current Background.*

2. Joseph C. Goulden, *Korea: The Untold Story of the War,* p. 555. For Dean Rusk's reaction to this reply, see "Briefing of Ambassadors," U.S. State Department, July 3, 1951.

3. The speech appears in the first edition of Kim Il Sung's selected works (4:230-231), and it is also available in Kim Il Sung, *Chayu wa tongnip ŭl wihan Chosŏn inmin ŭi chŏngŭi ŭi choguk haebang chŏnjaeng,* pp. 51-78.

4. Pak Chŏng-ae was one of the most powerful women of the North. She was born in August 1907 in Kyŏnghŭng, Hamgyŏng pukto, and was said to have studied in the Soviet Union. During the 1930s, she was arrested and imprisoned several times for her participation in the labor disputes in the Pyongyang Rubber Company. She was a common-law wife of the chairman of the North Korean

Branch Bureau of the Korean Communist Party, Kim Yong-bŏm. She was released from jail when Korea was liberated, and she was involved in a number of political groups shortly after the liberation, becoming chairman of the Central Committee of the Democratic Women's Union of the North. For the next two decades or so, Pak maintained her support for Kim and was one of the most powerful figures of the North.

5. These included Chang Si-u, Kim O-sŏng, An Ki-sŏng, Kim Kwang-su, Kim Ŭng-bin, Ku Chae-su, Yi Ch'ŏn-jin, Cho Pok-ye, and Yi Chu-sang.

6. The party bylaw revision committee consisted of Kim Il Sung, Pak Chŏng-ae, Pak Ch'ang-ok, Kim Il, Pak Yŏng-bin, Yi Ki-sŏk, Kim Kwang-hyŏp, Yi Kwŏn-mu, Han Sŏl-ya, Kang Mun-sŏk, Hwang T'ae-sŏng, Kim Yŏl, Ko Pong-gi, Kim Sŭng-hwa, and Pak Kŭm-ch'ŏl.

7. The serious fighting of the Korean War ended by June 1951 when the truce negotiations began, but during the 1952-1953 period of small-scale fighting and during the truce negotiations, the U.S. Air Force bombed North Korean cities, including Pyongyang, almost beyond recognition. See the North Korean account in *Pyongyang ŭi ŏje wa onŭl*, pp. 238-276. It was estimated that the destruction of property from the war amounted to 420 billion wŏn in old North Korean currency. See *Chosŏn nodongdang yŏksa kyojae*, p. 311.

8. The delegation consisted of Kim Il Sung, Pak Chŏng-ae, Chŏng Il-yong, Chŏng Chun-t'aek, Nam Il, and Kim Hoe-il. For details of Kim's visit to the Soviet Union, see *Chosŏn chungang yŏn'gam, 1954-55*, pp. 9-19; G. F. Kim, "Ekonomischeskoe razvitie Koreiskoi Narodno-Demokraticheskoe Respubliki."

9. For the details of Kim's trip to China and other countries see his comprehensive report of his trip to fraternal socialist countries in Kim Il Sung, *Hyŏngje kukka inmin dŭl ŭi kogwi han kukche chuŭijŏk wŏnjo*, pp. 2-60. The delegation to China consisted of Kim Il Sung, Hong Myŏng-hŭi, Pak Chŏng-ae, Chŏng Chun-t'aek, Nam Il, Kim Hoe-il, and two others.

10. Another delegation led by Yi Chu-yŏn left Pyongyang even before the end of the Korean War in June and returned on November 26, 1953, after visiting Czechoslovakia, Poland, East Germany, Hungary, Romania, and Bulgaria. This group received a number of machines, economic aid, and commitments from these countries to help develop heavy industries in the North. Slightly modified figures are in Pang Ho-sik, *Sahoe chuŭi chinyŏng naradŭl kanŭi kisul kyŏngjejŏk hyŏpcho*.

11. The three-year economic plan was approved on April 23, 1954, at the seventh session of the Supreme People's Assembly. The proposal was presented by Pak Ch'ang-ok on April 20 and was adopted on April 23. The plan was not adopted in 1953 after the war, as commonly alleged. See the details of Kim's policy on agricultural cooperativization in Kim Il Sung, *On Our Party's Policy for the Future Development of Agriculture*. The agricultural cooperatives were hinted at as early as August 1953 by Kim, but were not implemented until 1954. See *Agricultural Cooperativization in the Democratic People's Republic of Korea*, p. 85.

12. It is not my purpose here to give complete details of economic policies or statistical information on the economic development of the postwar North. Kim's

economic policy deserves a separate study. See two excellent studies by Cho Chae-
sŏn, *Kwadogi e issŏsŏ ŭi Chosŏn nodongdang ŭi kyŏngje chŏngch'aek; Chosŏn minju chuŭi
inmin konghwaguk sahoe kyŏngje chedo.* For a comprehensive coverage of agrarian
and industrial development in English, see Robert A. Scalapino and Chong-sik
Lee, *Communism in Korea*, 2:1011-1295.

13. Pak Il-u was one of the military figures from China. He was born in 1904
in P'yŏngan namdo and went to Manchuria when he was a boy. He went to mainland China for training and military activities against the Japanese there. Pak was
deputy commander of the Korean Revolutionary Army in China and one of the
leaders of the Korean Independence League in Yanan. Pak was identified as Boku
Ichiu (Japanese pronunciation of Pak Il-u) in Conrad Brandt, Benjamin Schwartz,
and John K. Fairbank, *A Documentary History of Chinese Communism*, p. 293.
When he returned to Korea Pak was Kim's first minister of interior and controlled some of the security forces in the North. He was a member of the Military
Committee during the Korean War and one of the few Korean military leaders
who worked closely with the Chinese Volunteer Army. Pak was minister of communication when he was purged. There is a report that Pak was sympathetic to
the cause of Pak Hŏn-yŏng and his group of South Korean Communists, but there
are no details of his antiparty activities other than those related here.

14. Kim Ch'ang-dŏk was a partisan who worked with Ch'oe Yong-gŏn in
northern Manchuria. Kim returned to Korea as commander of the 164th Division
of the Korean contingent in Manchuria in July 1949 and became head of the
Fifth Division of the Korean People's Army. Kim is said to have reported Pak
Il-u's antiparty and anti-Kim activities. For Kim's loyalty to the partisans, see Kim
Ch'ang-dŏk, "Chosŏn inmin'gun ŭn hangil ppalchisan ŭi hyŏngmyŏngjŏk aeguk
chŏnt'ong ŭl kyesŭng han hyŏngmyŏngjŏk mujangyŏk."

15. Kim's accusations of Pak Il-u, Pang Ho-san, Kang Mun-sŏk, O Ki-sŏp, and
others appear in his concluding remarks at the April 1955 plenum of the Central
Committee. See Kim's speech on April 4, 1955, in *Kim Il Sung sŏnjip*, 2d ed.,
4:254-286.

16. For the original speech see *Kim Il Sung sŏnjip*, 2d ed., 4:325-354. For the
revised version of this speech, see *Kim Il Sung chŏjak sŏnjip*, 3d ed., 1:560-585. For
the revised edition in English, see Kim Il sung, *On Eliminating Dogmatism and
Formalism and Establishing Juche in Ideological Work*. Kim's support for the Korean
Artists Proletarian Federation (KAPF) is truly ironic because he had just put away
one of its founders and the last chairman, Yim Hwa, who was sentenced to death
in the trial of Yi Sŭng-yŏp and the South Korean Communists.

17. Kim also condemned Pak Yŏng-bin in his speech on April 7, 1956. See Kim
Il Sung, *P'yŏngan pukto tang tanch'e dŭl ŭi kwaŏp*, pp. 2-66. Kim also attacked him
for his methods, which resembled an intelligence organization that gathers information on the people. Pak was supposed to have checked up on the number of
suits people owned. See *Kim Il Sung sŏnjip*, 2d ed., 5:397. Pak Yŏng-bin was
regarded as a revisionist in the North, and Kim condemned him often; see his
speeches on March 7, 1958, August 25, 1960, and January 23, 1961.

18. Kim's political thought is discussed in ch. 17.

19. For the complete text of Khrushchev's report, see N. S. Khrushchev, *Report of the Central Committee of the Communist Party of the Soviet Union to the 20th Party Congress.*

20. Other delegation members were Yi Hyo-sun and Hŏ Pin. Yi Hyo-sun is a brother of the late Yi Che-sun, who helped Kim make the Poch'ŏnbo raid. See *Yi Che-sun tongji ŭi saengae wa hwaltong.* Yi later became a member of the Political Committee of the party. Hŏ Pin was a Soviet-Korean who later became ambassador to Poland.

21. For Kim's speech, see Kim Il Sung, *P'yŏngan pukto tang tanch'e dŭl ŭi kwaŏp,* pp. 12-14. For the definition of collective leadership *(chipch'ejŏk chido),* see *Chŏngch'i sajŏn,* pp. 1084-1085. Many South Korean accounts claim that there was a March plenum, held March 28 and 29, but no such plenum was held. The last plenum of the Central Committee before the Third Party Congress was the December plenum of 1955. On collective leadership, see a good article by Chŏng In-sŏp, "Chipch'ejŏk chido rŭn tang mit kukkachedo ŭi ch'oego wŏnch'ŭk ida."

22. For the Korean text of Brezhnev's speech, see *Nodong sinmun,* April 25, 1956. The text is reprinted in *Chosŏn nodongdang che samch'a taehoe munhŏnjip,* pp. 479-486. This book is available in many languages, including English and Japanese; see *Documents and Materials of the Third Congress of the Workers' Party of Korea, April 23-29. 1956.* While the documents of the party congress were widely circulated, the minutes of the congress were not made public.

23. In addition to Brezhnev and Nie there were representatives from Poland, East Germany, Czechoslovakia, Romania, Hungary, Albania, Bulgaria, Mongolia, Vietnam, and Indonesia. They all spoke at the congress, offering congratulations to the delegates.

24. Kim for the first time called Kim Ku and Kim Kyu-sik teachers or elders *(sŏnsaeng)* in this speech. See *Kim Il Sung sŏnjip,* 2d ed., 4:518. Kim later commented that both Kim Ku and Kim Kyu-sik were opposed to communism, but they were on his side for communism before they died. See *Kim Il Sung sŏnjip,* 2d ed., 4:335-336. Nothing could be further from the truth. Kim Ku was assassinated in the South, and Kim Kyu-sik was kidnapped by the North Koreans during the Korean War and presumed dead in the North. See Kim's condemnation of these men in his earlier speeches – for example, Kim Il Sung, *Chosŏn minju chuŭi inmin konghwaguk surip ŭi kil,* p. 118.

25. For the text of Kim's entire speech, see Kim Il Sung's report to the Third Party Congress. This speech is not available in the latest edition of Kim's selected works. It is available only in the 2d ed., 4:433-571.

26. Yi was educated in Japan and regarded as one of the prominent intellectuals in the North. He was chairman of the History Department of Kim Il Sung University and also chairman of the History Compilation Committee of the North. He became Chairman of the Social Science Division of the Academy of Sciences of the North and was its leading member. His *Chosŏn kŭndaesa* was translated into Russian by A. M Pak, *Ocherki novoi istorii Korei;* into Chinese by Ding Zeliang and Xia Yuwwen, *Chaoxian jindaishi;* and into Japanese by Kawakubo Kōbu and

O Chae-yang, *Chōsen kindaishi kenkyū*. Yi was purged shortly thereafter, however, for allegedly giving credit to a magazine, *Chosŏn ji kwang*, an underground organ of the old Korean Communist Party in the 1920s and 1930s.

27. Examples are many, but most widely circulated is the book by Yi Na-yŏng. Yi said in the preface that it was written in response to the call by Kim Il Sung to study the partisans at the time of the Third Party Congress. Yi was purged sometime after the book was published. See Yi Na-yŏng, *Chosŏn minjok haebang t'ujaengsa*. See also *Chosŏn kŭndae hyŏngmyŏng undongsa*, and *Chosŏn t'ongsa*.

28. For Yi Song-un's discussion of Kim Il Sung's speech, see *Nodong sinmun*, April 25, 1956.

29. For Kim's criticism of Pak Mun-gyu, see Kim's speech on April 4, 1955, in the second edition of Kim's selected works, 4:283. He was criticized for his handling of agricultural production during the war. Pak was perhaps the only member of the domestic group who lasted under Kim Il Sung. He was a member of the inner circle of the domestic group and a close comrade of Yi Sŭng-yŏp and his followers. Pak was a student of Miyake Shikanosuke at Keijō Imperial University (Seoul National University) and was very active in the domestic group. He served in seven different cabinet posts under Kim Il Sung and was the first minister of agriculture. Pak was elected to the third, fourth, and fifth Central Committees of the party. He died on October 15, 1971, at the age of 65 after a long illness.

30. The eleven partisans who were members of the Central Committee included in rank order Kim Il Sung, Ch'oe Yong-gŏn, Kim Il, Pak Kŭm-ch'ŏl, Kim Kwang-hyŏp, Ch'oe Hyŏn, Yu Kyŏng-su, Kim Kyŏng-sŏk, Yi Yŏng-ho, Kim Ch'ang-dŏk, and Yi Song-un. The six partisans who were candidate members of the Central Committee included Sŏk San, O Chin-u, Ch'oe Kwang, Ch'oe Yong-jin, Kim Ch'ang-bong, and Sŏ Ch'ŏl. In addition to the four partisans, Kim Tu-bong and Pak Chŏng-ae constituted the top six members of the Central Committee.

31. For Pak's speech, see *Nodong sinmun*, April 20, 1956. For the text and explanation of the bylaws adopted at this congress, see *Chosŏn nodongdang kyuyak haesŏl*.

32. For the membership figures, see Kim's speech at the Third Party Congress; Kim Il Sung, *Chosŏn nodongdang che samch'a taehoe esŏ han chungang wiwŏnhoe saŏp ch'onggyŏl pogo*.

33. In addition to Kim Il Sung, the members of the delegation consisted of Pak Chŏng-ae, vice-chairman of the party; Nam Il, foreign minister; Yi Chong-ok, chairman of the State Planning Commission; Ko Chun-t'aek, vice-chairman of the Korean Democratic Party; Kim Pyŏng-je, vice-chairman of the Ch'ŏndogyo Young Friends Party; Ch'oe Hyŏn, vice-minister of the Ministry of Defense; Cho Kŭm-song, president of Kim Ch'aek Engineering College; and two labor heroes, Han Ki-ch'ang and Chŏn Sŏng-bok. See the details of the trip in *Kukche chuŭi ŭi ch'insŏn*.

34. It is not my purpose here to go into the details of economic development. For a comprehensive report on the first five-year economic plan of 1957-1961,

see the report by Yi Chong-ok at the first party conference, March 3-6, 1958, in *Nodong sinmun*, March 4, 1958. For the statistical figures, see *Nodong sinmun*, March 8, 1958.

35. Ch'oe Ch'ang-ik was born in 1896 in Onsŏng county, Hamgyŏng pukto. He was educated in Korea and Japan and participated in one of the first Korean Communist activities in Shanghai in 1921. He was arrested for his participation in the third Korean Communist Party Incident in Seoul in February 1928 and was imprisoned for six years. He was released from jail in 1934, fled to China the following year, and worked in various underground organizations in Nanjing, Wuhan, and Yanan. He was vice-chairman of the Korean Independence League in 1942 and was the leading member of the Yanan group. He was one of the vice-premiers of the North as well as the first minister of finance in Kim's first cabinet. At the time of his sixtieth birthday in 1956 he was decorated by Kim.

36. There are many highly unreliable accounts of this incident in the South. See *Pukkoe ŭi p'abŏl t'ujaengsa*; *Pukhan chŏnggwŏn ŭi amt'usang*, pp. 118-148.

37. Paek Pong, *Minjok ŭi t'aeyang Kim Il Sung changgun*, 2:399-403.

38. Kim made many facts public in his concluding speech at the first party conference on March 6, 1958. See the entire text of his speech under the title "For the Successful Fulfilment of the First Five-Year Plan," in *Kim Il Sung sŏnjip*, 2d ed., 5:359-393. A slightly edited version is in 3d ed., 2:101-131. About the August plenum, see an article by Yi Song-un in *Kŭlloja* (August 1959), no. 8, pp. 19-25.

39. Paek Pong, *Minjok ŭi t'aeyang Kim Il Sung changgun*, 2:401-403.

40. Kim made these facts public in his speech to the officers and men of the 324th Army Unit of the Korean People's Army on February 8, 1958. See the text of the speech in *Kim Il Sung sŏnjip*, 2d ed., 5:308-349. It is also available in the 3d ed., 2:64-100.

41. Interview records with defectors, So Chŏng-ja and Kim Nam-sik, were cited in Pang In-hu, *Pukhan Chosŏn nodongdang ŭi hyŏngsŏnggwa palchŏn*, p. 231. See also *Hyŏndaesa wa kongsan chuŭi*, pp. 369-378.

42. See ch. 5, n. 18 for Kim Tu-bong.

43. For criticism of these people by Kim Il Sung, see his concluding speech at the first party conference on March 6, 1958, in *Kim Il Sung sŏnjip*, 2d ed., 6:148. For the criticism of O Ki-sŏp, see Kim's speech on March 23, 1959, in *Kim Il Sung sŏnjip*, 2d ed., 6:321 and 327. Kim even ridiculed O for using too many foreign words and too much Russian in his speeches. His condemnation of O continued into the 1960s and 1970s. See Kim's speeches on January 3, 1964, February 23, 1965, and December 5, 1972.

44. The North Korean electoral districts are still divided into nine provinces and two cities: P'yŏngan namdo, P'yŏngan pukto, Hamgyŏng namdo, Hamgyŏng pukto, Hwanghae namdo, Hwanghae pukto, Yanggangdo, Chagangdo, Kangwŏndo, and the cities of Pyongyang and Kaesŏng.

45. For a number of Kim's articles in commemoration of the fortieth anniversary of the October Revolution, see *Pravda*, October 22, 1957, and November 7,

1957, and *Nodong sinmun*, October 29, November 5, November 7, and November 8, 1957. See also a pamphlet entitled *Widaehan siwŏl ŭi sasang ŭn sŭngni hago itta.* A portion of the article in this pamphlet appeared in *Mezhdunarodnaya Zhizn*, November 1957, pp. 31-49.

46. Much of the information described here comes from his speeches at this first party conference of March 1958. The party conference was a new invention at the time of the Third Party Congress to accomodate changes in the party between congresses. But article 41 of the bylaws stated that the party conference may not replace more than one-fifth of the members of the Central Committee. No changes were announced at this party conference.

47. For Kim's speech on the implementation of the judicial policy of the party, see *Kim Il Sung sŏnjip*, 2d ed., 5:438-458. This text is also available in the 3d ed., 2:132-150. For studies on North Korean law, see Pyong Choon Hahm, "Ideology and Criminal Law in North Korea," and also doctoral dissertation by Koo-chin Kang, "Law in North Korea," Harvard Law School, 1969.

48. Nikolai M. Gribachev, "Kim Ir Sen" [Kim Il Sung], in *Stikhotvoreniia i Poemy*, pp. 177-191. This is a narrative poem Gribachev wrote about Kim during the Korean War in October 1951. It relates many facts such as the death of Kim's wife and Kim's perception of South Korean politics.

PART IV. SEARCH FOR KOREAN IDENTITY

9. Mobilization Campaigns

1. The North Koreans have compiled sixteen volumes of tales and conversations Kim had with the people when he visited various localities. See *Inmindŭl sogesŏ.* Some of these stories were translated into English and began to appear in a number of pamphlets in the 1970s.

2. See *Kibon kŏnsŏl saŏp palchŏn ŭl wihan uri tang ŭi chŏngch'aek*, Kim Il Sung, *Nodong haengjŏng saŏp e taehan myŏkkaji munje*, pp. 3-21. For a good study of the North Korean economic system by the Economic and Law Research Institute of the Academy of Sciences of North Korea, translated into Japanese by Kim Ŭng-ji and Ko Sŭng-hyo see *Chōsen ni okeru shakai shugi no kiso kensetsu.*

3. "Ch'ŏllima" literally means "horse of a thousand *ri*." It was taken from a legendary horse that was capable of running one thousand *ri* per day. There is much literature on this movement. See *Ch'ŏllima undonggwa sahoe chuŭi kŏnsŏl taegojo e taehayŏ; Ch'ŏllima chagŏppan undong*; Kim Il Sung, *Ch'ŏllima kisudŭl ŭn uri sidae ŭi yŏngung imyŏ tang ŭi pulgŭn chŏnsa ida.*

4. Kim Il Sung, *Kŏnsŏl punya esŏ tang chŏngch'aek ŭl kwanch'ŏl halte taehayŏ*, pp. 2-19. For Kim's conversation with workers in the Kangsŏn steel mill, see Paek Pong, *Minjok ŭi t'aeyang Kim Il Sung changgun*, 2:407-412.

5. Kim Il Sung, *Sahoe chuŭi kŏnsŏl ŭi widaehan ch'udongyŏl in Ch'ŏllima chagŏppan undong ŭl tŏuk simhwa palchŏn sik'ija*, pp. 3-38. This was the speech Kim made on the second congress of the Ch'ŏllima workteam movement on May 11, 1968.

6. Paek Pong, *Minjok ŭi t'aeyang Kim Il Sung changgun*, 2:412-415.

7. Kim Il Sung, *Kim Il Sung sŏnjip*, 2d ed., 5:518-537. See also Kim Il Sung, *Kŏnsŏl ŭi chirŭl nop'igi wihayŏ*, pp. 2-15.

8. Kim Il Sung, *Kongsan chuŭi kyoyang e taehayŏ*, pp. 1-32.

9. Kim said that the collectivization of all farmland was completed by the end of August 1958. See his speech in English, "On the Victory of Socialist Agricultural Cooperativization and Further Development of Agriculture in Our Country," in *Documents on the National Congress of Agricultural Cooperatives*, pp. 1-56. This speech was widely circulated and translated into many languages, including English and Japanese.

10. The concept of *chipchung chido*, an intensive guidance system, should not be confused with *chipch'ejŏk chido*, collective leadership. Many defectors from the North claimed that the intensive guidance system was a method to weed out antiparty elements. There were other purposes, however, such as to devise new methods to boost production and improve the control mechanism of the central party organs. For these two terms and their differences, see *Chŏngch'i sajŏn*, pp. 1083-1085.

11. Kim criticized the mistakes of prominent local leaders such as Han Sang-du, Kim T'ae-gŭn, and Sŏ Ŭl-hyŏn. Han Sang-du, for example, was formerly chairman of the General Federation of Trade Unions. He was a member of the domestic group but survived Kim's criticism and later became minister of finance in Kim's fourth cabinet. Kim also condemned the crimes of Chang Sun-myŏng, who was from this region and was purged. See Kim's speech at the enlarged plenum of the Hamgyŏng pukto provincial committee in Kim Il Sung, *Hamgyŏng pukto tang tanch'e dŭl ŭi kwaŏp*.

12. I visited the Ch'ŏngsalli cooperative in May 1974. The place where Kim had stayed while leading his fifteen-day on-the-spot guidance was enshrined with monuments and mementos, and the tree he planted in commemoration of his visit had grown tall. With its nurseries, schools, and cultural and recreation halls, it was a showpiece of North Korea's agricultural cooperatives. The chairman of the cooperative informed me that their farm's grain production had more than doubled since Kim's visit.

13. Kim made three important speeches concerning his visit to Ch'ŏngsalli, the first at the Ch'ŏngsalli Party Committee meeting on February 8, 1960, the second at the Kangsŏ County Party Committee on February 18, 1960, and the third at the enlarged plenum of the Standing Committee of the party in Pyongyang on February 23, 1960. All are available in Kim Il Sung, *Sahoe chuŭi kyŏngje kwalli munje e taehayŏ*, 1:277-383.

14. There are two important speeches by Kim on the Taean work system. One is the speech he made at the Taean Electric Plant on December 16, 1961, entitled "On the Reform of Leadership and Management in Industry to Fit the New Circumstances;" the other, given on November 9, 1962, is entitled "On Further developing the Taean Work System." Both speeches are available in Kim Il Sung, *Sahoe chuŭi kyŏngje kwalli munje e taehayŏ*, 2:86-143 and 423-441. For a description of the Taean work system, see *Yŏksa sajŏn*, pp. 586-593.

15. Paek Pong, *Minjok ŭi t'aeyang, Kim Il Sung changgun*, 2:580.

16. The total party membership as of August 1, 1961, was 1,311,563 counting both regular and probationary members. This was an increase of 146,618 members during the five years since the Third Party Congress, when membership was reported to be 1,164,945. Kim reported that workers represented 30 percent of the members, an increase of 12.3 percent from the Third Party Congress when it was 17.3 percent. Indiscriminate recruitment of party members seems to have stopped sometime during the latter half of the 1950s, and Kim wanted to improve the ratio of workers (industrial proletariat) in the party. This was also the last congress at which the party disclosed its membership figures.

17. Four delegates spoke on the second day: Kozlov, Deng, Alfred Krehler of East Germany, and Miyamoto Kenji of Japan. There were 28 other delegates, and they spoke on the third, fourth, and fifth days of the congress.

18. This speech is available in many places in many languages. See the Korean original in Kim Il Sung, *Chosŏn nodongdang che sach'a taehoe esŏ han chungang wiwŏnhoe saŏp ch'onghwa pogo.* An English version is available in *Documents of the Fourth Congress of the Workers' Party of Korea,* pp. 1-157. It is also in *Kim Il Sung chŏjak sŏnjip.* 3:60-203.

19. For Kim Il's speech see the text in English in *Documents of the Fourth Congress of the Workers' Party of Korea,* pp. 159-260. Statistical figures were represented separately, and they are also available in *Atarashii sedai* [New era], (November 1961), no. 20, pp. 177-198.

20. Texts of both Kozlov and Deng's speeches are available in *Documents of the Fourth Congress of the Workers' Party of Korea,* pp. 254-271. For Korean text see *Nodong sinmun,* September 13, 1961.

21. Some changes were made, but the basic texts remained the same. The number of chapters was reduced from ten to nine and the number of articles was increased from sixty-two to seventy. The North Koreans did not publish the revised text of the party bylaws, but they are available from a South Korean source, *Pukhan ch'onggam,* pp. 671-678.

22. Those partisans who were reelected from the third to the fourth party Central Committee were: Kim Il Sung, Ch'oe Yong-gŏn, Kim Il, Pak Kŭm-ch'ŏl, Kim Kwang-hyŏp, Ch'oe Hyŏn, Kim Kyŏng-sŏk, Yi Yŏng-ho, Kim Ch'ang-dŏk, and Yi Song-un. General Yu Kyŏng-su, who was a member of the Central Committee of the Third Party Congress, died on November 19, 1958.

23. Those 25 partisans who were newly elected to the Central Committee of the Fourth Party Congress were: Sŏ Ch'ŏl, Sŏk San, Kim Ch'ang-bong, Hŏ Pong-hak, Ch'oe Yong-jin, Pak Sŏng-ch'ŏl, O Chin-u, Chŏn Mun-sŏp, Chŏn Ch'ang-ch'ŏl, Ch'oe Kwang, An Yŏng, Han Ik-su, Kim Tae-hong, Kim Tong-gyu, Pak Yŏng-sun, Ch'oe Ki-ch'ŏl, O Paek-yong, Kim Pyŏng-sik, Hŏ Sŏk-sŏn, Kim Ok-sun, Yim Ch'ŏl, Ch'oe Min-ch'ŏl, Kim Chwa-hyŏk, Chi Pyŏng-hak, and Hŏ Hak-song. For complete listings of changes between party congresses, see Dae-Sook Suh, *Korean Communism, 1945-1980,* pp. 309-359.

24. The 8 partisans were Paek Hak-nim, Yu Ch'ang-gwŏn, T'ae Pyŏng-yŏl, Pak U-sŏp, Chŏng Pyŏng-gap, Yi Kuk-chin, Hwang Sun-hŭi, and Pak Kyŏng-suk. Several factors seem to have been considered in choosing some partisans as

regular members and some as candidate members. Those who became candidate members were in general younger and lower-ranking military officers.

25. Nam Il was born on June 5, 1913, in Russia and was the son of a poor peasant from Kyŏngwŏn county, Hamgyŏng pukto. He is reported to have graduated from Smolensk Military School and also from a college in Tashkent. He apparently returned to Korea with the occupation forces as an officer of the Russian army. Nam died on March 7, 1976, at the age of 64. See his record in *Nodong sinmun*, March 8, 1976.

26. Kim Ch'ang-man was born in 1907 in Yŏnghŭng, Hamgyŏng namdo. He fled Korea in 1934 to join the anti-Japanese revolutionary activities in China. He is reported to have graduated from a college in Guangzhou and became an officer of the Korean Independence League, the Yanan group. Kim was purged in 1966.

27. Kim Ch'ang-man, *Modŭn kŏsŭn choguk kŏnsŏl e*. This was the book Kim had published shortly after he returned to Korea. It is an interesting work; see his accusation of Kim Ku on p. 27 and his praise of Kim Il Sung on p. 96.

28. Kim Ch'ang-man, "Chosŏn nodongdang yŏksa yŏn'gu esŏ chegi doenŭn myŏkkaji munje,"

29. *Hangil mujang t'ujaeng chŏnjŏkchi rŭl ch'ajŏsŏ*. A team of party cadres led by a partisan went to Manchuria and spent five months from May to October 1959 retracing the battlegrounds of Kim Il Sung. This book is the report of their visit.

30. Books concerning the partisans and their activities are too numerous to mention here. The standard twelve-volume reminiscence is *Hangil ppalchisan ch'amgajadŭl ŭi hoesanggi*. This was reorganized in chronological order and reprinted in a series known as *Inmin ŭi chayu wa haebang ŭl wihayŏ*.

31.There are many individual accounts such as the ones by Yim Ch'un-ch'u, *Hangil mujang t'ujaeng sigirŭl hoesang hayŏ*, and Pak Tal, *Choguk ŭn saengmyŏng poda tŏgwihada*. There are others by Ch'oe Hyŏn and Kim Myŏng-hwa in *Hyŏngmyŏng ŭi kiresŏ* [On the road of the revolution] available in two volumes. Some of these were translated into Japanese under such titles as *Fukutsu no uta* or *Hakutō no yamanami o koete*. For the heroes who died in Manchuria see *Hyŏngmyŏng sŏnyŏl dŭl ŭi saengae wa hwaltong*.

10. The Sino-Soviet Dispute and Kim Il Sung

1. It is not my intention to describe the Sino-Soviet dispute. Only certain issues relevant to North Korean relations with the Soviet Union and China are discussed here. For the dispute itself, see the standard works on the subject, such as Donald S. Zagoria, *The Sino-Soviet Conflict, 1956-1961*; David Floyd, *Mao Against Khrushchev*; W. E. Griffith, *The Sino-Soviet Rift*.

2. Most of Kim's references to Stalin are omitted from his works. See the original speeches of Kim – for example, his speeches on July 9, 1948, August 15, 1951, and December 15, 1952, in *Kim Il Sung sŏnjip*, 2:171-210; 3:252-280; 4:317-407.

3. In his speech at the third enlarged plenary meeting of the Fourth Central

Committee on March 8, 1962, Kim elaborated on the organizational and ideological work of the party. In the third part of his speech, Kim lashed out at the Korean revisionists and tried without success to clarify what the international revisionists meant to the domestic politics of the North. See the speech in *Kim Il Sung chŏjak sŏnjip*, 3:290-330.

4. There are a number of studies on the foreign policy of North Korea. See among others Byung Chul Koh, *The Foreign Policy Systems of North and South Korea*; Chin O. Chung, *P'yongyang Between Peking and Moscow*; and Ho-min Yang, "North Korea, Thirty Years between Moscow and Peking." See also John Bradbury, "Sino-Soviet Competition in North Korea," and Joseph C. Kun, "North Korea: Between Moscow and Peking."

5. For his trip of November 1958 to China and Vietnam, see *Yŏngwŏn han ch'insŏn*. For the activities and relationship of Zhou Baozhong and Li Yenlu with Kim, see part I of this study. Zhou Baozhong and Li Yenlu survived the war in Manchuria, and Zhou even became an alternate member of the Central Committee of the Chinese Communist Party. See their activities and the reunion meeting at the banquet in Howard L. Boorman, ed., *Biographical Dictionary of Republican China*, 1:415-416; Donald W. Klein and Anne B. Clark, *Biographic Dictionary of Chinese Communism, 1921-1965*, 1:225-228.

6. In this article Kim emphasized the past relationship between the Koreans and the Chinese, tracing the cooperative efforts from the partisan days in Manchuria through the Korean War. Kim also expressed appreciation to the Chinese people for their aid and said that trade between the two countries from 1945 to 1958 had increased 17 times. For the Chinese text, see *Renmin ribao*, September 26, 1959. It is also available in Russian in Kim Il Sung (Kim Ir-sen), *Izbrannye stat'i i rechi*, pp. 579-591. For the Korean original see *Kim Il Sung sŏnjip*, 2d ed., 6:440-454.

7. The only meeting from which Kim was conspicuously absent was the November 1960 meeting of the representatives of the workers' and Communist parties of the world in Moscow. Kim sent Kim Il in his place to represent the North. For the chronicles of the various trips to both Beijing and Moscow by various leaders of the North, see *Chosŏn chungang yŏn'gam* for the relevant years, particularly 1960 and 1961.

8. For the treaty between the Soviet Union and North Korea, see *Nodong sinmun*, July 7, 1961; *Izvestia*, July 7, 1961; and also *Chosŏn chungang yŏn'gam, 1962*, pp. 157-161. For the treaty between the People's Republic of China and North Korea, see *ibid.* pp. 161-163; *Nodong sinmun*, July 12, 1961; and D. M. Johnson and H. Chiu, *Agreements of the People's Republic of China, 1949-67: A Calendar*, pp. 124-125. For his visit to China, see Shi Licheng, *Chaoxian renmin gaoju hongqi qianjin*.

9. For Kim Il Sung's report on his participation in the twenty-second congress of the Communist Party of the Soviet Union, see *Kŭlloja* (December 1961), no. 12 (193), pp. 3-12; *Nodong sinmun*, November 28, 1961. An excerpt of this speech appeared in *Pravda*, December 4, 1961, and also in English in Alexander Dallin, ed., *Diversity in International Communism*, pp. 388-394.

10. "Cho-sso yangguk kanŭi pulp'ae ŭi tongmaeng" [The invincible alliance between Korea and the Soviet Union], *Nodong sinmun*, July 6, 1972; "Pulmyŏl ŭi ch'insŏn konggo han tongmaeng" [The eternal friendship and firm alliance], *Nodong sinmun*, July 11, 1962.

11. For the Chinese editorial entitled "Reexamination of Nehru's Philosophy in View of the Sino-Indian Border Problem," see *Renmin ribao*, October 27, 1962; it appeared in *Nodong sinmun* in Korean on October 31. 1962. For Zhou's letter in Korean see *Nodong sinmun*, November 23, 1962.

12. "Paekchŏn paeksŭng ŭi siwŏl kich'i" [The ever-victorious banner of October], *Nodong sinmun*, November 7, 1962.

13. Yi was one of the very few Communists of domestic origin who survived the purges and remained in high posts in the North. Born in 1903 in Tanch'ŏn, Hamgyŏng namdo, Yi was imprisoned from 1931 to 1936 for his participation in the Tanch'ŏn Peasant Union Incident. He served in a number of important positions, including ambassador to China during the Korean War, minister of commerce, minister of finance, minister of trade, and deputy premier; he was also a member of the Political Committee. He died on August 20, 1969.

14. "Sahoe chuŭi chinyŏng ŭi t'ongil ŭl suho hamyŏ kukche kongsan chuŭi undong ŭi tan'gyŏl ŭl kanghwa haja" [Let us protect the unity of the socialist camp and strengthen the solidarity of the international Communist movement], *Chosŏn chungang yŏn'gam, 1964*, pp. 80-84. See also *Nodong sinmun*, January 30, 1963. For Yi's undelivered speech, see *Nodong sinmun*, January 22, 1963.

15. Pak Kŭm-ch'ŏl represented the Supreme People's Assembly and visited China in June 1962. For the Chinese welcome of Pak, see *Zhong Chao yongshi tuanjie*. For Ch'oe Yong-gŏn's visit in June 1963, see the Chinese welcome in *Ch'oe Yong-gŏn weiyuanchang fangmen zhongguo*. For the editorial in *Nodong sinmun* about Ch'oe's visit, see June 5, 1963. The joint communiqué was issued and the text is available in *Nodong sinmun*, June 24, 1963. For Liu Xiaoqi's visit, see *Nodong sinmun*, September 15, 1963.

16. There are many articles about the promotion of self-resuscitation and the self-reliant economy in the North. See, for example, an excellent article in *Kŭlloja* (March 1962), no. 3, (196), pp. 2-7; *Charyŏk kaengsaeng ŭi hyŏngmyŏng sasang*; see also *Nodong sinmun* editorials on June 12, 1963, and October 26, 1963.

17. Kim Sŏk-hyŏng is the foremost Korean historian of the North. Born on November 7, 1915, Kim is a native of Kyŏngsang pukto and was educated at Keijō Imperial University. He is head of the History Research Center of the Academy of Sciences and professor of history at Kim Il Sung University. He led the North Korean delegation to the 25th International Orientalist Congress held in Moscow in August 1960. Among his many works on Korean history is *Chosŏn yŏksa*. He is a Communist historian who emphasizes the correct attitude in the study of Korean History. See his article in *Yŏksa kwahak* (1966), no. 6, pp. 1-7. Kim Hŭi-il is another leading historian of the North, specializing in the modern period. See his book *Miguk cheguk chuŭi ŭi Chosŏn ch'imyaksa* and other works. Son Yŏng-jong is a young scholar who specializes in Chosŏn dynasty history. See his articles in *Yŏksa kwahak* (1959), no. 5, pp. 42-61; (1966), no. 4, pp. 12-20.

18. Akademiia nauk, SSSR, *Vsemirnaia istoriia.* Ten volumes in chronological order were published from 1955 to 1965; three volumes were added from 1977 to 1983.

19. The entire text of the North Korean attack appeared first in *Nodong sinmun*, September 20, 1963. It was reprinted in *Kŭlloja* (September 1963), no. 18 (232), pp. 47-56.

20. For various sections on Korea in Akademiia nauk, SSSR, *Vsemirnaia istoriia*, see the following: (1957), 2:57; 3(3): 47-51; (2):537-541; 4:685-695; (1959), 6:434-444; (1960), 7:275-279; 8(3):427-432; (1965), 10(3):507-509; 11(3):160-169.

21. For North Korean studies of Korean history, see the standard work done by the History Research Institute of the Academy of Sciences of North Korea, *Chosŏn yŏksa.*

22. A good study of Kim Ok-kyun is *Kim Ok-kyun*, done jointly by members of the History Research Institute of the Academy of Sciences, including Kim Sŏk-hyŏng and Kim Hŭi-il.

23. There are many excellent studies by Soviet scholars on the contemporary history of Korea. See, among others, *Istoria Korei*; 2 vols.; F. I. Shabshina, *Narodnoe vosstanie 1919 goda v Koree*; and G. F. Kim and F. I. Shabshina, *Proletarian Internationalism and Revolutions in the East*, pp. 262-323.

24. See a stunning editorial entitled "Saohe chuŭi chinyŏngŭl ongho haja" [Let us defend the socialist camp] in *Nodong sinmun*, October 28, 1963. There is a good collection of pertinent editorials of *Nodong sinmun*, including this one, in Japanese in *Chōsen no kokusai rosen.*

25. For the Chinese editorial see *Renmin ribao*, November 2, 1963. This was reprinted under the title "Ssoryŏn kongsandang chidobuga indowa yŏnhap hayŏ chungguk ŭl pandae hago innŭn chinsang" [The true picture of the leadership of the Communist Party of the Soviet Union in collusion with India to oppose China], *Nodong sinmun*, November 3, 1963. For Pak's article, see Pak Kŭm-ch'ŏl, "Marŭk'ŭsŭ renin chuŭi kich'i rŭl nop'idŭlgo siwŏl hyŏngmyŏng ŭi wiŏp ŭl kyesŭng haja." See related articles in *Kŭlloja*, (November 1963), no. 21 (235), pp. 31-37; *Nodong sinmun*, November 7, 1963.

26. On the National Liberation movement, see *Nodong sinmun*, January 27, 1964. On revisionism, see *Nodong sinmun*, April 19, 1964. About the Japanese Communist Party, see "Ilbon kongsandang e taehan p'agoe ch'aektong ŭn kyŏlk'o hŏyong halsu ŏpta."

27. *Pravda*, August 18, 1964. A Korean version of this article appeared in *Nodong sinmun*, September 7, 1964.

28. Kim Il Sung gave a banquet for participants of the seminar and thanked them for holding the seminar in Pyongang. There were 34 countries represented. For Kim's speech at the banquet, see *Chosŏn chungang yŏn'gam, 1965*, pp. 34-35. About the seminar, see *Second Asian Economic Seminar: Pyongyang*. The first seminar was held in Colombo, Ceylon, in 1962; for the North Korean account, see *Nodong sinmun*, June 23, 1964.

29. Theja Gunawardhana of Sri Lanka was chairman of the Asian Economic

Bureau; the Soviet Union called her a Trotskyite. There were representatives from Japan, China, Sri Lanka, Vietnam, Indonesia, Pakistan, and North Korea. Many delegates representing 34 countries attended the seminar, but the Soviet Union and India were not invited. For the North Korean editorial, see *Nodong sinmun*, September 7, 1964.

30. For North Korean articles against the Soviet Union after the seminar, see *Nodong sinmun*, October 6, October 29, December 3, and December 21, 1964.

31. There are a number of sources reporting the alleged wall posters in China, but none of them is of Chinese or North Korean origin. There is a detailed account of this and subsequent allegations in a "restricted document" entitled *North Korea, 1945-67*, pp. 27-28. There are a number of South Korean accounts; see a representative one in *Pukhan chŏnsŏ*, 1:302-312. The Japanese also reported on the subject; see among others Hayashi Takehiko, *Kita Chōsen to minami Chōsen*, pp. 125-128.

32. Reported in Tanjug News Agency of Yugoslavia on February 19, 1967. This source was cited in *North Korea, 1945-67*, p. 28. See a similar report by Nakayasu Yosaku, "Chū-So kokkyō funsō to kita-Chōsen."

33. Havana Radio and Television of February 28 and March 1, 1967, were cited as sources in *North Korea, 1945-67*, p. 29. Some studies cite the Pyongyang radio broadcast as a source of the North Korean refutation of many of these charges; see, for example, Ho-min Yang, "North Korea, Thirty Years Between Moscow and Peking," pp. 155-156.

34. This is also available in *Current Background* (Hongkong: American Consulate-General) (April 3, 1968), no. 850, p. 27.

35. This minister was Pak Yŏng-sun, also known as Pak P'o-su. He was a famous partisan, and the stories of his partisan activities in Manchuria were well known. He is the one who invented a home-made grenade known as the *Yŏn'gil p'okt'an* (Yanji bomb), and he wrote a book by that name. He was head of the Communication Department of the party and became minister of communication in October 1962. He was also a member of the Central Committee of the Fourth Party Congress. He was reappointed minister of communication in December 1967.

36. It is assumed that he was married in the summer of 1963 because from May to July Kim Il Sung made no public appearances or speeches, the longest silence he has ever maintained. There is no information about Kim's wife, but she appears as the first lady of the North at official functions. Party cadres in North Korea told me that she has four children by Kim, three boys and a girl.

37. It is said that its pumice rock gives its crest a white color and it appears snow-capped even in summer, hence the name. See Shannon McCune, "Physical Basis for Korean Boundaries."

38. For the Korean chronicle of the negotiations, see *Sukchong sillok*, vol. 51, in *Chosŏn wangjo sillok*, 40:427-449. For Chinese studies, see Zhang Cunwu, "Qingdai zhonghan bianwu wenti tanyuan," and "Mukedeng suodingdi zhonghan guojie."

39. There are considerable difficulties in the name of the Tumen River. There

is another river that flows north to the Soviet border that is named Tumen (T'omun in Korean), and the Koreans understood the boundary to be this river rather than the current Tumen River, which is pronounced "Touman" in Chinese. Such an interpretation would include most of the Yanbian area of Northeast China, which is heavily populated by Koreans, in the territory of Korea. It was reported that China insisted that the river meant what was known as the Tumen River in 1880. See Yi Hong-jik, *Kuksa sajŏn*, p. 560; Ch'oe Nam-sŏn, *Paektusan kŭn ch'amgi*, pp. 202-229.

40. See a detailed description of a number of difficulties in Yi Sŏn-gŭn, "Paektusan kwa kando munje." In this article, the mountain is claimed as Korean.

41. See a representative of such maps, made by the noted Korean cartographer Kim Chŏng-ho in 1861, in Kim Chŏng-ho, *Taedong yŏ chido*, 2:7-8.

42. "The Korean Boundary Agreement," pp. C, app. 169-170; also cited in Shannon McCune, "Physical Basis for Korean Boundaries"; see also U. S. Department of State, *China-Korea Boundary* (June 29, 1962), no. 17, p. 3.

43. *Renmin huabuo*, November 1961. It is also available in the November 1961 issue of *China Pictorial*.

44. *Facts About Korea*, p. 1. The geographer of the State Department stated that this book was published in 1961 with the map captioned, prepared in August 1961, and speculated that the Chinese might have responded to this map in *China Pictorial*. It should be pointed out that as late as 1958 when the North Korean handbook was published, no question regarding the mountain was raised by the Chinese. The handbook said that the Korean mountain ranges start from Paektusan, situated on the border between Korea and China. It also added that "the main ranges extend along the north and east boundaries," *Democratic People's Republic of Korea*, pp. 1-3.

45. One study claimed that the Chinese and the North Koreans reached an agreement in September 1963 at the time of Liu Xiaoqí's visit to the North. See *Area Handbook for North Korea* (Washington, D.C.: GPO, 1969) p. 253; David Rees, "North Korea-China Rift." This article was based on an Indian article in *Amrita Bazar Patrika* of Calcutta. Since India was having its difficulties with China on their border, the information is highly suspect. There are a number of errors in the article as to the length of the border between China and Korea and various details of dates and locations. The disputed territory is estimated by the geographer of the State Department to be 600 square miles. See *The China-Korea Boundary*, p. 4. See also a North Korean travelogue to this area by Moon In-soo, "Mt. Baikdoo and Region."

46. The picture of Kim standing on top of the mountain, his hands folded behind, and looking at the lake, Ch'ŏnji, was widely circulated in 1969. See *Chosŏn chungang yŏn'gam, 1969*; Jiang Dao, "Zhonggong yu beihan di xinguojie," pp. 48-54.

47. *Korea Review*, p. 2; *Yŏksa sajŏn*, p. 976.

48. Kim was accompanied by Vice-Premier Kim Kwang-hyŏp, Foreign Minister Pak Sŏng-ch'ŏl and his wife, Yim Kye-ch'ŏl, Ch'ae Hŭi-jŏng, Hŏ Tam, and

a few others. See the details of his visit in *Korea Today* (May 1965), no. 108, pp. 25-36.

49. For the Soviet delegation see *Nodong sinmun*, August 13, 1965. There were two other veterans, one admiral and a navy captain. In his memoirs, General Chistiakov related that he visited Kim in 1968, and Kim took him to his former place of residence which was bombed by the Americans beyond recognition. See I. M. Chistiakov, "Voevoi puti 25-i armii," p. 60. Major General Lebedev told me that he has since become deputy chairman of the Soviet-Korean Friendship Association and has returned to Pyongyang several times.

50. For a complete list of the Chinese delegation, see *Nodong sinmun*, October 22, 1965. See also the Chinese celebration of the anniversary in China in *Renmin ribao*, October 25, 1965; "Chinese People's Volunteers' Anniversary," *Peking Review* (October 1965), no. 44, p. 4.

51. *Chajusŏng ŭl ongho haja*. This is a widely quoted article. It appeared in *Nodong sinmun*, August 12, 1966. B. C. Koh identifies this article as North Korea's declaration, "North Korea and the Sino-Soviet Schism."

52. Kim Il Sung, *Hyŏn chŏngse wa uridang ŭi kwaŏp*. This speech is also widely publicized. It is available in English in a pamphlet, Kim Il Sung, *The Present Situation and the Tasks of Our Party*, also in *Kim Il Sung chŏjak sŏnjip*, 3d ed., 4:317-403.

53. Apparently Kim was reluctant to send his troops to Vietnam while neither the Soviet Union nor China were sending theirs. But he was confronted with the fact that the South Korean authorities were sending their troops to Vietnam, and Kim had wanted to opt for international volunteers among the socialist countries in the style of the UN troops in the Korean war. At the time of the Sino-Soviet dispute, such an international volunteer force could hardly have been realized.

54. Reference here is to Chinese meddling in the internal affairs of the Japanese Communist Party. The North Koreans strongly supported the Japanese against the Chinese. See the details in Robert A. Scalapino, *The Japanese Communist Movement, 1920-66*, pp. 214-291.

PART V. PROBLEMS IN KIM'S INDEPENDENCE

11. The Rise of the Military

1. Kim Il Sung, *Sŏkt'an kongŏp ŭl ppalli palchŏn sik'igi wihayŏ*, pp. 3-34.

2. Kim Il Sung, *Kun nongŏp hyŏptong chohap kyŏngyŏng wiwŏnhoe rŭl naeolte taehayŏ*; Kim Il Sung, "Kun ŭi yŏkhwal ŭl kanghwa hamyŏ chibang kongŏp kwa nongcho'on kyŏngni rŭl tŏuk palchŏn sik'yŏ inmin saenghwal ŭl hwŏlsin nop'ija" [Let us radically improve the people's living standards by strengthening the role of the county and further developing local industry and agriculture], in *Kim Il Sung chŏjak sŏnjip*, 3:331-371; Kim Il Sung, "Kun hyŏptong nongjang kyŏngyŏng wiwŏnhoe rŭl tŏuk kanghwa palchŏn sik'ilte taehayŏ" [On further strengthening and developing the County Cooperative Farm Management Committee], *ibid.*, 3:438-460.

3. Kim Il Sung, *Sahoe chuŭi kyŏngje kwalli munje e taehayŏ*, 3:350-382; Kim Il Sung, *Chosŏn minju chuŭi inmin konghwaguk chŏngbu ŭi tangmyŏn kwaŏp e taehayŏ*.

4. For the report of Kim Kwang-hyŏp's visit, see *Nodong sinmun*, December 6, 1962. Only a short article indicating his return was featured, and there was no usual lengthy report of his visit to the Soviet Union.

5. The agenda for the fourth plenum of the Central Committee was kept secret. The plenum was held sometime between March and December 1962, and it might have been in this secret plenum that the crucial decision was made to strengthen the military. It has become the practice that whenever important problems were discussed in the plenum, both the agenda and date of the plenum were kept secret.

6. *Chosŏn chungang yŏn'gam, 1963*, pp. 157-162. See also the report on the plenum in *Nodong sinmun*, December 16, 1962. There is a huge sign bearing this slogan in the Revolutionary Museum in Pyongyang. When I was introduced to the Socialist Construction Section of the museum, I jokingly mentioned the slogan, implying that a man can neither shoot nor work with both hands occupied with arms, hammer, and sickle. This remark drew immediate anger and I quickly offered my apology. They were serious about the slogan. For Kim's reference to this slogan, see *Kim Il Sung chŏjak sŏnjip*, 4:365. See also *Chosŏn nodongdang yŏksa kyojae*, pp. 494-495.

7. Kim Il Sung, *The Present Situation and the Tasks of Our Party*, pp. 51-95.

8. The Red Young Guard were reorganized from the Student Worker-Peasant Red Guards at Kim's fifty-eighth birthday on April 15, 1970. The guards consisted mostly of North Korean high school students. See *Pukhan chŏnsŏ*, 1:37.

9. Kim Il Sung, *Uri hyŏngmyŏng esŏ ŭi chuch'e e taehayŏ*, 1:228-229.

10. The original Military Committee was established by decree of the Standing Committee of the Supreme People's Assembly of June 26, 1950, a day after the Korean War began. It was a seven-man committee headed by Kim Il Sung. Others were Pak Hŏn-yŏng, Hong Myŏng-hŭi, Kim Ch'aek, Ch'oe Yong-gŏn, Pak Il-u, and Chŏng Chun-t'aek. See *Chosŏn chungang yŏn'gam, 1951-52*, p. 82.

11. See Article 27 of the bylaws in *Pukhan chŏngch'iron*, pp. 574-575.

12. Kim Il Sung, *Uri ŭi hyŏngmyŏng kwa inmin kundae ŭi kwaŏp e taehayŏ*, pp. 148-216.

13. There are a number of interesting examples and much interesting information in Kim's speech. See *ibid*. This speech also appeared in *Kim Il Sung chŏjak sŏnjip*, 3:461-522, under the title of "Uri ŭi inmin kundaenŭn nodong kyegŭp ŭi kundae, hyŏngmyŏng ŭi kundae ida. Kyegŭp chŏngch'i kyoyang saŏp ŭl kyesok kanghwa hayŏya handa" [Our People's Army is an army of the working class, an army of the revolution. Class and political education should be continuously strengthened].

14. Kim Il Sung, "Uri inmin kundae rŭl hyŏngmyŏng kundae ro mandŭl myŏ kukbang esŏ chawi ŭi pangch'im ŭl kwanch'ŏl haja" [Let us transform our People's Army into a revolutionary army and implement the self-defense policy in the national defense], in *Uri hyŏngmyŏng esŏ ŭi chuch'e e taehayŏ*, 1:216-234.

15. For details on these ten goals, see *Chosŏn chungang yŏn'gam, 1963*, pp. 161-162.

16. *Nodong sinmun,* January 1, 1963. It also appears in *Chosŏn chungang yŏn'gam, 1964,* pp. 1-5.

17. Kim Il Sung, "Nongch'on e taehan noryŏk chiwŏn saŏp ŭl chŏn inminjŏk undong ŭro pŏllimyŏ kŏnsŏl e taehan chido ch'egye rŭl koch'ilte taehayŏ" [On developing the program to augment manpower in agriculture into the movement of the entire people and correcting the leadership system in construction], in *Sahoe chuŭi kyŏngje kwalli munje e taehayŏ,* 3:467-492.

18. This instruction was given to the workers in the Ŭnyul mines on January 22, 1965. Kim said that some workers made their eight-hour workday as little as a 190-minute workday and this should be corrected to have everyone work 480 minutes per day. See Kim Il Sung, *Soedol saengsan esŏ hyŏksin ŭl irŭk'ilte taehayŏ,* pp. 2-28.

19. Kim Il Sung, "Ch'ilgaenyŏn kyehoek ŭi kangch'ŏl kojirŭl chŏmnyŏng hagi wihayŏ" [For conquering the steel highland in the seven-year plan], in *Sahoe chuŭi kyŏngje kwalli munje e taehayŏ,* 3:92-114.

20. For the reference to the drinking of the workers, see *ibid.,* pp. 67-91. Kim also made known such movements as the Yi Man-sŏng movement and the Kim Tŭk-ch'an movement in transportation work. The details behind these movements were not mentioned, but Kim also mixed praise of this sort with stern criticism of the transportation workers. See Kim Il Sung, *Kim Il Sung chŏjak sŏnjip,* 4:13-30.

21. Kim Il Sung, *Yanggangdo tang chojik dŭl app'e nasŏnŭn kwaŏp,* pp. 2-54.

22. For some of Kim's writings during this period, see Kim Il Sung, *Theses on the Socialist Agrarian Question in Our Country; Kodŭng kyoyuk saŏp ŭl kaesŏn halte taehayŏ.* Some intellectuals wrote about the problems of economic development, specifically balance and speed; see, for example, Chŏng T'ae-sik, *Uri tang e ŭihan sokto wa kyunhyŏng munje ŭi ch'angjojŏk haegyŏl.* There are a number of newspaper editorials urging people to work hard for a self-sustaining economy. See, for example, a collection of such editorials for 1963 (all from *Nodong sinmun,* April 11, April 23, and October 26) in *Self-Reliance and the Building of an Independent Economy.*

23. See Kim's New Year address of January 1, 1965, in *Chosŏn chungang yŏn' gam, 1966-67,* pp. 1-5.

24. There were more than a dozen agreements signed between North Korea and the Soviet Union from 1965 to 1969, including two defense-related military agreements on May 31, 1965, and March 2, 1967. See George Ginsburgs and Roy U. T. Kim, *Calendar of Diplomatic Affairs, Democratic People's Republic of Korea, 1945-75,* pp. 91-123. For a number of individual agreements see, for example, *Izvestia,* February 24, 1965, March 14, 1965, February 16, 1967; *Pravda,* March 6, 1967; and *Nodong sinmun,* March 4, 1965. For a list of agreements, see the North Korean yearbooks, for example, *Chosŏn chungang yŏn'gam, 1966-67,* p. 394.

25. See Kim's New Year address on January 1, 1965. he also made reference to the problem in his speech at Aliarcham Academy of Social Science of Indonesia on April 14, 1965. See Kim Il Sung, *Kim Il Sung chŏjak sŏnjip,* 4:195-240.

26. See, for example, his instruction at the party meeting of the State Planning Commission in Kim Il Sung, *Inmin kyŏngje kyehoek ŭi irwŏnhwa, sebuhwa ŭi widae han saenghwllyŏk ŭl namgim ŏpsi palhwi hagi wihayŏ.* See also his speech on the twentieth anniversary of the founding of the Workers' Party of Korea on October 10, 1965, in *Kim Il Sung chŏjak sŏnjip,* 4:279-316. The North Koreans were indeed forced to follow the policy. See an editorial in *Nodong sinmun,* November 7, 1966.

27. The bylaws of the Third Party Congress stipulated that the party conference may not replace more than one-fifth of the members of the Central Committee (Article 41). However, at the Fourth Party Congress in 1961, this provision was dropped. See *Chosŏn nodongdang kyuyak haesŏl,* p. 12. For the bylaws after the Fifth Party Congress, see *Pukhan chŏngch'iron,* pp. 566-582. The First Party Conference was held in March 1958.

28. For Kim's speech on international relations, see the previous chapter; for his report on the revolution in South Korea, see chapter 12. For the text of the declaration of the party conference on the Vietnam problem dated October 12, 1966, see *Chosŏn chungang yŏn'gam, 1966-67,* pp. 130-131.

29. For the report on the eleventh plenum of the Central Committee, held in June and July 1965, and Kim Ch'ang-man's activities in it, see *Nodong sinmun,* July 2, 1965. There was an editorial after this plenum about upgrading higher education in Korea. See *Nodong sinmun,* July 4, 1965.

30. It is most likely that she was purged because it is customary that the activities of a party official of her stature are reported. In the case of Pak, the problem is more complicated because Kim Il Sung was married in 1963, and Kim's wife, Kim Sŏng-ae, was introduced in a number of political functions. In the past, when Kim was alone it was Pak Chŏng-ae who usually accompanied Kim. Pak was a common-law wife of Kim Yong-bŏm, first chairman of the North Korean Branch Bureau of the Korean Communist Party in Pyongyang shortly after the liberation of Korea. For the activities of Pak, see chapters 2 and 4. Pak was born in August 1907 in Kyŏnghŭng, Hamgyŏng pukto. There is no report of her whereabouts after 1967.

31. Nam Il was born on June 5, 1913, in the Soviet Union. His hometown in Korea was Kyŏngwŏn county of Hamgyŏng pukto. He was educated at Smolensk Military School and graduated from a college in Tashkent. When he returned to Korea he was a Soviet army officer with the rank of captain and became vice-minister of education. During the Soviet occupation of the North, he held a number of important posts; general of the army, first chief delegate to the armistice talks at Panmunjom, foreign minister, minister of railways, and chairman of state construction. Nam was one of the most durable officials. He was elected to the Supreme People's Assembly and was one of the very few who were elected to the Central Committee four times from the second (candidate member) to the fifth Central Committees. Nam died on March 7, 1976, at the age of 64. See *Nodong sinmun,* March 8, 1976.

32. The secretaries were Ch'oe Yong-gŏn, Kim Il, Pak Kŭm-ch'ŏl, Yi Hyo-sun, Kim Kwang-hyŏp, Sŏk San, Hŏ Pong-hak, Kim Yŏng-ju, Pak Yong-guk, and Kim To-man. Kim Il Sung was general secretary.

12. The South Korean Revolution

1. Kim Il Sung, *Chigŏp tongmaeng saŏp e taehayo*, pp. 166-214.

2. For example, see Kim's speeches at the Third Party Congress in April 1956, second and third Supreme People's Assembly speeches in September 1957 and October 1962, and the tenth anniversary speech of the founding of the Democratic People's Republic of Korea in September 1958. Even the proposal to create a Confederal Republic of Koryŏ was made at the tail end of the speech at the fifteenth anniversary commemorating the national liberation in August 1961. For Kim's lengthy speeches on unification problems, see his speeches at the tenth and fifteenth anniversaries of the founding of the Korean People's Army on February 8, 1958, and February 8, 1963.

3. The eighth plenum was held from February 25 to February 27, 1964. At this plenum Kim revealed the theses on the socialist agrarian questions, and in general the discussion of these theses overshadowed other important items on the agenda. Yi Hyo-sun, who was in charge of the party's South Korean operation, gave a long speech in connection with the unification issue. The third item was on strengthening the work with the masses, and Pak Kŭm-ch'ŏl also spoke on the subject. The speeches by Yi and Pak were not made public. For the reports of the eighth plenum, see *Nodong sinmun*, February 26 and February 28, 1964.

4. Kim Il Sung, *Choguk t'ongil wiŏp ŭl sirhyŏn hagi wihayŏ hyŏngmyŏng yŏngyang ŭl paekbang ŭro kanghwa haja*, pp. 1-24.

5. There are a number of speeches by Kim whose entire texts were kept secret, but this is the only document where one part of the text was blatantly omitted. For this omission, see *Kim Il Sung chŏjak sŏnjip*, 4:96.

6. For the details of the eighth plenum of February 1964, see *Chosŏn chungang yŏn'gam, 1965*, p. 44.

7. The Treaty on Basic Relations and Other Agreements between the Republic of Korea and Japan was signed on June 22, 1965. The South Korean National Assembly ratified it on August 14, 1965, and the National Diet of Japan on December 1, 1965. The instruments of ratification were exchanged on December 18, 1968. It is not my purpose here to discuss the controversy surrounding the normalization treaty or its content. For a study of the treaty see, among others, Kwan Bong Kim, *The Korea-Japan Treaty Crisis and the Instability of the Korean Political System*.

8. The Supreme People's Assembly decision condemning the treaty was issued on May 21, 1965. A memorandum on the crimes of the Korea-Japan Treaty by the Democratic People's Republic of Korea was issued on June 18, 1965. This was a long memorandum reviewing Korea-Japan relations throughout history. After the formal signing of the treaty, another memo was issued on June 23, 1965. See these documents in *Chosŏn chungang yŏn'gam, 1966-67*, pp. 63-64, 71-78, 90-92. Some writers equated this treaty with the treaty of 1905 that made possible the formal annexation of Korea by Japan. See, among others, Pae Pyŏng-du, "Kannichi kaidan to otsui hogo jōyaku." There are many editorials and articles about this treaty in newspapers and magazines; see among others, *Nodong sinmun*, August 25, 1965.

9. See, for example, Kim's reply to a question by Cuban reporters in Kim Il Sung, *Oeguk kijadŭl i chegihan chilmun e taehan taedap*, 1:32-45. Kim repeats the pledge in the interview with reporters from the United Arab Republic on September 14, 1965; *ibid.*, pp. 46-54. See the decision of the Supreme People's Assembly on May 20, 1965. There are numerous memoranda of the North Korean government about the Vietnam situation and Korea. See all these documents in *Chosŏn chungang yŏn'gam, 1966-67*, pp. 61-141.

10. Kim made these remarks in his speeches at the twentieth anniversary of the founding of the Workers' Party of Korea in October 1955 and at the Second Party Conference in October 1966. See Kim Il Sung, *Chosŏn nodongdang ch'anggŏn 20chunyŏn e chehayŏ.* See also Kim Il Sung, *The Present Situation and the Tasks of Our Party*, pp. 95-123.

11. For Kim's basic policy toward the South Korean revolution, see his speech on February 27, 1964. There are a number of articles supporting his policy. See, among others, "Namchosŏn hyŏnchŏngsewa namchosŏn hyŏngmyŏng e taehan tang ŭi kibon pangch'im" [The present condition of South Korea and our party's basic policy on the South Korean revolution], *Kŭlloja* (1966), no. 12 (298), pp. 18-27.

12. The official North Korean accounts did not disclose when the fifteenth plenum was held; the South Korean accounts estimated that the plenum was held in March 1976. The fifteenth plenum was held for five days from May 4 to May 8, 1967. See Paek Pong, *Minjok ŭi t'aeyang Kim Il Sung changgun*, 2:920. The sixteenth plenum was held from June 28 to July 3, 1967. Agendas of both plenums were kept secret. It is the general practice of the North Koreans that when important decisions are made, the dates and agendas of the plenums of the Central Committee are kept secret.

13. Hŏ was a partisan who was alleged to have infiltrated into Wŏnsan as an agent of Kim's partisan group on November 18, 1937, and was arrested. Hŏ, one of those rare intellectuals in the partisan group, headed the party school and worked in the propaganda section of the party. Kim To-man worked in the party's propaganda and agitation section from 1954 and became secretary of the party in October 1966. Ko Hyŏk was head of the party school of the Central Committee in 1961 and was vice-premier of the cabinet in September 1966. All these men were nonmilitary partisans.

14. This was a lecture given by Kim Il Sung to cadres of party and state organizations on October 11, 1969. For the complete text in English, see Kim Il Sung, *On Some Experiences of the Democratic and Socialist Revolutions in Our Country.* For the South Korean account of the purges, see, among others, *Pukhan chŏnsŏ*, 1:262-264.

15. Hŏ Pong-hak is a typical partisan general. He had joined the partisan group in the early 1930s and fought under another famous partisan, the late An Kil. He has written a number of articles reminiscing about the guerrilla days in Manchuria. There is a record of his participation in the campaign of the Third Directional Army in August 1939 with Ch'oe Hyŏn. An Kil, Kim Tong-gyu, and Pak U-sŏp. Hŏ was already a major general during the Korean War, became a full

general in 1963, and was director of the Political Bureau of the Korean People's Army. He was elected to the Central Committee of the party and to the Supreme People's Assembly, and when the partisan generals became politically prominent his speeches were printed in the newspapers. See, for example, his speeches in *Nodong sinmun*, October 26, 1963, and June 26, 1965. Hŏ's wife is also a partisan, Kim Ok-sun, former chairman of the Democratic Women's Union of Korea.

16. "Namchosŏn hyŏngmyŏng ŭl chŏkkŭk chiwŏn hayŏ uri sedae e kiŏk'o choguk t'ongil ŭl silhyŏn haja" [Let us assist the South Korean revolution and accomplish the fatherland unification in our generation], *Kŭlloja* (1968), no. 1 (311), pp. 16-24.

17. Kim Il Sung, *Let Us Embody More Thoroughly the Revolutionary Spirit of Independence, Self-Sustenance and Self-Defense in All Fields of State Activity*, pp. 20-29.

18. Kim Hyŏng-su, a native of Kyŏngsang pukto, defected to the North during the Korean War. He was trained as a espionage agent in the North and was sent back to his hometown to recruit his older brother, who was professor of medicine at Kyŏngbuk University in Taegu. The two brothers succeeded in recruiting some 13 men in Taegu, and after briefly training these men the agent, Kim Hyŏng-su, returned to the North. The two brothers maintained communication through shortwave radios, but Kim Tae-su and all 13 men were arrested on May 17, 1967. Kim briefly mentioned this incident in his speech on December 16, 1967. For the South Korean account of this incident, see, among others, Kim Chŏng-gi, *Pukkoe ŭi taenam chŏllyak ŭl haebu handa*, pp. 103-104.

19. Kim Il Sung, *Let Us Embody More Thoroughly the Revolutionary Spirit of Independence, Self-Sustenance and Self-Defense in All Fields of State Activity*, p. 28.

20. For the festivities planned, see *Nodong sinmun*, January 14, 1968. See a number of articles on January 6, 10, and 18, 1968.

21. Ch'oe Hyŏn was born on June 8, 1907, in Hunchun province, Jiandao, Manchuria. He grew up in his sister's home in Khabarovsk and did not attend school. He joined guerrillas several times before he joined the Northeast Anti-Japanese United Army. Ch'oe held about as high a position as Kim Il Sung did, and met for the first time in September 1933. Ch'oe was one of the founders of the North Korean military and one of the few who were already generals of the North Korean Army before the Korean War. He remained in the military establishment as a professional soldier but began to move into political circles from 1965, when he first became a member of the Central Committee of the party and also vice-minister of national defense. He was the fifth-highest member of the Political Committee at the time of the Fifth Party Congress. Ch'oe died on April 9, 1982.

22. One commando captured alive was Kim Sin-jo, who later confessed the entire undertaking from the recruitment and training to the execution. Most of the South Korean accounts of the incident come from his testimony. See, among others, Kim Chŏng-gi, *Pukkoe ŭi taenam chŏllyak ŭl haebu handa*, pp. 108-112; see also *Pukhan ch'onggam*, pp. 231-232; and *Tong-a ilbo*, January 22-February 28, 1968.

23. For various reports of South Korean revolutionary activities, see *Nodong*

sinmun, January 23–February 8, 1968. For the statistics and the description of a number of small incidents by North Korean news services, see *Chosŏn chungang yŏn'gam, 1969*, pp. 314-326. For Kim's encouragement, see his twentieth anniversary speech of the founding of the republic on September 7, 1968, in *Kim Il Sung chŏjak sŏnjip*, 5:133-200.

24. It is not my purpose here to discuss the *Pueblo* incident, but only its impact on North Korean domestic developments. For the North Korean official account of the incident, see the North Korean government declarations on January 27, 1968, and an article in *Chosŏn chungang yŏn'gam, 1969*, pp. 189-192 and 529. For the North Korean account of their release of the crew of the *Pueblo* in December 1968, see the statement by the Foreign Ministry spokesman on December 23, 1968, and the news release by the Korean Central News Agency on December 23, 1968; *ibid.*, pp. 550-551. For the capture of the *Pueblo*, see the *Nodong sinmun*, article on January 24, 1968, and an editorial on January 28.

25. For the text of his speech in English see a small pamphlet, Kim Il Sung, *On the 20th Anniversary of the Founding of the Korean People's Army.*

26. See his speech to the young people on April 13, 1968, in Kim Il Sung, *Ch'ŏngsonyŏn saŏpkwa sahoe chuŭi nodong ch'ŏngnyŏn tongmaeng ŭi immu e taehayŏ*, 2:484-522.

27. In the same speech, Kim boasted that North Korea was giving foreign aid to a less fortunate country, meaning Vietnam; *Kim Il Sung chŏjak sŏnjip*, 5:10-44.

28. For the congratulatory messages by Kim to these units, see *Invincible Is the Korean People's Army Founded and Trained by Ever-Victorious, Iron-Willed Genius Commander, Marshal Kim Il Sung*, pp. 14-34.

29. Direct infiltrations of the South are too numerous to mention here. See, for example, the Kim Tae-su incident. From Japan, operations were financed and directed by the Korean resident group in Japan; see, for example, the *Minjok ilbo* incident, for which Cho Yong-su, Song Chi-yŏng, and others were sentenced to death. There was even a North Korean agent (Yi Chae-sŏn) who subverted a Japanese Foreign Ministry official (Yamamoto) for espionage activities. In Europe, activities were directed mostly from East Berlin, where a former director of the Liaison Bureau (Pak Il-yŏng) was ambassador. The North Koreans attracted intellectuals and students in Europe and tried to convert them into agents to operate in South Korea. See Kim Chŏng-gi, *Pukkoe ŭi taenam chŏllyak ŭl haebu handa*, pp. 44-189.

30. Kim Chong-t'ae was born on November 24, 1926, in Naengch'ŏn-dong, Kŭmhomyŏn, Yŏngch'on county, Kyŏngsang pukto. There are a number of accounts of this incident from both the North and the South. For the North Korean accounts, see *Chosŏn chungang yŏn'gam, 1969*, pp. 311-314. See also *Chōsen shiryō* (August 1969), no. 99, pp. 2-9. For the South Korean account see, among others, *Pukhan chŏnsŏ*, 3:75-91. See also Kim Chŏng-gi, *Pukkoe ŭi taenam chŏllyak ŭl haebu handa.*

31. Yi was born in 1934, a native of P'yŏngan pukto. He fled the North shortly after the liberation of Korea and lived mostly in Taegu, Kyŏngsang pukto. Upon

graduation from high school, there, he attended Seoul National University, majoring in political science. He served in the South Korean air force as an officer after he graduated from college.

32. Others they mentioned were *Ch'ŏngnyŏn munhakka hyŏphoe* [Young Literary Writers' Council], *Tonghak hoe* [Eastern Learning Association], *Kitokkyo ch'ŏngnyŏn kyŏngje pokchihoe* [Christian Youth Economic Assurance Association], and *Songsan suyanghoe* [Songsan Disciplinary Association]. Most of these were organizations in name only with a token membership to justify the name. See *Chosŏn chungang yŏn'gam, 1967.*

33. Kim Chong-t'ae and his four accomplices, including Yi Mun-gyu, were sentenced to death, four others were sentenced to life imprisonment, and Kim's wife, Yim Yŏng-suk, and 21 people related to Kim's family were sentenced to various terms of imprisonment from two to twenty-five years.

34. The decision was made at the Political Committee meeting of the Central Committee on July 1, 1969. See the details in *Chosŏn chungang yŏn'gam, 1970,* p. 204.

35. For the full text of the documents, see *Chosŏn chungang yŏn'gam, 1970,* pp. 513-517. Kim said that the platform was made public in August 1969 by the party headquarters in Seoul. For Kim's reference to this platform, see *Kim Il Sung chŏjak sŏnjip,* 5:485.

36. For the text of Kim's speech on the twentieth anniversary of the founding of the republic on September 7, 1968, see *Kim Il Sung chŏjak sŏnjip,* 5:133-200. See also an article by Paek Kil-man, "Namchosŏn inmin dŭl ŭn ojik p'ongyŏk chŏk pangbŏp e ŭihaesŏman chugwŏn ŭl chaengch'wi halsu itta."

13. Disintegration of the Partisan Group

1. A number of statues were erected in 1968 honoring the partisans An Kil, Cho Chŏng-ch'ŏl, Ch'oe Ch'un-gŭn, Kang Kŏn, Kim Ch'aek, and Yu Kyŏng-su. There were numerous books published about the partisans who died before the liberation of Korea. See among others, *Hyŏngmyŏng sŏnyŏl dŭl ŭi saengae wa hwaltong.*

2. For the text of this speech by Kim Kwang-hyŏp, see *Nodong sinmun,* February 15, 1968.

3. The partisan generals dominated the political scene on every occasion and made speeches often. The texts of their speeches were often printed in full in newspapers. See, for example, Kim Ch'ang-bong's speeches of February 8 and June 28, 1968; Ch'oe Kwang's speech on July 27, 1968; and Yi Yŏng-ho's speech on July 29, 1968.

4. Kim Chung-nin is a native of Hamgyŏng pukto who has worked in his native provincial party organization for a long time. He was elected a candidate member of the Central Committee at the time of the Fourth Party Congress in 1961, but worked as a key member of the North Korean Red Cross, representing the North at Geneva Red Cross meetings. He facilitated the return of Koreans in Japan to North Korea. After the purge of the partisan generals, he became

prominent and was the tenth-ranking member of the Central Committee by the fifth congress in 1970.

5. The text of Kim's concluding remarks is available and no such order was issued. Kim spoke on the manpower administration on November 16, 1968, the last day of the plenum.

6. The plenums and party committee meetings of the army were never made public. This source reported that such a plenum was held from January 6-14, 1969, but this source, presumably a South Korean intelligence source, may not be accurate because Kim was participating in the festivities of the tenth anniversary of the Red Workers-Peasant Militia on January 13, 1969. For the South Korean sources see, among others, *Pukhan chŏnsŏ*, 1:263-265, and 2:31-33. See also *Pukhan chŏngch'iron*, pp. 258-267. For Kim's whereabouts in January 1969, see North Korean accounts in *Chosŏn chungang yŏn'gam, 1970*, p. 583.

7. This is a portion of a speech Kim made at the eighteenth plenum of the Central Committee on November 16, 1968, *Kim Il Sung chŏjak sŏnjip*, 5:284.

8. The entire speech Kim gave at the nineteenth plenum of the Central Committee on June 30, 1969, is not available. Only some excerpts were included in Kim Il Sung, *Sahoe chuŭi kyŏngje kwalli munje e taehayŏ*, 3:522-581.

9. This was Kim's speech at the P'yŏngan namdo party conference on February 15, 1969. Here again only excerpts are available; *ibid.*, pp. 481-494.

10. See Kim's speech on February 27, 1970, to the conference of industrial workers in *Kim Il Sung chŏjak sŏnjip*, 5:364-395.

11. *Chosŏn chungang yŏn'gam, 1970*, pp. 202-205.

12. None of these representatives was known either in the North or in the South. They have not been heard of since. The North Koreans have claimed the existence of the RPR in Seoul, but no such organization exists in the South.

13. For the full text, see Kim Il Sung, *Chosŏn nodongdang che och'a taehoe esŏ han chungang wiwŏnhoe saŏp ch'onghwa pogo*. This speech was delivered on the first day, November 2, 1970.

14. Kim later elaborated three major tasks of the technological revolution: to reduce the imbalance in the burden of heavy and light industry workers, to narrow the gap between the workloads of industrial and agrarian workers, and to free women from the heavy burdens of daily household chores. See *Kim Il Sung chŏjak sŏnjip*, 6:74-111.

15. Fot the text of Kim Kuk-hun's report, see *Nodong Sinmun*, November 4, 1970.

16. For details of the six-year economic plan, see *Chosŏn chungang yŏn'gam, 1971*, p. 101-116; for details of the Fifth Party Congress, see pp. 157-171.

17. See the complete roster of newly elected members and the analysis of the change in Dae-Sook Suh, *Korean Communism, 1945-1980*, pp. 309-337.

PART VI NORTH KOREA UNDER KIM

1. The reference can be found in one of the most important documents of the party, his report at the fifth joint plenum of the Central Committee held on December 15, 1952. It is important to see the first edition of Kim's work to find the reference because it was omitted from later versions of his selected works. See *Kim Il Sung sŏnjip*, 4:353-354.

14. South Korea and the Third World

1. From the Soviet Union came Sharaf R. Rashodov, the first secretary of the Uzbekistan Communist Party, in December 1971 and later Vice-Premier Yevgnity Novikov and Konstantin Katushev, secretary of the Central Committee of the Communist Party of the Soviet Union. In July 1971, the Chinese delegation headed by Li Xiannian, vice-premier of the State Council, and Li Desheng, director of the General Political Department of the People's Liberation Army, visited the North. Many delegations from the North went to Beijing and Moscow during 1971 and 1972, including such high government officials as Ch'oe Yong-gŏn, Chŏng Chun-t'aek, Hŏ Tam, and O Chin-u.

2. There are a number of references in Kim's speeches to Nixon's trip to China. See, among others, his speeches on December 2 and December 14, 1971, in *Kim Il Sung chŏjak sŏnjip*, 6:136-63 and 164-93. There was a report by Utsunomiya Tokuma in *Yomiuri shinbun* (August 19, 1975) that Kim Il Sung himself made a secret trip to Peking to celebrate Prince Sihanouk's fiftieth birthday in October 1972, but Utsunomiya's report was unfounded because Prince Sihanouk celebrated his fiftieth birthday in Pyongyang with Kim Il Sung on November 4, 1972. See Kim's speech on the occasion in *Chosŏn chungang yŏn'gam, 1973*. pp. 107-115.

3. The second plenum was held April 19-23, 1971, and discussed the unification problem, the technical revolution in orchards, and public health programs. The third plenum was held November 15-23 and discussed the quality of consumer goods. Kim Il Sung made a speech at the third plenum, but the text of his speech about unification was not made public. For the account of the plenums, See *Chosŏn chungang yŏn'gam, 1972*, pp. 267-270.

4. See the North Korean accounts of Kim's interview with reporters from *Asahi shinbun* and Kyōdō News Agency in *Kim Il Sung chŏjak sŏnjip*, 6:74-111. See also a similar reference in his speech at the fifth congress of the General Federation of Trade Unions of Korea on December 14, 1971, in Kim Il Sung, *On the Character and Tasks of the Trade Union in Socialist Society*, pp. 32-35.

5. See the report on the fifth session of the fourth Supreme People's Assembly in *Chosŏn chungang yŏng'am, 1972*, pp. 270-271; see also the North Korean account of the Red Cross talks on pp. 369-371. For Kim's speech on August 6, 1971 to welcome Prince Sihanouk to Pyongyang, see Kim Il Sung, *The Non-Alignment Movement Is a Mighty Anti-Imperialist Revolutionary Force of Our Times*, pp. 114-130.

6. There are seven articles in the communiqué. The first delineates three principles upon which the dialogue was to be conducted. For the text of the communiqué, see *Nambuk taehwa paeksŏ*, pp. 36-37. The same text can be found in North Korean publications in *Chosŏn chungang yŏn'gam, 1973*, pp. 336-337.

7. Agreement on the composition and operation of the North-South Coordinating Committee, *Nambuk chojŏl wiwŏnhoe*, was reached on November 4, 1972. The co-chairmen were Yi Hu-rak (director of the South Korean Central Intelligence Agency) and Kim Yŏng-ju (secretary and member of the Political Committee and brother of Kim Il Sung). In addition to the co-chairmen, there were four members from each side, and the committee consisted of ten men. The South Korean members were Chang Ki-yŏng (former vice-premier and member of the National Assembly), Ch'oe Kyu-ha (former foreign minister and assistant to the president on diplomatic affairs), Kang In-dŏk, and Chŏng Hong-jin (two bureau chiefs of the Central Intelligence Agency). The North Korean delegation consisted of Pak Sŏng-ch'ŏl, who acted on behalf of the North Korean co-chairman, Yu Chang-sik (member of the Central Committee and chairman of the party's external affairs section), Yi Wan-gi (councilor to the cabinet), Han Ung-sik and Kim Tŏk-hyŏn (two staff members of the Political Committee of the party).

8. There are numerous accounts of the South Korean position and their initial proposals. In addition to the white paper cited above, see *Pukhan chŏnsŏ*, 3:115-126.

9. For details of the North Korean position, see *Chosŏn chungang yŏn'gam, 1973*, pp. 340-341. The North Korean treatment of the Coordinating Committee was perfunctory at best when compared with the South Koreans, who had hoped for some sort of continued dialogue to reduce tension in Korea.

10. For the Red Cross conferences there are a number of pamphlets from the South, including serialized news bulletins, giving details of each session. See, among others, *The Dispersed Families in Korea*, pp. 219-295. Approximately 3 million North Koreans fled from the North to the South from 1945 to 1950, and it was estimated that approximately 85,000 people were either taken or voluntarily fled to the North during the Korean War.

11. The statement was made in answer to the question raised by reporters of *Mainichi shinbun* on September 17, 1972. See the North Korean version in Kim Il Sung, *On Some Problems of Our Party's Juche Idea and the Government of the Republic's Internal and External Policies*, p. 26.

12. See Kim's explanations in *On Some Problems of Our Party's Juche Idea*, pp. 15-32. See also his interview with the managing editor of *Sekai* magazine on October 6, 1972; Kim Il Sung, *Talk with the Managing Editor of the Japanese Politico-Theoretical Magazine, Sekai*, pp. 24-34.

13. The first proposal for confederation of the North and South was made on August 14, 1960, as a transitional step for ultimate unification. Kim has repeated this proposal on a number of occasions since then, but he has not revealed what the confederation of the two systems would entail. Nor has he ever defined what he meant by confederation as opposed to federation or any other form of unity. For his first reference, see Kim Il Sung, *Chosŏn inmin ŭi minjokchŏk p'ariro haebang*

15 chunyŏn kyŏngch'uk taehoe esŏ han pogo, pp. 34-35. Kim announced his five-point policy at the Pyongyang mass rally to welcome the party and government delegation of Czechoslovakia on June 23, 1973. See Kim Il Sung, *Let Us Prevent a National Split and Reunify the Country*, pp. 5-17.

14. It is not my purpose here to analyze the South Korean strategy in the North-South dialogue. The South Koreans have also contributed significantly to the deterioration of the dialogue.

15. For the condemnation of President Park's June 23 statement, see Kim Il Sung, *On the Five-Point Policy for National Reunification*, pp. 1–11. For Kim's denunciation of the South, see Kim Il Sung, *For the Independent, Peaceful Reunification of the Country*, pp. 238-245. For South Korean views on the dialogue, see five essays on the subject in *Theses on South-North Dialogue*.

16. For details of the assassination attempt by Mun Se-gwang that killed the president's wife, see *Korea-Japan Relations and the Attempt on the Life of Korea's President*, pp. 7-118. Kim disavowed any responsibility on the part of North Korea or the North Korean front organization in Japan; see Kim Il Sung, *On the Situation of Our Country and Tasks of the League of Korean Youth in Japan*, pp. 21-22.

17. The first tunnel was discovered on November 15, 1974, the second in March 1975, and the third in October 1978. See the details in *Secret Tunnel Under Panmunjom*, pp. 3-61.

18. See the unprecedented order for mobilization in *Nodong sinmun*, August 20, 1976. The earlier mobilization order at the time of the *Pueblo* was confined only to the armed forces, but this one included the Red Worker-Peasant Militia and Red Young Guards. For a detailed report of the incident see *Kita Chōsen kenkyū* (September 1976), no. 28, pp. 5-54.

19. See a representative article about the unification of Korea by Yu Kye-hang in *Nodong sinmun*, October 13, 1978.

20. Kim was awarded an honorary doctorate by Algiers University during his visit to Algeria in May 1975. See Kim Il Sung, *Speeches Delivered During the Visit to the Algerian Democratic and People's Republic*.

21. For the condemnation of Tito, see his speeches on December 15, 1945, October 23, 1962, and October 5, 1966, in Kim Il Sung, *Uri hyŏngmyŏng kwa kŏnsŏl esŏ inmin chŏnggwŏn ŭi kwaŏp e taehayŏ*, pp. 409-463. See also Kim Il Sung, *The Present Situation and the Task of Our Party*, pp. 2-51.

22. For Kim's speech at Ljublijana, Yugoslavia, see Kim Il Sung, *Speeches Delivered During the Visit to the Socialist Federal Republic of Yugoslavia*. For Kim's speech in Pyongyang during Tito's visit, see *Korea Today*, November 1977, pp. 29-31.

23. The first seven countries were the Soviet Union, Mongolia, Poland, Czechoslovakia, Romania, Hungary, and Bulgaria. Albania, China, East Germany, and Vietnam recognized the North by 1950 before the Korean War. See the North Korean account of their relationships, including the dates when they established diplomatic relations, in *Chosŏn chungang yŏn'gam, 1966-67*, pp. 505-506.

24. For a list of countries with diplomatic relations with North Korea, see Byung Chul Koh, *The Foreign Policy Systems of North and South Korea*, pp. 11-12; and Tai Sung An, *North Korea: A Political Handbook*, pp. 80-82.

25. In addition to Prince Sihanouk, who practically lived in China and visited the North often, visitors to the North included Daddah of Mauritania in 1967, Nyerere of Tanzania in 1968, Adassi of Syria in 1969, Nimeri of Sudan in 1970, and Ceausescu of Romania in 1971. During 1972, there were Barre of Somalia, Aini of Yemen, and Beavogui of Guinea; during 1973, Husak of Czechoslovakia, N'gouaubi of Congo, and Zhivkov of Bulgaria visited the North. There were seven in 1974: Boumedienne of Algeria, Senghor of Senegal, Eyadema of Togo, Daddah of Mauritania again, Assad of Syria, Ali of Yemen (D), and Mobutu of Zaire. Because of Kim's own trip in 1975, only two visited, Mintoff of Malta and Da Costa of Sao Tome and Principe. There were five in 1976: Traore of Mali, Ali Bhutto of Pakistan, Ratsiraka of Madagascar, Kerekou of Benin, and Khama of Botswana.

26. There were only three in 1977: Tito of Yugoslavia, Pol Pot of Kampuchea, and Honecker of East Germany. In 1978, there were Burnham of Guyana, Kokassa of Central Africa, Rene of Seychelles, Hua of China, Machel of Mozambique, Ceausescu of Romania, Yhomby-opango of Congo, Juvenal of Rwanda, Zia of Bangladesh, and Ratsiraka of Malagasy.

27. For the text of Kim's speech see among others, *Korea Today* (June 1975), no. 6, pp. 2-8; *Peking Review* (April 25, 1975), no. 17, pp. 14-17; and Kim Il Sung, *For the Independent Peaceful Reunification of Korea*, pp. 175-183.

28. Speeches Kim made in Romania, Algeria, Bulgaria, and Yugoslavia are in a number of English-language pamphlets published by the North Koreans, but all of them are also available in *Chosŏn chungang yŏn'gam, 1976*, pp. 58-99. Most conspicuously absent is the record of his visit to Mauritania.

29. Most of his interviews had been with reporters from the socialist and Communist countries in the past, but from the 1970s he did grant interview to reporters from nonaligned nations and even a few reporters from such capitalist countries as the United States and Japan. Reporters from the *New York Times* and the *Washington Post* as well as reporters from *Yomiuri shinbun* and *Asahi shinbun* interviewed Kim, and their reports were widely circulated. Reporters from *Yomiuri shinbun* interviewed him three times (January 10, 1972, September 28, 1975, and April 23, 1977); *Mainichi shinbun* twice (September 17, 1972 and November 25, 1975); *Asahi shinbun* on September 25, 1971; the *New York Times* (Harrison Salisbury) on May 25, 1972; and the *Washington Post* (Selig S. Harrison) on June 21, 1972. Most of these interview accounts are available in the respective newspapers. see the North Korean account of all interviews in Kim Il Sung, *Oeguk kijadŭl i chegihan chilmun e taehan taedap*.

30. See Kim's interview with Yasue Ryōsuke of the Japanese Magazine *Sekai* [The world] on March 28, 1976; Kim Il Sung, *Talk with the Editor-in-Chief of the Japanese Politico-Theoretical Magazine Sekai*, pp. 26-28.

31. See Kim's article about the nonalignment movement where he mentions the entry of the North into the conference of the nonaligned nations in Lima, Peru, in Kim Il Sung, *The Non-Alignment Movement Is a Mighty Anti-Imperialist Revolutionary Force of Our Times*, pp. 317-322.

32. Kim made a number of denunciations of the United Nations. See, for exam-

ple, his speech to the first session of the third Supreme People's Assembly on October 23, 1962, and his speech to the Korean People's Army unit on February 8, 1963, in Kim Il Sung, *Uri ŭi hyŏngmyŏng kwa inmin kundae ŭi kwaŏp e taehayŏ*, pp. 148-216.

33. Kim Il Sung, *On Some Problems of Our Party's Juche Idea*, pp. 15-23.

34. The proposal favoring the South (General Assembly Resolution 3390A) was passed by 59 to 51 with 29 abstentions, and the proposal favoring the North (General Assembly Resolution 3390B) was passed by 54 to 43 with 42 abstentions. The question was debated in the First Committee on October 29 and was voted on November 18, 1975, in the General Assembly. See the details in *Yearbook of the United Nations*, 24:193-204. See also the report in "Korea: Two Resolutions Sponsored by Differing Groups Approved."

35. Kim must have experienced a less than adequate welcome in Mauritania. For Kim's brief speech at the Nouakchott Mass Meeting in Mauritania, see *Korea Today* (1975), no. 8, pp. 36-38.

36. For the North Korean explanation for severing diplomatic relations with Mauritania, see *Nodong sinmun*, June 14, 1977.

37. The North Koreans claimed that their diplomatic mission was the target of surveillance and was also threatened by the authorities. See their explanation on June 18, 1977, about Argentina in *Kita Chōsen kenkyū* (June-July 1977), 4(37):27-29. For the report of severance with Australia, see *ibid.* (October 1975), 2(17):38-39.

38. While North Korean sources are relatively quiet about their adventure in Sri Lanka, it is generally regarded by the Third World countries that the North Koreans suffered a diplomatic setback in the fifth conference of the nonaligned nations in Colombo in 1976. See *Chōsen mondai chishiki no subete*, pp. 193-194.

39. There were a number of reports about the North Korean diplomats who were arrested and expelled from the Scandinavian countries. See a comprehensive report on the subject in *Kita Chōsen kenkyū* (November 1976), no. 30, pp. 10-14. They were also expelled from South Yemen in April 1975 and from Costa Rica in May 1975.

40. *Chōsen mondai chishiki no subete*, pp. 195-198. There are detailed accounts of various performances and exhibitions.

41. In the United States, there was a group known as the American-Korean Friendship and Information Center in New York. This group published irregularly a propaganda magazine called *Korea Focus* from fall 1971 to spring 1976, but it too was discontinued. For North Korean economic assistance to various Third World countries, there is a good survey by No Kye-hyŏn, "Pukhan ŭi pidongmaeng oegyo punsŏk."

42. The seminar was held from September 14 to September 17, 1977. There were no representatives from either China or the Soviet Union. See the speeches of the participants in *The International Seminar on the Juche Idea*.

15. The Shift from Party to State

1. It is not my purpose here to discuss political changes in the South. Only brief mention is made to give proper perspective on the changes that took place in the North. For the programs and constitution of the revitalized reform in the South, see the details of the amendment and the text of the constitution in Pak Il-gyŏng, *Yusin hŏnbŏp*, and *The October Revitalizing Reforms of the Republic of Korea*. The constitution of the Republic of Korea had been amended seven times, thrice by Rhee, once by the second republic, and thrice by Park Chung Hee, including the October Revitalized Constitution of October 1972.

2. For a slightly different interpretation of the new constitution see Chong-sik Lee, "The 1972 Constitution and Top Communist Leaders," in Dae-Sook Suh and Chae-Jin Lee, eds. *Political Leadership in Korea*, pp. 192-219.

3. For the text and analysis of the Socialist Constitution, the new 1972 constitution of the North, see *On the Socialist Constitution of the Democratic People's Republic of Korea*.

4. Article 76 stipulated that the Supreme People's Assembly has the right to elect or recall the vice-president of the republic, the secretary, and members of the Central People's Committee, but only on the recommendation of the president of the republic; *ibid.*, pp. 65-66.

5. There were 25 members of the first Central People's Committee in 1972, and it included all 15 members and candidate members of the Political Committee of the Central Committee except two, Sŏ Ch'ŏl and Han Ik-su. These two were elected to the Standing Committee of the Supreme People's Assembly. In addition to the 13 members and candidate members of the Political Committee of the party there were 12 new members of the Central People's Committee. For the composition of the Central People's Committee and other officers of the government elected at the fifth Supreme People's Assembly, see *Korea Today* (1973), no. 196, pp. 31-32.

6. For details of the discussion of farming at the twelfth plenum in October 1976, see *Külloja* (December 1976), pp. 2-8. For the report of the plenum, see *Nodong sinmun*, October 11, 1976.

7. See, for example, Kim's speech in *Kim Il Sung chŏjak sŏnjip*, 6:326-369. This speech was made at the first session of the fifth Supreme People's Assembly on December 25, 1972. He made a similar speech at the first session of the sixth Supreme People's Assembly on December 15, 1977. See Kim Il Sung, *Let Us Further Strengthen the People's Government*.

8. The open letter was adopted at the sixteenth plenum of the Central Committee held on January 8, 1978. For the report of Yi Chong-ok at the sixth Supreme People's Assembly, see *Pyongyang Times*, December 17 and December 24, 1977.

9. Ch'oe Yong-gŏn, perhaps the most famous partisan after Kim, died on September 19, 1976, at the age of 76. See the announcement of his death in *Nodong sinmun*, September 20, 1976. Chŏng Chun-t'aek, the foremost technocrat, who was appointed twelve times to five different cabinet posts, died on January 11, 1973. See the report in *Nodong sinmun*, January 12, 1973. Chŏng was 63 years

old when he died. Han Ik-su, partisan general and diplomat, died on September 5, 1978, at the age of 66. See *Nodong sinmun*, September 6, 1978.

10. The eighth plenum was held February 11-14, 1974, and the tenth plenum was held February 11-17, 1975. The ninth plenum was held sometime in between, most likely in the fall of 1974. The problem of succession might have been the agenda for this plenum, hence the silence.

11. For Kim's speech on the anniversary of the party, see Kim Il Sung, *On the Occasion of the 30th Anniversary of the Foundation of the Workers' Party of Korea.* For his speech on the anniversary of the government, see Kim Il Sung, *Let Us Step Up Socialist Construction Under the Banner of the Juche Idea.*

12. See the text of Kim's speech in English in Kim Il Sung, *Let Us Further Strengthen the People's Government.* This speech was made on December 15, 1977.

13. For Kim's reference to material incentives, see his speech at the enlarged meeting of the Political Committee of the party on February 1, 1973; *Kim Il Sung chŏjak sŏnjip*, 6:392-407.

14. For the reference about the young people learning foreign languages, see his speech in Kim Il Sung, *The Youth Must Take Over the Revolution and Carry It Forward*, pp. 182-229

15. The Three Revolutions refer to the ideological, technological, and cultural revolutions. It appeared in North Korean publications from about October 1973. See *Nodong sinmun*, October 22, 1973. For a discussion of the three-revolution policy, see *Kyŏngae hanŭn suryŏng Kim Il Sung tongji kkesŏ palk'yŏ chusin samdae hyŏngmyŏng nosŏn ŭi widaehan saenghwallyŏk.*

16. See Kim's speech on March 3, 1975; Kim Il Sung, *Samdae hyŏngmyŏng ŭl himikke pŏllyŏ sahoe chuŭi kŏnsŏl ŭl tŏuk tagŭch'ija.* In conjunction with this movement, see an article on the subject by a South Korean analyst, Yang Ho-min, "Samdae hyŏngmyŏng ŭi wŏllyu wa chŏn'gae."

17. There are a number of articles in both *Kŭlloja*, the party organ, and *Nodong sinmun*, the party daily, on the subject. A representative one is "Samdae hyŏngmyŏng pulgŭn'gi chaengch'wi undong ŭn onsahoe ŭi chuch'e sasanghwa rŭl tŏuk himikke tagŭch'yŏ nagagi wihan saeroun taejungjŏk undong" [The three-revolution Red Flag movement is the new mass movement for further developing the *Chuch'e* ideology throughout society], *Kŭlloja* (1976), no. 4 (408), pp. 43-50. See *Nodong sinmun*, November 11, 1976.

18. For the text of this speech, which was not included in the selected works, see the text in *Chosŏn chungang yŏn'gam, 1974*, pp. 8-24.

19. This speech was made in the Political Committee meeting held in Kangsŏ on March 14, 1973. The text is available in *Kim Il Sung chŏjak sŏnjip*, 6:415-445.

20. Kim's first reference to this phrase came as early as his speech on June 24, 1971. See Kim Il Sung, *The Youth Must Take Over the Revolution and Carry It Forward.* He repeated it again to the visiting Korean resident youth groups from Japan on August 31, 1973. For the Korean text of this speech, see *Kim Il Sung chŏjak sŏnjip*, 6:478-493.

21. For the reference to "human wave tactics," see his speech on March 14, 1973; *Kim Il Sung chŏjak sŏnjip*, 4:415-445; also available in *Kŭlloja* (1975), no. 3 (395), pp. 2-22.

22. Morgan E. Clippinger, "Kim Chong-il in the North Korean Mass Media: A Survey of Semi-Esoteric Communication," *Asian Survey* (March 1981), 21(3):289-309.

23. *Nodong sinmun*, January 14 and January 23, 1976. These campaigns were taking place in the Suan mines and 9-28 factories.

24. See a representative article by Ch'ŏn Se-bong, "Onsahoe ŭi chuch'e sasang hwa e ibajihanŭn hyŏngmyŏngjŏk munye chakp'um ŭl ch'angjak halte taehan tang ŭi t'agwŏlhan pangch'im."

25. "Widaehan suryŏng nimkke kkŭt ŏpsi ch'ungsil hayŏttŏn purgul ŭi kongsan chuŭi hyŏngmyŏng t'usa Kim Chŏng-suk tongji."

26. For the story about the museum, see Hwang Chŏng-hŭi, "Yŏngwŏn han ch'ungsŏng ŭro purŭnŭn hyŏngmyŏng ŭi chip." See Kim Sŏng-ae's speech on March 7, 1975, in commemoration of the sixty-fifth anniversary of International Women's Day, March 8; *Nodong sinmun*, March 9, 1975.

27. The full text was reproduced in a secret document by the Central Intelligence Agency in South Korea; *Pukkoe kanbu mit tangwŏn haksŭp charyo*, pp. 187-213. Portions of the text were reproduced in Japanese in *Kita Chōsen kenkyū* (March 1977), no. 34 pp. 5-9; and (June-July 1977), no. 37, pp. 50-55. See the report on the release of the document and the lecture series of the Chōsōren in February 1977 in *Mainichi shinbun*, February 12 and 13, 1977.

28. *Nodong sinmun*, October 15, 1980.

29. These were the theses presented to the eighth plenum of the Central Committee of the party on February 25, 1964. See the text in English, Kim Il Sung, *Theses on the Socialist Rural Question in Our Country*.

30. Inoue Shuhachi, *Modern Korea and Kim Jong Il*, pp. 114-115.

31. For Kim Jong Il's biographical information, see Ch'oe In-su, *Kim Jong Il: The People's Leader*; Nada Takashi, *A Paean of Great Love; Kim Jong Il and the People*. These are all North Korean official accounts, and simple fact about his life are hard to find.

32. For the guerrilla activities of Kang Kŏn and O Chung-hŭp, see Part 1 of this study.

33. Ch'oe In-su, *Kim Jong Il: The People's Leader*, 2:378-379.

34. In an interview with a Japanese socialist on May 13, 1978, Kim said that he often plays with his grandchildren on holidays. See *Shakai shinpō*, May 26, 1978; also in *Kita Chōsen kenkyū* (June 1978), no. 48, pp. 56-57. His children from his present wife are too young to give him grandchildren, and they must be from either his son Kim Jong Il or his daughter.

35. There are a number of reports indicating that his second wife has had two to four children by Kim. See, among others, the account of Nishitani Kunio, who spoke of two children, a boy and a girl, in *Mirai*, December 1970, p. 54. Others reported four (two boys and two girls) and identified the boys by the names of Kim Kyŏng-il and Kim Pyŏng-il and the girls by the names of Kim Sŏng-il and

Kim Yŏng-ja. When I visited the North, the party cadres' reply to my direct question about the number of children from Kim's second wife was that she had four children, three boys and a girl.

16. Semiretirement in the New Era

1. *Pyongyang Times*, April 12, 1986.
2. For the death of these men, see *Nodong sinmun*, January 10, 1983, and March 10, 1984.
3. *Nodong sinmun*, September 20, 1976.
4. *Nodong sinmun*, April 10, 1982.
5. Kim Il Sung, *Tasks of the People's Government in Modelling the Whole of Society on the Juche Idea.*
6. Kim Il Sung, *On the Korean People's Struggle to Apply the Juche Idea.*
7. Kim Il Sung, *Historical Experience of Building the Workers' Party of Korea.*
8. *Pyongyang Times,* September 11, 1983.
9. Texts of these interviews are available in English in individual pamphlets published by the Foreign Languages Publishing House in Pyongyang.
10. *The Leader Comrade Kim Il Sung's Official State Visit to the People's Republic of China* (Pyongyang: Foreign Languages Publishing House, 1982), P. 11.
11. *Nodong sinmun*, September 18 and 28, 1982.
12. *Pyongyang Times*, May 26, 1984.
13. *Pyongyang Times*, May 30 and June 6, 1987.
14. *Nodong sinmun*, July 12, 1985.
15. *Nodong sinmun*, April 10, 1985.
16. *Nodong sinmun*, August 9, 1985. For detailed discussion of the change in North Korea's reunification policy, see Dae-Sook Suh, "Changes in North Korean Politics and the Unification Policy," *Korea and World Affairs*, 9(4):684-706.
17. Those newly elected to the Central Committee included Chŏn Ha-ch'ŏl at the eighth plenum in December 1983 and Kang Sun-hŭi, Kim Wŏn-jun, and Chŏn Chin-su at the tenth plenum in December 1984. Those who were elected candidate members included Kim Kwang-jin, O Sŏng-yŏl, Ch'oe Kwang-yong, Ch'oe Tŏk-hong, Pak Yun-sŏk, Yim T'ae-yong, and Chu Ch'ang-jun at the eighth plenum in December 1983. At the tenth plenum, Kim Kwan-hak, Chŏng Ho-gyun, Nam Sang-hak, Kim Sŏng-gu, Ch'oe Pong-man, and Kim Ch'ol-myŏng were elected members of the Central Committee. See *Nodong sinmun*, December 11, 1984.
18. *Nodong sinmun*, October 2, 1985.
19. *Nodong sinmun*, February 17, 1985.
20. For the text of the joint-venture law in English see *Pyongyang Times*, September 15, 1984.
21. *Pyongyang Times*, May 31, June 7, July 19, 1986.

PART VII. CHUCH'E AND THE REPUBLIC

17. On Kim's Political Thought

1. There are many books on the subject of *chuch'e* by Kim, but these are all collections of his speeches, reports, and portions of interviews. See, among others, Kim Il Sung, *Chuch'e sasang e taehayŏ*; Kim Il Sung, *Uri hyŏngmyŏng esŏ ŭi chuch'e e taehayŏ*. For the study of the *chuch'e* idea, see such representative works as the three-volume study by the Social Science Institute of the Academy of Sciences, *Hyŏngmyŏng kwa kŏnsŏl e kwanhan Kim Il Sung tongji ŭi sasanggwa kŭ widaehan seanghwallyŏk* [The thought of Comrade Kim Il Sung on revolution and construction and its great strength] (Pyongyang: Sahoe kwahagwŏn ch'ulp'ansa, 1969). Another work by the same institute is entitled *Widaehan suryŏng Kim Il Sung tongji ŭi chuch'e sasang*. The same institute has begun to publish separate volumes on the implications of the *chuch'e* idea in various fields such as world revolution, socialist and Communist construction theories, socialist economic theories, the Three-Revolution Team theory, and language and linguistic theories. See, for example, *Chuch'e sasang e kich'ohan samdae hyŏngmyŏng iron; Chuch'e sasang e kich'ohan segyen hyŏngmyŏng iron*.

2. Kim Il Sung, "Report to the Fifth Congress of the Workers' Party of Korea on the Work of the Central Committee," in *Selected Works*, 5:500-501.

3. Kim Il Sung, *Uri tang ŭi chuch'e sasang kwa konghwaguk chŏngbu ŭi taenaeoe chŏngch'aek ŭi myŏt kaji munje e taehayŏ*, pp. 1-13.

4. *Hyŏngmyŏng kwa kŏnsŏl e kwanhan widaehan suryŏng Kim Il Sung tongji ŭi kyosi*, pp. 2-13.

5. For discussion of the idea of *chaju*, see *Widaehan suryŏng Kim Il Sung tongji ŭi chuch'e sasang*, pp. 153-170.

6. *Ibid.*, pp. 171-185. See also Kim Il Sung, *On Some Problems of Our Party's Juche Idea and the Government of the Republic's Internal and External Policies*, pp. 1-15.

7. *Widaehan suryŏng Kim Il Sung tongji ŭi chuch'e sasang*, pp. 185-204. See also Kim's speech to the company commanders and company political commissars of the Korean People's Army on October 11, 1973, in *Kim Il Sung chŏjak sŏnjip*, 6:494-523.

8. *Kim Il sung tongji ŭi hyŏngmyŏng sasang e taehayŏ*, pp. 18-49.

9. For Kim's discussion of national nihilism, *minjok hŏmu chuŭi*, see Kim Il Sung, *Sahoe kwahak immu e taehayŏ*, pp. 509-511. For his discussion of restorationism, *pokko chuŭi*, see *Kim Il Sung chŏjak sŏnjip*, 5:458-460. For the definition of these and other terms, see *Chŏngch'i sajŏn*.

10. *Kim Il Sung tongji ŭi hyŏngmyŏng sasang e taehayŏ*, pp. 27-28, 47-49, and 403-462.

11. His earlier biography had him back in middle school after his jailing in Jilin at this time, but this was later corrected and had him in Gelun speaking to the young people. For the text of his speech, see Kim Il Sung, *Chosŏn hyŏngmyŏng ŭi chillo*.

12. Published in the 1970s were speeches of June 30, 1930, May 20 1931, December 16, 1931, April 25, 1932, March 11, 1933, March 27, 1933, May 10 1933, March 27 1935, February 27, 1936, May 5, 1936, March 29, 1937, June 4, 1937, November 10, 1937, August 10, 1940, and September 15, 1943. Texts of all these speeches are available, mostly published in the 1970s in pamphlets.

13. This speech is said to have been delivered to the political cadres and political instructors of the Korean People's Revolutionary Army on September 15, 1943. They do not say where he delivered it, but Kim at this time was in the Russian Maritime Province. See the pamphlet, Kim Il Sung, *The Korean Revolutionaries Must Know Korea Well*.

14. Kim Il Sung, *Sasang saŏp esŏ kyojo chuŭi wa hyŏngsik chuŭi rŭl t'oech'i hago chuch'e rŭl hwangnip halte taehayŏ*. English versions of this speech were published once in 1964 and again in 1973.

15. Compare the edited version with the original. For the original see *ibid.*; for the latest edition without the reference to the rectification campaign, see *Kim Il Sung chŏjak sŏnjip*, 1:560-585.

16. During the eight-year period from December 1955 to February 1963, Kim once mentioned to party leaders of the Kangsŏ local party committee that they should not use heavy political jargon; those who used such words were leaders without *chuch'e*. This speech was on February 18, 1960; see *ibid.*, 2:480-504.

17. Kim Il Sung, *Uri ŭi hyŏngmyŏng kwa inmin kundae ŭi kwaŏp e taehayŏ*, pp. 148-216.

18. Kim Il Sung, *Uri hyŏngmyŏng esŏ ŭi chuch'e e taehayŏ*, pp. 216-234.

19. The speech he made in Indonesia is important in many respects. It revealed Kim's thought on *chuch'e*, his policy toward Third World countries, and his policy toward the South. See the complete text in *Kim Il Sung chŏjak sŏnjip*, 4:195-240.

20. See a lengthy exposition of the subject in his speech at the fourth Supreme People's Assembly on December 16, 1967, in Kim Il Sung, *Let Us Embody More Thoroughly the Revolutionary Spirit of Independence, Self-Sustenance and Self-Defense in All Fields of State Activity*.

21. *Kim Il Sung sŏnjip*, 2d ed., 5:216-249.

22. See Ch'oe Sŏng-uk, *Uri tang ŭi chuch'e sasang kwa sahoe chuŭijŏk aeguk chuŭi*.

23. There is a newsreel documentary on Hua's visit to the North, and any self-reliant Korean armed with the *chuch'e* idea would question such Korean subservience to the Chinese visitor. See a revealing photograph in a special issue of the North Korean pictorial *Democratic People's Republic of Korea*, special issue, 1978, pp. 4-5.

24. Compare his speeches of August 15, 1946, in *Kim Il Sung sŏnjip*, 1st ed., 1:147-181, with the same in the 2d ed., 1:142-166.

25. Find similar deletions in his speeches on February 19, June 14, and December 21, 1947, February 8, March 28, and August 23, 1948, April 22 and September 9, 1949, November 1, 1951, December 15, 1952, September 20, 1957, and others.

26. See Kim's speech on June 30, 1951, in Kim Il Sung, *Uri hyŏngmyŏng esŏ munhak yesul ŭi immu*, pp. 1-10.

27. *Kim Il Sung chuŭi hyŏngmyŏngnon*; Muhammad al Missuri, *Kimilsungism: Theory and Practice*.

18. The Republic by Kim

1. See Article 54 of the constitution. One of Kim's most difficult tasks after establishment of the state was the handling of Christians. He often said that there is freedom of religion in the North, but there is also freedom to demonstrate against religion, and he mobilized young people to demonstrate against church services on Sundays. There are no churches or Buddhist temples in the North today. For Kim's speech deriding Christianity, see *Kim Il Sung sŏnjip*, 4:414-415. for Kim's style of guaranteeing human rights for only selected people, see his speech on December 15, 1977, at the sixth Supreme People's Assembly in Kim Il Sung, *Let Us Further Strengthen the People's Government*, pp. 17-18.

2. The first assembly was held in September 1948 and the second one ten years later in 1957. Ever since the second assembly, the North Koreans have held their sessions of the Supreme People's Assembly once every five years, but the constitution still stipulates that it should be held once every four years. See Article 75 of the new constitution.

3. For Kim's reference to the constitution as a historic document, see his speech on December 25, 1972; Kim Il Sung, *Let Us Further the Socialist System of Our Country.*

4. Byung Chul Koh, "Political Leadership in North Korea: Toward a Conceptual Understanding of Kim Il Sung's Leadership Behavior".

5. Kim Il Sung, "Sacchosŏn kŏnsŏl kwa minjok t'ongil chŏnsŏn e taehayŏ," *Kim Il Sung sŏnjip*, 1:1-10.

6. See Kim's speech on December 15, 1952, at the fifth joint plenum of the Central Committee in Kim Il Sung, *Nodongdang ŭi chojikchŏk sasangjŏk kanghwa nŭn uri sŭngni ŭi kich'o*, pp. 2-57.

7. See *Pravda*, August 15, 1952. This article appeared only in the first edition of Kim's selected work and was dropped from subsequent selections. See *Kim Il Sung sŏnjip*, 4:255-279.

8. *Chosŏn chungang yŏn'gam, 1954-55*, pp. 14-15.

9. The Kim Il Sung flower very much resembles a common tropical orchid. See the story behind the flower in "Kimilsung Flower Abloom the World Over."

10. When I visited the museum, I asked the guide whether Kim Il Sung had ever personally visited the museum, for surely any man would react adversely to such elaborate personal glorification of both fact and fiction. The guide replied that he had not only visited once but many times and personally directed what should be displayed where in the museum.

11. For detailed statistical and other information concerning the activities of the 60th birthday, see *Chosŏn chungang yŏn'gam, 1972*, pp. 49-264.

12. For the South Korean claim of the Pyŏrori plenum, see Kim Ch'ang-sun, *Pukhan sibonyŏnsa*, pp. 121-131. This work was considered a standard account of the North at the time of publication, but it contains many errors in interpretation as well as in factual information about dates and places. Some of the errors were pointed out by Pang In-hu in his study of the Workers' Party of Korea in 1964. For the account of this particular monument, see *Chosŏn chungang yŏn'gam, 1972*, pp. 168-169.

13. The marker is erected atop the mountain near Lake Ch'ŏnji. See the text of the inscription in *Chosŏn chungang yŏn'gam, 1973*, p. 140.

14. Kim Il Sung, *Talk with the Editor-in-Chief of the French Newspaper Le Monde*, pp. 12-13. See the same in Korean in *Kŭlloja*, 1977, no. 8 (423), pp. 2-7.

Bibliography

Writings of Kim Il Sung

Chayu wa tongnip ŭl wihan Chosŏn inmin ŭi chŏngŭi ŭi choguk haebang chŏnjaeng [The just fatherland liberation war of the Korean people for freedom and independence]. Pyongyang: Chosŏn nodongdang ch'ulp'ansa, 1954.

Chigŏp tongmaeng saŏp e taehayŏ [On the work of the trade union]. Pyongyang: Chosŏn nodongdang ch'ulp'ansa, 1968.

Choguk t'ongil e kwanhan widaehan suryŏng Kim Il-sŏng tongji ŭi munhŏn [Documents of the great leader Comrade Kim Il Sung on the fatherland unification]. N.p.: Samhaksa, 1975.

Choguk t'ongil wiŏp ŭl sirhyŏn hagi wihayŏ hyŏngmyŏng yŏngyang ŭl paekbang ŭro kanghwa haja [Let us strengthen the revolutionary forces in every way to achieve the cause of reunification of the country]. Pyongyang: Chosŏn nodongdang ch'ulp'ansa, 1969.

Choguk ŭi t'ongil tongnip kwa minjuhwa rŭl wihayŏ [For the unification, independence, and democratization of the fatherland]. 2. vols. Pyongyang: Chosŏn nodongdang ch'ulp'ansa, 1949.

Ch'ŏllima kisudŭl ŭn uri sidae ŭi yŏngung imyŏ tang ŭi pulgŭn chŏnsa ida [Ch'ŏllima riders are heroes of our time and red fighters of our party]. Pyongyang: Chosŏn nodongdang ch'ulp'ansa, 1973.

Ch'ŏngsonyŏn saŏp e taehayŏ [For the work of the youth and children]. Pyongyang: Chosŏn nodongdang ch'ulp'ansa, 1966.

Ch'ŏngsonyŏn saŏfkwa sahoe chuŭi nodong ch'ŏngnyŏn tongmaeng ŭi immu e taehayŏ [The work of the youth and children and the task of the League of Socialist Working Youth]. 2 vols. Pyongyang: Chosŏn nodongdang ch'ulp'ansa, 1969.

Chŏnhu inmin kyŏngje pokku palchŏn ŭl wihayŏ [For the rehabilitation and development of the postwar people's economy]. Pyongyang: Chosŏn nodongdang ch'ulp'ansa, 1956.

Chosŏn hyŏngmyŏng ŭi chillo [The path of the Korean revolution]. Pyongyang: Chosŏn nodongdang ch'ulp'ansa, 1978.

Chosŏn inmin ŭi minjokchŏk myŏngjŏl p'ariro haebang 15 chunyŏn kyŏngch'uk taehoe esŏ han pogo [Report at the rally in commemoration of the fifteenth anniversary of the August 15 liberation, the national holiday of the Korean people]. Pyongyang: Chosŏn nodongdang ch'ulp'ansa, 1960.

Chosŏn minju chuŭi inmin konghwaguk chŏngbu ŭi tangmyŏn kwaŏp e taehayŏ [On the immediate tasks of the government of the Democratic People's Republic of Korea]. Pyongyang: Chosŏn nodongdang ch'ulp'ansa, 1962.

Chosŏn minju chuŭi inmin konghwaguk surip ŭi kil [The path to the establishment of the Democratic People's Republic of Korea]. Pyongyang: Pukchosŏn inmin wiwŏnhoe, 1947.

Chosŏn nodongdang ch'anggŏn 20chunyŏn e chehayŏ [On the occasion of the twentieth anniversary of the founding of the Workers' Party of Kora]. Pyongyang: Chosŏn nodongdang ch'ulp'ansa, 1965.

Chosŏn nodongdang che och'a taehoe esŏ han chungang wiwŏnhoe saŏp ch'onghwa pogo [Report on the work of the Central Committee to fifth congress of the Workers' Party of Korea]. Pyongyang: Chosŏn nodongdang ch'ulp'ansa, 1970.

Chosŏn nodongdang che sach'a taehoe esŏ han chungang wiwŏnhoe saŏp ch'onghwa pogo [Report on the work of the Central Committee to the fourth congress of the Workers' Party of Korea]. Pyongyang: Chosŏn nodongdang ch'ulp'ansa, 1961.

Chuch'e sasang e taehayŏ [On the idea of *chuch'e*]. Pyongyang: Chosŏn nodongdang ch'ulp'ansa, 1977.

For Correct Management of the Socialist Rural Economy in Our Country. Pyongyang: Foreign Languages Publishing House, 1977.

For Socialist Economic Construction. Pyongyang: Foreign Languages Publishing House, 1958.

For the Independent, Peaceful Reunification of Korea. Rev. ed. New York: Guardian Associates, 1976.

For the Independent, Peaceful Reunification of the Country. Pyongyang: Foreign Languages Publishing House, 1976; rev. ed. (New York: Guardian Associates, 1976).

Hamgyŏng pukto tang tanch'e dŭl ŭi kwaŏp [Tasks of the party organizations of North Hamgyŏng province]. Pyongyang: Chosŏn nodongdang ch'ulp'ansa, 1968.

Historical Experience of Building the Workers' Party of Korea. Pyongyang: Foreign Languages Publishing House, 1986.

Hyŏn chŏngse wa uridang ŭi kwaŏp [The present situation and the tasks of our party]. Pyongyang: Chosŏn nodongdang ch'ulp'ansa, 1966.

Hyŏngje kukka inmin dŭl ŭi kogwi han kukche chuŭijŏk wŏnjo [Precious international aid by the peoples of fraternal countries]. Pyongyang: Chosŏn nodongdang ch'ulp'ansa, 1953.

Inmin kyŏngje kyehoek ŭi irwŏnhwa, sebuhwa ŭi widaehan saenghwallyŏk ŭl namgim ŏpsi palhwi hagi wihayŏ [For the exhibition of great vitality of the unified and detailed planning of the national economy]. Pyongyang: Chosŏn nodongdang ch'ulp'ansa, 1969.

Izbrannye stat'i i rechi. Moscow: Gospolitizdat, 1962.

Juche! The Speeches and Writings of Kim Il Sung. Eldridge Cleaver, forword; Li Yuksa, ed. and introd. New York: Grossman, 1972.

Kim Il Sung chŏjakchip [Works of Kim Il Sung]. Pyongyang: Chosŏn nodongdang ch'ulp'ansa, 1979.

Kim Il Sung chŏjak sŏnjip. [Selected works of Kim Il Sung]. 3d ed. 6 vols. Pyongyang: Chosŏn nodongdang ch'ulp'ansa, 1969-1973.

Kim Il Sung, Selected Works. English text of *Kim Il Sung chŏjak sŏnjip.* 6 vols. Pyongyang: Foreign Languages Publishing House, 1971-72.

Kim Il Sung, Selected Works. English text of selected titles from *Kim Il Sung sŏnjip.* 2 vols. Pyongyang: Foreign Languages Publishing House, 1965.

Kim Il Sung sŏnjip [Selected works of Kim Il Sung]. 1st ed. 4 vols. Pyongyang: Chosŏn nodongdang ch'ulp'ansa, 1953-54.

Kim Il Sung sŏnjip [Selected works of Kim Il Sung]. 2nd ed. 6 vols. Pyongyang: Chosŏn nodongdang ch'ulp'ansa, 1960-64.

Kim Il Sung tongji ŭi chuyo munhŏnjip [Important documents of Comrade Kim Il Sung]. 3 vols. N.p.: Sahoe kwahaksa, 1971.

Kin nichi-sei senshū [Selected works of Kim Il Sung]. 3 vols. Tokyo: Sanichi shobō, 1952.

Kodŭng kyoyuksaŏp ŭl kaesŏn halte taehayŏ [On the reform in higher education work]. Pyongyang: Chosŏn nodongdang ch'ulp'ansa, 1973.

Kongsan chuŭi kyoyang e taehayŏ [On Communist education]. Pyongyang: Chosŏn nodongdang ch'ulp'ansa, 1960.

Kŏnsŏl punya esŏ tang chŏngch'aek ŭl kwanch'ŏl halte taehayŏ [On carrying out the party's policy in the construction sector]. Pyongyang: Chosŏn nodongdang ch'ulp'ansa, 1958.

Kŏnsŏl ŭi chirŭl nop'igi wihayŏ [For higher quality in construction]. Pyongyang: Chosŏn nodongdang ch'ulp'ansa, 1959.

The Korean Revolutionaries Must Know Korea Well. Pyongyang: Foreign Languages Publishing House, 1973.

Kun nongŏp hyŏptong chohap kyŏngyŏng wiwŏnhoe rŭl naeolte taehayŏ [On the formation of the County Cooperative Farm Management Committee]. Pyongyang: Chosŏn nodongdang ch'ulp'ansa, 1970.

Let Us Embody More Thoroughly the Revolutionary Spirit of Independence, Self-Sustenance and Self-Defense in All Fields of State Activity. Pyongyang: Foreign Languages Publishing House, 1967.

Let Us Further Strengthen the People's Government. Pyongyang: Foreign Languages Publishing House, 1977.

Let Us Prevent a National Split and Reunify the Country. Pyongyang: Foreign Languages Publishing House, 1973.

Let Us Step Up Socialist Construction Under the Banner of the Juche Idea. Pyongyang: Foreign Languages Publishing House, 1978.

Minju chuŭi inmin konghwaguk surip ŭl wihayŏ [For the establishment of the Democratic People's Republic of Korea]. Pyongyang: Pukchosŏn nodongdang ch'ulp'ansa, 1948.

Namchosŏn hyŏngmyŏng kwa choguk t'ongil e taehayŏ [The South Korean revolution and unification of the fatherland]. Pyongyang: Chosŏn nodongdang ch'ulp'ansa, 1969.

Nodong haengjŏng saŏp e taehan myŏkkaji munje [Some problems of manpower administration]. Pyongyang: Chosŏn nodongdang ch'ulp'ansa, 1972.

Nodongdang ŭi chojikchŏk sasangjŏk kanghwa nŭn uri sŭngni ŭi kich'o [The organizational and ideological consolidation of the party is the basis of our victory]. Pyongyang: Chosŏn nodongdang ch'ulp'ansa, 1953.

The Non-Alignment Movement Is A Mighty Anti-Imperialist Revolutionary Force of Our Times. Pyongyang: Foreign Languages Publishing House, 1976.

Oeguk kijadŭl i chegihan chilmun e taehan taedap [Answers to the questions raised by foreign correspondents]. 2 vols. Pyongyang: Chosŏn nodongdang ch'ulp'ansa, 1975.

On Juche in Our Revolution. 2 vols. Pyongyang: Foreign Languages Publishing House, 1975.

On Our Party's Policy for the Future Development of Agriculture. Pyongyang: Foreign Languages Publishing House, 1964.

On Some Experiences of the Democratic and Socialist Revolutions in Our Country. Pyongyang: Foreign Languages Publishing House, 1973.

On Some Problems of Our Party's Juche Idea and the Government of the Republic's Internal and External Policies. Pyongyang: Foreign Languages Publishing House, 1972.

On the Building of the People's Government. Pyongyang: Foreign Languages Publishing House, 1978.

On the Building of the Workers' Party of Korea. 2 vols. Pyongyang: Foreign Languages Publishing House, 1978.

On the Character and Tasks of the Trade Union in Socialist Society. Pyongyang: Foreign Languages Publishing House, 1974.

On the Five-Point Policy for National Reunification. Pyongyang: Foreign Languages Publishing House, 1977.

On the Korean People's Struggle to Apply the Juche Idea. Pyongyang: Foreign Languages Publishing House, 1983.

On the Occasion of the 30th Anniversary of the Foundation of the Workers' Party of Korea. Pyongyang: Foreign Languages Publishing House, 1975.

On the Situation of Our Country and Tasks of the League of Korean Youth in Japan. Pyongyang: Foreign Languages Publishing House, 1974.

On the 20th Anniversary of the Founding of the Korean People's Army. Pyongyang: Foreign Languages Publishing House, 1968.

On the Work with Children and Youth. Pyongyang: Foreign Languages Publishing House, 1978.

Pogŏn wisaeng saŏp ŭl palchŏn sik'igi wihayŏ [For the development of public health work]. Pyongyang: Chosŏn nodongdang ch'ulp'ansa, 1968.

The Present Situation and the Tasks of Our Party. Pyongyang: Foreign Languages Publishing House, 1968.

P'yŏngan pukto tang tanch'e dŭl ŭi kwaŏp [Tasks of the party organizations in P'yŏngan pukto]. Pyongyang: Chosŏn nodongdang ch'ulp'ansa, 1956.

Revolution and Socialist Construction in Korea: Selected Writings of Kim Il Sung. New York: International Publishers, 1971.

Sahoe chuŭi kŏnsŏl ŭi widaehan ch'udongyŏl in Ch'ŏllima chagŏppan undong ŭl tŏuk simhwa palchŏn sik'ija [Let us develop the Ch'ollima workteam movement in depth, a great impetus to socialist construction]. Pyongyang: Chosŏn nodongdang ch'ulp'ansa, 1968.

Sahoe chuŭi kyŏngje kwalli munje e taehayŏ [On the problems of socialist economic management]. 3 vols. Pyongyang: Chosŏn nodongdang ch'ulp'ansa, 1970.

Sahoe kwahak immu e taehayŏ [On the duty of the social sciences]. Pyongyang: Chosŏn nodongdang ch'ulp'ansa, 1969.

Samdae hyŏngmyŏng ŭl himikke pŏllyŏ sahoe chuŭi kŏnsŏl ŭl tŏuk ŭ tagŭch'ija [Let us further assist socialist construction by developing the three revolutions]. Pyongyang: Chosŏn nodongdang ch'ulp'ansa, 1975.

Sasang saŏp esŏ kyojo chuŭi wa hyŏngsik chuŭi rŭl t'oech'i hago chuch'e rŭl hwangnip halte taehayŏ [On eliminating dogmatism and formalism and establishing *Chuch'e* in ideological work]. Pyongyang: Chosŏn nodongdang ch'ulp'ansa, 1960.

Soedol saengsan esŏ hyŏksin ŭl irŭk'ilte taehayŏ [On the reform of ingot production]. Pyongyang: Chosŏn nodongdang ch'ulp'ansa, 1970.

Sŏkt'an kongŏp ŭl ppalli palchŏn sik'igi wihayŏ [For the rapid development of the coal industry]. Pyongyang: Chosŏn nodongdang ch'ulp'ansa, 1970.

Speeches Delivered During the Visit to the Algerian Democratic and People's Republic. Pyongyang: Foreign Languages Publishing House, 1976.

Speeches Delivered During the Visit to the Socialist Federal Republic of Yugoslavia. Pyongyang: Foreign Languages Publishing House, 1976.

Ssoryŏn ŭl pangmun han Chosŏn minju chuŭi inmin konghwaguk taep'yodan ŭi saŏp e taehayŏ [On the works of the government delegation of the Democratic People's Republic of Korea on their visit to the Soviet Union]. Pyongyang: Chosŏn nodongdang ch'ulp'ansa, 1949.

Talk with the Editor-in-Chief of the French Newspaper Le Monde. Pyongyang: Foreign Languages Publishing House, 1977.

Talk with the Managing Editor of the Japanese Politico-Theoretical Magazine, Sekai. Pyongyang: Foreign Languages Publishing House, 1972.

Tang tanch'e dŭl ŭi chojik saŏp esŏ ŭi myŏtkaji kyŏlham dŭl ŭi taehayŏ [On some defects in the organizational work of party organizations]. Pyongyang: Chosŏn nodongdang ch'ulp'ansa, 1951.

Tang ŭi konggohwa rŭl wihayŏ [For the strengthening of the party]. Pyongyang: Chosŏn nodongdang ch'ulp'ansa, 1951.

Tasks of the People's Government in Modelling the Whole of Society on the Juche Idea. Pyongyang: Foreign Languages Publishing House, 1982.

Theses on the Socialist Agrarian Question in Our Country. Pyongyang: Foreign Languages Publishing House, 1964.

Uri hyŏngmyŏng esŏ munhak yesul ŭi immu [Duty of literature and arts in our revolution]. Pyongyang: Chosŏn nodongdang ch'ulp'ansa, 1965.

Uri hyŏngmyŏng esŏ ŭi chuch'e e taehayŏ [On *chuch'e* in our revolution]. Pyongyang: Chosŏn nodongdang ch'ulp'ansa, 1970.

Uri hyŏngmyŏng kwa kŏnsŏl esŏ inmin chŏnggwŏn ŭi kwaŏp e taehayŏ [On the task of the people's government in our revolution and construction. Pyongyang: Chosŏn nodongdang ch'ulp'ansa, 1968.

Uri nara sahoe chuŭi nongch'on munje wa nongŏp kŭlloja tongmaeng saŏp e taehayŏ [On the work of the Agrarian Workers' Union and the problems of socialist agriculture in our country]. Pyongyang: Chosŏn nodongdan~ ch'ulp'ansa, 1968.

Uri tang ŭi chuch'e sasang kwa konghwaguk chŏngbu ŭi taenaeoe chŏngch'aek ŭi myŏt kaji munje e taehayŏ [Concerning several problems of our party's *chuch'e* ideology and domestic and foreign policy of our republic]. Pyongyang: Chosŏn nodongdang ch'ulp'ansa, 1969.

Uri ŭi hyŏngmyŏng kwa inmin kundae ŭi kwaŏp e taehayŏ [On the task of the People's Army and our revolution]. Pyongyang: Chosŏn nodongdang ch'ulp'ansa, 1968.

Widaehan siwŏl ŭi sasang ŭn sŭngni hago itta [The great thought of October is victorious]. Pyongyang: Chosŏn nodongdang ch'ulp'ansa, 1957.

Widaehan suryŏng Kim Il Sung tongji ŭi chungyo munhŏnjip [Collection of important documents of the great leader Comrade Kim Il Sung]. N.p.: Samhaksa, 1975.

Works. 30 vols. Pyongyang: Foreign Languages Publishing House, 1980-1987.

Yanggangdo tang chojik dŭl app'e nasŏnŭn kwaŏp [Tasks of the party organizations in Yanggang province]. Pyongyang: Chosŏn nodongdang ch'ulp'ansa, 1969.

Yŏngwŏn han ch'insŏn [Eternal friendship]. Pyongyang: Chosŏn nodongdang ch'ulp'ansa, 1959.

Yŏsŏng tongmaeng saŏp e taehayŏ [On the work of the Women's League]. Pyongyang: Chosŏn nodongdang ch'ulp'ansa, 1967.

The Youth Must Take Over the Revolution and Carry It Forward. Pyongyang: Foreign Languages Publishing House, 1976.

Archival Materials

National Archives Collection of Foreign Records Seized in 1941. Record Group 242: Records Seized by U.S. Military Forces in Korea. Washington, D.C., 1977.

Shipping Advice 2005
Box 1: items 24, 34; Box 2: items 2-3, 43, 51, 64, 80, 113; Box 3: items 1, 5, 15-21, 39; Box 5: items 3-10, 44; Box 6: items 1-20, 37-42; Box 7: item 22; Box 8: items 1-35, 36-59; Box 9: items 1-50; Box 10: items 6-13, 31-37, 38-48, 49-53;

Shipping Advice 2006
Box 1: items 1-80, 86, 107-112; Box 2: items 1-26, 27-38; Box 3: items 2-3; Box 4: items 1-5, 10, 27, 54-55, 57, 59; Box 6: item 68;

Shipping Advice 2007
Boxes 1-6; Box 9: item 8;

Shipping Advice 2008
Box 4: items 1-8, 9-27, 28-64; Box 8: items 2-70; Box 9: items 1-96, 99-101; Box 10: items 9, 16, 89-90, 94, 131;

Shipping Advice 2009
Box 1: items 1, 75, 95, 111, 195; Box 2: item 173; Box 3: item 232; Box 8: items 15, 96;

Shipping Advice 2010
Box 2: item 64; Box 3: item 107;

Shipping Advice 2011
Box 7: items 27-31, 35; Box 8: item 36;

Shipping Advice 2012
Box 3: item 17; Box 4: items 16, 17, 20, 31, 37; Box 5: items 45, 113; Box 6: item 23;

Shipping Advice 2013
Box 1: items 26, 34, 81, 111

Archives of the Japanese Ministry of Foreign Affairs: 1868-1945

"Kantō chihō heihi no bōdō to waga keisatsukan no katsudō oyobi kogun no shutsudō" [Riots by bandits, the activities of the police, and the dispatch of Japanese troops]. reel SP105, frames 9303, 9390, 9396, 9402, 9408, 9412-9413, 9418, 9420. Reel SP76, frame 3608.

"Manshū jihen oyobi sono igo" (The Manchurian Incident and thereafter]. Reel SP105, frames 9082-9087, 9599-9619.

"Zai Kirin sōryōjikan oyobi Tonka bunkan" [The consulate-general in Jilin and sub-consulate in Tunhua]. Reel SP86, frames 9640-9643, 9994-10,264.

Articles, Books, Documents

Agricultural Cooperativization in the Democratic People's Republic of Korea. Pyongyang: Foreign Languages Publishing House, 1958.
Akademiia nauk, SSSR. *Vsemirnaia istoriia* [World History]. E. M. Zhukov. 13 vols. Moscow: Gos. izd-vo polit. lit-ry, 1955-1983.
An, Tai Sung. *North Korea; A Political Handbook*. Wilmington, Del.: Scholarly Resources, 1983.

Area Handbook for North Korea. Washington D.C.: GPO, 1976.

Baianov, B. and M. Shafir. *Gosudarstvennyi stroi Koreiskoi Narodno-Demokraticheskoe Respubliki* [The structure of the Democratic People's Republic of Korea]. Moscow: Gosudarstvennyi Izd. Iu. Lit., 1957.

Baik Bong. *Kim Il Sung, Biography.* 3 vols. Tokyo: Miraisha, 1969.

Bokareta imbo [Uncovered plot]. Tokyo: Jundaisha, 1954.

Boorman, Howard L., ed. *Biographical Dictionary of Republican China.* 4 vols. New York: Columbia University Press, 1967.

Bradbury, John. "Sino-Soviet Competition in North Korea." *China Quarterly* (April-June 1961), no. 6, pp. 15-28.

Brandt, Conrad, Benjamin Schwartz, and John K. Fairbank. *A Documentary History of Chinese Communism.* Cambridge: Harvard University Press, 1952.

Chajusŏng ŭl ongho haja [Let us defend independence]. Pyongyang: Chosŏn nodongdang ch'ulp'ansa, 1966.

Charyŏk kaengsaeng ŭi hyŏngmyŏng sasang [The revolutionary thought of self-resuscitation]. Pyongyang: Chosŏn nodongdang ch'ulp'ansa, 1963.

Ch'ian-guk t'ükbyŏl chŏngbogwa. *Pukhan kongsan koeroe chŏnggwŏn e taehan koch'al* [Examination of the North Korean Communist puppet regime]. Seoul: Ch'ian-guk t'ŭngmu chŏngbogwa, 1958.

"Chinese People's Volunteers' Anniversary." *Peking Review* (October 1965), no. 44, p. 4.

Chistiakov, Ivan M. "Voevoi puti 25-i armii" [The battle path of the 25th Army]. In *Osvobozhdenie Korei* [Korean Liberation]. Moscow: Akademii nauk, 1976.

Cho Chae-sŏn. *Kwadogi e issŏsŏ ŭi Chosŭn nodongdang ŭi kyŏngje chŏngch'aek* [The economic policy of the Worker's Party of Korea during the transitional period]. Pyongyang: Chosŏn nodongdang ch'ulp'ansa, 1958.

Ch'oe Hyŏng-u. *Haeoe Chosŏn hyŏngmyŏng undong sosa* [Brief history of the Korean revolutionary movement abroad]. Seoul: Tongbang munhwasa, 1945.

Ch'oe In-su. *Kim Jong Il: The People's Leader.* 2 vols. Pyongyang: Foreign Languages Publishing House, 1983 and 1985.

Ch'oe Nam-sŏn. *Paektusan kŭn ch'amgi* [Record of the visit to Paektusan]. Seoul: Hansŏng tosŏ chusik hoesa, 1927.

Ch'oe Sŏng-uk. *Uri tang ŭi chuch'e sasang kwa sahoe chuŭijŏk aeguk chuŭi* [The chuch'e thought of our party and socialist patriotism]. Pyongyang: Chosŏn nodongdang ch'ulp'ansa, 1966.

Ch'oe Yong-gŏn weiyuanchang fangmen zhongguo [Chairman Ch'oe Yong-gŏn's visit to China]. Beijing: Renmin chubanshe, 1963.

Choguk t'ongil minju chuŭi chŏnsŏn kyŏlsŏng taehoe munhŏnjip [Documents of the founding congress of the Democratic Front for Unification of the Fatherland]. Pyongyang: Chosŏn minbosa, 1949.

Ch'ollima chagŏppan undong [The Ch'ŏllima workteam movement]. Pyongyang: Chigŏp tongmaeng ch'ulp'ansa, 1960.

Ch'ŏllima undonggwa sahoe chuŭi kŏnsŏl taegojo e taehayŏ [On the great socialist construction and the Ch'ŏllima movement]. Pyongyang: Chosŏn nodongdang ch'ulp'ansa, 1961.

Ch'ŏn Se-bong. "Onsahoe ŭi chuch'e sasang hwa e ibajihanŭn hyŏngmyŏngjŏk munye chakp'um ŭl ch'angjak halte taehan tang ŭi t'agwŏlhan pangch'im" [The party's superior policy to create revolutionary productions to transform the entire society into self-reliant thought]. *Kŭlloja* (1977), no. 12 (404), pp. 55-61.

Chŏng In-sŏp. "Chipch'ejŏk chido nŭn tang mit kukkachedo ŭi ch'oego wŏnch'ŭk ida" [Collective leaderhsip is the highest principle of the party and state]. *Inmin* (December 1955), no. 12, pp. 69-82.

Chŏng T'ae-sik. *Uri tang e ŭihan sokto wa kyunhyŏng munje ŭi ch'angjojŏk haegyŏl* [The creative solution of the problems of speed and balance by our party]. Pyongyang: Chosŏn nodongdang ch'ulp'ansa, 1964.

Chŏngch'i sajŏn [Dictionary of politics]. Pyongyang: Sahoe kwahak ch'ulp'ansa, 1973.

Chōsen mondai chishiki no subete [All the knowledge about the Korean problems]. Tokyo: Jitsugyō no sekaisha, 1977.

Chōsen ni okeru shakai shugi no kiso kensetsu [The basic construction of socialism in Korea]. Tokyo: Shin nippon shuppansha, 1962.

Chōsen no kokusai rosen [The international line of Korea]. Tokyo: Chōsen kenkyūjo, 1966.

"Chōsen rōdōtō dai yonkai daikai tokushū" [Special Collection of the Fourth Congress of the Workers' Party of Korea]. *Atarashii sedai* (November 1961), no. 20, pp. 13-314.

Chosŏn chŏnsa [Complete history of Korea]. 33 vols. Pyongyang: Sahoe kwahak yŏn'guso, 1979-1982.

Chosŏn chungang yŏn'gam [The Korean central yearbook]. Pyongyang: Chosŏn chungang t'ongsinsa, 1950-1985.

Chosŏn kŭndae hyŏngmyŏng undongsa [History of the modern Korean revolutionary movement]. Pyongyang: Kwahagwŏn ch'ulp'ansa, 1961.

Chosŏn minju chuŭi inmin konghwaguk ch'oego·inmin hoeŭi che ilch'a hoeŭirok [Minutes of the First Session of the Supreme People's Assembly of the Democratic People's Republic of Korea]. Pyongyang: Chosŏn minju chuŭi inmin konghwaguk ch'oego inmin hoeŭi sangim wiwŏnhoe, 1948.

Chosŏn minju chuŭi inmin konghwaguk sahoe kwahagwŏn yŏksa yŏn'guso. *Yŏksa sajŏn* [Dictionary of history]. Pyongyang: Chosŏn nodongdang ch'ulp'ansa, 1960.

Chosŏn minju chuŭi inmin konghwaguk sahoe kyŏngje chedo [The social and economic system of the Democratic People's Republic of Korea]. Pyongyang: Chosŏn nodongdang ch'ulp'ansa, 1958.

Chosŏn nodongdang che samch'a taehoe munhŏnjip [Collection of documents of the Third Party Congress of the Workers' Party of Korea]. Pyongyang: Chosŏn nodongdang ch'ulp'ansa, 1956.

Chosŏn nodongdang i kŏrŏon yŏnggwang sŭrŏun kil [The glorious path trodden by the Workers' Party of Korea]. Pyongyang: Chosŏn nodongdang ch'ulp'ansa, 1956.

Chosŏn nodongdang kyuyak haesŏl [Explanation of the bylaws of the Workers' Party of Korea]. Pyongyang: Chosŏn nodongdang ch'ulp'ansa, 1964.

Chosŏn nodongdang yŏksa kyojae [History text of the Workers' Party of Korea]. Pyongyang: Chosŏn nodongdang ch'ulp'ansa, 1964.

Chosŏn t'ongsa [History of Korea]. 3 vols. Pyongyang: Kwahagwŏn, 1956-1958.

Chosŏn yŏksa [Korean history]. Pyongyang: Kwahak paekkwa sajŏn ch'ulp'ansa. 1979-1982.

Chuch'e sasang e kich'ohan samdae hyŏngmyŏng iron [The Three-Revolution Team theory based on the thought of *chuch'e*]. Pyongyang: Sahoe kwahak ch'ulp'ansa, 1975.

Chuch'e sasang e kich'ohan segye hyŏngmyŏng iron [The world revolution theory based on the thought of *chuch'e*]. Pyongyang: Sahoe kwahak ch'ulp'ansa, 1975.

Chung, Chin O. *P'yongyang Between Peking and Moscow.* University: University of Alabama Press, 1978.

Chwaik sagŏn sillok [Record of the leftist incidents]. 11 vols. Seoul: Tae kŏm ch'alch'ŏng konganbu, 1968-74.

Cumings, Bruce. *The Origins of the Korean War: Liberation and the Emergence of Separate Regimes, 1945-1947.* Princeton: Princeton University Press, 1981.

Dallin, Alexander, ed. *Diversity in International Communism.* New York: Columbia University Press, 1963.

Democratic People's Republic of Korea. Pyongyang: Foreign Languages Publishing House, 1958.

Directory of Officials of the DPRK: A Reference Aid. N.P., 1981.

Dispersed Families in Korea. Seoul: National Red Cross, 1977.

Documents and Materials of the Third Congress of the Workers' Party of Korea, April 23-29, 1956. Pyongyang: Foreign Languages Publishing House, 1956.

Documents of the Fourth Congress of the Workers' Party of Korea. Pyongyang: Foreign Languages Publishing House, 1961.

Documents on Korean-American Relations, 1943-1976. Seoul: Research Center for Peace and Unification, 1976.

Documents on the National Congress of Agricultural Cooperatives. Pyongyang: Foreign Languages Publishing House, 1959.

Dongbei leishi jinianguan, ed. *Dongbei kangri lieshichuan* [Biographies of Northeast anti-Japanese fighters]. 3 vols. Harbin: Heilongjiang renmin chubanshe, 1980.

Economic Development in the Republic of Korea in Comparison with North Korea. Seoul: Naewoe Press, 1977.

Evemenko, A. I. *Stalingrad.* Moscow: Voennoe izdatelistbo ministerstva oboruni soyusa, SSR, 1961.

Facts About Korea. Pyongyang: Foreign Languages Publishing House, 1962.

Feng Zhongyun. *Dongbei kangri lienjun shih-ssu-nien k'u-tou chienshih* [A brief history of the 14-year bitter struggle of the Northeast Anti-Japanese United Army]. Harbin: Qingnian chubanshe, 1946.

Floyd, David. *Mao Against Khrushchev.* New York: Praeger, 1964.

Gendai Chōsen kenkyūkai. *Chōsen yōran* [Korea handbook]. Tokyo: Jiji tsūshinsha, 1973.

Gendaishi shiryō [Sources of modern history]. Vol. 30. Tokyo: Misuzu shobō, 1976.

Ginsburgs, George and Roy U. T. Kim. *Calendar of Diplomatic Affairs, Democratic People's Republic of Korea, 1945-1975.* Moorestown, N.J.: Symposia Press, 1977.

Goulden, Joseph C. *Korea: The Untold Story of the War.* New York: Times Books, 1982.

Gribachev, Nikolai M. *Stikhotvoreniia i poemy* [Verses and poems]. Moscow: Gos. Izd., 1958.

Griffith, W. E. *The Sino-Soviet Rift.* Cambridge: MIT Press, 1964.

Gunseibu gomonbu. *Manshū kysōsan hi no kenkyū* [Study of the Manchurian Communist bandits]. 2 vols. Shinkyō: Kōa insatsukyoku, 1937.

"Habarosuku yaei gakkō no jōkyō" [Conditions of the Khabarovsk Field School]. *Gaiji geppō* (November 1942), pp. 85-86.

Haebang hu simnyŏn ilchi, 1945-1955 [Ten-year chronicle after the liberation, 1945-1955]. Pyongyang: Chosŏn chungang t'ongsinsa, 1955.

Hahm, Pyong Choon. "Ideology and Criminal Law in North Korea." *American Journal of Comparative Law* (1969), 7(1):77-93.

Han Chae-dŏk. *Han'guk ŭi kongsan chuŭi wa pukhan ŭi yŏksa* [Korean communism and the history of North Korea]. Seoul: Naeoe munhwasa, 1965.

Han Kŭn-jo. *Kodang, Cho Man-sik.* Seoul: T'aegŭk ch'ulp'ansa, 1970.

Han Sŏl-ya. *Uri ŭi t'aeyang* [Our sun]. Pyongyang: Pukchosŏn yesul yŏnmaeng, 1946.

— *Yŏnung Kim Il Sung changgun* [Hero General Kim Il Sung]. Pyongyang: n.p., 1946.

Hangil mujang t'ujaeng chŏnjŏkchi rŭl ch'ajōsō [Visiting the battlegrounds of the anti-Japanese armed struggle]. Pyongyang: Chosŏn nodongdang ch'ulp'ansa, 1960.

Hangil ppalchisan ch'amgajadŭl ŭi hoesanggi [Reminiscence of the anti-Japanese partisan guerrillas]. 12 vols. Pyongyang: Chosŏn nodongdang ch'ulp'ansa, 1959-1969.

Han'guk e issŏsŏ ŭi kongsan chuŭi [Communism in Korea]. Seoul: Kongbobu, 1968.

Han'guk inmyŏng taesajŏn [Big dictionary of Koreans]. Seoul: Sin'gu munhwasa, 1974.

Hayashi Takehiko. *Kita Chōsen to minami Chōsen* [North Korea and South Korea]. Tokyo: Saimaru shuppankai, 1971.

History of the Just Fatherland Liberation War of the Korean People. Pyongyang: Foreign Languages Publishing House, 1961.

Hongqi biao biao [Red flag fluttering]. Vols. 5 and 8. Beijing: Zhongguo qingnian chubanshe, 1957-1958.

Hwang Chŏng-hŭi. "Yŏngwŏn han ch'ungsŏng ŭro purŭnŭn hyŏngmyŏng ŭi chip" [The revolutionary house of eternal loyalty]. *Ch'ŏllima* (December 1957), no. 200, pp. 29-31.

Hyŏndaesa wa kongsan chuŭi [Modern history and communism]. Seoul: Kongbobu, 1968.

Hyŏngmyŏng kwa kŏnsŏl e kwanhan Kim Il Sung tongji ŭi widaehan saenghwallyŏk [The thought of Comrade Kim Il Sung on revolution and construction and its great strength]. Pyongyang: Sahoe kwahagwŏn ch'ulp'ansa, 1969.

Hyŏngmyŏng kwa kŏnsŏl e kwanhan widaehan suryŏng Kim Il Sung tongji ŭi kyosi [Instructions of the supreme leader Comrade Kim Il Sung on revolution and construction]. Pyongyang: Chosŏn nodongdang ch'ulp'ansa, 1972.

Hyŏngmyŏng sŏnyŏl dŭl ŭi saengae wa hwaltong [Lives and activities of the revolutionary forerunners]. 2 vols. Pyongyang: Chosŏn nodongdang ch'ulp'ansa, 1964-1965.

"Ilbon kongsandang e taehan p'agoe ch'aektong ŭn kyŏlk'o hŏyong halsu ŏpta" [Destructive maneuvers against the Japanese Communist Party cannot be allowed]. *Kŭlloja* (July 1964), no. 14 (252), pp. 2-8.

Indomitable Revolutionary Fighter, Comrade Kim Hyong Gwon. Pyongyang: Foreign Languages Publishing House, 1976.

Inmin ŭi chayu wa haebang ŭl wihayŏ [For the liberation and freedom of the people]. 4 vols. Pyongyang: Chosŏn nodongdang ch'ulp'ansa, 1970.

Inmindŭl sogesŏ [Among the people]. 16 vols. Pyongyang: Chosŏn nodongdang ch'ulp'ansa, 1960-1978.

Inoue Shuhachi. *Modern Korea and Kim Jung Il.* Tokyo: Yuzankaku, 1984.

International Seminar on the Juche Idea. Pyongyang: Foreign Languages Publishing House, 1977.

Invincible Is the Korean People's Army Founded and Trained by Ever-Victorious, Iron-Willed Genius Commander, Kim Il Sung. Pyongyang: Foreign Languages Publishing House, 1968.

Istoria Korei [Korean history]. 2 vols. Moscow: Izdatelistvo nauk, 1974.

Ji Yunlong. *Yang Jingyu huo kanglien diyilujun* [Yang Jingyu and the First Route Army of the Northeast Anti-Japanese United Army]. N.p.: Dongbei, 1946.

Jiang Dao. "Zhonggong yu beihan di xinguojie" [New Agreement Between Communist China and North Korea]. *Zhonggong yanjiu* (September 1970), 4(9):48-54.

"Jinri chaoxiu jituan" [The Korean revisionist clique of today]. *Wenge tongxun* (February 15, 1968), no.1.

Johnson, D. M. and H. Chiu. *Agreements of the People's Republic of China, 1949-1967: A Calendar.* Cambridge: Harvard University Press, 1968.

Katō Toyotaka. *Manshūkoku keisatsu shoshi* [Brief history of the Manchurian Police]. 3 vols. Matsuyama: Gen zaigai kōmuin engōkai, 1968, 1974, and 1976.

Khrushchev, N. S. *Report of the Central Committee of the Communist Party of the Soviet Union to the 20th Party Congress.* Moscow: Foreign Languages Publishing House, 1956.

Kibon kŏnsŏl saŏp palchŏn ŭl wihan uri tang ŭi chŏngch'aek [Our party policy for the development of basic construction works]. Pyongyang: Chosŏn nodongdang ch'ulp'ansa, 1961.

Kim Ch'ang-dŏk. "Chosŏn inmin'gun ŭn hangil ppalchisan ŭi hyŏngmyŏngjŏk aeguk chŏnt'ong ŭl kyesŭng han hyŏngmyŏngjŏk mujangyŏk" [The Korean

People's Army is the revolutionary armed force that inherited the revolutionary tradition of the anti-Japanese partisans]. *Choguk powi rŭl wihayŏ* (1958), no. 6, pp. 4-8.

Kim Ch'ang-man. "Chosŏn nodongdang yŏksa yŏn'gu esŏ chegi doenŭn myŏkkaji munje" [Several problems in the research of the history of the Workers' Party of Korea]. *Kŭlloja* (January 15, 1960), no. 1, pp. 10-21.

— *Modŭn kŏsun choguk kŏnsŏl e* [All for the construction of the fatherland]. Pyongyang: Chosŏn nodongdang ch'ulp'ansa, 1947.

Kim Ch'ang-sun. *Pukhan sibonyŏnsa* [Fifteen-year history of North Korea]. Seoul: Chimun-gak, 1961.

— *Yŏksa ŭi chŭngin* [The witness of history]. Seoul: Han'guk asea pan'gong yŏnmaeng, 1956.

Kim Chŏng-gi. *Pukkoe ŭi taenam chŏllyak ŭl haebu handa* [Analyze the northern puppet's strategies toward South Korea]. Seoul: Han'guk sinmunsa, 1970.

Kim Chŏng-ho. *Taedong yŏ chido* [The maps of the Great East]. N.p.: reprinted by Han'guk sahakhoe, 1965.

Kim Chun-yŏp and Kim Ch'ang-sun. *Chosŏn kongsan chuŭi undongsa* [History of the Korean Communist movement]. 5 vols. Seoul: Asea munje yŏn'guso, 1976.

Kim, G. F. "Ekonomicheskoe razvitie Koreiskoi Narodno-Demokraticheskoi Respubliki" [Economic development of the Democratic People's Republic of Korea]. *Voprosy Ekonomiki* (1955), no. 8, pp. 108-120.

Kim, G. F. and F. I Shabshina. *Proletarian Internationalism and Revolutions in the East.* Moscow: Nauka Publishing House, 1972.

Kim Hak-chun. *Han'guk munje wa kukche chŏngch'i* [The Korean problem and international politics]. Seoul: Pagyŏngsa, 1975.

Kim Hŭi-il. *Miguk cheguk chuŭi ŭi Chosŏn ch'imyaksa* [The history of the American imperialist invasion of Korea]. Pyongyang: Chosŏn nodongdang ch'ulp'ansa, 1964.

Kim Hyong-jik. Pyongyang: Foreign Languages Publishing House, 1968.

Kim Il Sung chuŭi hyŏngmyŏngnon [The revolutionary theory of Kimilsungism]. N.p.: Samhaksa, 1974.

Kim Il Sung kwa Kim Sŏng-ju [Kim Il Sung and Kim Sŏng-ju]. Seoul: Kongsan kwŏn munje yŏn'guso, 1970.

Kim Il Sung tongji ŭi hyŏngmyŏng sasang e taehayŏ [On the revolutionary thought of Kim Il Sung]. Pyongyang: Chosŏn nodongdang ch'ulp'ansa, 1972.

Kim, Kwan bong. *The Korea-Japan Treaty Crisis and the Instability of the Korean Political System.* New York: Praeger, 1971.

Kim Nam-sik. *Sillok, namnodang* [The true record of the Workers' Party of South Korea]. Seoul: Sin hyŏnsilsa, 1975.

Kim Ok-kyun. Pyongyang: Sahoe kwahagwŏn ch'ulp'ansa, 1964.

Kim Pyŏng-sik. *Kin Nichisei shusō no shisō* [Thoughts of Premier Kim Il Sung]. Tokyo: Yomiuri shinbunsha, 1972.

Kim Sŏk-hyŏng. *Chosŏn yŏksa* [Korean history]. Tokyo: Hagu sŏbang, 1954.

Kim Tu-bong. "Pukchosŏn nodongdang ch'angnip taehoe pogo" [Report to the

Founding Congress of the Workers' Party of North Korea]. *Kŭlloja* (October 25, 1946), no. 1, pp. 19-30.

"Kimilsung Flower Abloom the World Over." *Korean Nature* (1977), no. 2, pp. 5-6.

"Kin Nichisei no katsudō jōkyō" [Conditions of the activities of Kim Il Sung]. *Tokkō gaiji geppō* (November 1944), pp. 76-78.

Kin Seimei. *Chōsen dokuritsu undō, kyōsan shugi undō hen* [The Korean independence movement, the Communist movement section]. Tokyo: Hara shobō, 1967.

Kiyosaki, Wayne S. *North Korea's Foreign Relations.* New York: Praeger, 1976.

Klein, Donald W. and Ann B. Clark. *Biographical Dictionary of Chinese Communism, 1921-1945.* 2 vols. Cambridge: Harvard University Press, 1971.

Koh, Byung Chul. *The Foreign Policy of North Korea.* New York: Praeger, 1969.

— *The Foreign Policy Systems of North and South Korea.* Berkeley: University of California Press, 1984.

— "North Korea and the Sino-Soviet Schism." *Western Political Quarterly* (December 1969), pp. 940-962.

— "Political Leadership in North Korea: Toward a Conceptual Understanding of Kim Il Sung's Leadership Behavior." *Korean Studies* (1978), 2:139-157.

Korea-Japan Relations and the Attempt on the Life of Korea's President. Seoul: Pan National Council for Probe into August 15 Incident, 1974.

Korea Review. Pyongyang: Foreign Languages Publishing House, 1974.

"Korea: Two Resolutions Sponsored by Differing Groups Approved." *UN Monthly Chronicle* (December 1975), 12(11):18-21.

"The Korean Boundary Agreement." in *Third Annual Report on Reform and Progress in Korea, 1909-1910.* Seoul: Govenment-General of Chosen, 1910.

Kukche chuŭi ŭi ch'insŏn [Friendship of internationalism]. Pyongyang: Chosŏn chungang t'ongsinsa, 1957.

Kuksa p'yŏnch'an wiwŏnhoe. *Ilche ch'imyak haŭi han'guk samsimyungnyŏnsa* [Thirty-six-year history of Korea under the Japanese invasion]. Seoul: T'amgudang, 1971.

Kun, Joseph C. "North Korea: Between Moscow and Peking." *China Quarterly* (July-September 1967), no. 31, pp. 48-58.

Kyŏngae hanŭn suryŏng Kim Il Sung tongji kkesŏ palk'yŏ chusin samdae hyŏngmyŏng nosŏn ŭi widaehan saenghwallyŏk [The great strength under the three-revolution policy as shown by the respected supreme leader, Comrade Kim Il Sung]. Pyongyang: Chosŏn nodongdang ch'ulp'ansa, 1975.

Lebedev, N. G. "S Soznaniem ispolnennogo dolga" [In consciousness of fulfilled duty]. In *Osvobozhdenie Korei.* Moscow: Akademii nauk, 1976.

Lee, Chong-sik. "Kim Il Sung of North Korea." *Asian Survey* (June 1967), 7:374-382.

— "Korean Communists and Yenan." *China Quarterly* (January-March 1962), no. 9, pp. 184-185.

— *Revolutionary Struggle in Manchuria: Chinese Communism and Soviet Interests, 1922-1945.* Berkeley: University of California Press, 1983.

Lee, Chong-sik and Ki-wan Oh. "The Russian Faction in North Korea." *Asian Survey* (April 1968), 7(4):275-276.

Lei Ding. *Dongbei yiyongjun yundong shihua* [Historical stories of the Northeast Volunteer Army movement]. Shanghai: Tianma shudian, 1937.

Li Du, Zhou Baozhong, et al. *Dongbei di heian yu guangming* [Darkness and brightness in Manchuria]. Shanghai: Lishi zuliao gongyingshe, 1946.

Liu Baiyu. *Huanxing dongbei* [Return to the Northeast]. Shanghai: Fangsheng chubanshe, 1946.

Ma Yi, ed. *Chaoxian geming shihua* [Stories of Korean revolutionary history]. Zhongjing: n.p., 1944.

Magnolias of Mangyongdae. Pyongyang: Foreign Languages Publishing House, 1978.

Mangyongdae. Pyongyang: Foreign Languages Publishing House, 1978.

Manshūkoku chianbu keimushi. *Manshūkoku keisatsushi* [History of the Manchukuo Police]. Seoul: Manshūkoku chianbu keimushi, 1942.

Manshūkokushi [History of Manchukuo]. Tokyo: Manmo tōhō engokai, 1971.

Matsumoto Seichō. *Kita no shijin* [Poet of the north]. Tokyo: Kōbunsha, 1967.

McCune, Shannon. "Physical Basis for Korean Boundaries." *Far Eastern Quarterly* (May 1946), pp. 272-288.

McLellan, David S. "Dean Acheson and the Korean War." *Political Science Quarterly* (March 1968), 83(1):16-39.

Mijeguk chuŭi koyong kanch'ŏp Pak Hŏn-yŏng, Yi Sŭng-yŏp todang ŭi Chosŏn minju chuŭi inmin konghwaguk chŏnggwŏn chŏnbok ŭmmo wa kanch'ŏp sagŏn kongp'an munhŏn [Trial records of the espionage incident and the conspiracy to overthrow the government of the Democratic People's Republic of Korea by the American imperialist spies Pak Hŏn-yŏng and Yi Sŭng-yŏp]. Pyongyang: Chosŏn minju chuŭi inmin konghwaguk ch'oego chaep'anso, 1956.

Missuri, Muhammad al. *Kimilsungism: Theory and Practice*. Pyongyang: Foreign Languages Publishing House, 1982.

— *Kimilsungist: Cause Admirably Carried Forward*. Pyongyang: Foreign Languages Publishing House, 1982.

"Modŭn kŏsun minju yŏngyang chunbi rŭl wihayŏ" [All for the preparation of the democratic force]. *Kŭlloja* (October 25, 1946), no. 1, pp. 7-18.

Moon In-soo. "Mt. Baikdoo and Region." *Korea Today* (January 1965), no. 104, pp. 45-47.

Mother of Korea. Pyongyang: Foreign Languages Publishing House, 1978.

Mrs. Kang Ban-sok, Mother of the Great Leader of Korea. Pyongyang: Foreign Languages Publishing House, 1968.

Nakayama Yosaku, "Chū-so kokkyō funsō to kita Chōsen" [The Sino-Soviet border disputes and North Korea]. *Ajia* (June 1969), pp. 122-126.

"Nam Chosŏn hyŏn chŏngse wa nam Chosŏn hyŏngmyŏng e taehan tang ŭi kibon pangch'im" [The present condition of South Korea and our party's basic policy on the South Korean revolution]. *Kŭlloja* (1966), no. 12 (298), pp. 18-27.

"Nam Chosŏn hyŏngmyŏng ŭl chŏkkŭk chiwŏn hayŏ uri sedae e kiŏk'o choguk t'ongil ŭl silhyŏn haja" [Let us assist the South Korean revolution and accomplish fatherland unification in our generation]. *Kŭlloja* (1968), no. 1 (311), pp. 16-24.

Nambuk Chosŏn che chŏngdang sahoe tanch'e taep'yoja yŏnsŏk hoeŭi chungyo charyojip [Collection of important documents of the joint conference of the representatives of the political and social organizations of the North and South]. Seoul: Sinhŭng ch'ulp'ansa, 1948.

Nambuk taehwa paeksŏ [White Paper on the North-South dialogue]. Seoul: Nambuk chojŏl wiwŏnhoe, 1975.

Nishimura Shigeo. *Chūkoku kindai tōhoku chiekishi kenkyū* [Study of modern Chinese northeastern regional history]. Kyōto: Hōritsu bunkasha, 1984.

No Kye-hyŏn. "Pukhan ŭi pidongmaeng oegyo punsŏk" [Analysis of nonaligned diplomacy of North Korea]. *T'ongil chŏngch'aek* (1978), 4(3):198-215.

Noble, Harold Joyce. *Embassy at War.* Seattle: University of Washington Press, 1975.

North Korea, 1945-1967. N.p.: n.p., n.d.

O Yŏng-jin. *Hana ŭi chŭngŏn* [One testimony]. Seoul: Chungang munhwasa, 1952.

October Revitalizing Reforms of the Republic of Korea. Seoul: East-West Crosscurrent Center, 1972.

On the Socialist Constitution of the Democratic People's Republic of Korea. Pyongyang: Foreign Languages Publishing House, 1975.

Osvobozhdenie Korei [Korean liberation]. Moscow: Akademii nauk, 1976.

Otnosheniia Sovetskogo Soiuza s narodnoi Koreei, 1945-1980: dokymentii i materiallii [Relations Between the Soviet Union and the Korean people, 1945-1980: Documents and materials]. Moscow: Izd. nauka, 1981.

Pae Pyŏng-du. "Kannichi kaidan to otsui hogo jōyaku" [The Korea-Japan Conference and the Protection Treaty of 1905]. *Chōsen shiryō* (February 1965), no. 45, pp. 28-34; and (August 1965), no. 54, p. 9-17.

Paek Kil-man. "Namchosŏn inmin dŭl ŭn ojik p'ongyŏk chŏk pangbŏp e ŭihaesŏman chugwŏn ŭl chaengch'wi halsu itta" [The South Korean people can win sovereigny only through violent means]. *Kŭlloja* (1969), no. 3 (325), pp. 53-58.

Paek Nam-un. *Ssoryŏn insang* [Impression of the Soviet Union]. Pyongyang: Nodong sinmun ch'ulp'ansa, 1950.

Paek Pong. *Minjok ŭi t'aeyang Kim Il Sung changgun* [Sun of the nation, Marshal Kim Il Sung]. 2 vols. Pyongyang: Inmun kwahaksa, 1968-1969.

Paige, Glenn D. *The Korean Decision: June 24-30, 1950.* New York: Free Press, 1968.

Pak Hŏn-yŏng. "Manifesto of the South Korean Workers' Party." *For a Lasting Peace, for a People's Democracy* (March 24, 1950), no. 12 (72), pp. 3-4.

Pak Il-gyŏng. *Yusin hŏnbŏp* [The revitalized constitution]. Seoul: Pagyŏngsa, 1972.

Pak Kŭm-ch'ol. "Maruk'ŭsŭ renin chuŭi kich'i rŭl nop'idŭlgo siwŏl hyŏngmyŏng ŭi wiŏp ŭl kyesŭng haja" [Let us continue the great work of the October Revolution with raising high the banner of Marxism and Leninism]. *Külloja* (November 1963), no. 22 (236), pp. 2-15.

Pak Tal. *Choguk ŭn saengmyŏng poda tŏgwihada* [The fatherland is more precious than life]. Pyongyang: Minch'ŏng ch'ulp'ansa, 1960.

Pang Ho-sik. *Sahoe chuŭi chinyŏng naradŭl kanŭi kisul kyŏngjejŏk hyŏpcho* [Technical and economic cooperation among the socialist countries]. Pyongyang: Chosŏn nodongdang ch'ulp'ansa, 1958.

Pang In-hu. *Pukhan Chosŏn nodongdang ŭi hyŏngsŏnggwa palchŏn* [Formation and development of the Workers' Party of Korea in North Korea]. Seoul: Asea munje yŏn'guso, 1967.

Puk Chosŏn inminhoeŭi che ilch'a hoeŭi hoeŭirok [Minutes of the first session of the North Korean People's Assembly]. Pyongyang: Puk Chosŏn inmin hoeŭi sangim wiwŏnhoe, 1947.

Puk Chosŏn inminhoeŭi hoeŭirok [Minutes of the North Korean People's Assembly]. Pyongyang: Puk Chosŏn inmin hoeŭi sangim wiwŏnhoe, 1947-1948.

Puk Chosŏn inminhoeŭi t'ŭkpyŏl hoeŭi hoeŭirok [Minutes of the special session of the North Korean People's Assembly]. N.p.: n.p., n.d.

Puk Chosŏn nodongdang ch'angnip taehoe, checharyo [The founding congress of the Workers' Party of North Korea, documents]. Pyongyang: Puk Chosŏn nodongdang chungang ponbu, 1946.

Puk Chosŏn nodongdang ch'angnip taehoe hoeŭirok [Minutes of the founding congress of the Workers' Party of North Korea]. N.p.: n.p., n.d.

Puk Chosŏn nodongdang che ich'a chŏndang taehoe che chaeryojip [Collection of documents of the Second Party Congress of the Workers' Party of North Korea]. Pyongyang: Puk Chosŏn nodongdang chungang ponbu, 1948.

Puk Chosŏn nodongdang che ich'a chŏndang taehoe hoeŭirok [Minutes of the Second Congress of the Workers' Party of North Korea]. Pyongyang: Puk Chosŏn nodongdang chungang wiwŏnhoe, 1948.

Pukhan chŏngch'iron [North Korean politics]. Seoul: Kŭktong munje yŏn'guso, 1976.

Pukhan ch'onggam [North Korea yearbook]. Seoul: Kongsan'gwŏn munje yŏn'guso, 1968.

Pukhan chŏnggwŏn ŭi amt'usang [Secret struggle in North Korean politics]. Seoul: Naeoe munje yŏn'guso, 1966.

Pukhan chŏnso [North Korean reviews]. 3 vols. Seoul: Kŭktong munje yŏn'guso, 1970-1974.

Pukhan inmyŏng sajŏn [Biographical dictionary of North Korea]. Seoul: Chungang ilbosa, 1981.

Pukhan koejip chŏnsul munhŏnjip [Collection of documents on the strategies of the North Korean puppet regime]. Seoul: Taehan pan'gongdan, 1957.

Pukkoe kanbu mit tangwŏn haksŭp charyo [Study text of the party members and cadres of the northern puppets]. Seoul: Chungang chŏngbobu, 1977.

Pukkoe ŭi p'abŏl t'ujaengsa [History of factional struggles of the North Korean puppets]. Seoul: Naeoe munje yŏn'guso, 1966.

Pulgul ŭi hyŏngmyŏng t'usa Kim Ch'ŏl-chu tongji [The indomitable revolutionary

Comrade Kim Ch'öl-chu]. Pyongyang: Chosön nodongdang ch'ulp'ansa, 1980.

Pulgŭn haebal area hangil hyŏngmyŏng 20nyŏn [Twenty years of the anti-Japanese struggle under the red banner]. 5 vols. Pyongyang: Chosön nodongdang ch'ulp'ansa, 1980.

Pyongyang ŭi ŏje wa onŭl [Pyongyang yesterday and today]. Pyongyang: Kungnip chu'ulp'ansa, 1957.

P'yŏngyangji [Record of Pyongyang]. Pyongyang: Kungnip ch'ulp'ansa, 1957.

Ranseikai. *Manshū kokugun* [The Manchurian Army]. Tokyo: Ranseikai, 1970.

Rees, David. "North Korea-China Rift." *Atlas* (September 1969), 18(3):50-51.

Saikin ni okeru Chōsen chian jōkyō [Recent security conditions in Korea]. Keijō: Chōsen sōtokufu, 1936 and 1939.

Samsonov, A. M. *Stalingradskaya bitva* [Battle of Stalingrad]. Moscow: Izdatelistvo nauka, 1968.

Sapozhnikov, B. G. "Iz istorii sovetsko-koreiskoi druzvy" [From the history of Soviet-Korean friendship]. In *Osvobozhdenie Korei*. Moscow: Akademii nauk, 1976.

Sapozhnikov, B. G. and A. T. Iakimov. "Propaganda sredi Iaponskikh voisk i aseleniia Severo-Vostochnogo Kitaia i Severnoi Korei, Is opita rabot i politorganov Krasnoi Armii v 1945 g" [Propaganda among the Japanese troops and the population in Northeast China and North Korea, from the experiences of the political organizing work of the Red Army in 1945]. *Narodi Azii i Afriki* (1975), no. 5, pp. 40-49.

Satō Katsumi. *Waga taikenteki Chōsen mondai* [Korean problems through my experience]. Tokyo: Tōyō keizai shinbosha, 1978.

Scalapino, Robert A. *The Japanese Communist Movement, 1920-1966*. Berkeley: University of California Press, 1967.

Scalapino, Robert A. and Chong-Sik Lee. *Communism in Korea*. 2 vols. Berkeley: University of California Press, 1972.

Second Asian Economic Seminar: Pyongyang. 2 vols. Colombo: Asian Economic Bureau, 1964.

Secret Tunnel Under Panmunjom. Seoul: Korea Overseas Information Service, 1978.

Self-Reliance and the Building of an Independent Economy. Pyongyang: Foreign Languages Publishing House, 1965.

Shabshina, F. I. *Narodnoe vosstanie 1919 goda v Koree* [The popular uprising of 1919 in Korea]. Moscow: Izd-vo. Akademii nauk, 1952.

Shchetinin, B. V. "V Koree posle osvobozhdenie" [Korea after the liberation]. In *Osvobozhdenie Korei*. Moscow: Akademii nauk 1976.

— "Vozniknovenie narodnykh komitetov v severnoi Koree" [The rise of the People's Committee in North Korea]. *Sovetskoe Gosudarstvo i Pravo* (1947), no. 4, pp. 62-72.

Shi Licheng. *Chaoxian renmin gaoju hongqi qianjin* [Progress of the Korean people with hoisted red flag]. Beijing: Shijie zhishi chubanshe, 1963.

Shihōshō, Keiji-kyoku, dai go-ka. *Manshū ni okeru kyōsan shugi undō* [The Communist movement in Manchuria]. N.p.: n.p., 1938.

"Shinkyō kōtō kensatsu chōnai shisō jōsei" [Thought conditions within the jurisdiction of the Changchun high prosecutor's office]. *Shisō geppō* (November 1940), pp. 150-152.

Statistical Return of National Economy of the Democratic People's Republic of Korea. Pyongyang: Foreign Languages Publishing House, 1964.

"Soren busō Chōsen jin chōsa no sennai sennyū jiken" [Incident of a Korean spy infiltration into Korea with Russian arms]. *Tokkō gaiji geppō* (September 1943), pp. 109-113.

Suh, Dae-Sook. "Communist Party Leadership." In *Political Leadership in Korea.* Seattle: University of Washington Press, 1976.

— *Documents of Korean Communism.* Princeton: Princeton University Press, 1970.

— *Korean Communism, 1945-1980.* Honolulu: University of Hawaii Press, 1981.

— *The Korean Communist Movement, 1918-1945.* Princeton: Princeton University Pess, 1967.

— "A Peconceived Formula for Sovietization: North Korea." In T. T. Hammond, ed., *The Anatomy of Communist Takeover.* New Haven: Yale University Press, 1975.

Suh, Dae-Sook and Chae-Jin Lee, eds. *Political Leadership in Korea.* Seattle: University of Washington Press, 1976.

Sukchong sillok [The records of King Sukchong]. In *Chosŏn wangjo sillok* [The records of the Korean kingdom]. Vol. 40. Seoul: Kuksa p'yŏnch'an wiwŏnhoe, 1973.

Sun Jie. *Dongbei kangri lianjun disijun* [The Fourth Army of the Northeast Anti-Japanese United Army]. Paris: Jiuguo chubanshe, 1936.

Suzuki Shōji. "Manshū kyōsan shugi undō kenkyū no gendankai." *Gunji shigaku* (December 1985), 21(3):35-44.

Takashi, Nada. *A Paean of Great Love: Kim Jong Il and the People.* Pyongyang: Foreign Languages Publishing House, 1984.

Tamaki Motoi. *Chōsen minshu shugi jinmin kyōwakoku no sinwa to genjitsu* [Myth and reality of the Democratic People's Republic of Korea]. Tokyo: Korea hyōronsha, 1978.

— *Kin Nichisei no shisō to kōdō* [Ideology and practice of Kim Il Sung]. Tokyo: Korea hyōronsha, 1978.

"Tang saŏp pangbŏpkwa chakp'um ŭl kyŏlchŏngjŏk ŭro kaesŏn haja" [Let us reform decisively the methods and products of the party work]. *Tang kanbu egye chunŭn ch'amgo charyo* (1959), no. 4, pp. 2-11.

Theses on South-North Dialogue. Seoul: South-North Coordinating Committee, 1978.

Tsuboe Senji. *Hokusen no kaihō jūnen* [Ten-year liberation of North Korea]. Tokyo: Nikkan rōdō tsūshinsha, 1956.

United States Arms Control and Disarmament Agency. *World Military Expenditures and Arms Trade, 1963-1973.* Washington, D.C.: GPO, 1975.

United States Department of State. *Foreign Relations of the United States, 1947.* Vol. 6: The Far East. Washington, D.C.: GPO, 1972.

— *Foreign Relations of the United States, 1950*. Vol. 7: Korea. Washington, D.C.: GPO, 1978.

— *North Korea: A Case Study in the Technique of Takeover*. Washington, D.C.: GPO, 1961.

— *The Record on Korean Unification, 1943-1960*. Washington, D.C., GPO, 1960.

Uri ŭi t'aeyang [Our sun]. Pyongyang: n.p., 1946.

Wada Haruki, "Kin Nichisei to Manshū no kōnichi busō tōsō [Kim Il Sung and anti-Japanese armed struggle in Manchuria]. *Shisō* (July 1985), pp. 55-83; (September 1985), pp. 38-71.

Wardman, Alan. *Plutarch's Lives*. Berkeley: University of California Press, 1974.

Wei dongbei di heping minzhu er douzheng [The struggle for peace and democracy in the northeast]. Vol. 1. N.p.: Dazhong wenhua, n.d.

Wei Manzhouguoshi [History of puppet Manchukuo]. Jilin: Renmin chubanshe, 1980.

Whiting, Allen S. *China Crosses the Yalu*. New York: Macmillan, 1960.

Who's Who in Communist China. Hongkong: Union Research Institute, 1966.

"Wicked History of P'eng Teh-huai." *Current Background* (April 26, 1968), no. 851, pp. 8-9.

Widaehan suryŏng Kim Il Sung tongji chŏn'gi [Biography of the great leader Kim Il Sung]. 3 vols. Pyongyang: Chosŏn nodongdang ch'ulp'ansa, 1982.

Widaehan suryŏng Kim Il Sung tongji ŭi chuch'e sasang [The *chuch'e* thought of the great leader, Comrade Kim Il Sung]. Pyongyang: Sahoe kwahak ch'ulp'ansa, 1975.

"Widaehan suryŏng nimkke kkŭt ŏpsi ch'ungsil hayŏtton purgul ŭi kongsan chuŭi hyŏngmyŏng t'usa Kim Chŏng-suk tongji" [The indomitable Communist revolutionary fighter, Comrade Kim Chŏng-suk, who was faithful to the great leader]. *Kŭlloja* (1975), no. 9 (401), pp. 21-28.

Xinghuo liaoyuan [A single spark can start a prairie fire]. Beijing: Renmin wenxue chubanshe, 1961.

Yang Ho-min. "North Korea, Thirty Years Between Moscow and Peking." *Chinese Affairs* (July 1976), 1(2):105-172.

— *Pukhan ŭi ideorogi wa chŏngch'i* [Ideology and politics of North Korea]. Seoul: Asea munje yŏn'guso, 1967.

— "Samdae hyŏngmyŏng ŭi wŏllyu wa chŏn'gae" [Origin and development of the three revolutions]. *Pukhan hakpo* (1977), no. 1, pp. 11-50.

Yearbook of the United Nations. Vol. 29. New York: Office of Public Information of the United Nations, 1978.

Yi Che-sun tongji ŭi saengae wa hwaltong [Life and activities of Comrade Yi Che-sun]. Pyongyang: Chosŏn nodongdang ch'ulp'ansa, 1965.

Yi Ch'ŏng-wŏn. *Chosŏn kŭndaesa* [Modern history of Korea]. Translated into Russian by M. N. Pak, *Ocherki novoi istorii Korei* (Moscow: Izd-vo insotrannoi litry, 1952); into Chinese by Ting Zeliang and Xia Chaowen, *Chaoxian jindaishi* (Beijing: Sanlian shudian, 1955); into Japanese by Kawakubo Kobu and O Chae-yang, *Chōsen kindaishi* (Tokyo: Daigetsu shoten, 1956).

Yi Hong-gŭn. *Ssoryŏn kunjŏng ŭi simal* [Beginning and end of the Soviet military occupation]. Seoul: n.p., 1950.

Yi Hong-jik. *Kuksa sajŏn* [Dictionary of Korean history]. Seoul: Chimun'gak, 1971.

Yi Kang-guk. *Minju chuŭi Chosŏn ŭi kŏnsŏl* [The establishment of democratic Korea]. Seoul: Chosŏn inminbosa, 1946.

Yi Myŏng-yŏng. *Kim Il Sung yŏlchŏn* [Biography of Kim Il Sung]. Seoul: Sinmunhwasa, 1974.

— "Tongman ŭi p'ung-un-a O Sŏng-yun" [An adventurer of Eastern Manchuria, O Sŏng-yun]. *Chungang* (July 1973).

Yi Na-yŏng. *Chosŏn minjok haebang t'ujaengsa* [History of the Korean people's liberation struggle]. Pyongyang: Chosŏn nodongdang ch'ulp'ansa, 1958.

Yi Sŏn-gŭn. "Paektusan kwa kando munje" [Paektusan and the problems of Jiandao]. *Yŏksa hakpo* (June 1962), nos. 17-18, pp. 547-570.

Yim Ch'un-ch'u. *Hangil mujang t'ujaeng sigirŭl hoesang hayŏ* [Recollecting the times of the anti-Japanese armed struggle]. Pyongyang: Chosŏn nodongdang ch'ulp'ansa, 1960.

Yim Ŭn. "Suryŏng ŭi ch'angsegi, Kim Il Sung ilsa" [Genesis of the supreme leader, biography of Kim Il Sung]. Handwritten manuscript.

Yŏksa sajŏn [Dictionary of history]. Pyongyang: Sahoe kwahak ch'ulp'ansa, 1971.

Yŏm Han-guk. "Ossi kajok ŭi p'iŭi kirok" [The bloody record of the family of Mr. O]. *Saechosŏn (October 1948), pp. 32-36.*

Yŏn'gil p'okt'an [Yanji bomb]. Pyongyang: Chosŏn nodongdang ch'ulp'ansa, 1968.

Yŏngwŏn han ch'insŏn [Eternal friendship]. Pyongyang: Chosŏn nodongdang ch'ulp'ansa, 1959.

Yun Se-p'yŏng. "Kim Il Sung changgun ŭi hangil mujang t'ujaeng." *Yŏksa chemunje* (September 1949), 11:61-75.

Zagoria, Donald S. *The Sino-Soviet Conflict, 1956-1961.* Princeton: Princeton University Press, 1962.

Zhang Cunwu. "Mukedeng suodingdi zhonghan guojie" [The Sino-Korean border by Mukedeng]. *Zhongyang yanjiuyuan guoji hanxue huiyi linwenji* (October 1981), pp. 1347-1365.

— "Qingdai zhonghan bianwu wenti tanyuan" [Research on the problem of the Sino-Korean border in the Qing dynasty]. *Jindaishi yanjiusuo jikan (1971), 2:463-501.*

Zhong-Chao yongshi tuanjie [Eternal unity of the Chinese and Korean Peoples]. Beijing: Renmin chubanshe, 1962.

Zhou Baozhong. *Zhandou zai baishan heisui* [Struggles in white mountain and black waters]. Shenyang: Liaoning renmin chubanshe, 1983.

Zhou Erfu. *Dongbei henduanmien* [Across the northeast]. N.p.: Jinri chubanshe, 1946.

Index

The East Asian Institute
of Columbia University

The East Asian Institute is Columbia University's Center for research, publication, and teaching on modern East Asia. The Studies of the East Asian Institute were inaugerated in 1962 to make available the results of significant new research on Japan, China, and Korea.

Studies of the East Asian Institute

The Ladder of Success in Imperial China. Ping-ti Ho. New York: Columbia University Press, 1962.

The Chinese Inflation, 1937–1949. Shun-hsin Chou. New York: Columbia University Press, 1963.

Reformer in Modern China: Chang Chien, 1853–1926. Samuel Chu. New York: Columbia University Press, 1965.

Research in Japanese Sources: A Guide. Hershel Webb, with the assistance of Marleigh Ryan. New York: Columbia University Press, 1965.

Society and Education in Japan. Herbert Passin. New York: Teachers College Press, 1965.

Agricultural Production and Economic Development in Japan, 1873–1922. James I. Nakamura. Princeton: Princeton University Press, 1966.

Japan's First Modern Novel: Ukigumo of Futabatei Shimei. Marleigh Ryan. New York: Columbia University Press, 1967.

The Korean Communist Movement, 1918–1948. Dae-Sook Suh. Princeton: Princeton University Press, 1967.

The First Vietnam Crisis. Melvin Gurtov. New York: Columbia University Press, 1967.

Cadres, Bureaucracy, and Political Power in Communist China. A. Doak Barnett. New York: Columbia University Press, 1968.

The Japanese Imperial Institution in the Tokugawa Period. Herschel Webb. New York: Columbia University Press, 1968.

Higher Education and Business Recruitment in Japan. Koya Azumi. New York: Columbia University Press, 1969.

The Communists and Peasant Rebellions: A Study in the Rewriting of Chinese History. James P. Harrison, Jr. New York: Atheneum, 1969.

How the Conservatives Rule Japan. Nathaniel B. Thayer. Princeton: Princeton University Press, 1969.

Aspects of Chinese Education. C. T. Hu, ed. New York: Teachers College Press, 1970.

Documents of Korean Communism, 1918–1948. Dae-Sook Suh. Princeton: Princeton University Press, 1970.

Japanese Education: A Bibliography of Materials in the English Language. Herbert Passin. New York: Teachers College Press, 1970.

Economic Development and the Labor Market in Japan. Koji Taira. New York: Columbia University Press, 1970.

The Japanese Oligarchy and the Russo-Japanese War. Shumpei Okamoto. New York: Columbia University Press, 1970.

Imperial Restoration in Medieval Japan. H. Paul Varley. New York: Columbia University Press, 1971.

Japan's Postwar Defense Policy, 1947–1968. Martin E. Weinstein. New York: Columbia University Press, 1971.

Election Campaigning Japanese Style. Gerald L. Curtis. New York: Columbia University Press, 1971.

China and Russia: The "Great Game." O. Edmund Clubb. New York: Columbia University Press, 1971.

Money and Monetary Policy in Communist China. Katharine Huang Hsiao. New York: Columbia University Press, 1971.

The District Magistrate in Late Imperial China. John R. Watt. New York: Columbia University Press, 1972.

Law and Policy in China's Foreign Relations: A Study of Attitudes and Practice. James C. Hsiung. New York: Columbia University Press, 1972.

Pearl Harbor as History: Japanese-American Relations, 1931–1941. Dorothy Borg and Shumpei Okamoto, eds., with the assistance of Dale K. A. Finlayson. New York: Columbia University Press, 1973.

Japanese Culture: A Short History. H. Paul Varley. New York: Praeger, 1973.

Doctors in Politics: The Political Life of the Japan Medical Association. William E. Steslicke. New York: Praeger, 1973.

The Japan Teachers Union: A Radical Interest Group in Japanese Politics. Donald Ray Thurston. Princeton: Princeton University Press, 1973.

Japan's Foreign Policy, 1868–1941: A Research Guide. James William Morley, ed. New York: Columbia University Press, 1974.

Palace and Politics in Prewar Japan. David Anson Titus. New York: Columbia University Press, 1974.

The Idea of China: Essays in Geographic Myth and Theory. Andrew March. Devon, England: David and Charles, 1974.

Origins of the Cultural Revolution. Roderick MacFarquhar. New York: Columbia University Press, 1974.

Shiba Kokan: Artist, Innovator, and Pioneer in the Westernization of Japan. Calvin L. French. Tokyo: Weatherhill, 1974.

Insei: Abdicated Sovereigns in the Politics of Late Heian Japan. G. Cameron Hurst. New York: Columbia University Press, 1975.

Embassy at War. Harold Joyce Noble. Frank Baldwin, Jr., ed. and intro. Seattle: University of Washington Press, 1975.

Rebels and Bureaucrats: China's December 9ers. John Israel and Donald W. Klein. Berkeley: University of California Press, 1975.

Deterrent Diplomacy. James William Morley, ed. New York: Columbia University Press, 1976.

House United, House Divided: The Chinese Family in Taiwan. Myron L. Cohen. New York: Columbia University Press, 1976.

Escape from Predicament: Neo-Confucianism and China's Evolving Political Culture. Thomas A. Metzger. New York: Columbia University Press, 1976.

Cadres, Commanders, and Commissars: The Training of the Chinese Communist Leadership, 1920–1945. Jane L. Price. Boulder, Colo.: Westview Press, 1976.

Sun Yat-Sen: Frustrated Patriot. C. Martin Wilbur. New York: Columbia University Press, 1977.

Japanese International Negotiating Style. Michael Blaker. New York: Columbia University Press, 1977.

Contemporary Japanese Budget Politics. John Creighton Campbell. Berkeley: University of California Press, 1977.

The Medieval Chinese Oligarchy. David Johnson. Boulder, Colo.: Westview Press, 1977.

The Arms of Kiangnan: Modernization in the Chinese Ordnance Industry, 1860–1895. Thomas L. Kennedy. Boulder, Colo.: Westview Press, 1978.

Patterns of Japanese Policymaking: Experiences from Higher Education. T.J. Pempel. Boulder, Colo.: Westview Press, 1978.

The Chinese Connection: Roger S. Greene, Thomas W. Lamont, George E. Sokolsky, and American-East Asian Relations. Warren I. Cohen. New York: Columbia University Press, 1978.

Militarism in Modern China: The Career of Wu P'ei-Fu, 1916–1939. Odoric Y.K. Wou. Folkestone, England: Dawson, 1978.

A Chinese Pioneer Family: The Lins of Wu-Feng. Johanna Meskill. Princeton: Princeton University Press, 1979.

Perspectives on a Changing China. Joshua A. Fogel and William T. Rowe, eds. Boulder, Colo.: Westview Press, 1979.

The Memoirs of Li Tsung-Jen. T. K. Tong and Li Tsung-Jen. Boulder, Colo.: Westview Press, 1979.

Unwelcome Muse: Chinese Literature in Shanghai and Peking, 1937–1945. Edward Gunn. New York: Columbia University Press, 1979.

Yenan and the Great Powers: The Origins of Chinese Communist Foreign Policy. James Reardon-Anderson. New York: Columbia University Press, 1980.

Uncertain Years: Chinese-American Relations, 1947–1950. Dorothy Borg and Waldo Heinrichs, eds. New York: Columbia University Press, 1980.

The Fateful Choice: Japan's Advance into Southeast Asia. James William Morley, ed. New York: Columbia University Press, 1980.

Tanaka Giichi and Japan's China Policy. William F. Morton. Folkestone, England: Dawson, 1980; New York: St. Martin's Press, 1980.

The Origins of the Korean War: Liberation and the Emergence of Separate Regimes, 1945–1947. Bruce Cumings. Princeton: Princeton University Press, 1981.

Class Conflict in Chinese Socialism. Richard Curt Kraus. New York: Columbia University Press, 1981.

Education under Mao: Class and Competition in Canton Schools. Jonathan Unger. New York: Columbia University Press, 1982.

Private Academies of Tokugawa Japan. Richard Rubinger. Princeton: Princeton University Press, 1982.

Japan and the San Francisco Peace Settlement. Michael M. Yoshitsu. New York: Columbia University Press, 1982.

New Frontiers in American-East Asian Relations: Essays Presented to Dorothy Borg. Warren I. Cohen, ed. New York: Columbia University Press, 1983.

The Origins of the Cultural Revolution: II, The Great Leap Forward, 1958–1960. Roderick MacFarquhar. New York: Columbia University Press, 1983.

The China Quagmire: Japan's Expansion on the Asian Continent, 1933–1941. James William Morley, ed. New York: Columbia Univeristy Press, 1983.

Fragments of Rainbows: The Life and Poetry of Saito Mokichi, 1882–1953. Amy Vladeck Heinrich. New York: Columbia University Press, 1983.

The U.S.-South Korean Alliance: Evolving Patterns of Security Relations. Gerald L. Curtis and Sung-joo Han, eds. Lexington, Mass.: Lexington Books, 1983.

Japan and the Asian Development Bank. Dennis Yasutomo. New York: Praeger, 1983.

State and Diplomacy in Early Modern Japan. Ronald Toby. Princeton: Princeton University Press, 1983.

Discovering History in China: American Historical Writing on the Recent Chinese Past. Paul A. Cohen. New York: Columbia University Press, 1984.

The Foreign Policy of the Republic of Korea. Youngnok Koo and Sung-joo Han, eds. New York: Columbia University Press, 1984.

Japan Erupts: The London Naval Conference and the Manchurian Incident. James W. Morley, ed. New York: Columbia University Press, 1984.

Japanese Culture. 3d ed. rev. Paul Varley. Honolulu: University of Hawaii Press, 1984.

Japan's Modern Myths: Ideology in the Late Meiji Period. Carol Gluck. Princeton: Princeton University Press, 1985.

Shamans, Housewives, and Other Restless Spirits. Laurel Kendall. Honolulu: University of Hawaii Press, 1985.

Human Rights in Contemporary China. R. Randle Edwards, Louis Henkin, and Andrew J. Nathan. New York: Columbia University Press, 1986.

The Manner of Giving: Strategic Aid and Japanese Foreign Policy Dennis T. Yasutomo. Lexington: Lexington Books—D.C. Heath, 1986.

Security Interdependence in the Asia Pacific Region. James W. Morley, ed. Lexington: Lexington Books—D.C. Heath, 1986.

The Pacific Basin: New Challenges for the United States. James William Morley, ed. New York: Academy of Political Science, 1986.

Anvil of Victory: The Community Revolution in Manchuria. Steven I. Levine. New York: Columbia University Press, 1987.

China's Satellite Parties. James D. Seymour. Armonk, N.Y.: Sharpe, 1987.

China's Political Economy: The Quest for Development Since 1949. Carl Riskin. London: Oxford University Press, 1987.

Single Sparks: China's Rural Revolutions. Kathleen Hartford and Steven M. Goldstein, eds. Armonk, N.Y.: Sharp, 1987.

Urban Japanese Housewives: At Home and in the Community. Anne E. Imamura. Honolulu: University of Hawaii Press, 1987.

Remaking Japan: The American Occupation as New Deal. Theodore Cohen. Herbert Passin, ed. New York: Free Press, 1987.

Border Crossings: Studies in International History. Christopher Thorne. Oxford and New York: Blackwell, 1988.

Contending Approaches to the Political Economy of Taiwan. Edwin A. Winkler and Susan Greenhalgh, eds. Armonk, N.Y.: Sharpe, 1988.

The Japanese Way of Politics. Gerald L. Curtis. New York: Columbia University Press, 1988.

The Indochina Tangle: China's Foreign Policy, 1975–1979. New York: Columbia University Press, 1988.